2 yr

neqx

DISCARD

a

BOHN'S PHILOSOPHICAL LIBRARY

THE WORKS OF GEORGE BERKELEY
VOL. I

GEORGE BELL & SONS

LONDON : YORK STREET, COVENT GARDEN
NEW YORK : 66, FIFTH AVENUE, AND
BOMBAY : 53, ESPLANADE ROAD
CAMBRIDGE : DEIGHTON, BELL & CO.

George Berkeley D.D.
Bishop of Cloyne.

from the picture by John Smibert, in the National Portrait Gallery.

THE WORKS OF
GEORGE BERKELEY, D.D.
BISHOP OF CLOYNE

EDITED BY
GEORGE SAMPSON

WITH A BIOGRAPHICAL INTRODUCTION BY
THE RT. HON. A. J. BALFOUR, M.P.

VOL. 1

LONDON
GEORGE BELL AND SONS
1897

CHISWICK PRESS :—CHARLES WHITTINGHAM AND CO.
TOOKS COURT, CHANCERY LANE, LONDON.

PREFACE.

EDITIONS of Berkeley are not so numerous as to compel apologies for the appearance of a new issue. Beyond this present edition, there exists only the magnificent one of Professor Campbell Fraser (Oxford, 1871), which, however, leaves a considerable part of the reading public quite untouched; and thus one of the most attractive figures in the history of English letters remains comparatively unknown for lack of easy means of access. Then, again, fear of the matter of Berkeley's work has lost him many readers; nor is confidence restored when he is presented with a vast apparatus of discussions and explanations portending dulness. It is right that a full philosophical edition should exist; it is not right that such an edition should exist alone. To furnish a cheap and accurate text of a writer whose subtle grace of expression is quite equal to his vast importance in the history of philosophy is the chief aim of the present edition.

Berkeley considerably modified his books in the successive issues of his lifetime; and while every work is given in the order of its first appearance, the text is that of the final revision. However, after a careful collation of the original editions, any variation of the

least importance is given in the notes. No attempt
has been made to supply commentary or discussion ;
but, instead, an appendix to the third volume will give
references to every criticism of any value.

An editor of Berkeley is but a poor gleaner in the
field where Professor Fraser has so vigorously wrought;
and to him, both for aid from his published work and
for much private help generously given, the editor
desires to offer his sincere acknowledgments and
thanks.

The introductory essay by Mr. Balfour has been
reprinted with the author's permission, and after some
slight revision for the present purpose, from a volume
of his Essays and Addresses.

The portrait which forms the frontispiece to this
volume has been reproduced by Messrs. Walker and
Boutall from the picture in the National Portrait
Gallery, painted by John Smibert in 1728.

CONTENTS.

VOL. I.

PAGE

BIOGRAPHICAL INTRODUCTION. By the Right Hon.
ARTHUR J. BALFOUR, M.P. ix

ARITHMETIC DEMONSTRATED WITHOUT EUCLID
OR ALGEBRA. 1

MATHEMATICAL MISCELLANIES 39

AN ESSAY TOWARDS A NEW THEORY OF VISION 67

A TREATISE CONCERNING THE PRINCIPLES OF
HUMAN KNOWLEDGE 153

PASSIVE OBEDIENCE. 253

THREE DIALOGUES BETWEEN HYLAS AND PHI-
LONOUS 291

BIOGRAPHICAL INTRODUCTION.

I.

BERKELEY'S chief title to fame must always rest on his philosophy. It is as a descendant in the true line of succession from Locke to the modern schools of thought, which are either a development of Locke's principles or a reaction against that development, that he is, and that he deserves to be, chiefly remembered. Yet his life and character had for his contemporaries, and may have for us, an interest quite apart from the details of metaphysical discussion. We may look at him, as they looked at him, not principally as the successor of Locke and the predecessor of Hume, as the almost impersonal author of a subtle philosophical theory, but as the worthy associate of the men who rendered the first fifty years of the eighteenth century illustrious in English literature, as an Irish patriot, as an American philanthropist, as a religious controversialist, as a man of delightful character and converse, simple, devoted, and unworldly. Though it be true, therefore, that—philosophy apart— Berkeley effected little; though he did not write enough to rank in the first class among men of letters, nor perform enough to be counted a successful man of action; though he was neither a great social power, nor a great missionary, nor a great ecclesiastic, it is also true that scarce any man of his generation touched contemporary life at so many points. In reading his not very voluminous works we find ourselves not only in the thick of every great controversy—theological, mathematical, and philosophical — which raged in England during the first half of the eighteenth century, but we get glimpses of life in the most diverse conditions : in the seclusion of Trinity College, Dublin, in the best literary and fashionable society in London, among the prosperous colonists of Rhode Island, among the very far from prosperous peasants and squireens of Cork. And all this in the company of a man endowed with the subtlest of intellects, lit up with a humour the most delicate and urbane.

It is not creditable to the piety with which we cherish the memory of our literary ancestors, that no serious effort should have been made till 120 years after Berkeley's death to collect his scattered writings, and to place on record all that can be discovered of his life. But we may perhaps console ourselves for the fact that some valuable material has thus been lost beyond recall, by reflecting that the work, though begun too late, has at last been admirably carried out. Professor Fraser, in his recent edition of Berkeley's collected works,[1] has not only provided the philosophic student with all the assistance he can possibly require, but (which is more to my present purpose) has enriched it with a most excellent life of his author. Our obligations to him, however, do not end there. Since the publication of the life and letters, some new

[1] "Works of George Berkeley," &c., ed. Professor Fraser. Clarendon Press (1871). "Life and Letters," ditto.

biographical details of much interest have come to light. Professor Fraser has taken the opportunity, afforded him by the issue of the series of " Philosophic Classics,"[1] to insert them in the volume devoted to Berkeley, and has thereby earned a new title to the gratitude of Berkeley's admirers. In this little work Professor Fraser has, with remarkable skill, woven into an organic whole much of the material he formerly divided (in the complete edition) between the works and the life : so that the reader may now obtain an adequate account of the opinions of the philosopher, illustrated by the circumstances under which those opinions were formed and given to the world. This is, without doubt, the proper way to obtain a true view of the life and writings of any author, and not least of Berkeley. But it unfortunately presupposes a wider knowledge of philosophical subjects than most readers possess or care to acquire : and I may, therefore, be doing a service if, by a free use of the materials which Professor Fraser has supplied, I can succeed, without lapsing into metaphysics, in giving an interesting portrait of one of the most interesting figures in our literary history.

For few purposes but those of the almanack-maker does the period we call the "eighteenth century" begin with the year 1701. The precise limits of it can, indeed, be hardly determined ; and the terms which we fix for it must not only be to some extent arbitrary, but must vary according to the point of view from which we happen to be considering it. Yet, we may say roughly, that for the purposes respectively of

[1] "Berkeley" (Blackwood's Philosophic Classics), by Professor Fraser (1881).

science, philosophy, and theology, it began (in England at least) with Newton's "Principia," published in 1687; Locke's "Essay," published in 1690; and (let not the reader be shocked at the descent) Toland's deistical work, "Christianity not Mysterious," published in 1696. Trinity College, Dublin, then just beginning to recover from the civil wars which in Ireland accompanied the Revolution, was profoundly affected by all three works, With a readiness to accept new doctrine which has not always been shown by academic societies, the " Principia " and the " Essay " became at once part of the studies of the place, and though I do not know whether the ponderous " Logics " of Burgersdicius and Smiglecius, on which it is alleged that Swift's university career so nearly made shipwreck a few years before,[1] were discarded from the "curriculum," there can be no doubt that the whole current of opinion ran violently against scholastic methods, and in favour of Newton's physics and Locke's philosophy.   As for Toland, the effect of his work in Dublin was more violent and, for our present purpose, nearly as important.   "Christianity not Mysterious" was burnt by the common hangman, censured by the Irish Parliament, denounced from every pulpit in the city, whilst its author, much delighted at the turmoil he had raised, found it expedient to leave the country.   " A sermon against his errors was as much expected," says Mr. Hunt,[2] " as if it had been prescribed in the rubric : and an Irish peer gave it as a reason why he had ceased to attend church, that once he heard something there about his Saviour,

[1] Berkeley was born at Killenn (co. Kilkenny), on the 12th of March, 1685.   Swift took his degree in that year.

[2] " Religious Thought in England," vol. ii. p. 244.

Jesus Christ, but now all the discourse was about one John Toland." This took place in 1697. In 1700, Berkeley, at the age of fifteen, matriculated at Trinity College.

At the most receptive period of his precocious youth he thus found himself plunged in the middle stream of eighteenth century thought, already running with a full tide though still so near its source. For more than thirty years the character of his speculative writings turned on questions in debate during the period in which he began his first residence at Trinity College. His philosophical batteries are always directed so as to present a threefold opposition to the metaphysics of Locke, certain mathematico-physical assumptions which he ascribed to Newton, and the theological inferences of the Deists and Free-thinkers. But it must never be forgotten that, in his opposition to the new ideas, he did not represent the age that was going out, but (though in a peculiar manner) the age that was coming in. He was not engaged in the last desperate stand made along the old lines, with the old argumentative weapons, against invading innovations. In so far as he opposed the new conclusions, it was in the spirit of the new premises. If he attacked Locke, it was not as a disciple of the schoolmen. If he criticised Newton, it was not as a disciple of Descartes. And, though his orthodoxy was beyond suspicion, we may look through his theological writings in vain for that learned discussion of dogmatic subtleties which was dear to the seventeenth century, of which his own contemporaries produced more than one admirable example, but which was on the whole alien to the taste of the eighteenth century, whether believing or sceptical, whether lay or clerical. It would be a more natural, but not a less important error, to suppose that Berkeley's habits of thought [1] anticipated something of the spirit of the nineteenth century. He is, as every one knows, an " idealist " : and it might be concluded that his speculations had something of the imaginative vagueness which characterised the idealistic reaction against the shallow rationalism of the pre-revolutionary period. But it is not so. Berkeley emphatically belonged to his age. The same impatience of authority in matters of speculation, the same passion for clearness and simplicity, the same dislike of what was either pedantic on the one side or rhetorical on the other, the same desire to clothe his thoughts in an agreeable literary dress, is found in him as in any French philosopher who undertook to acquaint admiring *salons* with the latest fashion in infidelity. His creed, indeed, was a very different one from theirs, but he belonged to the same century, intellectually as well as chronologically.

On these and on other points connected with the development of Berkeley's modes of thought, we have most interesting evidence in his "Commonplace Book," [2] a collection of miscellaneous notes and memoranda connected with his philosophical studies, jotted down, apparently, between the years 1705-1707, *i.e.*, when Berkeley was little more than twenty. That a collection of this kind, never intended to meet any eyes but those of its author, should contain much that is crude and even absurd, that there should be frequent repeti-

---

[1] From all these remarks I exclude the " Siris," the work of his last years, of which I shall have to speak later.

[2] First published by Professor Fraser in 1871.

tion and no method, is, of course, inevitable. A soliloquy from which these characteristics are absent is most surely intended to be overheard. To my taste, therefore, these defects, if defects they be, only add to the vividness, and, therefore, to the interest, of the fragment of intellectual autobiography so fortunately preserved. We have here, in casual and detached utterances, almost the whole substance of the philosophy which, in a form exquisitely polished and developed, Berkeley afterwards gave to the world. But we have much more than this. We are allowed to watch all the emotions which, in the mind of its author, accompanied the birth of the new Idea.[1] His hopes, his fears, his good resolutions, his confidence in the value of his discovery, his misgivings as to its reception, are put before us in the liveliest way in notes of almost ejaculatory brevity, or fragments of dialogue with imaginary opponents.

" I wonder not," he tells us,[2] "at my sagacity in discovering the obvious tho' amazing truth ; I rather wonder at my stupid inadvertency in not finding it out before—'tis no witchcraft to see."

And again—

"MEM.—That I was distrustful at eight years old, and consequently by nature disposed to these new doctrines.[3]

"All things in the Scripture which side with the vulgar against the learned, side with me also. I side in all things with the mob. I know there is a mighty sect of men will oppose me, but yet I may expect to be supported by those whose minds are not overgrown with madness.[4]

[1] *I.e.*, The non-existence of independent matter.
[2] " Life and Letters," p. 489.   [3] *Ibid.* p. 488.   [4] *Ibid* p. 420.

I.   *b*

"MEM.—To be eternally banishing Metaphysics, etc., and recalling men to common sense. [1]

"My end is not to deliver Metaphysics in a general scholastic way, but in some way to accommodate them to the sciences, etc. [2]

"I abstain from all flourish and powers of words and figures, using a great plainness and simplicity of simile, having oft found it difficult to understand those that use the lofty and Platonic or subtil and scholastic strain." [3]

These are some of the notes which might be quoted as being pertinent to the foregoing account of Berkeley's frame of mind while at Trinity College. Let me add to them a maxim which, fortunately for the world, Berkeley only very imperfectly observed, viz.:

"N.B.—To rein in ye satyrical nature." [4]

And another for which it is strange he should even have thought he had any occasion :

"N.B.—To use utmost caution not to give least offence to the Church or Churchmen." [5]

Possibly, when he penned the last of these admonitions to himself, he was thinking of the wearisome controversy which arose out of the offence given to the too sensitive orthodoxy of Bishop Stillingfleet by Locke's doctrine of substance.

However this may be, Berkeley had no hesitation in openly ranging himself with "the Church and Churchmen ;" for within a very short time of his penning the words, namely, in 1709, he took orders, and in the same year, at the age of twenty-four, he gave to the

---

[1] "Life and Letters," p. 445. [2] *Ibid.* p. 482.
[3] *Ibid.* p. 492. [4] *Ibid.* p. 433.
[5] *Ibid.* p. 451.

world his first philosophical book—the "New Theory of Vision." This dealt with but a small number of the problems on which, as the "Commonplace Book" shows, he had for some time arrived at novel and interesting conclusions; but it was rapidly followed by the "Principles of Human Knowledge" (1710), which contain what we are in the habit of calling the "Berkeleian Philosophy," in a tolerably complete form; while in the next two years were written the dialogues between Hylas and Philonous, which presented his early speculations in their final and most elaborate shape.

Before he was twenty-eight, therefore, Berkeley had finished the work on which his position in the history of philosophy chiefly depends. His life was not half run out, and the part which still remained to him was not only far more full of incident and interest than the few quiet years spent in excogitating his new "Principle" in the studious retirement of Trinity College, but must have seemed to his contemporaries far more reasonably employed. We, on the other hand, shall, perhaps, be rather inclined to wonder that a man who had done so much before he was thirty, had not done much more by the time he was sixty. The precocity of his genius and its comparative barrenness may seem to us almost equal matters of surprise. The strangeness of both, however, diminishes on reflection. Philosophy is nearly as likely to be done well in early as in later life. It needs neither profound knowledge of human nature, nor that superficial acquaintance with the ways of mankind which goes by the name of "knowledge of the world." It is wholly independent of experience, and nearly independent even of book learning. It scarcely requires, therefore, for its successful cultivation any of the accomplishments, for the full development of which Time is a necessary condition. What it demands from its successful votaries is the instinct which tells them where, along the line of contemporary speculation, that point is to be found from which the next advance may best be made, and that speculative faculty which is as much a natural gift as an aptitude for mathematics or a genius for poetry. Should they lack the first of these requisites, they will be left, whatever their ability, like Berkeley's contemporaries, Clarke and Malebranch, out of the main current of thought in a kind of philosophical back-water ; should they lack the second, they have made a mistake as to their true calling, which neither industry nor learning will do anything to remedy. Berkeley possessed both gifts. We need not wonder, therefore, that like many other philosophers—like Hume, Fichte, Schelling, and Schopenhauer—he produced valuable original work at an early age. That he produced so little in his maturer years is doubtless due in part to temperament, and to the distractions of an unsettled and wandering life, but it must also be largely attributed to the almost total absence of intelligent criticism, either from friends or foes, under which Berkeley suffered throughout the whole period during which such criticism might have roused him to make some serious effort to develop or to defend the work of his youth. Professor Fraser has given us, from unpublished sources, an account of one ineffectual effort which Berkeley made to get his views discussed by a competent critic. In 1711 his friend Sir John Percival, to whom Berkeley had applied for information as to the reception of the " Principles," reported that the book had fallen into Dr. Clarke's hands. Clarke, it appears, read it, disagreed with it, but refused to give his reasons ; and was, moreover, alleged to have expressed an opinion that Berkeley's labours were "of little use on account of their abstruseness." Poor Berkeley, who flattered himself that his treatise did away with the " chief causes of error and difficulty in the sciences," and destroyed the "grounds of scepticism, atheism, and irreligion," was naturally distressed at a criticism which, it must be confessed, came with rather an ill grace from the author of the metaphysical " Demonstration of the Being and Attributes of God." The rest of the world has so long and so unanimously said of philosophers that their labours are " useless to mankind on account of their abstruseness," that philosophers should in common decency refrain from saying it of each other.

Berkeley, however, was now to be in a position to judge for himself, and at first hand, what the world thought of his system. Early in January, 1713, he gave up his academic life in Dublin, and, with the manuscript of his unpublished " Dialogues " in his pocket, started for London. He was there only seven months. He had the assistance neither of wealth nor of family connection, and did not even carry with him, so far as we know, any powerful recommendations from his native country ; for the reputation of having written a book which those who had read it thought useless, and those who had not, thought mad, can hardly be so esteemed.[1] Yet we find him almost

[1] It is true, however, that Berkeley alleges that Steele was interested in his account of the " Principles of Human Knowledge," and that Arbuthnot was a convert to the " Dialogues."

immediately received into the intimate society of
Whig men of letters, like Steele and Addison, and
of Tory men of letters, like Swift and Arbuthnot.
He was engaged to write in the "Guardian." Pope
presented him with a copy of a "very ingenious new
poem," "Windsor Forest." He went to Court, he was
introduced to ministers and statesmen, and finally
obtained an appointment as chaplain to a special
embassy of Lord Peterborough.

The foundation of this rapid success was doubtless
due to Berkeley's extraordinary charm of manner.
The effect of this on all who met him seems to have
been instantaneous and lasting. The words in which
Atterbury recorded his first impression of him are
almost as well known as the line in which Pope
attributes to him "every virtue under heaven." Less
well known, but equally characteristic, is the anecdote
which records that he had to escape by stratagem
from the hospitality of Wilton, so unwilling was Lord
Pembroke to be deprived of the pleasures of his
society. But it may be doubted whether any charm
of character or manner would, under ordinary circumstances, have so soon produced its natural fruits,
even though its possessor had enjoyed in addition the
reputation of having written a book which nobody
could understand. The explanation is rather to be
sought in the fact that while his nationality gained
Berkeley an introduction through his countrymen,
Steele and Swift, into the best literary society of
the day, the best literary society had, in relation to
the best society of other kinds, a position in Queen
Anne's time which it has never exactly occupied
either before or since. Lord Macaulay would have us

believe [1] that this was due to the fact that after the
Revolution statesmen felt the growing necessity of
appealing to public opinion outside the walls of
Parliament, and, at a time when debates were conducted with closed doors, could only do so by means
of the press : so that, as a natural consequence, men
of letters ceased to be merely the objects of their
patronage, and became their allies and their associates.
That this explanation partly accounts for the facts
I am far from denying, but that it does so only
in part is clear from the circumstance that the
alleged cause existed long after the alleged consequence had disappeared.   In the time of Walpole,
who valued this kind of assistance so highly that
he is said to have spent £50,000 in ten years to
secure it, there was no privileged literary circle of
any consequence, and no men of letters received
high political appointments.   Moreover, while in the
preceding period a writer so useful to ministers, as,
for example, Defoe, was paid for his services in
hard cash, and not either in posts of distinction or in
social consideration, it would be hard, I think, to show
that there was more than a very general connection
between the political writings and the politico-social
successes of such men as Prior, Addison, or even
Swift.   Prior began the diplomatic career, in which he
finally became ambassador and plenipotentiary, in
1690 ; but I am not aware that he contributed anything but verses to party controversy, except some
numbers of the " Examiner " in 1710.   Addison's
political writings are a mere fraction of his works ;
and if the places and pensions which he at various

[1] " Essay on Addison."

times obtained are to be considered as a payment for
them, it must at all events be admitted that they were
a payment conducted on very strange principles. He
had received a pension and had been made under-
secretary before writing anything political at all. A
single pamphlet in defence of the war was followed by
his appointment to the Irish Chief Secretaryship.
From the time the Whigs went out in 1710, till they
came in again on the death of the Queen, he wrote, I
believe, but one political pamphlet besides the Whig
"Examiner;" and the Whig "Examiner" he dis-
continued just when the Tory "Examiner," in Swift's
hands, became most formidable. There never was a
time when his party was more in need of a powerful
pen than during this season of their adversity; but
Addison devoted almost all his energies during it to
purely literary work, and did his best to dissuade Steele
from taking a different course. Yet so far were his
friends from thinking that they had reason to complain
of his remissness, that on their return to office, they
immediately re-appointed him to the Irish Chief
Secretaryship. The services which Swift's pen did to
his party, it would, indeed, be difficult to overrate.
But no one can doubt that, from whatever motives the
Tory Ministers began to receive him into a flattering
intimacy, they continued to do so not because they
wanted to buy him as a writer, but because they
valued him as an adviser, and loved him as a friend.

The main cause, therefore, of the unique position of
men of letters in the first quarter of the last century,
is to be found, I believe, not in any law of social
evolution, but in a mere coincidence—in the coincidence,
namely, of two men, both in the very first rank of

literary ability, both entirely devoid of literary jealousy, both zealous and disinterested friends to their literary brethren, both combining great independence with the rarest social gifts, and both ready to do political as well as literary work—in the coincidence (I say) of two such men existing together at a time when the leaders of both political parties were eminently quali-fied to appreciate their excellences. When we speak of the men of letters in the age of Queen Anne, we are usually thinking principally of Addison and "his little senate," of Swift and the Scriblerus Club; the rest were "Grub Street," and suffered neither a better nor a worse fate under Queen Anne than under the first Georges. My contention is that the explanation of the unexampled influence of the former is to be found, not in the mere fact that the statesmen of that day desired to secure the services of writers capable of producing "The Freeholder" or "The Conduct of the Allies," but in the fact that men like Addison and Swift were contemporaries of men like Somers and Halifax, Oxford and Bolingbroke.

However this may be, and I have perhaps paused too long over a question which is but indirectly con-nected with my subject, there is no doubt that Berkeley greatly profited by the state of things he found exist-ing in London. Neither then, nor at any other time, did he mix himself up in party controversy. In ecclesiastical matters he was apparently a moderate High Churchman, in politics a moderate Tory. But at a time when both ecclesiastical and political party feeling ran very high, his interests seem always to have centred in other, broader, and perhaps less practical, issues; and he therefore associated on perfectly easy

terms with men whose difference of opinion debarred
them from associating on perfectly easy terms with
each other. If this circumstance prevented him being
an actor in the stormy politics of the period, it enabled
him to be an impartial spectator of more than one
scene interesting in our literary history. At Easter,
1713, Addison's tragedy of "Cato" was acted for the
first time. Most people know Macaulay's lively
account of this celebrated "first night," though comparatively few know anything else about what was,
according to Voltaire, the first "regular" tragedy that
had ever been brought on the English stage. The
success of the play, so far as success may be measured
by applause, was certain from the first. For in the
then condition of politics, everybody was determined
to find in it a political intention ; and as neither party
would permit the other to appropriate to itself the fine
sentiments with which its speeches abounded, Whig
and Tory clapped against one another in noisy but
undiscriminating emulation. Pope tells us how the
author "sweated behind the scenes with concern to
find the applause proceeded more from the hand than
the head ;" and Berkeley writes that he "was present
with Mr. Addison and a few more friends in a side
box, where we had a table and two or three flasks of
Burgundy and Champagne, with which the author
(who is a very sober man) thought it necessary to
support his spirits. . . . Lord Harley, who sat in the
box next us, was observed to clap as loud as any in
the house all the time of the play." [1]   The picture is

---

[1] Bishop Hurd amusingly remarks, in his note to "Cato":
"While the *present humour* of idolising Shakespeare continues,
no quarter will be given to this poem."

amusing, and the testimony to Addison's habitual
sobriety is interesting on account of the accusation of
intemperance which has been brought against him.

From another letter which Professor Fraser has
brought to light, and which I cannot resist quoting,
we learn that in March Berkeley breakfasted with
Addison and Swift at the lodgings of the latter. This
incident (which is not mentioned, I believe, in the
Journal to Stella) is interesting, as throwing light on
the relations of two eminent men, whose friendship
was sometimes sorely strained, but never quite broken,
by political differences.

" I breakfasted," says Berkeley, " with him [*i.e.* with
Addison] at Dr. Swift's lodgings in Bury Street. His
coming when I was there, and the good temper which
he showed, I construed as a sign of the approaching
coalition of parties. Dr. Swift is admired by both
Steele and Addison, and I think him one of the best-
natured and most agreeable men in the world."

The prophecy suggested in this extract had more of
charity in it than of foresight. Not many months had
passed before " the best-natured man in the world "
was gibbeting Steele in " The Importance of the
' Guardian ' considered." In little more than a year
Swift was an exile in his native land, and the Tory
chiefs were either imprisoned or were flying for their
lives.

Before this wreck of all his hopes Swift was able to
do for Berkeley one of the many kindnesses which, in
the days of his power, he conferred on his literary
brethren. He got him appointed chaplain to the
special embassy of which the celebrated Lord Peterborough was the head. The service he thus did his

friend was greater than may at first appear. In the
last century, travelling meant something more than
hurrying through picture galleries, staring at churches,
and seeing a little of everything in foreign countries
except their inhabitants. But while its advantages
were greater, so also was its cost. A man, without
introductions or powerful connections, could not enjoy
its full benefits ; and a man without money, or the
assistance of those who had money, could scarcely
hope to enjoy them at all. Under these circumstances,
there were two methods by which a poor man might
obtain direct knowledge of foreign society or foreign
art. He might become companion, probably tutor, to
some richer person, or he might obtain an appointment on some embassy. Addison, Gray, Adam
Smith, are examples of the first method ; Locke and
Hume of the second. Berkeley enjoyed both. In
1713-14, as chaplain to Lord Peterborough's mission,
from 1716-20, as tutor to the son of Ashe, Bishop of
Clogher, he travelled on the Continent under favourable circumstances, visiting France, Italy, and Sicily.

It is not necessary to pause over his wanderings.
Of part of them we have a very full record in a journal
which has been preserved, and which Professor Fraser
has, for the first time, rendered accessible. From this
it is easy to discern the spirit in which he wandered
through Italy and Sicily, lingering with delight in
what he describes, in an admirable letter to Pope, as
the "romantic" scenery of Ischia, or penetrating into
the little-known recesses of Calabria. He does not
indulge largely in historical or political reflections, nor
are his pages loaded with classical reminiscences,
though these are not wanting ; but he notes the

external aspect of the country and its inhabitants, the character of the agriculture, of the scenery, and, even more particularly, of the architecture.   He is, besides, a keen scientific investigator.   He sent home to Arbuthnot, and Arbuthnot communicated to the Royal Society, an excellent account of an ascent of Vesuvius during an eruption.   He inquired with great care, though with no very conclusive result, into the phenomena of Tarantism—*i.e.*, into the effects that were supposed to follow the bite of the Tarantula ; and he made a collection of the flora of Sicily.   All this has for us now only a biographical interest ; and even if the second part of the " Principles of Human Knowledge," which he wrote in Sicily, and which was lost at sea, had been preserved, it may be doubted whether much of permanent value would have been added to what we know of his philosophy from other sources.   But it cannot be doubted that the effect of his travels on Berkeley himself was great, and that when he returned to England at the end of 1720, he brought back from the Continent a knowledge of men and things, and a cultivated sensibility to the beauties of nature and art, which have left permanent traces in his writings.

The inner connection of the events which occurred in the three years immediately succeeding his return home are, at first sight, difficult to discover.   But the events themselves are easily told.   He arrived in England during the very crisis of the South Sea mania.   This, and what else he saw of the condition of society, startled him into writing an "Essay towards the Prevention of the Ruin of Great Britain," of which it is sufficient to say here that it is one of those

energetic protests against national vices to which no
nation, standing gravely in need of it, would be likely
to pay much attention.   This done, and acquaintance
renewed with the survivors among his old literary
friends, he seems to have laid himself out for ecclesiastical preferment.   The architectural knowledge acquired in Italy recommended him to the architectural
Lord Burlington, through whose influence he became
chaplain to the Duke of Grafton, then just appointed
Lord-Lieutenant of Ireland.   The post seems to have
been little to Berkeley's liking.   But if, as is probable,
he accepted it as a step to one more congenial to his
tastes, he certainly succeeded better than his friend
Swift, who had occupied a similar position with similar
hopes many years before, with no better reward than
the living of Laracor.   The more fortunate Berkeley
was appointed, in rapid succession, by his College to
several lectureships, and by the Lord-Lieutenant to a
living and two deaneries.[1]   The deanery of Dromore,
on account of some legal obstacle, he seems never to
have enjoyed.   With regard to the deanery of Derry
there were no such difficulties.   But he had no sooner
entered into undisturbed possession of it than he
astonished his friends by expressing the most ardent
wish to leave it, in order to execute a scheme for the
conversion of America.

It certainly seems strange at first sight that Berkeley
should thus for some years have sought ecclesiastical
preferment with no other apparent object than to
resign it as soon as it was obtained.   But the fact
seems to be that during those years his scheme of life
underwent a complete change.   Doubtless, he returned,

[1] He returned to Ireland in 1721.

after his long wanderings, anxious for a settled home and determinate work, and with the intention of finding these in the ordinary development of a clerical career. But the spectacle of the corrupt society of the early Georgian period, rendered more repulsive by the shameless fraud and avarice that accompanied the South Sea speculation, shocked his unaccustomed gaze. He conceived a profound dislike of a civilisation eaten into, and, as he believed, fatally undermined, by idleness, self-indulgence, and irreligion. He turned, as others in a like position have turned, to a younger and more hopeful society across the ocean. There gradually grew up in his mind the strange but fascinating dream of a missionary college, which should be a centre of civilisation to the rising Empire in the West. His imagination filled itself with the vision of a learned and devout company of friends, far removed from luxury and the snares which beset the search for wealth, devoting themselves, under the serene skies of Bermuda, to the instruction of native Americans, who were in their turn to teach their brethren on the mainland those truths of Christian morality which in Europe men continued to profess, but had long ceased to value. If, however, the vision was to become a reality, the first and most important step was to convince a sceptical age of his own unselfish belief in its possibility. And it may well have seemed to Berkeley that, as a means towards attaining this end, he could not do better than obtain that ecclesiastical preferment which he had probably originally sought from other and more ordinary motives. A missionary scheme which would have received scant attention while advocated by a literary clergyman of no established position, unsupported by any powerful connection, might wear a very different complexion when promoted by a dean who was prepared to sacrifice his deanery to assist it. A man who was not only ready, but anxious to give up two thousand a year at home in order to get a hundred a year in the middle of the Atlantic, might be visionary, but must certainly be disinterested ; and Berkeley knew well enough that in order to get people to believe in his scheme, it was first necessary to make them believe in himself.

If this was his object, it must be admitted that, in the first instance at least, it was thoroughly attained. His unrivalled powers of personal persuasion were unsparingly used to further his cause. Every one knows the anecdote narrated by Warton, on the authority of Lord Bathurst, which tells how the members of the Scriblerus Club agreed to rally Berkeley on his project, how, after hearing all that they had to say, he asked to be heard in his turn, and how the eloquence of the philanthropic philosopher so moved them, that those who came to scoff remained to subscribe. The story, though strange, may be believed, since we have it on no less evidence than the Statute Book, that he performed the far more amazing feat of obtaining a grant of money (£20,000) from the State, and this at a time when Sir Robert Walpole was responsible for its finances. Nobody was more surprised at such a result than Sir Robert himself, who attributed it, and with good reason, not to the merits of the project, but to the persuasive powers of the projector. These were, in truth, used without stint. The King's Court at St. James's and the Princes' Court at Leicester Fields, the world of letters and the world of fashion, as well as every individual member of the House of Commons, were canvassed on behalf of the scheme, and with such effect that, as we have seen, the nation promised money, the King granted a charter, Walpole himself subscribed, Bermuda became the fashion, and even Bolingbroke talked of emigrating, *not* in a missionary capacity, to Berkeley's ideal island.

Yet the scheme seems now so impracticable, that we may well wonder how any single person, let alone the representatives of a whole nation, could be found to support it. In order that religion and learning might flourish in America, the seeds of them were to be cast in some rocky islets severed from America by nearly six hundred miles of stormy ocean. In order that the inhabitants of the mainland and of the West Indian colonies might equally benefit by the new university, it was to be placed in such a position that neither could conveniently reach it. In order that no taint of luxury should corrupt its morals, it was to be removed far from every source of wealth and every centre of industry to a place where, as Berkeley flattered himself, there was no more lucrative occupation possible than that of making straw hats. It was to spring from no natural want, it was to follow no natural growth, it was to be thrown as it were from without to a population which had never expressed any desire for it, and in whom a desire was not likely to be excited by a gift which, however valuable in itself, was presented to them for the first time in so singular and so inconvenient a shape.

Berkeley, it may be observed, was not moved to adopt his scheme by any such Utopian views, either of the European colonists or the native Americans, as became fashionable on the Continent at a later period of the century. He did not believe that a society which, by force of circumstances, was free from the vices incident to an ancient and complex civilisation was therefore virtuous; nor yet that in hordes of ignorant savages was to be found the perfect and uncorrupted work of Nature. On the contrary, in the curious pamphlet in which he recommended his project to the public, he expressly mentions the "avarice, the licentiousness, the coldness in the practice of religion, and the aversion from propagating it," of which the colonists on the mainland were accused; and tells us that "no part of the Gentile world are so inhuman and barbarous as the savage Americans, whose chief employment and delight consist in cruelty and revenge." But he certainly believed that in the New World there was not only the largest, but also the most hopeful field for missionary effect. Society there might be corrupt, but it was not, like society in Europe, grown old in corruption. The native Indians might be ignorant and brutal, but "if they were unimproved by education, they were also unencumbered with that rubbish of superstition and prejudice which is the effect of a wrong one." He imagined that if only the religion and learning of the Old World, purified from its pedantry and its vice, could be brought to bear on the New while this was yet young and plastic, the eyes of posterity might be gladdened by the sight of a new Golden Age; and he bursts into a strain of almost prophetic rapture as, in vigorous verses, he describes the new Arts and new Empire, "not such as Europe breeds in her decay," which were to rise in the West, the "last and noblest" birth of Time.

Reflections such as these suggested, we may be sure, the main outlines of his scheme. The character of its details was probably due to his special idiosyncrasies. Ten years before, in one of his papers in the "Guardian," he had drawn a picture of University life as it might be, as it had been, perhaps, to him, but as it certainly was not, in his day, to the majority of students. The same vision haunted his declining years. And doubtless, while still in the prime of life, a project which should enable him to further the interests of a continent, while holding himself aloof, in academic retirement, from the noise, the dust, and the contamination of the struggling multitude, had, as it might well have, irresistible fascination. But this was not all. His fancy lingered lovingly over the picture drawn by poets and travellers of the scenery in the western isles. With Ischia and Sicily still fresh in his recollection, he dwelt on the orange-groves and cedars, the cloudless skies, and the perpetual spring which were to be found in Bermuda. He even dreamed of rearing amid these natural beauties collegiate buildings, which his architectural knowledge should render not unworthy of their setting.

The vision, it must be owned, was a fascinating one; but it was never to be realised, even in the smallest particular. Fortunately, as I hold, for Berkeley, his scheme was not even tried sufficiently to show its incurable vices. In pursuance of his mission, he left England, it is true, in 1728 with his newly-married wife,[1] but he never reached Bermuda. In Rhode

---

[1] Anne, daughter of John Forster, Chief Justice of Common Pleas (Ireland), whom he married on August 1st, 1728. He sailed on September 4th.

Island, where he arrived after a long and tedious passage, he waited, perhaps with diminishing belief in his own plans, for the funds which never came. Sir Robert Walpole had been forced by an unexpected vote to promise a sum of £20,000, but there was nothing to force him to pay it. " If you put the question to me as a Minister," he said, " I can assure you that the money shall most undoubtedly be paid— as soon as suits public convenience ; but if you ask me as a friend whether Dean Berkeley shall continue in America expecting the payment of £20,000, I advise him by all means to return to Europe."

To Europe accordingly Berkeley returned in February, 1732. Of Bermuda we hear no more. But he long retained a lively interest in the colony in which for nearly three years he had, as it were by accident, found a home. To Yale and to Harvard colleges he sent, soon after his arrival in England, a gift of books ; and to the former he left his farm near Newport (the scenery of which he has so exquisitely described in "Alciphron") for the perpetual sustentation of three scholarships. The foundation exists, I believe, to the present day, and has not only served the purpose for which it was immediately founded, but has aided the education of some of those who have most earnestly devoted themselves to raising the condition of the North American Indians. This is the only contribution which Berkeley has made to the cause for which he left England ; and it is, perhaps, the most permanent and important result of an enterprise begun with vast aims and lofty hopes, the record of which remains, indeed, a splendid testimony to the personal charm, to the self-forgetful zeal, to the disinterested benevolence of its author ;

but also a standing proof of how little in the region of action these high qualities avail, dissociated from the practical instinct which distinguishes between what does and what does not deserve to be attempted.

II.

IF Berkeley's journey to America did not materially further the object for which it was undertaken, it was not, on the other hand, wholly barren of results. During the three years of enforced but agreeable leisure which he spent in Rhode Island, he composed the longest, and, in his own lifetime, the most considered of all his writings—" Alciphron, or the Minute Philosopher."

This work—a series of seven dialogues directed against the Deists—contains Berkeley's chief polemical contribution to the great religious controversy of his generation. During the thirty-seven years that intervened between the publication of Toland's " Christianity not Mysterious " and that of " Alciphron," this controversy had never flagged. But, though the points in debate are not widely removed from those which profoundly stir men's interests now, they are just sufficiently removed to make the discussion of them empty and unsatisfactory to modern ears. Objections to revealed religion founded upon textual criticism, history, and science, were put then as they are put now, but they were put and answered by men to whom criticism , history, and science, in the modern use of those terms, were practically unknown. The consequence of this has been that, with the one exception of Butler's " Analogy," the merely argumentative part of that voluminous controversy has lost all but a historic interest, and only those fragments of it can now be read with pleasure which are preserved from neglect by their purely literary merits.

This is hard upon the Deists ; for, whatever may have been the intrinsic strength of their arguments, it is generally admitted that all the wit (to say nothing of the learning) was on the side of their opponents. The deistical writings are now antiquated, but they were always dull ; and there is scarcely a single piece deliberately intended to further their distinctive opinions which can now be read with any sort of satisfaction. The fact is remarkable. In an age in which so large a proportion of the best literary work, whether in prose or verse, was satirical ; in which even those who, like Gray and Akenside, would least have desired to be remembered as satirists seemed to write with unwonted ease and vigour when they trespassed on satiric ground, it is strange that no one could be found able and willing to retaliate in kind on the attacks of Swift, Steele, Bentley, and Berkeley. Even Pope, whose " Essay on Man " was mainly founded on the writings of one Deist and the conversations of another, has nothing but sneers for the "smart free-thinker," and took occasion to pillory their most con-siderable authors in the " Dunciad ; " while Shaftes-bury, though he loudly recommended the use of ridicule as a cure for "enthusiasm" and "superstition," was, unfortunately, denied by nature the gifts neces-sary for supplementing his precepts by his example. It was not till Deism had been transplanted from its original home to the more congenial soil of France, that the balance was redressed.   Voltaire, who added little to the argumentative armoury of Collins, Tindal, and the rest, for the first time succeeded in making infidelity amusing, while, unlike his English predecessors, he met with nothing in the field of literature deserving the name of resistance.

Berkeley, it will be recollected, had been interested from his earliest Dublin days in the Deistic controversy. The very title pages of his " Principles of Human Knowledge," and of the " Dialogue of Hylas and Philonous," proclaimed the fact that his philosophic speculations were intended as a remedy for " Scepticism," " Atheism," and " Irreligion."   But he soon found that his remedy, whatever might be its intrinsic value, was scarcely adapted for general use. Ordinary men were not prepared to admit that a Deity was necessary because matter was impossible. In the " Guardian " he accordingly adopted a more popular style, well suited to readers who knew little of theology and nothing of metaphysics, but who required to be reminded that religion had some claims to the gratitude and reverence of mankind, and that the pretensions of those who attacked it provided no measure of their merits.

Who, then, were these enemies of religion ? By their opponents they were not unfrequently described as persons who, in matters practical, were of relaxed morals, and in matters speculative might be called almost indifferently Deists, freethinkers, and atheists. Yet nothing is more certain than that Shaftesbury, for instance, and Collins, were perfectly respectable members of society, and that while all the more important writers on the unorthodox side would have repudiated the name of atheist, Shaftesbury, at least, made ardent and, doubtless, sincere professions of Theism. Are we then to attribute the language of the orthodox party to the mere heat and prejudice of controversy? In part, I think, we must. The almost incredible coarseness with which, under cover of a learned tongue, men of learning and piety had in preceding ages not unfrequently conducted their disputes, was in the eighteenth century greatly mitigated But the practice of exaggerating the errors of an opponent, in order to gibbet them with more effect, prevailed to a serious extent. The High Churchman was denounced as a Papist. The Low, or (as we should now say) Broad Churchman, was denounced as a Latitudinarian; the Latitudinarian was denounced as a Socinian; the Socinian as a Deist; the Deist as an atheist. But, admitting all this, it must be remembered that it would be most unjust to estimate the controversial moderation of the orthodox divines in the first half of the last century, by a bare comparison of their language with the official utterances of their opponents. Berkeley, especially, can never be understood, unless we keep in mind that he interpreted the text of Shaftesbury, Collins, and Mandeville by the light of the social facts of his own day. The Deist movement did not appear to him as it does to us, in the form of a certain number of treatises directed against the received theology, for the most part tedious, of slight literary merit, containing nothing either to agitate or instruct the modern reader, and predestined, in England at least, to bear little permanent fruit. In his view, these were rather the more prominent and public signs of a widespread attack on religion, conducted orally on much more extreme lines, and with great and growing success. He believed in the existence of freethinking clubs, where those who, in their published writings were content to advocate Deism, professed in private to demonstrate that no Deity could possibly exist. He believed that Society was honeycombed with a religious scepticism, not arising from any disinterested pursuit of truth, but from mere libertinism in thought, at once the effect and the cause of libertinism in conduct ; and he traced a direct connection between the relaxed morality of the Georgian era and the contemptuous tone towards Christianity rendered fashionable by the Deistical writers.

The consequence of this is that, while his contemporary, Butler, addresses himself entirely to producing a convincing reply to the formal arguments of the freethinkers, Berkeley seeks also to attack them on what we may term their social side. His strokes are aimed not only at Shaftesbury and Collins, but at the Coffee-house infidels ;—the would-be men of fashion, who thought that there was no greater proof of enlightenment than to sneer at Christianity, or of wit than to cut jokes on a parson. He is never weary of dilating on the pretentious ignorance of these gentlemen.

" Who," says Euphranor (one of the orthodox speakers in " Alciphron "), " are these profound and learned men that of late years have demolished the whole fabric which philosophers, lawgivers, and divines have been erecting for so many ages ? "

" Lysicles (the infidel man of fashion), hearing these words, smiled, and said that he believed Euphranor had figured to himself philosophers in square caps and long gowns; but, thanks to these happy times, the reign of pedantry is over. 'Our philosophers,' said he, 'are of a different kind from those awkward students. . . . I will undertake a lad of fourteen, bred in the modern way, shall make a better figure and be more considered in any drawing-room than one of four-and-twenty, who hath lain by a long time at school or college. He shall say better things, in a better manner, and be more liked by good judges.'

"*Euphranor.* Whence doth he pick up all this improvement?

"*Crito* (ironically). Where our grave ancestors would never have looked for it—in a drawing-room, a coffee-house, a chocolate-house, at the tavern or groom porters."

And so forth.

To us, who are directly acquainted with nothing but the literary remains of the controversy, the laugh seems so clearly to be on the side of Orthodoxy, that we have some difficulty in recollecting that to Berkeley and Berkeley's contemporaries the fact must have seemed exactly reversed. The "raillery" which Shaftesbury recommended as the test of truth was, in society, freely employed against "priestcraft" in general, and the clergy of the Established Church in particular; who, when not denounced as bigots, were ridiculed as musty pedants.

"I have often observed," says Crito, "that the Freethinking sect run into two faults of conversation, declaiming and bantering, just as the tragic or comic humour prevails. Sometimes they work themselves into a high passion, and are frightened at spectres of their own raising. In those fits every country curate passes for an inquisitor. At other times they affect a sly, facetious manner, expressing little, insinuating much, and upon the whole seeming to divert themselves with the subject and their adversaries." "Can no method be found," he exclaims in a later dialogue, "to free them from the terror of that fierce and bloody animal, an English parson?"

Arguments may be refuted, but "who," it has been asked, "can answer a sneer?" Berkeley in "Alciphron" attempted to answer both the arguments and the sneer. It was this double object which probably induced him to employ the most difficult of all forms of composition to manage with effect—the Dialogue. He had already, it is true, used it with extraordinary skill in the region of pure exposition. The three dialogues between Hylas and Philonous have never in their peculiar style been equalled in English; they will, I suppose, never be surpassed. Yet what reader, anxious rather to get at the substance of Berkeley's doctrine, than to spend his time over a literary luxury, would not prefer to these admirable conversations the straightforward statement contained in the "Principles of Human Knowledge?" But in the case of "Alciphron," its author pursued a more complex end. *There* dialogue was not merely one of the two possible forms by which his aim could be reached; it was the only possible form. It was only by bringing his opponents actually on the stage, by dramatising their conversation, by exhibiting the weaknesses of their character as well as the errors of their logic, that his intention could be accomplished in all its fulness. To my thinking, Berkeley was wonderfully successful.

Mr. Leslie Stephen, indeed, declares " Alciphron " to be the "least admirable of all its author's admirable works." But I cannot help thinking that this excellent critic, in forming his judgment, was thinking rather of what he desired to find in the book, than of what its author desired to put into it. It may at once be granted that " Alciphron " is not, like the " Analogy," a great original contribution to theology. Many portions of it are now wholly antiquated; many other portions contain arguments which have since, by frequent repetition, become the mere commonplaces of apologetics. But there remains more than one admirable application of Berkeley's peculiar philosophy to the theory of religion ; there remain the slight but exquisite descriptions of incident and scenery which form the setting of the piece ; and there remains, above all, the literary skill displayed in the dramatic and polemical elements of the dialogue and in the art with which these are woven together into an organic whole.

It was an inevitable defect in the structure of the piece that, as all the varieties of the genus Freethinker are represented in it by two persons, unity of character cannot be sustained throughout the seven dialogues. Nothing, for instance, can make it natural for Lysicles, the freethinking man of pleasure, who says in one place—" For my part, I find no fault with the Universities; all I know is that I had the spending of three hundred pounds a year in one of them, and think it the cheerfullest time of my life. As for their books and style, I had not leisure to mind them"— nothing, I say, can make it natural for such a man to quote, as he does in another dialogue, Spinoza and Hobbes, and to argue about the metaphysical doctrine of substance. But this is a trifling defect. A far more serious charge has been brought against Berkeley by Sir James Mackintosh, and, more recently, by Professor Fowler in his excellent biography of Shaftesbury, to the effect that, in the third dialogue and elsewhere, the latter has been treated with gross unfairness. I admit at once that Professor Fowler is right in saying that Berkeley does not examine Shaftesbury's doctrines in the spirit "which befits one philosopher examining the works of another." But I cannot admit that, in Sir James Mackintosh's phrase, he "sinks to the level of a railing polemic."

Shaftesbury is not, to me at least, an attractive writer. His constant efforts to figure simultaneously as a fine gentleman and a fine writer, are exceedingly irritating; and the very moderate success which has attended his efforts in the latter character, suggests the doubt, justified by his general style, whether he can really have shone in the former. His pretensions to taste are quite unjustified by what we know of his opinions. Like most of his contemporaries he despised Gothic architecture, yet he saw nothing to admire in Wren; while he theorised about painting till he persuaded himself that the merits of a picture were wholly independent of its colouring. At the same time it must be acknowledged that eminent authorities have found in him distinguished merits. Mr. Leslie Stephen tells us, that "on the rude stock of commonplace Whiggism he grafted accomplishments strange to most of his countrymen." He reminded Warburton of Plato, and has been so fortunate as to remind Professor Fowler of Marcus Aurelius. Moreover, by writers on Moral Philosophy he is naturally

and properly regarded as a moral philosopher who
occupies an important position in the history of ethical
speculation as the predecessor of Butler and Hutche-
son, the originator of a new method of procedure in
moral inquiries.

But Berkeley, it must be recollected, regarded the
author of the "Characteristics" from a very different
point of view. He was not concerned with the
ethical system, which may with more or less success
be extracted from these very unsystematic essays;
nor yet with the hints contained in them, which have
in other hands become important in the history of
thought. His interest in Shaftesbury's writings was
practical, not speculative. He looked at them not as
"one philosopher examining the works of another,"
but as a man profoundly interested in the actual condition of religious thought must look at a book by
which that condition was powerfully affected. It was
the general tendency of the theological parts of the
"Characteristics," therefore, and not the special doctrines which might be supported by isolated passages
in them, that moved him to attack Shaftesbury: and
I do not think that the account he gives of that
tendency, though perhaps one-sided, is justly chargeable with gross unfairness. If, however, it be alleged
that Berkeley has, for controversial purposes, credited
Shaftesbury with holding opinions which the latter
has distinctly repudiated: I reply that Shaftesbury
has no right to complain of any critic who appeals
from specific statements in his writings to their general
animus, since he himself has never scrupled to make
professions of respect for theological dogmas which
we know him to have held in contempt.

I cannot admit, therefore, that Berkeley is guilty nearly to the full extent of the charge made against him ; and I must also point out that, if I read his character aright, and if the account I have given of his intentions in writing "Alciphron" be true, Shaftesbury must, of all writers, have been the one he found most difficult to treat in a spirit of perfect charity. Berkeley, partly from a natural feeling of *esprit de corps*, and partly from a higher motive, strongly objected to the tone adopted towards the clergy in some sections of society.   Shaftesbury speaks of them with all the airs of superiority which a "free writer" and a wit in those days thought himself justified in using towards "pedants" and "bigots."   Berkeley was weighed down with a sense of the wickedness and corruptions of his generation.   Shaftesbury's creed was a shallow optimism.   Berkeley, intent upon the regeneration of the lowest and most brutal of mankind, felt keenly that the forces arrayed on the side of virtue were all too weak as they stood ; and that they did but a small service to morality who, by undermining a belief in a system of future rewards and punishments, "while they extolled the beauty of virtue, attempted to lessen her dower." [1]   Shaftesbury, on the other hand, strong in the possession of £10,000 a year, and a feeble constitution, really talks sometimes as if virtue was mainly an object of æsthetic sensibility ; certain on its own merits to be appreciated by gentlemen of "taste and breeding," but sadly injured, from the point of view of Art, by superfluous references to Heaven and Hell.

Nor was Berkeley's opposition to the sentiment of

[1] Essay in the "Guardian."

the elder author likely to be softened by admiration for his style. In "Alciphron" he levels more than one sarcasm at it; and it must be admitted that Shaftesbury's laborious struggles after an "easy way" of writing, his vulgar affectation of refinement, his strange experiments in search of the sublime, and the pedantic trifling which does duty in his writings for "raillery and humour," were not likely to be more agreeable to a man of Berkeley's literary taste, than were Shaftesbury's opinions to a man of Berkeley's religious convictions.

Two years after the appearance of "Alciphron" occurred the last great change in the external circumstances of its author. He was appointed to the Bishopric of Cloyne, through the influence of Queen Caroline, 1734. This remarkable woman, wife of George II., and by far the most distinguished Queen Consort England has ever possessed, not content with being, next to Walpole, the greatest political power in the country, amused her leisure hours by dabbling in all the theological and philosophical controversies of the period. Berkeley, in the days when he was canvassing for his Bermuda scheme, had been obliged to discuss in her presence, and presumably for her amusement, his philosophical tenets with Clarke, not, as he pathetically observed, because he loved Courts, but because he loved America. Clarke himself, till his death in 1729, was constantly in her society, and but for his scruples respecting the Athanasian doctrine of the Trinity, which permitted him, apparently, to hold a rectory but not to accept a bishopric, would long before, through her favour, have obtained high ecclesiastical preferment. Butler, who a little later than this succeeded to Clarke's position with the Queen, was by her recommendation raised to the See of Bristol. When I add that she caused the whole of the controversy between Clarke and Leibnitz to pass through her hands, it will be seen that few persons—not philosophers—have ever taken a keener or more practical interest in the philosophy of their day. How far she was really competent, by study or natural aptitude, for such inquiries, it is hard to say. She was supposed, perhaps on insufficient evidence, to be unsettled, if not unorthodox, in her religious convictions. If so, it is possible that, like many others in similar circumstances, she was driven to investigations, for which she was perfectly unfitted, by the hope of there finding an anodyne for an unquiet spirit. Horace Walpole,[1] who represents the social tradition respecting her, declares that she was incapable of understanding Butler's "Analogy." Clarke, on the other hand, professed a high admiration for her philosophic capacity. The evidence of neither witness is very satisfactory. Clarke was too good a courtier to be a very good judge; while Walpole and his set would certainly be unwilling to believe that any one, much less any woman, least of all any Queen, could find a meaning in abstract arguments which they themselves had never taken the trouble to understand. However this may be, it is unquestionably to her enlightened patronage that

---

[1] "The Bishop of Durham (Chandler) is dead : he is succeeded by Butler of Bristol, a metaphysic author, much patronised by the late Queen. She never could make my father read his book, and which she certainly did not understand herself : he told her his religion was fixed, and that he did not want to change or improve it."—*Walpole to Mann.*

the Churches of England and Ireland owed the two most distinguished bishops of the eighteenth century. The appointment of Berkeley is the more creditable, since he had nothing but his merits to recommend him, and was quite unprovided with any of the ordinary titles to Irish ecclesiastical preferment. If he belonged to either Party in the State, he was a Tory ; and in Tories who were not Jacobites the Government saw little either to love or to fear. He was wholly unfitted by taste, character, and abilities, for carrying out the political functions sometimes so strangely associated with the Episcopal office in Ireland. And, besides all this, he had powerful enemies near the person of the Queen ; for Hoadley, her favourite bishop, and Lord Hervey, her favourite courtier, liked neither him nor his writings, which, indeed, it must be owned, they were very little fitted to comprehend.

Berkeley's eighteen years of recluse life in his diocese of Cloyne give little material to the biographer. It was a period marked by declining health and increasing infirmities, loss of friends and of children ; nor was there anything in the condition of public affairs, on either side of St. George's Channel, to lighten the burden of these private afflictions. Yet he seems to have been on the whole not unhappy. The glimpses we get of his home life are not very numerous, but they are attractive ; the studious retirement which he loved he could indulge in to his heart's content ; and though disease and advancing years had sapped the natural energy of his character, he could still on occasion show something of the old fire. We find him, for instance, in 1745, when the Pretender was on his march to Derby, and when fears were naturally entertained lest Ireland should catch the contagion of rebellion from the sister island, writing thus to Dean Gervais :

"Our Militia have been arrayed, that is, sworn : but, alas! we want not oaths, we want muskets. I have bought up all I could get, and provided horses and arms, for four and twenty of the Protestants of Cloyne, which with a few men," etc.

Two episodes there are, however, in these uneventful years, to which more particular allusion must be made : the publication of the " Querist " (1735-37), and the " Tar Water " enthusiasm, which followed soon after.

The " Querist," as my readers are probably aware, is, to all intents and purposes, an essay on the social state of Ireland thrown into the form of a series of questions. Of all the mass of literature which has been devoted to the distresses of that distressful country, this is probably the most original. Its form alone would seem to distinguish it from every other production of a similar kind. It consists of 595 interrogatories, averaging three or four lines in length, and entirely without connecting passages. Sustained eloquence under these conditions is clearly out of the question. It is difficult to understand by what literary arts such a production can even be made readable. Yet readable it certainly is ; and not only readable, but impressive. Berkeley has, in truth, chosen his instrument with remarkable skill. He was enabled by its peculiarities to give his argument on certain rather dry subjects—banks, for instance and paper currency—with a brevity which no other form of literary composition would have permitted, and a force which in no other form could have been excelled ; while his opinions on the state of the nation lose nothing either by the conciseness with which they are expressed, or the interrogatory form into which they are thrown. Paragraphs like these, for example, serve Berkeley's purpose as well as a whole page of sensational description :

" 19. Whether the bulk of our Irish peasantry are not kept from thriving by that cynical content in dirt and beggary which they possess to a degree beyond any other in Christendom ?

" 456. Whether it be not certain that the matrons of this forlorn country send out a greater proportion of its wealth for fine apparel than any other females on the whole surface of this terraqueous globe ?

" 106. Whether the dirt, famine, and nakedness of the bulk of our people might not be remedied, even though we had no foreign trade ?

" 132. Whether there be upon earth any Christian or civilised people so beggarly wretched, and destitute, as the common Irish ?

" 133. Whether, nevertheless, there is any other people whose wants may be more easily supplied from home ? "

Many of the " queries " are, it must be added, enlivened by Berkeley's peculiar turn of irony ; for example :

" 111. Whether the women (of Ireland) may not sew, spin, weave, embroider, sufficiently for the embellishment of their persons, *and even enough to raise envy in each other*, without being beholden to foreign countries ?

" 330. What right an eldest son hath to the worst education?

" 405. Whether an expense in building and improvement doth not remain at home, pass to the heir, and adorn the public? *And whether any of these things can be said of claret?*"

Yet this method of writing was not without its dangers. It lent itself with unfortunate facility to the intellectual habits which increasing infirmities were bringing on Berkeley. As in " Siris," of which I shall presently speak, there are hints and adumbrations of a new philosophy strangely tacked on to reflections upon a new medicine ; so in the " Querist " there are fragments of a new political economy mixed up with schemes for the social regeneration of Ireland. And it is, I think, clear that in both cases the fragmentary methods of exposition were in part chosen because the ideas to be expounded, though fruitful and original, and though in other hands they have since received a fuller development, were, in the mind of their author, themselves fragmentary and ill-compacted. Take, as an example of this, Berkeley's opinion upon what is called the " mercantile theory " of commerce—the theory which taught that a nation is benefited by a foreign trade in proportion as that trade brought money or bullion into the country. This absurd doctrine is absolutely exploded in the " Querist," it is demonstrated to be wrong in theory and wrong in practice ; yet some of the queries (*e.g.* 161-2) seem to assume its truth. Again, nothing can be more explicit than Berkeley's proof that, for currency purposes, notes and gold may perform exactly the same function. Yet so great is his hatred of the doctrine that money

is a source of wealth that, though anxious to increase
the amount of the circulation in the country, he is unwilling to increase the amount of gold, and seems
almost to hold that, though notes may be a substitute
for coin, coin is not a substitute for notes.[1]

My business, however, is not with Berkeley's political economy, any more than with his philosophy, but
rather with the temper and qualities of the man himself ; and if we would see how these make themselves
felt in the treatment of the Irish problem, let us compare the "Querist" with Swift's tracts on Ireland
which appeared in the preceding decade. In their
diagnosis of the diseases under which that unhappy
country was suffering, these two eminent friends
agreed with each other, and with the majority of subsequent observers. The idleness, squalor, and poverty
of the "native Irish," the absence of manufactures,
the ignorance and extravagance of the gentry, their
want of care for the real interests of their tenantry
and their country,—these are topics common to both.
It is when they set themselves to make straight the
crooked ways that the difference between them
appears. Berkeley tells his countrymen that the
remedy for the evils under which they suffer lies, in
the main, in their own hands. Let the upper classes
give up a stupid and tasteless extravagance. Let
their women buy fewer silks and laces, and their men
drink less claret. Let luxury be checked, if need be,
by sumptuary laws. Let the "standard of comfort"
of the peasantry be raised, and thereby something
done to destroy their lazy contentment in an exist-

---

[1] Cf. "Querist," 227, 283.

ence more squalid and wretched than that of the savage Americans. Let manufacturing enterprise be stimulated by an improved currency, an improved machinery of credit, and by the increase of a home demand for home products. But let nobody imagine that any good was done by sitting down and complaining of the tyranny of England. Though it were true that England had hampered their commerce and destroyed their woollen trade, yet nations had flourished, and were flourishing, whose external trade was insignificant. England and Ireland were one nation, and what was good for the part was good for the whole. If Englishmen had forgotten this truth as regards Irishmen, let not Irishmen forget it either as regards Englishmen or as regards each other. Foreign commerce was not necessary to the solid well-being of the country. But it *was* necessary that the manufacturers of the North should not be jealous of the manufacturers of the South ; that the landlord should not suppose that he could be prosperous when his tenantry was squalid and miserable ; that the Protestant minority should not suppose that they could be rich and flourishing when the Roman Catholic majority were poor and oppressed.

Whatever may be thought of Berkeley's specific proposal, it will not be denied that he treated his subject in the spirit of true patriotism and sound wisdom. So did not Swift. He detested Ireland ; he never called himself an Irishman ; he would never have set foot in Ireland could he have avoided it. But if he was an Irishman by the visitation of Heaven, he was a partisan by the very necessity of his nature. As a Tory, he hated the Whigs. As an Anglican, he

hated both the Irish Roman Catholics and the Irish
Presbyterians. As a member of the Lower House of
Convocation, he hated the Bishops. As a member of
the dominant race he would doubtless have hated the
native population had they been formidable enough
to provoke any sentiment stronger than a pitying
contempt. And so, when compelled to become an
Irishman, it was inevitable that he should also become
an Irish patriot.

Irish patriotism took the form then, as it has often
done since, not so much of helping Ireland as of
thwarting England; and, doubtless, the task of thwarting England was doubly agreeable to Swift because
England meant primarily the Whig Ministry and the
commercial classes, who were at once the chief support
of the Whigs and the greatest curse to Ireland. Like
Berkeley, he recommended his countrymen to consume
their own manufactures; not like Berkeley, because
he thought it would benefit the Irish, but because he
hoped it might hurt the English. In the famous
controversy respecting " Wood's halfpence," he went
much farther. All the arts, legitimate and illegitimate,
of the most accomplished political pamphleteer that
ever lived were used to inflame the passions of the
people against the attempt of the English Government to give them, not anything injurious, not even
anything indifferent, but something they were urgently
in need of. Swift, as every one knows, triumphed.
One Lord-Lieutenant had to resign ; another had to
yield. The Government had to put up with a loss
of credit. The country had to put up with the loss of
a much-wanted currency. Angry feeling was roused
on all sides, and so far as I know, no good was done

to any human being. Now, I am far from denying
that, in the course he thus took, Swift was partly
animated by a disinterested hatred of the monstrous
injustice to which Ireland was habitually subjected by
England. What I wish to point out is that, while he
belongs to the large class of Irish politicians whose
chief public motive is a desire to avenge the wrongs
of their country, Berkeley belongs to the very small
class whose first desire is to remedy her woes.

Their respective claims on the general gratitude
were acknowledged as might have been expected.
Berkeley, who in single-minded sincerity had pointed
out the true course of national improvement, lived
unknown and died unlamented by the mass of his
countrymen ; even in his own neighbourhood and
among his own people, the memory of him did not
long survive his departure. Swift pursued a different
course and underwent a different fate. If he did not
love the people among whom he was compelled to
live, at least he hated their enemies. Though he did
nothing to mitigate their sufferings, he embodied and
gave effect to their passions. Therefore he became
the idol of the mob. Their pathetic fidelity never
wavered through his years of inaction, sickness, and
idiocy. His death was an occasion of public mourning,
and his memory still lives as that of one of Ireland's
greatest patriots.

Soon after Berkeley had published the last instal-
ment of the " Querist," his thoughts were drawn from
the general and chronic miseries of the country to the
acute calamities of his own district. The terrible
winter of 1739-40 was followed by famine, famine
was followed by disease, and Berkeley's mind was

actively turned towards the discovery of expedients for mitigating both these evils. It so happened that his American experience had made him acquainted with *tar water, i.e.,* water containing the soluble constituents of tar. With characteristic enthusiasm he now took up the idea that this simple medicine was, if not a cure, at least a palliation for most of the physical ills to which flesh is heir. He dosed himself, his children, and his neighbours with it. He investigated the best method of making and administering it. He induced his friend Prior to assist in advertising its merits; and he recommended it to the world in the most singular treatise which has probably ever proceeded from the pen of an Anglican divine. "Siris," as it is called, was written when its author was occupied half in treating his sick, and half in the lofty, but somewhat vague speculations dear to him in his later years. The book accordingly takes its whole character from these strangely-assorted sources of inspiration. It begins by enumerating the diseases for which tar water may be successfully prescribed; and few inventors of quack remedies, I should imagine, have presumed further upon the public credulity than did Berkeley, in all good faith, when he published this imposing catalogue. Consumption, erysipelas, ulcers, dropsy, asthma, pleurisy, gout, fevers, small-pox, and *all* inflammations, are some of the maladies which this panacea was expected to cure. Little more than a third of the treatise, however, is devoted to this wondrous drug. By a rapid transition at the end of the 119th section, Berkeley leaves tar water and plunges into chemistry; from chemistry he ascends easily to physics; from physics to metaphysics; from metaphysics to theology; so that when the astonished reader reaches the end of the book he finds that he has, step by step, been led from the purely utilitarian, if not vulgar, topics with which it began, to the airiest heights of mystical philosophy.

The destiny of "Siris" has been as remarkable as are its contents. It had an immediate success far exceeding that of any other of its author's works. Horace Walpole wrote about this time: "We are now mad about the water, on the publication of a book written by Dr. Berkeley, Bishop of Cloyne. The book contains every subject from tar water to the Trinity; however, all the women read it and understand it no more than if it were intelligible. A man came into an apothecary's shop the other day: ' Do you sell tar water?' 'Tar water?' replied the apothecary, 'why, I sell nothing else!'" Three editions were called for in the year of its publication; two more soon followed. It was translated into French and into German. The remedy it recommended became the fashion, and the doctors trembled for their monopoly. Since then, times have changed. Tar water, so suddenly elevated to the dignity of a universal medicine, has again sunk to the position of the humblest drug in the Pharmacopeia. But the philosophy of the book, which before was only rendered palatable by its medicine, has now found admirers for its own sake. In the speculations of "Siris," later thinkers have seen not only a development of its author's early philosophy, but an anticipation of systems which have not even yet received their final expression. As in his youthful writings Berkeley is the teacher of Hume, so in those of his declining years he is regarded as the forerunner of the speculative movement of which a reaction against Hume was the most notable cause. Without discussing this question at length, I may say that while the actual value of these metaphysical fragments have, in my judgment, been exaggerated, their biographical interest is very great. They show a remarkable development in the philosopher, though not a development which has been of much value to philosophy. Berkeley's early work is distinguished not only by the admirable qualities of originality, lucidity, and subtlety, but by a less excellent characteristic, which I can only describe as a certain *thinness* of treatment. At the time when he produced these immortal speculations he had read little, and felt little. No experience of the weary entanglement of concrete facts had yet suggested to him that a perfect solution of the problem of the universe is beyond our reach. He easily exaggerated, therefore, the scope of his discovery, and his youthful self-confidence found no difficulty in believing that, by a simple correction in our theory of perception, all puzzles would be unravelled and all mysteries made plain. Very different was his attitude of mind when, richer by thirty years of experience and study, he gave to the world the fragments of his later Philosophy ; and the difference is perceptible on the most cursory comparison of his works at the two dates. In the " Principles of Human Knowledge " its author found little occasion to mention previous systems, except to express his dissent from them, In " Siris " the appeal to authority is so persistent as sometimes to become almost wearisome. In the "Three Dialogues" he designs, so he informs us, " plainly to demonstrate the reality and perfection of human knowledge." In

"Siris" he tells us that "with respect to the universe of things we, in this mortal state, are like men educated in Plato's cave," and that "we must be satisfied to make the best of those glimpses within our reach." The earlier works are remarkable for the easy confidence of their reasoning, the clearness and definiteness of their conclusions. In "Siris" there is little that deserves the name of argument, and its teaching is mystical and ill-defined. It is as if by the same intellectual light, which in his youth he had concentrated with such admirable results on a restricted area, he strove, in his later years, to explore the vast and shadowy spaces in which the sages of the ancient world had vainly sought for Absolute Truth, but found that the rays which formerly yielded such definite images now showed only in faint and doubtful outline the eternal framework on which, as Berkeley thought, is reared the fleeting world of sense.

It is rather, therefore, the spirit in which "Siris" is written, than its direct teaching, which appeals to the sympathy of the modern reader. Its fragmentary character, its uncritical wealth of erudition, the crudeness of its science, and the incompleteness of its philosophy, are easily forgiven, on account of its suggestiveness, the large toleration it displays towards widely-different modes of thought, and a certain quality of moral elevation and speculative diffidence alien both to the literature and the life of the eighteenth century. The whole book is, in truth, an anachronism. It draws its inspiration sometimes from the Neo-platonists, sometimes, even, from the alchemists, while sometimes it foreshadows metaphysical systems still in process of formation. But if its mystical speculations were not in harmony with an age taught by Voltaire and Hume, neither were such reflections as the following likely to suit the taste of a nation governed by Walpole or Newcastle :

" Whatever the world thinks, he who hath not much meditated upon God, the human soul, and the *summum bonum*, may possibly make a thriving earthworm, but will most indubitably make a sorry patriot and a sorry statesman."

By utterances such as these Berkeley spiritually severed himself from a generation not much given to meditation—at least in his fashion—either upon God, the soul, or the *summum bonum*. But his work in it was nearly done. The last years at Cloyne were overshadowed by increasing infirmities and domestic losses.[1] Less and less able for business, anxious only for repose, he turned again to his early dream of a life spent in academic retirement. Though it does not appear that he had Oxford friends, he had seen Oxford many years before, and the external aspect of the place (in 1752 much the best part of it) had lingered in his memory as that of a spot where such a dream might well be fulfilled. Thither, accordingly, he removed, 1752. The change of air seemed at first to benefit him. He was able to superintend the republication of some of his earlier works, and was in better health than he had been for some years. But the end came suddenly. On the 14th of January, 1753, in the midst of his family, without warning and without pain, he passed away: leaving behind him writings which will perpetuate his fame as one of the most admirable

---

[1] His second son, William, died in 1751 at the age of sixteen.

of English philosophers, and the memory of a character not, I think, to be surpassed in individuality, or in charm, by any recorded in the history of English men of letters.

ARTHUR JAMES BALFOUR.

ARITHMETIC

DEMONSTRATED WITHOUT EUCLID OR ALGEBRA.

BY * * * * BACHELOR OF ARTS,

TRINITY COLLEGE, DUBLIN.

1707.

[THESE two tracts formed Berkeley's first published matter. They appeared anonymously in 1707, written in Latin. They cannot be said to have any value other than the author's name gives them. The translation used here is that of the Rev. G. N. Wright ("Works of Berkeley", 1843).]

DEDICATION.

To that very promising youth, WILLIAM PALLISER, the only son of the most reverend the ARCHBISHOP of CASHEL, endowed with genius, sagacity, and learning beyond his years, and born with every quality suited to afford some great light and increase to the sciences, this treatise on arithmetic is, as a small pledge of devoted attachment, offered and dedicated by

THE AUTHOR.

PREFACE.

I PERCEIVE and regret, that most votaries of mathematical science are blindfolded on the very threshold. Inasmuch as the mode of learning mathematics, at least with us, first to apply to arithmetic, then geometry, then algebra; and as we read Tacquet's arithmetic, which no one can thoroughly understand without having some knowledge of algebra, it hence happens, that most students in mathematics, whilst they carefully and successfully master the demonstrations of theorems of inferior utility, leave untouched the principles and reasonings of arithmetical operations, though these last are of such efficacy and value, that they give the most important aid, not only to other branches of mathematics, but to the interests of men of all denominations. Wherefore if any one, after a mathematical course, turn his attention back to Tacquet's work, he will observe many things demonstrated in an obscure manner, so as not so much to enlighten as to force conviction on the mind, being environed with a repulsive array of porisms and theorems.

Nor has any one else, that I am aware of, demonstrated the rules of arithmetic without the aid of algebra. Thinking, then, that it would be of service to beginners if I should set forth my thoughts on these subjects, I now publish them, after they have almost all been kept by me for nearly three years. Now as I have not only given the rules for working questions, but also the demonstrations of those rules, drawn from the proper and genuine principles of arithmetic, some will perhaps be surprised that this treatise is of less size than the common works on arithmetic, though they contain merely the practice. The reason of this is that I have been very brief, both as regards precept and example, in explaining the "wherefore" of operations, on which writers on arithmetic are, in general, very tedious: and yet this brevity, as I hope, has not caused any obscurity. For although the blind require that a guide should lead them by the hand at every step, yet for one proceeding by the clear light of demonstration, it is sufficient to be furnished with even a slender clue. Wherefore I am anxious, that all votaries of mathematics should apply their minds to master the reasons and grounds of the rules of arithmetic.

This is not so difficult as some might suppose. The demonstrations here brought forward are, if I mistake not, easy at once and concise, nor are the principles drawn from any other quarter; nothing borrowed from algebra or Euclid is taken for granted here; I always prefer to prove an operation by obvious and familiar reasoning *à priori*, than to have recourse to an *argumentum ad absurdum*, by means of a tedious chain of consecutive demonstrations. I have endeavoured to derive the theory of square and cube roots from the nature itself of arithmetical involution, which, in my opinion, seems better suited to explain complicated extraction of roots, than what is generally applied to this purpose from the second book of Euclid, or from the analysis of algebraical powers. The common rule for the alligation of various things is demonstrated with difficulty and in particular instances. I have therefore substituted for it one of my own, which scarcely needs demonstration. I have rejected "the rule of false," as it is ineffectual and nearly useless.

I have copied no one; I have trespassed on the intellectual stores of none. For my original purpose was to deduce the rules of arithmetical operations from their principles for my own amusement and exercise, and so to employ my leisure hours. I could not on this occasion, without justly incurring the charge of ingratitude, omit mention of the name of the Rev. John Hall, doctor of divinity, Vice-Provost of this college, and the worthy professor of Hebrew. To that excellent man I acknowledge my obligations on many accounts, and not the least, that by his exhortations I was excited to the delightful study of mathematics.

I have now explained my aim: impartial judges will decide how far I have attained it. To their candid examination I cheerfully submit these first-fruits of my studies, little regarding what sciolists or the malignant may think.

ARITHMETIC.

PART I.

CHAPTER I.

OF NOTATION AND THE STATEMENT OF NUMBERS.

THERE are nine numeral signs 1, 2, 3, 4, 5, 6, 7, 8, 9, employed with the cypher (o) for expressing unlimited classes of numbers. The whole of this contrivance depends on the value of these signs increasing in a tenfold proportion. The series of numbers rising in value according to that law is divided into members or periods for convenience of statement. The subjoined table will completely explain this :

Series of Numeral Signs.

Hundreds	} 349 .	of Quintillions.
Tens		
Units		
Hundreds	} 758 .	Quadrillions.
Tens		
Units		
Hundreds	} 192 .	Trillions.
Tens		
Units		
Hundreds	} 003 .	Billions.
Tens		
Units		
Hundreds	} 505 .	Millions.
Tens		
Units		
Hundreds	} 739 .	Thousands.
Tens		
Units		
Hundreds	} 047.	Integers.
Tens		
Units }		
Unesimal }		

Decimal	} 32 .	Parts.
Centesimal		
Unesimal		
Decimal	} 568 .	Thousandths.
Centesimal		
Unesimal		
Decimal	} 918 .	Millionths.
Centesimal		
Unesimal		
Decimal	} 300 .	Billionths.
Centesimal		
Unesimal		
Decimal	} 052 .	Trillionths.
Centesimal		
Unesimal		
Decimal	} 704	Quadrillionths.
Centesimal		

in which is exhibited a series of numeral signs, set forth by threes, the members or periods advancing in thousandfold proportion, and the places in tenfold proportion. For instance, the figure in the units place, and marked by a point placed under it, denotes seven individuals, integral, or considered at least as integral; the next number on the right hand, three tenth parts of that integer, and the number which immediately precedes it denotes four tens of the same integers, and in this tenfold proportion each place exceeds that following it, and is exceeded by that preceding it.

Still further, since by an infinite multiplication and division of units, the series of signs is infinitely extended in each direction, from the units place, and so innumerable places for expressing their exact value, there is need merely of the continual repetition of three numbers, provided that each collection of threes, or period, be designated by its own name, as is the case in the table; for, in proceeding from the units place, towards the left, the first period marks units, or integers, the second thousands, the third millions, the fourth billions, and so on. In the same way, preserving the analogy, in the periods descending below units, first occur the parts simply, then thousandths, then millionths, then billionths, and so on ; and these last are to be divided into unesimal or unit parts, tenths, hundredths, the others to be collected into units, tens, hundreds.

If then we wish to state the number expressed by any

figure of the series, we must, 1st, note the simple value of
the figure ; 2nd, the value of the place ; lastly, of the period.
For instance, let the number selected be 9, in the fifth period
towards the left. The figure, taken simply, has the value of
nine ; in consequence of its place, it has the value of nine
tens ; and in consequence of its period, of nine tens of
trillions. Let 5 be chosen in the third period : taken simply,
it signifies five ; in consequence of its place, five units ; in
consequence of its period, five units of millions, or five
millions. In the second period below unit, let 8 be chosen :
the simple value of the figure is eight : in consequence of its
place, eight hundredths ; in consequence of its period, eight
hundredths of thousandths.

If the number to be stated have not words affixed, to
denote the value of the periods and of the places, it should
be pointed into threes towards the right and left, from the
units place, and then should be expressed by the name
assigned to the place and period. For instance, let the
numbers proposed be 73,480,195. The figures being divided
into periods, I first inquire what is the value of the figure in
the first place on the left, which, since it is in the second
place of the third period, is seven tens of millions ; but
since the numbers advance in tenfold proportion, the value
of the first figure being known, the values of the rest follow
in due order. We shall therefore thus express the proposed
number : seven tens, and three units of millions ; four hundreds, and eight tens of thousands ; one hundred, nine tens,
and five units : or more concisely, seventy-three millions,
four hundred and eighty thousand, a hundred and ninety-
five. Hence we perceive that a cypher, though in itself of
no value, must of necessity be expressed, for the purpose of
assigning a proper place to each figure.

There will be no difficulty in writing and expressing the
largest numbers, if due attention be given to what has been
just laid down, an acquaintance with which will also afterwards be of the greatest importance ; for nature itself teaches
us the way of working arithmetical questions on the fingers,
but there is need of science to perform these operations
accurately, with respect to greater numbers ; all turning
upon this, that whereas the limited nature of our faculties
does not permit the work to be done at once, and with a

single effort, we divide it into various operations, by separately inquiring the aggregate or sum, the difference, the product, and then combining them, express the ultimate sum total, remainder, or product ; the whole reason and contrivance of the operations resulting from the simple progression of the places, and being ultimately founded on it.

N.B.—I am aware that some arithmeticians divide the series otherwise than I do ; for compounding the denominations, they use sixes instead of threes. But as others [1] follow the method pursued by me, I have thought it advisable to retain it as simpler.

CHAP. II.

ON ADDITION.

In addition, the sum of two or more numbers is required ; to obtain which the numbers to be added should be set down, so that units should be placed under units, tens under tens, and decimal parts under decimals, and so forth. On this account, when decimal parts are added, the units place should be marked by the insertion of a comma. Then commencing from the right, the figures in the first place should be added, and if any tens result, they should be carried over to the next place, and be added to the sum of the figures of that place, the tens which belong to the next place being reserved, and so the process should be continued. For instance, in the first example of the operations below, 9 and 5 make 14 ; I therefore reserve the 10 and proceed with the 4 ; 4 and 8 make 12, therefore I reserve the 10, and going on to the next place I find 6, to which I add 2, on account of the tens reserved in the first place ; and as 8 and 2 make 10, I reserve that, and set down the 1 which remains, and proceed in the same way.

[1] For instance, the celebrated Wallis in his "Universal Mathesis," and Father Lamy, in his "Elements of Mathematics."

Addend.	2 0 1 8· 8·2 2·5· 4 3 6 9	523,9702 81,35 60,2005	£ s. d. 7 8 9 3 12 5 0 7 2
Sum	1 4 6 1 2	665,5207	11 8 4

If the things to be summed up be of different kinds, we should proceed in the same way, taking into account, however, the proportions according to which the different denominations advance. For instance, the denominations of pounds, shillings, and pence, do not advance as those of numbers; for 12 pence, not 10 pence, make a shilling: 20 shillings, and not 10 shillings, make a pound. On this account, in adding such quantities, instead of tens, twelves should be carried from the pence, twenties should be carried from the shillings to the next place.

CHAP. III.

ON SUBTRACTION.

In subtraction, the difference of two numbers is required, or what remains after one has been taken from the other; for ascertaining which the less quantity of each denomination should be placed under the greater; then beginning from the right, the first denomination of the quantity to be subtracted is to be taken from that written above it, and the remainder set down below, and the work continued in this way until the whole subtraction be effected.

If, however, it should happen that any number be too small to admit of the lower quantity being taken from it, such upper number should be increased by ten, that is, by a unit borrowed from the next place.

Let it be required to subtract 1189 from 32034; the numbers being set down as in the adjoined example, I set about subtracting the first figure 9 from the 4 placed over it; but as 4 does not even once contain 9, a ten must be added to it, so as to make 14, and then 9 taken from 14 leaves 5. Proceeding then to the left, I have to subtract 8 from 2, not from 3, because we should take into account the ten which has been borrowed, and as 8 cannot be subtracted from 2, I subtract it from 12, and 4 remains. The next figure of the quantity to be subtracted is 1, which, however, cannot be subtracted from nothing or o ; in place of the cipher o I use 9 ; now I use 9 because the ten which is borrowed must be diminished by the unit which has been added to the preceding figure; continuing the process in this manner, 1 taken from 1 leaves nothing. Finally, the subtraction being completed, 3 remain, which I set down below.

In a similar manner, the subtraction of different denominations is effected : only we should observe that ten is not necessarily to be used, but such a number as declares how many of the denominations in question are in the next denomination, and this number should be borrowed to supply the defect of any particular figure.

			£ s. d.
Subtract.	32034 1189	7329,645 3042,100	4 8 3 2 6 5
Rem.	30845	4287,545	2 1 10

N.B.—From what has been here laid down, it is plain that the science of arithmetic, as far as we have treated it, consists in doing in detail that which cannot be done at once ; and that the reason of reserving tens in addition, and of borrowing them in subtraction, altogether depends on the tenfold advance in the value of the places.

CHAP. IV.

ON MULTIPLICATION.

In multiplication the multiplicand is taken as often as the multiplier requires ; or in other words, a number is sought

bearing the same ratio to the multiplicand that the multiplier does to unity. That number is called the product,
or rectangle; the factors or sides of which are called respectively, the multiplicand, and the number by which it is
multiplied.

For finding the product of two numbers, the multiplying
number being written under the multiplicand, this last should
be multiplied by each figure of the former, beginning from
the right hand : the first figure of the product should be
written directly under the multiplying figure, and the rest in
order towards the left.

The multiplication being finished, the several products
should be collected into one sum, the number of decimal
places in which should be equal to those in both the
factors.

Let 30,94 be the number to be multiplied by 26,5. Five
times 4 produce 20, the first figure of which (0) I place
under the multiplying figure (5), and carry the remaining 2 ;
then 5 multiplied into 9 produces 45 ; 5 with the 2 carried
make 7, which I set down, carrying 4 to the next place. and
so on.

	30,94 26,5	52886 24	6000 56
	15470 18564 6188	211544 105772	36 30
Prod. tot.	819,910	1269264	336000

As there is a twofold value of each number, this should be
taken into account, so that the multiplication be rightly
effected, that is, that each figure be multiplied as well
according to the simple value of the multiplying figure,
as according to that which it has from its place. Hence the
figure of each respective product is written under the multiplying figure. For instance, in the multiplier of the second
example, the figure 2 has the value, not of 2 units, but of 2
tens ; therefore, when multiplied into 6, the first figure of
the multiplicand, it will produce, not 12 units, but 12 tens ;

therefore, the first figure of the product should be set down in the place of tens, that is, directly under the multiplying figure 2.

For the same reason, when there are (decimal) parts in the factors, the number produced by the multiplication of the first figure of the multiplier into the first of the multiplicand, is to be removed as far below the multiplied figure as the multiplier is to the right hand below unity; so that as many (decimal) places in the entire product are to be marked off as there were in both factors.

N.B.—If there be ciphers continuously to the right of each or of both factors, the multiplication should be performed on the other figures merely, and the ciphers afterwards annexed to the entire product; for since the places advance in value in a tenfold proportion, it is clear that a number becomes tenfold, a hundredfold, a thousandfold itself, if it be advanced one, two, or three places.

CHAP. V.

ON DIVISION.

DIVISION is the reverse of multiplication, its object being to resolve or divide that quantity which the latter produces. The number found by division is called the quotient, because it declares how often the dividend contains the divisor, or, what is the same, the ratio of the dividend to the divisor, or finally, the part of the dividend denominated from the divisor.

In division, having written down the dividend and divisor, as in the first of the subjoined examples, commencing from the left, that part of the dividend containing the divisor, or having the least excess above the containing number, should be marked off by a point. I mean in this instance the simple values. It should then be ascertained how often the divisor is contained in that member of the dividend, and the resulting number will be the first figure of the quotient; the divisor should then be multiplied into the figure thus found, and the product subtracted from the member of the dividend,

and the remainder set down below; to which should
be annexed the next figure of the dividend, and a new
dividend thus obtained, from whence must be ascertained
the next figure of the quotient, which being multiplied into
the divisor, and the product subtracted from the dividend
just divided, the remainder with the next figure of the original
dividend annexed will form a new member, and so on, until
the operation is finished. The decimal places of the divisor
being then subtracted from those in the dividend, the
remainder will indicate what number of places should be in
the quotient; but if this subtraction be not feasible, so
many decimal cyphers should be added to the dividend as
are necessary.

If, after the division has been completed, there should be
a remainder, by adding decimal cyphers the division can be
continued until either nothing remain, or it be so minute
that it need not be taken into account, or the remaining
figures may be set down and the divisor under them.

If both the dividend and divisor end in cyphers, an equal
number of these should be struck off in both: but if the
divisor alone end in cyphers they should not be taken into
account in the operation, but the same number of the last
figures of the dividend should be struck off, and at the end
of the work set down, a line drawn below them, and the
divisor written underneath.

Let it be required to divide 45832 by 67. Since the
divisor is greater than 45 let another figure be added, and
the member taken for division be 458, which I separate
from the rest of the dividend by a point. 6 is contained in
45 seven times, with three remainder; but, as 7 is not also
contained seven times in 38, the quotient must be taken less.
Let 6 therefore be taken; and, as 6 is contained 6 times in
45 and 9 remains, and 98 contains 7 six times, the first
figure of the quotient should be 6. This, multiplied into
the divisor, produces a subtrahend 402, which being taken
from 458, there will be a remainder 56; to which I annex 3,
the next figure of the dividend, by which means a new
dividend is formed 563, which I divide as the former, and
find 8 for the second figure of the quotient; and, as 8 multiplied into 67 produces 536, I subtract this from 563, and,
adding to the remainder 2, the next figure of the dividend, I

obtain 272 as a new dividend, which, when divided, gives 4, which, being first set down in the quotient, and then multiplied into the divisor, and the product subtracted from 272, there remains 4, which should be annexed to the quotient, a line being drawn under it, and the divisor then written below it.

The operation is more speedy when the subtraction immediately follows the multiplication of each figure, and the multiplication proceeds from left to right. For instance, let it be proposed to divide 12199980 by 156, as in the third example; the divisor being written under 1219, the first member of the dividend, it is plain that the one is contained 7 times in the other; and, in consequence, 7 is put down in the quotient. Seven times 1 make 7; which, being subtracted from 12, I strike out both the multiplied figure 1 and 12, the part of the member from which the product was subtracted, setting down above the remainder 5; then I proceed to 5, the next figure of the divisor; 7 multiplied into 5 makes 35, and 35 being subtracted from 51, there remains 16, which I write above and strike out 51 and 5. I then multiply 7 into 6, and the product 42 being subtracted from 69 there remain 27, which I set down, striking out both 69 and 6, the last figure of the dividend. The divisor being now entirely struck out, I set it down, moved one place to the right, and with it I divide the member written above it, which indeed is made up of the remainder of the last divided member increased by the following figure. In this way the divisor should be moved until it goes through the whole dividend.

67)458.32(684$\frac{4}{67}$	200)8200	
402		
——	2)82(41	
563	8	
536	—	
——	02	
272	2	
268	—	
——	00	
004		

In the next place the reason of the rules will be given; and first, it is plain why we should seek for the quotient by separate divisions.

2ndly, It may, for instance, be asked why, in the example above given, 6 should be taken as the quotient of the first member, divided by the divisor; for 67 is contained in 458 hundreds, not six times but six hundred times, for they are not units but hundreds, since they are distant two places to the left from units.

To this I answer, that in reality not merely 6 but 600 is written in the quotient, for two figures afterwards ascertained follow it, and thus the proper value is assigned to the quotient; for as many places are set down after each figure in the quotient as there are after that member of the dividend from which they are obtained.

3rdly, Since each figure of the quotient indicates how often that member of the dividend from which it was obtained contains the divisor, it is proper that the subtrahend should be formed by multiplying the divisor into the figure last found; for then the divisor is subtracted exactly as often as it is contained in the dividend, unless it should happen that the number last set down in the quotient should be too large or too small: if the first be the case the product will be so large that it cannot be subtracted; if the latter be the case, then the resulting product will be so small, that after performing the subtraction the remainder will be equal to or greater than the divisor.

4thly, The reason why so many (decimal) places should be marked off in the quotient that with those which are in the divisor they may be equal to those in the dividend, is that the dividend is the product resulting from the multiplication of the divisor into the quotient, and consequently it should have as many decimal places as those two, as we have shown when treating of multiplication.

5thly, It is clear that decimal cyphers, annexed to the end of the dividend, do not affect its value; for as to the integers, those which are removed for the same distance from the units place, have the same value, but decimals are not diminished in value unless the cyphers be placed before them.

6thly, Since the quotient expresses or denominates the ratio of the dividend to the divisor, it is clear, that as long as that continues the same the quotient must be the same; but the common cyphers, being cast away, the ratio of the numbers to each other is not in the slightest degree altered. Thus, for instance, 200 bears the same ratio to 100—that is, 200 contains 100 as often as 2 contains 1, which is sufficiently manifest by itself.

CHAP. VI.

ON FORMING SQUARES AND FINDING THEIR ROOTS.

THE product of a number multiplied into itself is called its *square;* and the number by the multiplication of which into itself the square is produced is called the *square root* or *side;* and the operation by which we search for the root of the given square is called the *extraction of the square root;* for understanding which it will be necessary to consider the manner in which the square is produced, the parts of which it is composed, their order, and relative position.   And since it is best in acquiring a knowledge of any thing to proceed from the simplest and easiest, let us commence with the consideration of the production of a square, resulting from a binomial root.

We should, in the first place, closely consider what takes place when a number, consisting of two figures, is multiplied into itself.   And first it is plain that the first figure on the right of the root is multiplied into the one placed above it, that is, into itself, and thence results the square of the lesser number.   Then, by multiplying the same figure into the next part of the multiplicand, a rectangle results contained by both members of the root.   Having then finished the multiplication of the whole multiplicand by the first figure of the root, we come to the second, which, being multiplied into the first figure of the multiplicand, there results again a rectangle, contained under the two figures of the binomial root; then the second figure of the multiplicand multiplied into itself, gives the square of the second member of the binomial root.   We ascertain from this that any square produced from a binomial root consists, in the first place, of the

square of the lesser member; in the second, of double the
rectangle contained under the members; in the third, of the
square of the greater member.

Let it be required to square a binomial root, for instance,
23, according to what has been laid down in chap. iv.
I first multiply 3 into 3, which gives 9, as the square of
the first member; I secondly multiply 3 into 2, the
other figure of the root, and obtain 6, the rectangle
contained by both; thirdly, from 2 multiplied into 3
arises a second time, the rectangle contained under the members; in the fourth place, 2 multiplied into 2 produces 4
the square of the greater member.

$$\begin{array}{r} 23 \\ 23 \\ \hline 69 \\ 46 \end{array}$$

Let us now proceed to the production of a square, from a
root of three members. In this operation, the first figure of
the root multiplied into the whole root, produces, in the first
place, the square of the first member; in the second place,
the rectangle contained under the first and second member;
in the third place, the rectangle contained under the first and
third member. Now for the second figure, this multiplied
into the root gives first the rectangle contained under the first
and second member; secondly, the square of the second
member; thirdly, the rectangle contained under the second
and third members. Lastly, from the third figure of the
root, multiplied into the root, results first, the rectangle contained under the first and third members; secondly, the
rectangle contained under the second and third members;
and thirdly, the square of the third member.

From this we ascertain, that a square, produced from a
trinomial root comprises, first, the square of the first figure
of the root; secondly, double the rectangle contained under
the first figure and the two others; in the third place, the
square of the two others, that is, the square of each, and also
double the rectangle contained under both, which we have
before shown, constitute the square of the two figures.

In the same way, it can be shown, that the square of four,
five, or any number of figures, contains, first, the square of
the figure of lowest value; secondly, double the rectangle resulting from the multiplication of the figure of lowest value
into all the others; thirdly, the square of all the other figures,
which itself, as is plain from what has been stated, contains
the square of the figure next from the right, double the

rectangle of that same figure multiplied into all the others, the square of all the other figures, which in the same way contains the square of the third figure, two rectangles of it, and the others, and the square of these, and so on, until we come to the square of the highest figure of the root.

The parts of which the square is composed being ascertained, we should next consider, concerning their arrangement and place. If therefore, beginning from the right, we divide the square into periods of twos, from the mode of production which we have explained above, it is plain that the first member from the left will be occupied by the square of the first or highest figure, and at the same time, of that portion of double the rectangle resulting from the multiplication together of the first and second figures, which is redundant above the first place of the following period of two ; that the first place of the second period contains double the rectangle mentioned, and besides whatever of the square of the second figure is over ; that the second contains the square of the second figure, and whatever is over of double the rectangle of the two first figures, multiplied into the third as far as the lowest figure at the first place of the third two, and so on.

For instance, in the annexed example, the first member 10 contains 9, the square of the first figure 3, besides 1 by which 12 (double the rectangle of the figure 3 multiplied into the following 2) exceeds the first place of the second member. The first place of the second two contains 2 (the remainder of the double rectangle of the figures 3 and 2), and also that which is over the next following place, and so on, &c.

$$
\begin{array}{r}
321 \\
321 \\
\hline
321 \\
642 \\
963 \\
\hline
10.30.41
\end{array}
$$

Having thus considered the formation of the square, let us proceed to its analysis. Let any number, for instance 103041, be proposed, the square root of which is required. This should be pointed off by twos, beginning from the right in case the number be even, as if otherwise the last member will consist of but one figure. I then inquire, what is the greatest square contained in 10, the first member towards the left, and 3, the root of this, is the first figure of the root required, the square of which (9) I

$$
\begin{array}{r}
10.30.41(321 \\
9 \\
\hline
6)13\cdot0 \\
12\cdot4 \\
\hline
64)641 \\
641 \\
\hline
000
\end{array}
$$

subtract from (10) the member. From the remainder (1), with
(3) the first figure of the following member added, is formed
a dividend (13), which I divide by the found figure doubled
(6), the quotient (2) will be the second figure of the root;
which being multiplied first into the divisor, and then into
itself, and the sum of the product, taken so, however,
that the latter be removed one place to the right (124), I
take away this from the dividend (13), increased by 0, the
remaining figure of the second member. To the remainder
6, I add 4, the first figure of the third two, and so a new
dividend (64) is produced, which being divided by 64, twice
the root already found, gives 1, the third of the required root;
this being then multiplied into itself and the products added
up, I subtract the sum (641) from the dividend, increased by
the addition of the other figure of the third member, and in this
way we must proceed to whatever length the operation may
be carried.

If after the last subtraction there be a remainder, it shows
that the given number was not a square; however by adding
to it decimal cyphers, the operation can be continued to any
extent thought desirable.

If there be any decimal places in the number, for the root
of which we are searching, their number divided by two, will
show how many should be in the root. The reason of this
appears from chap. iv.

The reason of the mode of proceeding is quite clear from
what has been stated. For as a divisor I employed 6, the
double of the found figure, because, from the formation of
the square as it has been explained, I knew that double
the rectangle of that figure, multiplied into the following
one, comprised the dividend; consequently, if this were
divided by the double of one factor (3), that the other
factor (2), that is, the next figure of the root, could be obtained. So likewise I have formed a subtrahend from double
the rectangle of the quotient and the divisor, and the square
of the quotient added together, because I found that those
two rectangles and the square were contained in that order
in the remainder and the following member from which the
subtraction was made, and so the evolution of the power is
easily effected from its involution or formation.

CHAP. VII.

CONCERNING THE INVOLUTION AND EVOLUTION OF THE CUBE.

THE root multiplied into the square produces the cube. To prepare the way for the analysis we should, as has been done in the former chapter, begin with the composition of the power. In the production then of the cube from a binomial root, the first member of the root, in the first place, meets with its own square, whence results the cube of the first figure; secondly, double the rectangle of the members, whence double the solid of the square of the first figure multiplied into the other; thirdly, the square of the other member, whence the solid produced from the first figure and the square of the second. In the same way, when the multiplication takes place by the second member, there arises the solid of the second figure and of the square of the first; in the second place double the solid of the first figure and of the square of the second; in the third place the cube of the second member.

Therefore the cube produced from the binomial root contains the cubes of the two members and six solids, that is to say, three made from the square of each member, multiplied into the other.

The reasoning being continued according to the analogy of the preceding chapter, it will follow, that if, as the square should be divided into twos, the cube resulting from any root be distributed into threes, that the three, or member first from the left, contains the cube of the figure first on the left, and also the excess, if there be any, of three solids of the square of the same, multiplied into the second; that the first place of the second contains the said solids and the excess of the three solids of the square of the second figure, multiplied into the first; that the second place contains the same three solids and the excess of the cube of the second figure; and that the third is occupied by the said cube and the excess of the three solids produced from the square of the preceding figures, multiplied into the third; and that the solids just mentioned fill the first place of the third member, and so on. From this we shall easily derive the following manner of extracting the cube root.

Beginning from the right, I divide, by means of points, the resolvend (80621568) into threes, except the last member, which can be less. I then take the greatest cube (64) contained in the first member towards the left, and having written down its root (4) for the first figure of the sought root, I annex to the remainder (16) the next figure (6) of the resolvend, whence results a dividend (166), which I divide by 48, thrice the square of the figure which has been found: the quotient (3) is the second figure of the root. I multiply this first into the divisor, secondly its square into three times the first figure, and thirdly itself into itself twice. The products then being collected in this way, that the second be set down one place to the right of the first, the

third one place to the right of the second. $\left\{ \begin{matrix} 144 \\ 108 \\ 27 \end{matrix} \right\}$ I subtract

it from the dividend increased by the addition of the two remaining figures of the second member. In this way, however prolonged the operation, a dividend will always result from the remainder, with the addition of the first figure of the following member, and a divisor from three times the square of the figures of the root already found, and a subducend from the figure last found, the square of the same multiplied into three times the preceding figures, lastly its cube, and these collected in the manner set forth.

```
80.621.568(432
64
─────
48)16621
   15507
─────
5547)1114568
     1114568
─────
     0000000
```

If the resolvend be not a cube, by adding decimals to the remainder you can carry its exhaustion to infinity.

The root should have a third part of the decimal places of the resolvend.

N.B.—Synthetical operations can be examined by means of analytical, and analytical by means of synthetical; so if either number, being subtracted from the sums of two numbers, the other remains, the addition has been rightly performed; and *vice versâ*, subtraction is proved to be right when the sum of the subtrahend and remainder is equal to the greater number. So if the quotient multiplied into the divisor produce the dividend, or the root multiplied into itself produce the resolvend, it is a proof that the division or evolution has been correct.

ARITHMETIC.

PART II.

CHAP. I.

ON FRACTIONS.

IT has been before mentioned that division is signified by setting down the dividend with the divisor under it, and separated from it by a line drawn between them. Quotients of this kind are called broken numbers, or fractions, because the upper number, called also the numerator, is divided or broken into parts, the denomination of which is fixed by the lower, which is therefore called the denominator. For instance, in the fraction $\frac{2}{4}$, 2 is the dividend or numerator, 4 the divisor or denominator, and the fraction indicates the quotient which arises from 2 divided by 4, that is the fourth of any two things whatever, or two-fourths of one, for they mean the same.

N.B.—It is clear that numbers which denote decimal parts, and which are commonly called decimal fractions, can be expressed as vulgar fractions, if the denominator be written beneath. For instance, ·25 is equivalent to $\frac{25}{100}$, ·004 is equivalent to $\frac{4}{1000}$, &c., which we must either do, or understand to be done, as often as those are to be reduced to vulgar fractions, or conversely these are to be reduced into those, or any other operation is to take place equally affecting both fractions, decimal and vulgar.

CHAP. II.

OF ADDITION AND SUBTRACTION OF FRACTIONS.

1. IF fractions, whose sum or difference is sought, have the same denominator, the sum or difference of the nu-

merators should be taken, and the common denominator written under, and this will be the answer.

2. If they be not of the same denomination let them be reduced to the same denomination. The denominators multiplied into each other will give a new denominator, but the numerator of each fraction multiplied into the denominators of the others will give a numerator of a new fraction of equal value. Then the new fractions should be treated as above.

3. If an integer is to be added to a fraction or subtracted from it, or *vice versâ*, it should be reduced to a fraction of the same denomination as the given one; that is, it is to be multiplied into the given denominator, and that denominator to be placed under it.

Addition.	$\frac{1}{6}$ to $\frac{2}{6}$ sum $\frac{3}{6}$	
Subtraction.	$\frac{1}{6}$ from $\frac{2}{6}$ rem. $\frac{1}{6}$	
Addition.	$\frac{2}{3}$ to $\frac{3}{4}$, that is $\frac{8}{12}$ to $\frac{9}{12}$, sum $\frac{17}{12}$	
Subtraction.	$\frac{2}{3}$ from $\frac{3}{4}$, that is $\frac{8}{12}$ from $\frac{9}{12}$, rem. $\frac{1}{12}$	
Addition.	3 to $\frac{5}{8}$, that is $\frac{24}{8}$ to $\frac{5}{8}$, sum $\frac{29}{8}$	
Subtraction.	$\frac{5}{8}$ from 3, that is $\frac{24}{8}$, rem. $\frac{19}{8}$	

In the first place, it should be explained why fractions should be reduced to the same denomination before we treat them; and it is on this account, that numbers enumerating heterogeneous things cannot be added together, or subtracted from each other. For instance, if I wish to add three pence to two shillings, the sum will not be 5 shillings, or 5 pence, nor can it be ascertained before that the things mentioned be brought to the same sort, by using 24 pence instead of 2 shillings, to which if I add 3 pence, there results a sum of 27 pence; for the same reason, if I have to add 2 thirds and 3 fourths, I do not write down 5 parts either thirds or fourths, but, instead of them I employ 8 twelfths and 9 twelfths, the sum of which is 17 twelfths.

Secondly.   I wish to show that fractions after such reduction are of the same value as before, for instance, $\frac{2}{3}$ and $\frac{8}{12}$; since both numerator and denominator are multiplied by the same number (4); but every fraction represents the ratio of the numerator or dividend to the denominator, or divisor, and consequently as long as that remains the same, the fraction retains the same value, but each term of the ratio being multiplied by the same number, it is certain that the ratio is not changed : for instance, if the half of one thing be double the half of another, that whole will be double this whole, which is so plain that it does not require proof.

Thirdly. An integer reduced to a fraction is not altered in value, for if the rectangle of two numbers be divided by one of them, the other will be quotient ; but, in the reduction of an integer to a fraction, it is multiplied into the given denominator, and also divided by it, therefore the fraction has the same value as the given integer.

N.B.—It will sometimes be useful to reduce a fraction to a given denominator, for instance, $\frac{2}{8}$ to another whose denominator is 9, which is done by means of the rule of three (laid down subsequently), by finding a number to which the given denominator will be as the denominator of the given fraction to its numerator ; that will be the numerator of the fraction of which the name has been given, and the value will be the same as of the former, for, in each instance the ratio between the terms of the fraction is the same.

CHAP. III.

OF THE MULTIPLICATION OF FRACTIONS.

1. IF a fraction is to be multiplied into a fraction, the numerators of the given fractions multiplied into each other will give the numerator of the product, and the denominators in the same way will give the denominators.

2. If a fraction is to be multiplied into an integer, the given integer should be multiplied into the numerator of the fraction, the denominator remaining the same.

3. If in either factor, or in both, integers occur, or hetero-

geneous fractions, they, for the sake of clearness, should be collected together.

Examples of Multiplication.

Multiply	$\frac{2}{3}$ by $\frac{5}{8}$, prod. $\frac{10}{24}$, $\frac{4}{7}$ by 2, prod. $\frac{8}{7}$.
Multiply	2 and $\frac{2}{5}$ by $\frac{1}{2}$ and $\frac{2}{3}$, that is, $\frac{12}{5}$ by $\frac{7}{6}$.

1. It is plain that the quotient is increased in the same proportion as is the dividend : for instance, if 2 be contained three times in 6 it will be contained twice three times in twice 6. It is plain also that it is diminished in the same proportion as the divisor increases : for instance, if the number 3 be contained 4 times in 12, twice 3 will be contained only twice in 12 ; therefore when I multiply $\frac{2}{3}$ by $\frac{5}{8}$, the fraction $\frac{2}{3}$ is to be increased in a fivefold ratio, since it is to be multiplied by 5 ; and to be diminished in an eightfold ratio, since it is multiplied, not actually by 5, but only by its eighth part ; consequently I multiply the dividend 2 by 5, and the divisor 3 by 8.

2. As to the second rule, it is plain that twice 4 of any things are equal to 8 things of the same denomination, whatever it may be.

CHAP. IV.

ON DIVISION OF FRACTIONS.

1. A FRACTION is divided by an integer, by multiplying the given integer into the denominator of the given fraction.

2. If a fraction is to be divided by a fraction, the numerator of the divisor multiplied into the denominator of the dividend will give the denominator of the quotient ; and its denominator multiplied into the numerator of the dividend will give the numerator of the quotient.

3. Whenever integers or fractions of different denominations are mixed, the easiest way of proceeding will be to collect the members of each, as well dividend as divisor, into two sums.

Examples of Division.

Divide $\frac{3}{4}$ by 2, quot. $\frac{3}{8}$.
Divide $\frac{4}{9}$ by $\frac{2}{5}$, quot. $\frac{20}{18}$.
Divide $2\frac{1}{3} \times \frac{3}{2}$ by $3\frac{2}{5}$, that is, $\frac{21}{6}$ by $\frac{17}{5}$.

1. As to the first rule, it is clear from the preceding chapter that a fraction is lessened or divided in the same proportion as the denominator is multiplied.

2. Since to divide one fraction by another, for instance, $\frac{4}{9}$ by $\frac{2}{5}$, I have multiplied the denominator 9 into 2, the fraction $\frac{4}{18}$ only expresses how often 2 is contained in the dividend; but the fifth of it will indicate how often the fifth part of the number 2 is contained in it; wherefore I multiply the first quotient $\frac{4}{18}$ by 5, whence results $\frac{20}{18}$.

N.B.—If the given fractions be homogeneous, the shorter and more elegant way is to divide the numerator of the dividend by the numerator of the divisor as often as it measures it. Thus, $\frac{6}{8}$ being divided by $\frac{3}{8}$, the quotient will be 2, for whatever things are enumerated by 6 contain 3 twice.

2. If a root is to be extracted from a given fraction, the root of the denominator, placed under the root of the numerator, will form a fraction, which is the root sought. For instance, $\frac{2}{3}$ is the square root of the fraction $\frac{4}{9}$, and the cube root of the fraction $\frac{8}{27}$; for, from what we have said about multiplication it is clear that $\frac{2}{3}$ multiplied into $\frac{2}{3}$ produces $\frac{4}{9}$; and that $\frac{2}{3}$ multiplied into $\frac{4}{9}$ produces $\frac{8}{27}$.

CHAP. V.

OF THE REDUCTION OF FRACTIONS TO THEIR LOWEST TERMS.

1. Since the value of fractions is most easily ascertained when they are at their lowest terms, it is of advantage when

feasible to divide fractions by a common measure. The greater that common divisor may be so much less will be the quotients or terms of the fraction equal to the given one. It is necessary, therefore, when two numbers are given, to have a method of finding their greatest common measure, that is to say, the greatest divisor which will divide the given divisor without a remainder. Such is the following :

2. Divide the greater of the given numbers by the less, and that divisor by the remainder of the division ; and, if still there be a remainder, you should by it divide the former divisor—that is, the last remainder, and so on until you come to a divisor which exhausts or measures its dividend, that is, the greatest common measure of the two.

For instance, let 9 and 15 be the given numbers. I divide 15 by 9, and 6 remains ; I divide 9 by 6, and 3 remains ; I divide 6 by 3, and nothing remains. Therefore 3 is the greatest common measure of the two numbers 9 and 15, which I show thus.

(*a*) 3 measures 6, but (*b*) 6 measures 9, if 3 be taken away. Therefore 3 measures 9, if 3 be taken away ; but 3 measures itself, therefore it measures the whole 9 ; but (*c*) 9 measures 15, 6 being taken away ; therefore 3 measures 15, 6 being taken away ; but it measures 6, therefore it measures the whole number 15. Hence it is clear, that 3 is the common measure of the given numbers, 9 and 15. It remains for me to show that it is the greatest common measure. If not, let there be some other common measure, say 5. Now since (*d*) 5 measures 9, (*e*) but 9 measures 15, 6 being taken away ; it is plain that 5 measures 15, 6 being taken away ; but it measures the whole 15 (by hypothesis), therefore it measures 6 ; but 6 measures 9, 3 being taken from it ; therefore 5 measures 9, 3 being taken from it. Therefore since 5 measures both the whole of 9, and 9, 3 being taken from it : it will also measure 3 itself, that is, (*f*) the lesser number, which is absurd.

The greatest common measure being found, it is plain that the fraction $\frac{9}{15}$ can be lowered to this fraction $\frac{3}{5}$, which I thus show to be equal to the former. Every fraction denotes the quotient of the numerator divided by the denominator ;

(*a*) By construction.   (*b*) By construction.   (*c*) By construction.   (*d*) By hyp.   (*e*) By construction.   (*f*) By hyp.

but in division the quotient expresses the ratio of the dividend to the divisor; whilst the ratio therefore remains the same, the quotient or fraction will be the same. Moreover, it is very clear, that the ratio is not changed, its terms being equally divided; for instance, if anything be double of another, or triple, the half of that will be double or triple of the half of the other.

Those who can divide and multiply fractions by integers will find no difficulty in reducing fractions of fractions to integers. For instance, this fraction of a fraction $\frac{3}{4}$ of $\frac{2}{5}$, what else is it, than three times the fourth part of the fraction $\frac{2}{5}$, or $\frac{2}{20}$ multiplied into the integer 3? In like manner, the numerators and denominators being mutually multiplied into the fraction of a fraction of a fraction, is reduced to an integer. Since these things are so clear and manifest, it is amazing by what circuitous processes, what a tedious apparatus of theorems, quotations, and species they are demonstrated, or rather obscured.

ARITHMETIC.

PART III.

CHAP. I.

OF THE RULE OF PROPORTION.

THE rule of *Proportion* is that by which, three numbers being given, a fourth, proportional to them, is found. Its use is frequent and very great, and hence it is called the *golden rule*. It is also called the Rule of Three, on account of the three given terms. We directly find the fourth proportional by multiplying the second term by the third, and dividing the product by the first; for instance, if as 2 is to 6, so should 4 be to the number required; multiply 4 into 6, and divide the product 24 by 2, the quotient 12 will be the fourth proportional required, which I demonstrate as follows.

In four proportionals the product of the extremes is equal

to the product of the intermediate terms. For, since the
numbers are proportional, that is, have the same ratio between themselves, but ratio is estimated by division, if the
second term be divided by the first, and the fourth by the
third, the quotient will be the same, which, according to the
nature of division, multiplied into the first term will produce
the second, and into the third will produce the fourth. If
therefore we multiply the first term into the fourth, or which
is the same thing, into the third and common quotient, and
the third term into the second, or which is the same thing,
into the first and common quotient, it is clear that the products will be equal, as the factors are in each case the same.
But from the nature of multiplication and division, it is clear
that the product being divided by one of the factors, the other
is the quotient; therefore if I divide the product of the two
intermediate terms (6 and 4) by the first (2), the quotient
(12) will be the fourth proportional sought.

Question 1. A traveller in 3 hours goes 15 miles: how
many will he go in 9 hours? Answer 45. For it is clear
from the question, that as 3 is to 15, so is 9 to the number
required; that is, 3 : 15 : : 9 : therefore 135, the product of
9 into 15, divided by 3, will give the number required, that
is 45.

Question 2. If 2 workmen in 4 days earn 2s., how much
will 5 earn in 7 days? that is, as 2 multiplied by 4 are to 2,
so are 5 multiplied by 7 to the number sought; or as 8 : 2
: : 35 to the number sought; and thus the hire sought is
found to be 8s. 9d.

Question 3. Three merchants forming a partnership, gain
£100. The first spent £5, the second £8, the third £10.
It is sought how much each gained. The sum of the ex-
penditure is £23. Say therefore, as 23 is to 5, so is £100
to the sum sought. The resulting number will indicate how
much is due to the first from the common gain, for it is fair
that, as the expense of each is to the sum of the expenses,
so should be his gain to the sum of the gains. Further, in
the same way by saying 23 : 8 : : 100 &c., and 23 : 10 : :
100, &c., the gains of the others will appear.

The inverse rule of proportion is easily resolved into
simple. For instance, 2 men expend £5 in 6 days: in how
many days will 8 men expend £30? Say first 2 : 5 : : 8 : &c.

and the answer will be 20 ; say therefore, then as 20 : 6: : 30 : &c. and you will find the number required. It is superfluous to explain, why the sought term immediately is found by means of this rather intricate rule.

Question 4. Four pipes fill a cistern in 12 hours : in how many hours will it be filled by 8 of the same size ? We should say, as 8 : 4 : : 12 : &c. ; then 4, multiplied into 12, that is, 48 divided by 8, give the answer, that is 6. Nor in this case, when the proportion is inverted, is there any new difficulty ; for the terms being properly arranged, we shall have two equal rectangles of one, of which both sides are known, but the other is produced from the known term, multiplied into the unknown ; and by dividing that first product by the known side or factor, the unknown term will come out. But it will appear from the question itself, in what order the terms are to be arranged.

CHAP. II.

ON ALLIGATION.

The rule called Simple Alligation is that by which, two things being given, of different price or weight, &c., there is found some third sort, so compounded of the given, that its price, weight, &c., be equal to a given price, weight, &c., intermediate between the given. For instance, a cubic inch of gold weighs 18 ounces, a cubic inch of silver weighs 12 ounces. It is required to have a cubic inch of metal compounded of both, and weighing 16 ounces : in which problem, the intermediate weight 16, exceeds the weight of silver by 4, and is exceeded by the weight of gold, by 2. Now if we take $\frac{2}{6}$ of a cube inch of silver and $\frac{4}{6}$ of a cube of gold, it is clear that these, if combined, will make up a cube inch, as they are equal to unity. But it is also plain, that the weight of this mixed metal is equal to the intermediate 16 ; for we took 2 parts of silver, which is lighter by 4, therefore the defect is 2 in 4 ; but of gold, which is heavier by 2, we took 4 parts, so the excess is 4 in 2 ; that is, equal to the defect, so that they counterbalance each other.

Hence results a rule for the alligation of two things. The

quantity of the greater, which is to be taken, is indicated by a fraction, the denominator of which is the sum of the differences, and the numerator, the difference between the middle and less ; and in the next place, that which has the same denominator, and for numerator the difference between the greater and middle, shows the less quantity which is to be taken.

Question. There are two kinds of silver : the ounce of finer is worth 7, that of inferior quality is worth 4 ; we want to find 3 ounces of silver which are each worth 5. Answer. It is clear, that if I take $\frac{2}{3}$ of the inferior, and $\frac{1}{3}$ of the finer, there will be one ounce of the mixed compound, and three times this will be the quantity required.

If the things to be alligated are more than two, the rule is called Compound Alligation. For instance, there are five kinds of wine, the strength of massic is 1, of chian 3, of falernian 5, of cæcuban 7, of corcyræan 9 : I require a mixture, the strength of which is 4. The strength of a mixture of equal parts of massic and chian, will be 2, being half of the sum of that of the given quantities 1 and 3, as is plain ; so the strength of a mixture of equal parts of falernian, cæcuban, and corcyræan will be 7 ; that is $\frac{1}{3}$ of the number 21, or of the sum of the strengths of the components of the mixture. I alligate 2 and 7 with the given intermediate strength 4, and the defect is 2, the excess 3, the sum of the differences 5 ; consequently there should be taken $\frac{3}{5}$ of the first mixture, $\frac{2}{5}$ of the latter, then $\frac{2}{5}$ being divided by 2, the quotient shows how much of each, chian and massic, should be taken. In the same way $\frac{2}{5}$ divided by 3, will indicate how much of falernian, &c., should be in the required mixture. So $\frac{3}{10}$ massic, $\frac{3}{10}$ chian, $\frac{2}{15}$ falernian, $\frac{2}{15}$ cæcuban, $\frac{2}{15}$ corcyræan, will give the answer.

Hence we perceive how compound alligation may be reduced to simple. The prices, magnitudes, weights, or whatever else should be alligated, ought to be collected into two sums, which are to be divided each by the number of terms which constitute it ; the quotients should be alligated with the intermediate term ; the resulting fractions, divided each by the number of things entering into the sum to which they refer, will express the quantity of each to be taken. The demonstration is plain, from what has been said.

N.B.—In alligation of several things, each question admits of innumerable solutions, and this for two reasons ; first, the deficient terms can be combined with the exceeding ones in several ways, whence will result various quotients to be alligated with the given intermediate term. Care should be taken, however, lest the quotients be together greater, or together less, than the mean ; for if this happen, it is plain that the question is impossible ; secondly, it is allowable frequently to repeat the same term, whence its share or portion will be increased, but those of the others diminished.

I am glad here, for the gratification of the studious, to give a solution of that famous problem given to Archimedes by Hiero.

Question : A crown is made of an alloy of gold and silver : it is asked how much gold, how much silver, is in it, and the king does not allow the crown to be broken up. Ans. Two masses should be taken, one of gold, another of silver, each of equal weight with the crown, which being done, it is manifest that the problem could be proposed in another form, as follows : a pound of gold and a pound of silver being given to find a pound of an alloy made up of both, which shall be of the given intermediate mass. Now, as the solid contents of the crown cannot be ascertained geometrically, there is need of contrivance. Each of the masses should be separately immersed in a vessel full of water, and the quantity of water which flows out on each immersion should be measured, it being obvious that it must be equal in bulk to the immersed mass ; suppose the gold being immersed, let the bulk of displaced water be 5, of the silver 9, of the crown 6. The question, therefore, comes to this ; there being given a pound of gold of the magnitude of 5, and a pound of silver of the magnitude of 9, it is required how much of each we should take to have a pound of an alloy of the magnitude of 6. Then if 9 and 5 be alligated with the intermediate magnitude 6, the quantity of gold will be ascertained, that is, $\frac{3}{4}$ of the quantity of gold, and $\frac{1}{4}$ of the quantity of silver, combined in the crown.

Hence it appears how little difficulty there is in the problem on the solution of which Archimedes of old exclaimed Ἕυρηκα.

CHAP. III.

ARITHMETICAL progression is a name given to a series of numbers increasing or diminishing by a common difference. For instance, in this series 1, 4, 7, 10, 13, 16, 19, 22, 25, 3 is the common excess by which the second term exceeds the first, the third the second, the fourth the third, and so on; and in this other series of decreasing numbers 15, 13, 11, 9, 7, 5, 3, 1, 2 is the common quantity by which each number falls short of the preceding.

Now, from considering this series and the definition which we have laid down, it is manifest that each term contains the lesser extreme, and the common difference multiplied by the number of places by which it is removed from that lesser extreme. For instance, in the first series the number 13 consists of the lesser extreme 1, and the common difference 3 multiplied into 4, the number of places by which it is removed from the lesser extreme. Hence the lesser extreme and the common difference being given, any term, for example the eleventh from the lesser exclusive, can be easily found, by multiplying the difference 3 into 11, and adding the product 33 to the lesser extreme 1. If the greater extreme, the common difference, and the number of places intervening between the term sought and the greater extreme be given, the term sought may be found by multiplying the difference into the number of places, and taking the product from the greater extreme. It is clear also how the first term is assigned, if any term, its index, and common difference be given; and how the common difference may be obtained if any term, its index, and the lesser extreme be given; and also how the index of any term may be obtained if the term, the difference, and lesser extreme, be given. It is also clear that the half of the sum of two terms is equal to the arithmetical mean proportional. For instance, 7 and 13 make 20, whose half, 10, is a mean between the given terms. Any one can easily deduce these and many other problems and theorems, and their solutions, from the nature of arithmetical progression, especially if he use skilful symbolical computation. I therefore leave them to beginners for points of practice.

GEOMETRICAL progression is the name given to a series of numbers increasing or decreasing by the same continued ratio. For instance, 3, 6, 12, 24, 48, 96 are in a geometrical progression, the common ratio of which is twice, as each term is twice the preceding one. In like manner the numbers of this decreasing series 81, 27, 9, 3, 1, proceed in a subtriple ratio, that is, each term is in a subtriple ratio to the preceding, or $\frac{1}{3}$; where it should be observed that each term is composed of the power of the common ratio, bearing the same name with it, multiplied into the first term. For instance, 48, the fourth term, exclusively, is produced from 16, the fourth power of the number 2 (that is, that which produced from 2 multiplied three times into itself, since the root itself is called the first power,) multiplied by the first term 3. Wherefore what has been laid down concerning arithmetical progression holds good here, if, instead of addition and subtraction, we use multiplication and division ; and instead of multiplication and division, involution and evolution, or the extraction of roots.[1] For instance, as in arithmetical progression the sum of the extremes divided into two equal parts gives the arithmetical mean, so in geometrical progression the mean proportional is the root of the product of the extremes. Therefore, as regards theorems and problems, we shall not longer dwell upon deducing them, since they easily result from the mere consideration of the series.

But there is one theorem of geometrical progression from which the knowledge of logarithms was originally derived, and on which they still rest ; and which therefore it is fit to explain here. In a geometrical progression, the commencement of which is unity, the rectangle of any two terms is equal to the term of the same progression, which has for index the sum of the index of the factors. For instance, if in the following series.$\left\{\begin{array}{l} 1,\ 2,\ 4,\ 8,\ 16,\ 32,\ 64, \\ 0,\ 1,\ 2,\ 3,\ \ 4,\ \ 5,\ \ 6, \end{array}\right\}$ the second

[1] N.B.—A careful reader can investigate how the roots of any powers may be extracted by means of the method which we followed when treating of the cube, the square, and their roots.

term 2 be multiplied into the fourth 8, the product, 16, is the fifth term, the index of which, 4, is the sum of the indexes of the second and fourth. The reason is manifest; for each power, multiplied into any other power of the same root, produces a third, in which there are as many dimensions as there were in both of the generating powers. But in a geometrical progression, of which the first term is unity, it is clear that all the other subsequent ones are powers produced from the common ratio, and that each have as many dimensions as their places are distant from unity. Therefore, if to an infinite geometrical progression there were annexed also an infinite series of indices, to obtain the rectangle of two terms it would not be necessary to multiply one by the other; but, merely adding the indices to find an index equal to the sum, and this would show the sought rectangle annexed to it. In like manner, if one term is to be divided by another, the difference of the indices, if the square or cube root is to be extracted, $\frac{1}{2}$ or $\frac{1}{3}$ as an index, would show the required quotient or root.

Hence it is plain that the more difficult operations in arithmetic could be singularly abridged, if tables were formed in which the numbers placed in natural order should have each a corresponding index annexed; for then multiplication can be effected by addition alone; division by subtraction; the extraction of roots by halving or trisecting the indices: but to accommodate those indices or logarithms to numbers, "this is the task, this the labour," in effecting which numbers of mathematicians have toiled.

The first who formed tables generally proceeded in this way. To the numbers 1, 10, 100, 1000, &c., in decuple progression, they assigned the logarithms 0.0000000, 1.0000000, 2.0000000, 3.0000000, &c. Then to find the logarithm of any number, for instance, 4, between 1 and 10, seven cyphers being added to each, they sought a mean proportional between 1.0000000 and 10.0000000; and if it were less than 4, the mean proportional was to be sought between it and 10.0000000, but if greater, between it and 1.0000000 ; and then they finally sought a mean proportional between this (if it were less than 4) and the next greatest, but if greater, and the next less, and so on until they came to a number differing by a very small part, for instance, $\frac{1}{100000}$, from the proposed 4. Then the logarithm of this was had by finding an arithmetic mean between the logarithms of the numbers 1 and 10, and another between it and the logarithm of ten, &c. Now if the logarithm of the number 4 be halved, the logarithm of 2 is found; the same when doubled gives the logarithm of the number 16; and if to the logarithm of 4 be added the logarithm of 2, the sum will be the logarithm of 8.

In the same way, from one logarithm of the number 4, others innumerable can be obtained. In this manner, when logarithms were adapted to other numbers between 10 and unity, they supplied very many others to their sum and difference. But of this enough; for we have not undertaken to give all things which bear on logarithms. It was merely proposed to a certain extent to explain their nature, use, and invention.

MATHEMATICAL MISCELLANIES:

SOME THOUGHTS

CONCERNING

SURD ROOTS, THE ATMOSPHERIC TIDE, AN EQUILATERAL
CONE AND CYLINDER CIRCUMSCRIBED ABOUT THE
SAME SPHERE, ON THE ALGEBRAIC GAME,

AND SOME PERSUASIVES TO

THE STUDY OF MATHEMATICS, ESPECIALLY ALGEBRA.

BY * * * * BACHELOR OF ARTS,

TRINITY COLLEGE, DUBLIN.

1707.

D. SAMUEL MOLYNEUX,

FELLOW COMMONER IN DUBLIN COLLEGE, SON OF THE
EMINENT WILLIAM MOLYNEUX, CUT OFF A FEW YEARS
AGO, BY A FATE LAMENTABLE BOTH FOR HIS COUNTRY
AND THE INTERESTS OF LITERATURE.

EXCELLENT YOUTH,

Such was the esteem in which your father when living was
held by the learned, that I consider I would do them a
grateful service, if I should show that he has left a son, who
inherits his penetration and sagacity. It must indeed be
allowed, that your uncle,[1] a man of a remarkably enlarged
and well-informed mind, had previously done something of
the kind. For that eminent man had perceived your disposition as you approached maturity, that it was probable
you would follow in the footprints of your father. The
authority of such a man influenced me so far, that I from
that thenceforth conceived great hopes of you. But now
when becoming acquainted with the nature of your studies,
I perceive you devoting yourself to sound philosophy and
mathematics, when I perceive that the thorns which seem
to beset mathematics, and usually deter others from its study,
on the contrary, spur you on to a more speedy progress ;
when I also see, that high intellectual powers accompany
that industry and desire of knowledge, I cannot restrain my
joy from manifesting itself to the learned world, and expressing my undoubting anticipation that, if God grant you
life and health, you will be one of the chief ornaments of the
rising age. Wherefore, presenting to you the following
pieces, whatever may be their merit, I wished to seize the
opportunity of communicating publicly with, as well that I
might gratify my affection towards you, as well as, that
expectation being raised respecting you, you might by some
tie, and that no ungrateful one, be attached to the study of
such excellent objects.

[1] See a letter of Thomas Molyneux, M.D., to the Bishop of Clogher,
in Philosoph. Transac. No. 282.

OF SURD ROOTS.

IT formerly occurred to me to think that algebraical operations would be rendered more easy, if, discarding the radical
signs, some other method could be contrived of computing
the roots of imperfect powers which would be less at variance
with the forms used in other processes. For, as in arithmetic, fractions are rendered much more manageable by
being reduced from vulgar to decimal, for then, the place of
each figure serving as a denominator, they are abridged in one
part and expressed as integers, and form the same sort of
series as they do, and are regulated by the same rules : so if
from symbolical computations we removed that radical sign
($\sqrt{\ }$), which, as the denominator marks the difference between
integers and fractions, points out a difference in treating
radicals and surds, unquestionably the mode of treating them
would be simplified.

Wherefore should we not, therefore, designate surd roots
like rational, merely by letters, and substitute c or d for $\sqrt{b}$?
for if they were expressed in this way there will be no distinction between them and the roots of perfect powers, and
addition, subtraction, multiplication, &c., will be managed in
the same manner in each case. But there is a ready objection, that quantities multiplied in this way confuse calcula-
tions more than radical signs do. To this I answer, a remedy
can be applied if we use the letters of the Greek alphabet for
expressing roots, by writing β for $\sqrt{b}$, γ for $\sqrt{d}$, &c. ; in
which way not so much the letters themselves as the
characters will be varied, and each substituted figure will so
far correspond to the primitive that there will be no room for
scruple. The root of a quantity produced from the multiplication or division of others, will be marked by their roots
simply multiplied and divided, for instance, $\sqrt{bc} = \beta\kappa$, and
$\sqrt{\frac{bdm}{e}} = \frac{\beta\delta\mu}{\epsilon}$

But if a multinomial quantity, or one consisting of many members, in which there is no unknown quantity connected by the signs + or −, be proposed, their aggregate might be expressed (as is often the case) by some one letter. For instance, let $a + b − c = g$, the root of which is γ. You will perhaps ask, what is to be done where unknown and known quantities are connected; for instance, if the imperfect power be $f + x$: for if we use ϕ and ξ as the roots of the parts, the root of the whole cannot be determined from them. Why, then, could we not render the given imperfect power equal to some perfect one; as for instance, $f + x = ff + 2f\xi + \xi\xi$, or $fff + 3f\xi + 3f\xi\xi + \xi\xi\xi$, &c.? For then $f + \xi = \sqrt[2]{f + x}$ or $\sqrt[3]{f + x}$, &c.

But it has been omitted how we are to ascertain of what sort is the root; whether quadratic, cube, or biquadratic; and whether, Greek characters being left to quadratics, others should be used for the rest. Or rather, the characters remaining the same, we should by means of one point placed above, denote a square root, by two a cube root, by 3 a bi-quadratic root, &c.; in the same way as first, second, third, &c., fluxions are expressed. Or, finally, should consider it suffi-cient that the denominator of the root might appear by re-trogression; since in the course of the operation it is of no import of what kind the root may be, since all expressed without a radical sign are subject to the same laws, and treated in the same manner.

These things are, indeed, crude and imperfect; and I am aware of how little value is that which I am proposing. But you, illustrious youth, who have both leisure and abilities, can perhaps extract some good from this refuse. However I am not certain whether the thing which we have been discussing may not be of some use to beginners, for I know others will little regard them; and whether by their aid the thread of analytic investigation may not be disentangled when the radical sign being laid aside, the heterogeneous operations which accompany it may also disappear. However this may be, I am convinced that these being partially set forth, I could more briefly and clearly explain the common theory of surds than I am aware that it has been done by anyone. I now proceed to do it.

Surd roots are said to be commensurable when their mutual ratio can be expressed by rational numbers, but if this cannot be done they are called incommensurable. If there be given two surd roots, and it be required to ascertain whether they be commensurable or not, let there be found an exponent of the ratio existing between the powers to which the radical sign is prefixed; if this be a perfect power, having the same index as the proposed roots, they will be commensurable; but otherwise, then they should be regarded as incommensurable. For instance, let the proposed roots be $^2\sqrt{24}$ and $^2\sqrt{54}$, the fraction $\frac{4}{9}$ squared, expresses the ratio of one power, 24, to the other, 54; and consequently the roots are commensurable: that is to say, $^3\sqrt{24} : ^3\sqrt{54} :: 2 : 3$. Let $^3\sqrt{320}$ and $^3\sqrt{135}$ be the given quantities, the ratio of the number 320 to 135 is expressed by $\frac{64}{27}$, a perfect cube; the root of which, $\frac{4}{3}$, indicates the ratio of the one root, $^3\sqrt{320}$, to the other, $^3\sqrt{125}$. The demonstration is manifest, since all know that square roots are in subduplicate ratio, cube roots in subtriplicate, biquadratic in subquadruplicate, and so on of the respective powers.

If the roots, the ratio of which is required, be heterogeneous, they should be reduced to one kind by involving the numbers affixed to the radical sign, each according to the index of the other root, which being thus involved, the radical sign is to be prefixed, with an index produced by multiplying together the indexes originally given. For instance, let the heterogeneous surd roots be $^2\sqrt{5}$ and $^3\sqrt{11}$; if 5 be cubed and 11 be squared, they will become 125 and 121. The radical sign, prefixed with the index 6, produces the homogeneous roots $^6\sqrt{125}$, $^6\sqrt{121}$. That the reason of this operation may be perceived, let $^2\sqrt{5}$ be denoted by some simple sign, suppose b, and $^3\sqrt{11}$, by c, and $^2\sqrt{bb}$ will be $= ^2\sqrt{5}$, and $^3\sqrt{ccc} = ^3\sqrt{11}$, and $^6\sqrt{bbbbbb} = ^6\sqrt{125}$, and $^6\sqrt{ccccc} = ^6\sqrt{121}$; where it is plain that $^6\sqrt{bbbbbb} = ^2\sqrt{bb}$, $^6\sqrt{ccccc} = ^3\sqrt{cc}$.

As to the addition of surd roots, if they are commensurable it is done by prefixing the sum of the terms to the radical sign of the ratio, under which the common divisor is to be placed, by means of which the terms of the common ratio were denoted. For instance, $^2\sqrt{24} + ^2\sqrt{54}$

$= 5\sqrt[2]{6}$. For, from what has been already observed, and from what follows concerning multiplication, $\sqrt[2]{24} = 2\sqrt[2]{6}$, and $\sqrt[2]{54} = 3\sqrt[2]{6}$. In the same way is subtraction managed, only that the difference of the terms is prefixed to the radical sign of the exponent. If incommensurable surd roots are to be added or subtracted, they should be connected by the signs $+$ or $-$. For instance, $\sqrt{6} + \sqrt{3}$ and $\sqrt{6} - \sqrt{3}$ are the sum and difference of the roots of the numbers 6 and 3; in which way, also, rational numbers are added to or subtracted from surds. If the surd root is to be multiplied by another homogeneous, the radical sign and the common index should be prefixed to the rectangle of the powers. For instance, the $\sqrt[2]{3} \times \sqrt[2]{7} = \sqrt[2]{21}$, and $\sqrt[3]{g} \times \sqrt[3]{x} = \sqrt[3]{gx}$. For demonstrating which operation, let the roots of the numbers 3 and 7 be denoted by b and d, so that $bb = 3$ and $dd = 7$, and it is manifest that $\sqrt[2]{bbdd} = bd$; that is, the square root of the product is equal to the products of the square roots. The same thing can be demonstrated in the same way concerning any other roots, cubic, biquadratic, &c. Heterogeneous roots, before they are multiplied, should be reduced to homogeneous. If a rational number is to be multiplied into a surd, it should be raised to a power of the same denomination with the given imperfect one, to which is prefixed the radical sign and the index of the same power, and then proceed as before. For instance, $5 \times \sqrt[3]{4} = \sqrt[3]{125} \times \sqrt[3]{4} = \sqrt[3]{500}$; or more compendiously thus: $5\sqrt[3]{4}$, and generally $b \times \sqrt[a]{c} = \sqrt[a]{b^a c}$, or $b^a \sqrt[a]{c}$.

As to division, as often as the dividend and divisor are both surd roots, having removed what is heterogeneous, if there be any, the radical sign prefixed to the quotient of the powers, with the proper index, will exhibit the required quotient. For instance, $\sqrt[2]{7} \div \sqrt[2]{3} = \sqrt[2]{\frac{7}{3}} = \sqrt[2]{2\frac{1}{3}}$. But if of two numbers only one be under the radical sign, the other, involved according to the index of the given root, should be placed under the radical sign, and proceed as before. For instance, $\sqrt[3]{96} \div 4 = \sqrt[3]{96} \div \sqrt[3]{64} = \sqrt[3]{\frac{96}{64}}$

$= \sqrt[3]{\frac{3}{2}}$; or without preparation, $\dfrac{\sqrt[3]{96}}{4}$; and generally $\sqrt[a]{c}$

$\div\ b = {}^a\sqrt{\dfrac{c}{ba}}$ or $\dfrac{{}^a\sqrt{c}}{ba}$. These are, as well as the former, easily demonstrated.

ON THE ATMOSPHERIC TIDE.

SOME time since I met with a book bearing the title, "On the Influence of the Sun and Moon on the Human Body," by an eminent doctor of medicine and F.R.S. I am well aware how celebrated he is and how insignificant I am. But that I may freely declare my opinion, I thoroughly receive the opinion concerning the atmospheric tide as he there explains it, and how it is based on the principle of the celebrated Newton. I am not, however, convinced that the ingenious author has rightly ascertained the causes of some phenomena connected with it. How far my doubts may be well founded, you, with whose acuteness I am well acquainted, will best judge.

That eminent man considers that there is a swelling out of the spheroidal figure of the earth about the equinoctial line. He attributes to the same cause the difference between the swelling of the air caused in the oblique sphere by the meridional, and (if I may use the expression) antimeridional moon. But I do not think that the explanation of either of those phenomena should be sought in the oblate spheroid. On this account, because though the opinion that the aëreo-terrestrial mass is of that figure is supported both by mathematical and physical grounds, and also agrees well with some phenomena, still it is not so fully received by all, but that some, and those of note too, hold the opposite opinion. And indeed I remember that Dr. Chardellou, who is profoundly skilled in astronomy, informed me that he had ascertained that the axis of the earth is longer than the diameter of the equator, and consequently, that the earth is a spheroid, but such as Burnet describes it, rising at the poles and lower at the equator. But as for me, I would rather call in question the observations of that eminent man, than reject the arguments for the earth being oblate. Still since that opinion does not equally please all, I should be reluctant to adopt it as a principle for explaining any phenomenon, unless the thing could not otherwise be explained. But in the next place, so far from the explanation of the above-mentioned effects requiring necessarily a spheroidal figure of the earth, that it gains not a particle of light from it, and I will try to show this, by adding what that eminent man writes on the subject : " The air rises above its usual level about the two equinoxes, because when the equinoctial line corresponds with that circle of the terrestrial globe which has the greatest diameter, each of the heavenly bodies, while in it, is nearer to the earth." On the Influence of the Sun and Moon, p. 9. However, it may be well doubted, whether that nearer position of the luminaries be adequate to raise the air above the usual level. For so slight is the difference

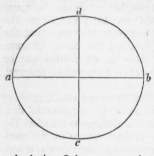

between the transverse and conjugate axis of the ellipse, by the revolution of which the terrestrial spheroid is generated, that it approaches very near to a sphere. But that we may consider the question more accurately, let *a c b d* denote a section of the aëreo-terrestrial mass through the poles *d c* being the axis, *a b* the diameter of the equator. Now by calculation I have ascertained, that the attractive power of the moon is not $\frac{1}{4000}$ part stronger at *a* or *b* than it would be at *c* or *d* if it directly were above either pole, and, therefore, that so small a difference would be altogether unequal to producing any sensible effect. It should also be considered, that the moon is never distant from the equator a third part of the arc *b d*, and that consequently the aforesaid difference must be still very much restricted. But what we have said of the moon must be still further the case as to the sun, since it is many times further distant. It is true indeed that Dr. Mead has adduced, besides other causes of the tide being higher near the equinoxes, to wit, " the greater agitation of a fluid spheroid revolving in a greater circle, besides the centrifugal force having a much greater influence there." As to the first, although at first it appears of some import, I must confess that I do not altogether perceive how any thing bearing on the distinct explanation of the subject can be concluded from that. As to the second, it is plain that the centrifugal force is far the greatest near the equator, and on that account that the aëreo-terrestrial mass has the figure of an oblate spheroid ; but I do not see what consequence results from this. But although we should allow that the air, for the causes mentioned by this eminent man, should about the equinoxes swell out near the equator, it does not, however, appear thence, how with us, who live so far from the equator, it then should be higher than usual, but rather the contrary seems to follow. Mead writes thus in the following page : " To conclude, in the same parallels where the declination of the moon is towards that pole of the heavens which rises highest, the attraction is the strongest, when it comes to the meridian of the place, but least, when it comes to the meridian of the opposite place ; the contrary of which happens in the opposite parallels. The cause is in the spheroid figure of the earth and atmosphere." But I do not think that the cause is in the figure of the earth and ambient atmosphere, because if we assume the earth to be perfectly spherical, or even oblong, the same thing will certainly happen, as will be shown below.

It remains for me to attempt the explanation of these things, especially on this account, because a reason drawn from the spheroidal figure of the earth was regarded by me with suspicion ; for without taking it at all into account, the affair could be most clearly and easily explained.

Newton, in his Physico-mathematical work, book iii., prop. 24, where he explains the phenomena of the tides of the sea, has this passage : " The influence of each luminary also depends on its declination, or distance from the equator. For if the luminary were placed at the pole it would constantly attract every particle of water without increase or diminution of its action, and so would cause no reciprocation of motion. Therefore the luminaries, in proceeding towards the pole from the equator, will gradually lose their effects, and on that account will cause less tides in the solstitial than in the equinoctial syzygies." But no other cause need be sought for any phenomenon of the atmospheric tide, than is sufficient for producing a similar effect in the tide of the sea. But that

I may explain more fully that which has been rather briefly, and therefore obscurely by the most eminent man in the world, in the former figure let *a d b c* be the meridian, and *a b* the axis of the aëreo-terrestrial mass, and let the sun and moon be conceived to be placed at the poles. It is clear that each part of the aerial mass, *d* for instance, during the diurnal revolution retains an equal distance from the luminary, and so is equally attracted towards their bodies; so that the air is not at one time elevated, at another depressed, but through the whole day remains at the same altitude. But secondly let *a c b d* represent the equator, or some parallel, and let the luminaries be in the equinoctial plane; at that time it is plain that the equator itself, as well as each parallel, assumes an elliptical figure. It is manifest also that the air which now is at *a*, the summit of the transverse axis, and is the highest six hours afterwards, will be at *c*, the extreme of the conjugate axis and lowest, and that the greatest reciprocation of motion results. To finish the whole work at once, let us suppose the swellings of the tidal spheroid to have a threefold position, either in the poles, or in the equator, or in the intermediate parts. In the first case the plane of diurnal rotation would be perpendicular to the axis of the spheroid, and therefore a circle; whence there would be no tide; in the second, it would be parallel to the same, and consequently an ellipse, between the axes of which would be the greatest difference, consequently the tides be greatest; in the third, in proportion as it approached nearer to the perpendicular position, it would be more nearly a circle, and consequently the tides would be less.

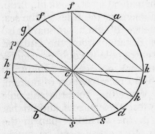

It remains that I should demonstrate that the difference which exists in an oblique sphere between any tide and the following one, when the moon is away from the equator, will result indifferently, the earth being assumed either oblate, or exactly spherical, or oblong. Let *a b* be the axis of the world, *g d* the equator, *k* any place, *f k* the parallel of the place, *h l* the axis of the tidal spheroid, swelling on both sides principally by the influence of the moon. Let the moon's place be near l. It is to be demonstrated that $c\,k$, the height of the air when the moon is near the meridian, is greater than $c\,f$, the height of the air when the moon has passed the meridian of the opposite place. Let $p\,s$ be drawn, a parallel corresponding to the former on the opposite side, and let $c\,k\,c\,f$ be produced to p and s. By construction the arc $p\,h$ is equal to the arc $k\,l$, therefore the arc $f\,h$ is greater than the arc $k\,l$; therefore on account of the ellipse the right line $f\,s$ is less than the right line $k\,p$, and $f\,c$ less than $k\,c$. Q. E. D.

OF THE EQUILATERAL CONE AND CYLINDER DESCRIBED ROUND THE SAME SPHERE.

LEMMA.

THE side of an equilateral triangle is to the diameter of the inscribed circle as $\sqrt{3}$ to 1, and the perpendicular, let fall from any angle to the opposite side, is to the same as 3 to 2.

These things are plain to anyone at all acquainted with algebra and geometry.

PROBLEM.

To find the ratio between the cylinder and equilateral cone circumscribed about the same sphere.

Let the diameter and periphery of the base of the cylinder be each unity. Then by lemma the diameter and the periphery of the base of the cone will be each $\sqrt{3}$. Then $1 \times \frac{1}{4} = \frac{1}{4} =$ base of cylinder; and $\frac{1}{2} =$ the sum of the bases. And $\sqrt{3} \times \frac{1}{4}\sqrt{3} = \frac{3}{4} =$ base of the cone, and surface of the cylinder, or four times the base is equal to 1. And the simple surface of the cone is equal to $\frac{3}{2} = \dfrac{\sqrt{6}}{4} \times \sqrt{6}$; for $\sqrt{\frac{3}{2}}$ (that is, a mean proportional between $\sqrt{3}$, the side of the cone, and radius of the base or $\sqrt{\frac{3}{4}}$) is the radius of a

E

circle equal to the surface of the cone; and by the preceding $1 + \frac{1}{2} = \frac{3}{2} =$ surface of whole cylinder, and $\frac{3}{2} + \frac{3}{4} = \frac{9}{4} =$ surface of whole cone. Consequently, by lemma and hypothesis the axis of the cylinder is 1, and of the cone $\frac{3}{2}$. But the solid contents of the cylinder $= \frac{1}{4} \times 1 = \frac{1}{4}$, and the solid contents of the cone $= \frac{3}{4} \times \frac{1}{2} = \frac{3}{8}$. Hence, the homogeneous quantities being compared together, there will result the following.

THEOREM.

Between an equilateral cone and cylinder circumscribed about the same sphere, there is the same sesquialterate ratio as to the whole surfaces, the solids, altitudes, and bases. Two years ago I discovered that theorem to my no small surprise. I did not wonder at my own talents or peculiar sagacity, as the thing is so easy, but merely that Tacquet, a celebrated professor of mathematics, prided himself so much on a discovery, to which a beginner is competent. His discovery, which is but a part of that stated above, is, "that an equilateral cone is sesquialterate in solid contents and entire surface, of a cylinder circumscribed about the same sphere," and that consequently, "there is a continued ratio" between an equilateral cone, cylinder, and sphere.

This is that proposition, to which reference is made by the figure, which is with an inscription placed on the title-page of that author's work on the select theorems of Archimedes. The reader may still further consult what the Jesuit states in his preface, in the scholium to Prop. 32, and at the end of the 44th proposition of the same work, where he puts forward his theorem as a wonderful invention, and rivalling those of Archimedes. And not only Tacquet, but the celebrated Wallis also, brings it out in the additions and emendations to the 81st chapter of his Algebra, as having been demonstrated by Caswell by means of the arithmetic of infinites; which is also done, as to one part, by Dechales, in the 20th proposition of his book about indivisibles. However, the method of indivisibles and the arithmetic of infinites founded on it, are by some scarcely allowed to be geometrical.

But the whole theorem has been demonstrated before by

no one that I know. However, if it be true, as Tacquet thinks, that amongst the other various and celebrated dis-coveries of Archimedes, he was most pleased with that in which he shows that the cylinder is sesquialterate of the in-scribed sphere in solid contents and surface, because there is one connected proportion of the bodies and of the surfaces containing them. If this was the reason that he wished the cylinder circumscribed about the sphere to be sculptured on his tomb, what would the old Sicilian have done had he dis-covered that the one connected proportion held in a fivefold respect as to the two bodies. But we have just noticed how easily that follows from his inventions.

In much the same way as we have done that, it will not be difficult to discover and demonstrate all the theorems which Tacquet annexes to the Archimedean, and a hundred more of the same sort, if necessary.

ON THE ALGEBRAIC GAME.

I INVENTED the algebraic game about the same time that I did that theory. For when I saw some of my acquaintance, perhaps for half a day, intent on chess, wondering at their close pursuit of trifling, I asked what it was on which they were so closely occupied, and was answered, a delightful exercise of the mind. Turning this over in my thoughts, I wondered why so few applied their minds to mathematics, a pursuit at once so pleasing and so useful. Is it on account of difficulty? but many have great abilities, and decline no toil in trifles. Or is it because it is not a pleasing exercise of the mind? But what discipline or occupation whatsoever, I would ask, could better exercise skill, penetration, sagacity, every faculty of the mind? Are mathematics a game? They are no less agreeable; however, if they were to present them-selves in that guise, perhaps those nice fellows, who spend their time in games, might devote themselves to this study. To this was added, the advice of that profound thinker, John Locke, on a similar occasion. I then contrived the following game as an exercise in algebra, with no great reach of mind,

I allow, but such as will, I hope, easily be excused in a youth, especially one engaged in other studies.

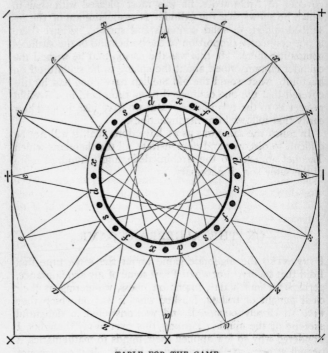

TABLE FOR THE GAME.

Algebraical problems consist of given equations, which in determinate questions bring out sought quantities equal to a number. But each equation consists of two members, connected by a sign of equality, in each of which are for consideration, first, the sorts, whether they denote given or sought quantities; then, the signs by which they are connected. It is our object, then, to contrive that all these come out, to produce questions from chance, and a game, as well from the formation of the questions as from their solution. On a small board, such as is commonly used for

the game of draughts, or of chess, let there be marked out
a circle, inscribed in a square, and everything set down as
in the adjoining plan, except that in place of black spots
there should be holes. We then shall have the table for the
game. There should also be provided a slender peg of wood,
which could fit in any of the holes. We now shall proceed
to explain the use of these.

It may be observed that the symbols of calculation are set
down at the sides and angles of the squares; moreover the
sides give signs to the first, the angles to the latter members
of equations. The inscribed circle is divided by sixteen
points into as many equal parts, so that three points are
directed to each side and angle, but some directly, some
obliquely. Those which are directed obliquely to any side
or angle, are common to the side and angle, but those which
directly point to any side belong to no angle, but are referred
equally to each adjacent one; and *vice versa*, those which
are directly pointed towards any angle belong to no side,
but are to be considered referable equally to each of the
adjacent ones.

In forming, then, the question, our attention should be
first directed to the point which the peg marks, and the side
and angle to which it belongs. These signs should be noted
as those which, as we have said, connect the sorts of each
member of the equation; then the peg being placed at the
letter written at the said point number 1, and that being
transferred to the opposite side by means of the direction of
right line (as the astrologers do, assigning the reason of
names by which feasts are designated) number 2. Then
proceeding to the other extremity of the line, as if it were
continued through the intermediate ring number 3, and so
on, until the letter adjacent to the first point recurs, and so
on. Hence descending by the right line to the point terminated in the convexity of the interior circle, fix the peg in
either adjacent hole. The number last enumerated will
show how many sought quantities, or, which is the same,
how many given equations there are in the question. The
former members of these are constituted by the unknown
quantities taken alternately, and connected with the lateral
sign, the latter, by the unknown or known quantities (as may
be determined by the letter written at the internal point)

connected with the sought by the angular. Moreover, d shows that various sorts of known quantities are to be used, s that only one, f the numeral figures 2, 3, 4, &c., x that the sought quantities are to be repeated. But it is to be observed, in the latter member of each equation no other unknown quantities are set down than those which are found in the first member of the following equation. What has been said will be illustrated by examples.

Let us say now, that the peg occupies the hole marked by a star, and the point to which it refers will belong to the side, the sign of which is $+$, and to the angle, the sign of which is $\times$; which signs I set down on paper, the lateral on the left, or first, then the angular. Moreover, e is written at the point at which I reckon 1 ; thence (but it is allowable of two lines to follow the direction of either) proceeding towards the left, I come on a, at which I reckon 2 ; thence, turning to z, I reckon 3 ; then proceeding across, I meet with e, the letter placed at the first point, at which, reckoning 4, I proceed directly to the interior point marked by the letter d. There will, therefore, be four sought quantities in the question ; which, connected alternately by the lateral sign $+$, will constitute the first members of the given equation. But the latter will be constituted of various known and unknown quantities (on account of d), connected by $\times$, the angular sign, in this way :—

$$
\begin{aligned}
a + e &= yb & a &= \,? \\
e + y &= zc & e &= \,? \\
y + z &= ad & y &= \,? \\
x + a &= ef & z &= \,?
\end{aligned}
$$

Wherefore, if we say that the peg is in the preceding hole, so that it will directly be directed to the lateral $+$, and we follow the direction of the left line, there will result three quantities to be investigated ; and the interior point will have the letter f. Whence the number of the given equations, and the signs of the former members of the same, and the species of the latter are determined. But since in this case the point is circumstanced indifferently with respect to the two adjacent angles, therefore their signs are to be employed alternately ; from which conditions results a question of this kind :—

$$a + e = 2y \qquad a = ?$$
$$e + y = 3—a \qquad e = ?$$
$$y + a = 4e \qquad y = ?$$

But if we say that the peg is to be fixed in the following hole, the peg point should be directed towards + angular, and will equally have reference to the lateral signs + and —. Then, if you be inclined to take the right path, according to the rules laid down above, the following question will result:—

$$a + e = ey \qquad a = ?$$
$$e - y = ay \qquad e = ?$$
$$y + a = ae \qquad y = ?$$

[1] But it should first be observed, that the rules laid down admit some variety in the combinations of signs and sorts, whence it is that the point and direction being determined, various questions arise.

Secondly, that although we have already said, that a stop should be made at the recurrence of the first letter, that rule, however, can be changed at the will of each; so that we may proceed until a, e, z, x, successively turn up, or some of them twice; or until we reach some other limit. But we hasten to the game. First, then, let some of the players form a question for himself, according to the method just laid down. The other must do the same, then, by the same rules. So the question of each being made out, each should set himself about the solution of that which chance has given him. Then let each set down a fraction, the numerator of which is to be the number of quantities sought in his problem, and the denominator the number of degrees or equations which, whilst the question was solving, he set down on paper. He is to be the winner whose fraction is the largest.

Then, if fugitive quantities elude the eager algebraist, he must be considered to have lost all hope of victory. Nor altogether unreasonably, since it must happen rather by the fault of the selector than by mischance, that the question is undeterminate.

As often as in the sport we come to an equation adfected beyond quadratic, there will be no need of a tedious process,

[1] See Appendix.

or construction by parabola; it is sufficient if an unknown root, its kind being changed, be regarded as known.

The solution of all the questions being finished, each should examine the work of the other, for which purpose parchment margins are convenient. As to pledges and fines, each may settle that as he pleases, for I leave these to others.

As regards the problems, they are not difficult, for otherwise they would be ill suited for amusement; but they are of that kind the solution of which will redound to the great advantage of the players whilst they strive to reach the proper path, whilst they, in their minds, run over long trains of consequences, and try to comprehend the whole series of analysis in a very brief glance. Permit me now, excellent youth, briefly to address others, for you, whom the difficulty itself attracts, have no need of an exhorter. I address you, college youths, who have energy of mind, sagacity, and penetration, but are averse from sad seclusion in the study and the lives of those generally called *Pumps*, thinking better to show your talents among your fellow idlers in play and games. You see what a mere game is algebra, and that both chance and science find place in it. Why should you not, then, come to this gaming table? For you need not here dread that which happens in cards, chess, draughts— that whilst some play others stand idly by; for whoever wish to play, can at once play and study; and some, too, make a little money. But I think I hear some one exclaiming in these words, Do you think that we can be deceived? We are not to be lured by presenting the appearance of a game, into learning a very difficult science, which must be mastered with great pains. I answer, that algebra is so far difficult as is required for a game; for if you take away all difficulty, you also take away all recreation and amusement. For all plays are so many arts and sciences. Nor is there any distinction between this and the others, but that they only regard present gratification; but from this, besides most delightful occupation, other abundant fruits are obtained. But, so far is this from having a pernicious tendency, that he is in every respect praiseworthy, according to the expression of the poet, "and has gained every point, who has combined the useful with the agreeable."

But what are those fruits which you extol? To enumerate them, mathematics in all their extent; the arts and sciences, advancing civil and military affairs, should be reviewed. For through all these is diffused the wonderful power of algebra. It is styled by all, the great, the wonderful art, the highest pinnacle of human knowledge, the kernel and key of all mathematics; and, by some, the foundation of all sciences. And, indeed, how difficult would it be to assign the limits of algebra, when it has latterly extended to natural philosophy and medicine, and daily sets about the most valuable arguments. That I may pass over other things, in the Philosophical Transactions, No. 257, there are algebraic theorems on the certainty of human evidences and traditions; and it may be laid down for certain that wherever greater and less are brought forward, wherever any ratio or proportion can be admitted, there algebra finds a place.

But perhaps some one may say, that he cares neither for mathematics, nor for anything treated mathematically. Be it so; let us so far indulge the desire, the ignorance of persons; for I venture to maintain that this contempt proceeds from ignorance of the most exalted pursuits, and "which distinguish us from barbarians." [1] But is there anyone who thinks slightingly of a capacious intellect, a sagacious genius, a sound judgment? If there be anyone so devoid of reason, let him then disregard mathematics, the great importance of which, for forming all the best habits of the mind, is allowed by all.

Bacon somewhere, in what he has written concerning the advancement of knowledge, has observed a sort of analogy between the play of hand-ball and mathematics. To wit, as by means of that, besides the pleasure primarily aimed at, we attain other more valuable objects, agility and strength of body, quicksightedness; so mathematical studies, besides their proper aims and uses, have that collateral one, that they abstract the mind from the senses, sharpen and confirm the talents. The ancients formerly, the wiser of the moderns now, allow this. The efficacy of algebra in rearing the intellectual powers is shown, amongst others, by Descartes, and more at length by Malbranche's Inquiry into Truth, book vi.,

[1] See an Essay in English, on the Gardens of Epicurus, by Sir William Temple, Bart.

part i., chap 5, and part ii., chap. 8 ; and many other places.
And those excellent rules which, in book vi., part ii., chap. 1,
he lays down to be observed in the solution of questions, and
which are so admirable, that an ingenious author considers
that an angel could not give better ; these angelic rules, I say,
seem taken from algebra.   Why need I mention others, when
John Locke, who, if anyone did, knew well all the defects of
the human intellect and their remedies, recommends, as
infinitely useful, the study of mathematics in general, and of
algebra especially, to all raised above the populace ?   See his
Posthumous Works, pp. 30, 31, 32, &c., Treatise on the
Conduct of the Understanding, a small and imperfect work
indeed, but which may well be preferred to the vast and
elaborate volumes of others.   But an author of great name
thinks that mathematical pursuits require too severe meditation, and which is less suitable for a man of rank and devoted
to pleasure.   I answer, as Locke exhorts, that the judgment
of the dissentient, St. Evremont, is set against it to no
purpose.   For he must be regarded an incompetent judge
who, as is most probable from his life and writings, had
scarcely entered the threshold.   But if the bark seem hard
and dry, what wonder is it ?   But that I may state the affair
as it is, the best way is that each, making trial of the matter,
follow their own judgment.   Nor is there reason for raising
up great difficulties because the word algebra has I know not
what harsh and fearful sound.   For anyone can, in the short
space of a month, learn the art as far as may be requisite for
the game.

Having now explained our game and views, I request the
mathematical reader to receive candidly these scanty first-
fruits of my studies, as I will probably produce others better
hereafter.   For the present other studies engage, which, dry
and jejune enough, have taken the place of delightful mathematics.   In the meantime do you, excellent youth, accept
this rhapsody of trifles as a sort of emblem of regard for yourself.   Adieu.

APPENDIX.

THAT anyone may fully comprehend my purpose, I have thought it advisable to place before the view, in the following pages, all the variations of combinations and sorts in the questions which the above-stated conditions of playing admit of.

But it should be observed, in the first place, that the following formulæ, according to the modes of combination and sorts of quantities, but not all according to the number of the given equations, belong to the respective points; for often more than three quantities are to be investigated.

Secondly, that as all formulæ of questions may be had, various limits are to be laid down ; otherwise only two of the four classes can belong to any one point.

I call the first point that which is directed to the lateral +, the second that next to it on the right, and so on.

TO THE READER.

I HAVE sometimes regretted too late to have given forth these efforts of my youth, struggling for some knowledge of mathematics only occasionally, and from my own resources. And I would still regret it, but that hence has arisen an occasion of emulation for a noble pair of geniuses, growing up as the hope of the rising generation. Nor do I boast any other claim on the republic of letters. Let these things be considered a deprecation of envy, of censure, on account of my rashness ; if, indeed, I have given occasion of any.

First Point.

$$a + e = b \times ee - bb \times yy - be \times bb - ey \times bb - y$$
$$e + y = b - yy \times bb - aa \times by - bb \times ya - bb \times a$$
$$s \quad y + a = b \times aa - bb \times ee - ba \times bb - ae \times bb - e$$

$$a + e = b \times ee - bb \times yy - be \times bb - ey \times bb - y$$
$$e + y = c - yy \times cc - aa \times cy - cc \times ya - cc \times a$$
$$d \quad y + a = d \times aa - dd \times ee - da \times dd - ae \times dd - e$$

$$a + e = 2 \times ee - 22 \times yy - 2e \times 22 - ey \times 22 - y$$
$$e + y = 3 - yy \times 33 - aa \times 3y - 33 \times ya - 33 \times a$$
$$f \quad y + a = 4 \times aa - 44 \times ee - 4a \times 44 - ae \times 44 - e$$

$$a + e = e \times ye - ye \times yy - e$$
$$e + y = y - ay \times aa - ya \times y$$
$$x \quad y + a = a \times ea - ea \times ee - a$$

Second Point.

$$a + e = b \times eb \times y$$
$$e + y = b \times yb \times a$$
$$s \quad y + a = b \times ab \times e$$

$$a + e = b \times eb \times y$$
$$e + y = c \times yc \times a$$
$$d \quad y + a = d \times ad \times e$$

$$a + e = 2 \times e2 \times y$$
$$e + y = 3 \times y3 \times a$$
$$f \quad y + a = 4 \times a4 \times e$$

$$a + e = e \times y$$
$$e + y = y \times a$$
$$x \quad y + a = a \times e$$

Third Point.

$$a + ea - e = e \times by \times b$$
$$s \quad e - ye + y = y \times ba \times b$$
$$y + ay - a = a \times be \times b$$

$$a + ea - e = e \times by \times b$$
$$d \quad e - ye + y = y \times ca \times c$$
$$y + ay - a = a \times de \times d$$

$$a + ea - e = e \times 2y \times 2$$
$$f \quad e - ye + y = y \times 3a \times 3$$
$$y + ay - a = a \times 4e \times 4$$

$$a + ea - e = e \times y$$
$$x \quad e - ye + y = y \times a$$
$$y + ay - a = a \times e$$

Fourth Point.

$$a - e = b \times e\, b \times y$$
$$s \quad e - y = b \times y\, b \times a$$
$$y - a = b \times a\, b \times e$$

$$a - e = b \times e\, b \times y$$
$$d \quad e - y = c \times y\, c \times a$$
$$y - a = d \times a\, d \times e$$

$$a - e = 2 \times e\, 2 \times y$$
$$f \quad e - y = 3 \times y\, 3 \times a$$
$$y - a = 4 \times a\, 4 \times e$$

$$a - e = e \times y$$
$$x \quad e - y = y \times a$$
$$y - a = a \times e$$

Fifth Point.

$$a - e = e \times bb \div ey \times bb \div yb \times ee \div bb \times yy \div b$$
$$s \quad e - y = y \div bb \times ya \div bb \times ab \div yy \times bb \div aa \times b$$
$$y - a = a \times bb \div ae \times bb \div eb \times aa \div bb \times ee \div b$$

$$a - e = e \times bb \div ey \times bb \div yb \times ee \div bb \times yy \div b$$
$$d \quad e - y = y \div cc \times ya \div cc \div ac \div yy \times cc \div aa \times c$$
$$y - a = a \times dd \div ae \times dd \div ed \times aa \div dd \times ee \div d$$

$$a - e = e \times 22 \div ey \times 22 \div y2 \times ee \div b2 \times yy \div 2$$
$$f \quad e - y = y \div 33 \times ya \div 33 \times a3 \div yy \times c3 \div aa \times 3$$
$$y - a = a \times 44 \div eo \times 44 \div e4 \times aa \div d4 \times ee \div 4$$

$$a - e = e \times ye \div ye \times yy \div b$$
$$x \quad e - y = y \div ay \times aa \div ya \times y$$
$$y - a = a \times ea \div ea \times ee \div a$$

Sixth Point.

$$a - e = b \div eb \div ye \div by \div b$$
$$s \quad e - y = b \div yb \div ay \div ba \div b$$
$$y - a = b \div ab \div ea \div be \div b$$

$$a - e = b \div eb \div ye \div by \div b$$
$$d \quad e - y = c \div yc \div ay \div ea \div c$$
$$y - a = d \div ad \div ea \div de \div d$$

$$a - e = 2 \div e2 \div ye \div 2y \div 2$$
$$f \quad e - y = 3 \div y3 \div ay \div 3a \div 3$$
$$y - a = 4 \div a4 \div ea \div 4e \div 4$$

$$a - e = e \div yy \div e$$
$$x \quad e - y = y \div aa \div y$$
$$y - a = a \div ee \div a$$

Seventh Point.

$$a - ea \times e = e \div bb \div ey \div bb \div y$$
$$s \quad e \times ye - y = y \div bb \div ya \div bb \div a$$
$$y - ay \times a = a \div bb \div ae \div bb \div e$$

$$a - ea \times e = e \div bb \div ey \div bb \div y$$
$$d \quad e \times ye - y = y \div cc \div ya \div cc \div a$$
$$y - ay \times a = a \div dd \div ae \div dd \div e$$

$$a - ea \times e = e \div 22 \div ey \div 22 \div y$$
$$f \quad e + ye - y = y \div 33 \div ya \div 33 \div a$$
$$y - ay \times a = a \div 44 \div ae \div 44 \div e$$

$$a - ea \times e = e \div yy \div e$$
$$x \quad e + ye - y = y \div aa \div y$$
$$y - ay \times a = a \div ee \div a$$

Eighth Point.

$$a \times e = e \div bb \div ey \div bb \div y$$
$$s \quad e \times y = y \div bb \div ya \div bb \div a$$
$$y \div a = a \div bb \div ae \div bb \div e$$

$$a \times e = e \div bb \div ey \div bb \div y$$
$$d \quad e \times y = y \div cc \div ya \div cc \div a$$
$$y \times a = a \div dd \div ae \div dd \div e$$

$$a \times e = e \div 22 \div ey \div 22 \div y$$
$$f \quad e \times y = y \div 33 \div ya \div 33 \div a$$
$$y \times a = a \div 44 \div ae \div 44 \div e$$

$$a \times e = e \div yy \div e$$
$$x \quad e \times y = y \div aa \div y$$
$$y \times a = a \div ee \div a$$

Ninth Point.

$$a \times e = b + ee \div bb \div yy \div be + bb \div ey + bb \div y$$
$$s \quad e \times y = b + yy + bb \div aa \div by \div bb \div ya \div bb \div a$$
$$y \times a = b + aa \div bb \div ee \div ba \div bb \div ae \div bb \div e$$

$$a \times e = b + ee \div bb \div yy \div be + bb \div ey + bb \div y$$
$$d \quad e \times y = c \div yy \div cc \div aa \div cy \div cc \div ya \div cc \div a$$
$$y \times a = d + aa \div dd \div ee \div da \div dd \div ae \div dd \div e$$

$$a \times e = 2 + ee \div 22 \div yy \div 2e \div 22 \div ey \div 22 \div y$$
$$f \quad e \times y = 3 \div yy \div 33 \div aa \div 3y \div 33 \div ya \div 33 \div a$$
$$y \times a = 4 + aa \div 44 + ee \div 4a \div 44 \div ae \div 44 \div e$$

$$a \times e = e + ye \div ye + yy \div e$$
$$x \quad e \times y = y \div ay + aa \div ya \div y$$
$$y \times a = a + ea \div ea + ee \div a$$

Tenth Point.

$$s \begin{cases} a \times e = e + by + b \\ e \times y = y + ba + b \\ y \times a = a + be + b \end{cases}$$

$$d \begin{cases} a \times e = e + by + b \\ e \times y = y + ca + c \\ y \times a = a + de + d \end{cases}$$

$$f \begin{cases} a \times e = e + 2y + 2 \\ e \times y = y + 3a + 3 \\ y \times a = a + 4e + 4 \end{cases}$$

$$x \begin{cases} a \times e = e + y \\ e \times y = y + a \\ y \times a = a + e \end{cases}$$

Eleventh Point.

$$s \begin{cases} a \times ea \div e = e + by + b \\ e \div ye \times y = y + ba + b \\ y \times ay \div a = a + be + b \end{cases}$$

$$d \begin{cases} a \times ea \div e = e + by + b \\ e \div ye \times y = y + ca + c \\ y \times ay \div a = a + de + d \end{cases}$$

$$f \begin{cases} a \times ea \div e = e + 2y + 2 \\ e \div ye \times y = y + 3a + 3 \\ y \times ay \div a = a + 4e + 4 \end{cases}$$

$$x \begin{cases} a \times ea \div e = e + y \\ e \div ye \times y = y + a \\ y \times ay \div a = a + e \end{cases}$$

Twelfth Point.

$$s \begin{cases} a \div e = b + eb + y \\ e \div y = b + yb + a \\ y \div a = b + ab + e \end{cases}$$

$$d \begin{cases} a \div e = b + eb + y \\ e \div y = c + yc + a \\ y \div a = d + ad + e \end{cases}$$

$$f \begin{cases} a \div e = 2 + e2 + y \\ e \div y = 3 + y3 + a \\ y \div a = 4 + e4 + e \end{cases}$$

$$x \begin{cases} a \div e = e + y \\ e \div y = y + a \\ v \div a = a + e \end{cases}$$

Thirteenth Point.

$$a \div e = e + bb - ey + bb - yb + ee - bb + yy - b$$
$$s \quad e \div y = y - bb \times ya - bb + ab - yy + bb - aa + b$$
$$v \div a = a + bb - ae + bb - eb + aa - bb + ee - b$$

$$a \div e = e + bb - ey + bb - yb + ee - bb + yy - b$$
$$d \quad e \div y = y - cc + ya - cc + ac - yy + cc - aa + c$$
$$y \div a = a + dd - ae + dd - ed + aa - dd + ee - d$$

$$a \div e = e + 22 - ey + 22 - y2 + ee - 22 + yy - 2$$
$$x \quad e \div y = y - 33 + ya - 33 + a3 - yy + 33 - aa + 3$$
$$y \div a = a + 44 - ae + 44 - e4 + aa - 44 + ee - 4$$

$$a \div e = e + ye - ye + yy - e$$
$$x \quad e \div y = y - ay + aa - ya \times y$$
$$y \div a = a + ea - ea + ee - a$$

Fourteenth Point.

$$a \div e = b - eb - ye - by - b$$
$$s \quad e \div y = b - yb - ay - ba - b$$
$$y \div a = b - ab - ea - be - b$$

$$a \div e = b - eb - ye - by - b$$
$$d \quad e \div y = c - yc - ay - ca - c$$
$$y \div a = d - ab - ea - de - d$$

$$a \div e = 2 - e2 - ye - 2y - 2$$
$$f \quad e \div y = 3 - y3 - ay - 3a - 3$$
$$y \div a = 4 - a4 - ea - 4e - 4$$

$$a \div e = e - yy - e$$
$$x \quad e \div y = y - aa - y$$
$$y \div a = a - ee - a$$

Fifteenth Point.

$$a \div ea + e = e - by - bb - eb - y$$
$$s \quad e + ye \div y = y - ba - bb - yb - y$$
$$y \div ay + a = a - be - bb - ab - e$$

$$a \div ea + e = e - by - bb - eb - y$$
$$d \quad e + ye \div y = y - ca - cc - yc - a$$
$$y \div ay + a = a - de - dd - ad - e$$

$$a \div ea + e = e - 2y - 22 - e2 - y$$
$$f \quad e + ye \div y = y - 3a - 33 - y3 - a$$
$$y \div ay + a = a - 4e - 44 - a4 - a$$

$$a \div ea + e = e - yy - e$$
$$x \quad e + ye \div y = y - aa - y$$
$$y \div ay + a = a - ee - a$$

Sixteenth Point.

$$a + e = e - by - bb - eb - y$$
$$s \quad a + y = y - ba - bb - yb - a$$
$$y + a = a - be - bb - ab - e$$

$$a + e = e - by - bb - eb - y$$
$$d \quad e + y = y - ca - cc - yc - a$$
$$y + a = a - de - dd - ad - e$$

$$a + e = e - 2y - 22 - e2 - y$$
$$f \quad e + y = y - 3a - 33 - y3 - a$$
$$y + a = a - 4e - 44 - a4 - e$$

$$a + e = e - yy - e$$
$$x \quad e + y = y - aa - y$$
$$y + a = a - ee - a$$

N.B.—There is also another variety in the first member of the equations, where the analytic sign is found ; that is, if we transpose the sorts. For instance, if in the fourth point we use $\begin{Bmatrix} e-a \\ y-e \\ a-y \end{Bmatrix}$ in the twelfth $\begin{Bmatrix} e \div a \\ y \div e \\ a \div y \end{Bmatrix}$ the questions will be doubled.

Lest anyone should perchance suppose that in our game all possible questions are exhibited by our tables, it should be observed that they are, in fact, innumerable. For these stops can be varied without end ; whence arise innumerable questions, in each of which, however, no other methods are to be followed in determining signs, combinations, and sorts, than those which are set forth in the questions alone of each odd number except unit of the quantities sought, and these are accordingly exhibited in the tables which we have given.

AN ESSAY

TOWARDS

A NEW THEORY OF VISION.

FIRST PRINTED IN THE YEAR 1709.

[THE "Essay" first appeared in 1709. A second edition, slightly altered, and containing an Appendix, followed in the same year. In 1732 an edition, further modified, and without the Appendix, was added to the second volume of "Alciphron," because of the connection between the "Essay" and the Fourth Dialogue. This was the author's last revision, and the text of that year (1732) is therefore adopted in this edition. The Appendix, however, has been restored. The student should beware of expecting from Berkeley's terms, the nice significance of their modern counterparts; thus, *perception* and *sensation* are used generally rather than philosophically: *ideas*, in his own phrase elsewhere, are the "objects of the understanding," and not "fictions and fancies of the mind": and *touch* means sometimes contact, and sometimes muscular effort or locomotion. The Theory was, as Mackintosh styles it, "a great discovery in Mental Philosophy," and seems the more wonderful when we regard the youth of the discoverer.]

AN
ESSAY
Towards a
New Theory
O F
VISION.

By George Berkeley M. A.
Fellow of *Trinity College Dublin*

DVBLIN:

Printed by Aaron Rhames, at the Back of
Dick's Coffee-House, for Jeremy Pepyat,
Bookseller in *Skinner-Row*, MDCCIX.

ESSAY

Towards a

New Theory

OF

VISION.

By George Berkeley, M.A.
Fellow of Trinity College, Dublin.

DUBLIN

Printed by Aaron Rhames, at the Back of
Dick's Coffee-House, for Jeremy Pepyat,
Bookseller in Skinner-Row, MDCCIX.

RIGHT HON. SIR JOHN PERCIVALE, BART.

SIR,

I COULD not, without doing violence to myself, forbear upon this occasion to give some public testimony of the great and well-grounded esteem I have conceived for you, ever since I had the honour and happiness of your acquaintance. The outward advantages of fortune, and the early honours with which you are adorned, together with the reputation you are known to have amongst the best and most considerable men, may well imprint veneration and esteem on the minds of those who behold you from a distance. But these are not the chief motives that inspire me with the respect I bear you. A nearer approach has given me the view of something in your person infinitely beyond the external ornaments of honour and estate. I mean, an intrinsic stock of virtue and good sense, a true concern for religion, and disinterested love of your country. Add to these an uncommon proficiency in the best and most useful parts of knowledge; together with (what in my mind is a perfection of the first rank) a surpassing goodness of nature. All which I have collected, not from the uncertain reports of fame, but from my own experience. Within these few months that I have the honour to be known unto you, the many delightful hours I have passed in your agreeable and improving conversation have afforded me the opportunity of discovering in you many excellent qualities, which at once fill me with admiration and esteem. That one at those years, and in those circumstances of wealth and greatness, should continue proof against the charms of luxury and those criminal pleasures so fashionable and predominant in the age we live in ; that he should preserve a sweet and modest behaviour, free from that insolent and assuming air so familiar to those who are placed above the ordinary rank of men ; that he should manage a great fortune with that prudence and inspection, and at the same time expend it with that generosity and nobleness of mind, as to shew himself equally remote from a sordid parsimony and a lavish inconsiderate profusion of the good things he is intrusted with —this, surely, were admirable and praiseworthy. But, that he should, moreover, by an impartial exercise of his reason, and constant perusal of the sacred Scriptures, endeavour to attain a right notion of the principles of natural and revealed religion ; that he should with the concern of a true patriot have the interest of the public at heart, and omit no means of informing himself what may be prejudicial or advantageous to his country, in order to prevent the one and promote the other ; in fine, that, by a constant application to the most severe and useful studies, by a strict observation of the rules of honour and virtue, by frequent and serious reflections on the mistaken measures of the world, and the true end and happiness of mankind, he should in all respects qualify himself bravely to run the race that is set before him, to deserve the character of great and good in this life, and be ever happy hereafter—this were amazing and almost incredible. Yet all this, and more than this, SIR, might I justly say of you, did either your modesty permit, or your character stand in need of it. I know it might deservedly be thought a vanity in me to imagine that anything coming from so obscure a hand as mine could add a lustre to your reputation. But, I am withal sensible how far I advance the interest of my own, by laying hold on this opportunity to make it known that I am admitted into some degree of intimacy with a person of your exquisite judgment. And, with that view, I have ventured to make you an address of this nature, which the goodness I have ever experienced in you inclines me to hope will meet with a favourable reception at your hands. Though I must own I have your pardon to ask, for touching on what may possibly be offensive to a virtue you are possessed of in a very distinguishing degree. Excuse me, SIR, if it was out of my power to mention the name of SIR JOHN PERCIVALE without paying some tribute to that extraordinary and surprising merit whereof I have so clear and affecting an idea, and which, I am sure, cannot be exposed in too full a light for the imitation of others. Of late, I have been agreeably employed in considering the most noble, pleasant, and comprehensive of all the senses. The fruit of that (labour shall I call it or) diversion is what I now present you with, in hopes it may give some entertainment to one who, in the midst of business and vulgar enjoyments, preserves a relish for the more refined pleasures of thought and reflexion. My thoughts concerning Vision have led me into some notions, so far out of the common road that it had been improper to address them to one of a narrow and contracted genius. But, you, SIR, being master of a large and free understanding, raised above the power of those prejudices that enslave the far greater part of mankind, may deservedly be thought a proper patron for an attempt of this kind. Add to this, that you are no less disposed to forgive than qualified to discern whatever faults may occur in it. Nor do I think you defective in any one point necessary to form an exact judgment on the most abstract and difficult things, so much as in a just confidence of your own abilities. And, in this one instance, give me leave to say, you shew a manifest weakness of judgment. With relation to the following *Essay*, I shall only add that I beg your pardon for laying a trifle of that nature in your way, at a time when you are engaged in the important affairs of the nation, and desire you to think that I am, with all sincerity and respect,

SIR,

Your most faithful and most humble servant,

GEORGE BERKELEY.[1]

---

[1] This Dedication appears only in the first edition.

CONTENTS.

SECT.
1. Design.

2. Distance of itself invisible.
3. Remote distance perceived rather by experience, than by sense.
4. Near distance thought to be perceived by the angle of the optic axes.
5. Difference between this and the former manner of perceiving distance.
6. Also by diverging rays.
7. This depends not on experience.
8. These the common accounts, but not satisfactory.
9. Some ideas perceived by mediation of others.
10. No idea which is not itself perceived can be the means of perceiving another.
11. Distance perceived by means of some other idea.
12. Those lines and angles mentioned in optics are not themselves perceived.
13. Hence the mind does not perceive distance by lines and angles.
14. Also because they have no real existence.
15. And because they are insufficient to explain the phenomena.
16. The ideas that suggest distance are—*First*, the sensation arising from the turn of the eyes.
17. Betwixt which and distance there is no necessary connexion.
18. Scarce room for mistake in this matter.
19. No regard had to the angle of the optic axes.
20. Judgment of distance made with both eyes, the result of experience.
21. *Secondly*, confusedness of appearance.
22. This the occasion of those judgments attributed to diverging rays.
23. Objection answered.
24. What deceives the writers of optics in this matter.
25. The cause why one idea may suggest another.
26. This applied to confusion and distance.
27. *Thirdly*, the straining of the eye.
28. The occasions which suggest distance have in their own nature no relation to it.
29. A difficult case proposed by Dr. Barrow as repugnant to all the known theories.
30. This case contradicts a received principle in catoptrics.
31. It is shewn to agree with the principles we have laid down.

SECT.
32. This phenomenon illustrated.
33. It confirms the truth of the principle whereby it is explained.
34. Vision, when distinct and when confused.
35. The different effects of parallel, diverging, and converging rays.
36. How converging and diverging rays come to suggest the same distance.
37. A person extremely purblind would judge aright in the forementioned case.
38. Lines and angles why useful in optics.
39. The not understanding this a cause of mistake.
40. A query, proposed by Mr. Molyneux in his " Dioptrics," considered.
41. One born blind would not at first have any idea of distance by sight.
42. This not agreeable to the common principles.
43. The proper objects of sight not without the mind, nor the images of anything without the mind.
44. This more fully explained.
45. In what sense we must be understood to see distance and external things.
46. Distance, and things placed at a distance, not otherwise perceived by the eye than by the ear.
47. The ideas of sight more apt to be confounded with the ideas of touch than those of hearing are.
48. How this comes to pass.
49. Strictly speaking, we never see and feel the same thing.
50. Objects of sight twofold—mediate and immediate.
51. These hard to separate in our thoughts.

52. The received accounts of our perceiving magnitude by sight, false.
53. Magnitude perceived as immediately as distance.
54. Two kinds of sensible extension, neither of which is infinitely divisible.
55. The tangible magnitude of an object steady, the visible not.
56. By what means tangible magnitude is perceived by sight.
57. This farther enlarged on.
58. No necessary connexion between confusion or faintness of appearance and small or great magnitude.
59. The tangible magnitude of an object more heeded than the visible, and why.
60. An instance of this.
61. Men do not measure by visible feet or inches.
62. No necessary connexion between visible and tangible extension.
63. Greater visible magnitude might signify lesser tangible magnitude.
64. The judgments we make of magnitude depend altogether on experience.
65. Distance and magnitude seen as shame or anger.
66. But we are prone to think otherwise, and why.
67. The moon seems greater in the horizon than in the meridian.
68. The cause of this phenomenon assigned.
69. The horizontal moon, why greater at one time than another.
70. The account we have given proved to be true.

SECT.

71. And confirmed by the moon's appearing greater in a mist.
72. Objection answered.
73. The way wherein faintness suggests greater magnitude illustrated.
74. Appearance of the horizontal moon, why thought difficult to explain.
75. Attempts towards the solution of it made by several, but in vain.
76. The opinion of Dr. Wallis.
77. It is shewn to be unsatisfactory.
78. How lines and angles may be of use in computing apparent magnitudes.
79. One born blind, being made to see, what judgment he would make of magnitude.
80. The *minimum visibile* the same to all creatures.
81. Objection answered.
82. The eye at all times perceives the same number of visible points.
83. Two imperfections in the visive faculty.
84. Answering to which, we may conceive two perfections.
85. In neither of these two ways do microscopes improve the sight.
86. The case of microscopical eyes considered.
87. The sight admirably adapted to the ends of seeing.

88. Difficulty concerning erect vision.
89. The common way of explaining it.
90. The same shewn to be false.
91. Not distinguishing between ideas of sight and touch cause of mistake in this matter.
92. The case of one born blind proper to be considered.
93. Such a one might by touch attain to have ideas of "upper" and "lower."
94. Which modes of situation he would attribute only to things tangible.
95. He would not at first sight think anything he saw, high or low, erect or inverted.
96. This illustrated by an example.
97. By what means he would come to denominate visible objects, "high" or "low," &c.
98. Why he should think those objects highest which are painted on the lowest part of his eye, and *vice versâ*.
99. How he would perceive by sight the situation of external objects.
100. Our propension to think the contrary no argument against what hath been said.
101. Objection.
102. Answer.
103. An object could not be known at first sight by the colour.
104. Nor by the magnitude thereof.
105. Nor by the figure.
106. In the first act of vision, no tangible thing would be suggested by sight.
107. Difficulty proposed concerning number.
108. Number of things visible would not, at first sight, suggest the like number of things tangible.
109. Number, the creature of the mind.

SECT.

110. One born blind would not, at first sight, number visible things as others do.

111. The situation of any object determined with respect only to objects of the same sense.

112. No distance, great or small, between a visible and tangible thing.

113. The not observing this, cause of difficulty in erect vision.

114. Which otherwise includes nothing unaccountable.

115. What is meant by the pictures being inverted.

116. Cause of mistake in this matter.

117. Images in the eye not pictures of external objects.

118. In what sense they are pictures.

119. In this affair we must carefully distinguish between ideas of sight and touch.

120. Difficult to explain by words the true theory of vision.

121. The question, whether there is any idea common to sight and touch, stated.

122. Abstract extension inquired into.

123. It is incomprehensible.

124. Abstract extension not the object of geometry.

125. The general idea of a triangle considered.

126. Vacuum, or pure space, not common to sight and touch.

127. There is no idea, or kind of idea, common to both senses.

128. First argument in proof hereof.

129. Second argument.

130. Visible figure and extension not distinct ideas from colour.

131. Third argument.

132. Confirmation drawn from Mr. Molyneux's problem of a sphere and a cube, published by Mr. Locke.

133. Which is falsely solved, if the common supposition be true.

134. More might be said in proof of our tenet, but this suffices.

135. Farther reflection on the foregoing problem.

136. The same thing doth not affect both sight and touch.

137. The same idea of motion not common to sight and touch.

138. The way wherein we apprehend motion by sight, easily collected from what hath been said.

139. *Ques.* How visible and tangible ideas came to have the same name, if not of the same kind?

140. This accounted for without supposing them of the same kind.

141. *Obj.* That a tangible square is liker to a visible square than to a visible circle.

142. *Ans.* That a visible square is fitter than a visible circle to represent a tangible square.

143. But it doth not hence follow that a visible square is like a tangible square.

144. Why we are more apt to confound visible with tangible ideas, than other signs with the things signified.

145. Several other reasons hereof assigned.

146. Reluctancy in rejecting any opinion no argument of its truth.

SECT.

147. Proper objects of vision the Language of the Author of Nature.
148. In it there is much admirable and deserving our attention.

149. Question proposed concerning the object of geometry.
150. At first view we are apt to think visible extension the object of geometry.
151. Visible extension shewn not be the object of geometry.
152. Words may as well be thought the object of geometry as visible extension.
153. It is proposed to inquire, what progress an intelligence that could see, but not feel, might make in geometry.
154. He cannot understand those parts which relate to solids, and their surfaces, and lines generated by their section.
155. Nor even the elements of plane geometry.
156. The proper objects of sight incapable of being managed as geometrical figures.
157. The opinion of those who hold plane figures to be the immediate objects of sight considered.
158. Planes no more the immediate objects of sight than solids.
159. Difficult to enter precisely into the thoughts of the above-mentioned intelligence.
160. The object of geometry, its not being sufficiently understood, cause of difficulty and useless labour in that science.[1]

---

[1] There was in the first edition a section 160.

AN ESSAY

A NEW THEORY OF VISION.

1.

M Y design is to shew the manner wherein we perceive by sight the distance, magnitude, and situation of objects. Also to consider the difference there is betwixt the ideas of sight and touch, and whether there be any idea common to both senses.[1]

2. It is, I think, agreed by all that distance of itself, and immediately, cannot be seen. For distance being a line directed endwise to the eye, it projects only one point in the fund of the eye—which point remains invariably the same, whether the distance be longer or shorter.

3. I find it also acknowledged that the estimate we make of the distance of objects considerably remote is rather an act of judgment grounded on experience than of sense. For example, when I perceive a great number of intermediate objects, such as houses, fields, rivers, and the like, which I have experienced to take up a considerable space, I thence form a judgment or conclusion, that the object I see beyond them is at a great distance. Again, when an object appears faint and small which at a near distance I have experienced to make a vigorous and large appearance, I instantly conclude it to be far off.—And this, it is evident, is the result of experience; without which, from the faintness and littleness, I should not have inferred anything concerning the distance of objects.

[1] In the first edition (1709) there followed this passage : "In treating of all which, it seems to me, the writers of optics have proceeded on wrong principles."

4. But, when an object is placed at so near a distance as that the interval between the eyes bears any sensible proportion to it, the opinion of speculative men is, that the two optic axes (the fancy that we see only with one eye at once being exploded), concurring at the object, do there make an angle, by means of which, according as it is greater or lesser, the object is perceived to be nearer or farther off.[1]

5. Betwixt which and the foregoing manner of estimating distance there is this remarkable difference :—that, whereas there was no apparent necessary connexion between small distance and a large and strong appearance, or between great distance and a little and faint appearance, there appears a very necessary connexion between an obtuse angle and near distance, and an acute angle and farther distance. It does not in the least depend upon experience, but may be evidently known by anyone before he had experienced it, that the nearer the concurrence of the optic axes the greater the angle, and the remoter their concurrence is, the lesser will be the angle comprehended by them.

6. There is another way, mentioned by optic writers, whereby they will have us judge of those distances in respect of which the breadth of the pupil hath any sensible bigness. And that is the greater or lesser divergency of the rays, which, issuing from the visible point, do fall on the pupil— that point being judged nearest which is seen by most diverging rays, and that remoter which is seen by less diverging rays ; and so on, the apparent distance still increasing, as the divergency of the rays decreases, till at length it becomes infinite when the rays that fall on the pupil are to sense parallel. And after this manner it is said we perceive distance when we look only with one eye.

7. In this case also it is plain we are not beholden to experience : it being a certain, necessary truth that, the nearer the direct rays falling on the eye approach to a parallelism, the farther off is the point of their intersection, or the visible point from whence they flow.

8. Now, though the accounts here given of perceiving near distance by sight are received for true, and accordingly made use of in determining the apparent places of objects, they do

[1] See what Descartes and others have written on this subject.— AUTHOR.

nevertheless seem to me very unsatisfactory, and that for these following reasons :—[1]

9. It is evident that, when the mind perceives any idea, not immediately and of itself, it must be by the means of some other idea. Thus, for instance, the passions which are in the mind of another are of themselves to me invisible. I may nevertheless perceive them by sight, though not immediately, yet by means of the colours they produce in the countenance. We often see shame or fear in the looks of a man, by perceiving the changes of his countenance to red or pale.

10. Moreover, it is evident that no idea which is not itself perceived can be to me the means of perceiving any other idea. If I do not perceive the redness or paleness of a man's face themselves, it is impossible I should perceive by them the passions which are in his mind.

11. Now, from sect. ii., it is plain that distance is in its own nature imperceptible, and yet it is perceived by sight. It remains, therefore, that it be brought into view by means of some other idea, that is itself immediately perceived in the act of vision.

12. But those lines and angles by means whereof some men pretend to explain the perception of distance, are themselves not at all perceived, nor are they in truth ever thought of by those unskilful in optics. I appeal to anyone's experience, whether, upon sight of an object, he computes its distance by the bigness of the angle made by the meeting of the two optic axes ? or whether he ever thinks of the greater or lesser divergency of the rays which arrive from any point to his pupil ? nay, whether it be not perfectly impossible for him to perceive by sense the various angles wherewith the rays, according to their greater or lesser divergence, do fall on the eye ? Everyone is himself the best judge of what he perceives, and what not. In vain shall any man tell me, that

---

[1] In the first (1709) edition section eight reads thus : "I have here set down the common current accounts that are given of our perceiving near distances by sight, which, though they are unquestionably received for true by mathematicians, and accordingly made use of by them in determining the apparent places of objects, do nevertheless seem to me very unsatisfactory, and that for these following reasons :—"

The section was revised as above in the second edition.

I.   G

I perceive certain lines and angles which introduce into my mind the various ideas of distance, so long as I myself am conscious of no such thing.

13. Since therefore those angles and lines are not themselves perceived by sight, it follows, from sect. x., that the mind does not by them judge of the distance of objects.

14. The truth of this assertion will be yet farther evident to anyone that considers those lines and angles have no real existence in nature, being only an hypothesis framed by the mathematicians, and by them introduced into optics that they might treat of that science in a geometrical way.

15. The last reason I shall give for rejecting that doctrine is, that though we should grant the real existence of those optic angles, &c., and that it was possible for the mind to perceive them, yet these principles would not be found sufficient to explain the phenomena of distance, as shall be shewn hereafter.

16. Now, it being already shewn that distance is suggested to the mind, by the mediation of some other idea which is itself perceived in the act of seeing, it remains that we inquire what ideas or sensations there be that attend vision, unto which we may suppose the ideas of distance are connected and by which they are introduced into the mind.—And, *first*, it is certain by experience, that when we look at a near object with both eyes, according as it approaches or recedes from us, we alter the disposition of our eyes, by lessening or widening the interval between the pupils. This disposition or turn of the eyes is attended with a sensation, which seems to me to be that which in this case brings the idea of greater or lesser distance into the mind.

17. Not that there is any natural or necessary connexion between the sensation we perceive by the turn of the eyes and greater or lesser distance. But—because the mind has, by constant experience, found the different sensations corresponding to the different dispositions of the eyes to be attended each with a different degree of distance in the object—there has grown an habitual or customary connexion between those two sorts of ideas; so that the mind no sooner perceives the sensation arising from the different turn it gives the eyes, in order to bring the pupils nearer or farther asunder but it withal perceives the different idea of distance which was wont to be connected with that sensation. Just as

upon hearing a certain sound, the idea is immediately suggested to the understanding which custom had united with it.

18. Nor do I see how I can easily be mistaken in this matter. I know evidently that distance is not perceived of itself—that, by consequence, it must be perceived by means of some other idea, which is immediately perceived, and varies with the different degrees of distance. I know also that the sensation arising from the turn of the eyes is of itself immediately perceived, and various degrees thereof are connected with different distances, which never fail to accompany them into my mind, when I view an object distinctly with both eyes whose distance is so small that in respect of it the interval between the eyes has any considerable magnitude.

19. I know it is a received opinion that, by altering the disposition of the eyes, the mind perceives whether the angle of the optic axes, or the lateral angles comprehended between the interval of the eyes and the optic axes, are made greater or lesser; and that, accordingly, by a kind of natural geometry, it judges the point of their intersection to be nearer or farther off. But that this is not true I am convinced by my own experience, since I am not conscious that I make any such use of the perception I have by the turn of my eyes. And for me to make those judgments, and draw those conclusions from it, without knowing that I do so, seems altogether incomprehensible.

20. From all which it follows, that the judgment we make of the distance of an object viewed with both eyes is entirely the result of experience. If we had not constantly found certain sensations, arising from the various disposition of the eyes, attended with certain degrees of distance, we should never make those sudden judgments from them concerning the distance of objects; no more than we would pretend to judge of a man's thoughts by his pronouncing words we had never heard before.

21. *Secondly*, an object placed at a certain distance from the eye, to which the breadth of the pupil bears a considerable proportion, being made to approach, is seen more confusedly. And the nearer it is brought the more confused appearance it makes. And, this being found constantly to be so, there ariseth in the mind an habitual connexion between

the several degrees of confusion and distance; the greater confusion still implying the lesser distance, and the lesser confusion the greater distance of the object.

22. This confused appearance of the object doth therefore seem to be the medium whereby the mind judgeth of distance, in those cases wherein the most approved writers of optics will have it judge by the different divergency with which the rays flowing from the radiating point fall on the pupil. No man, I believe, will pretend to see or feel those imaginary angles that the rays are supposed to form according to their various inclinations on his eye. But he cannot choose seeing whether the object appear more or less confused. It is therefore a manifest consequence from what has been demonstrated that, instead of the greater or lesser divergency of the rays, the mind makes use of the greater or lesser confusedness of the appearance, thereby to determine the apparent place of an object.

23. Nor doth it avail to say there is not any necessary connexion between confused vision and distance great or small. For I ask any man what necessary connexion he sees between the redness of a blush and shame? And yet no sooner shall he behold that colour to arise in the face of another but it brings into his mind the idea of that passion which hath been observed to accompany it.

24. What seems to have misled the writers of optics in this matter is, that they imagine men judge of distance as they do of a conclusion in mathematics; betwixt which and the premises it is indeed absolutely requisite there be an apparent, necessary connexion. But it is far otherwise in the sudden judgments men make of distance. We are not to think that brutes and children, or even grown reasonable men, whenever they perceive an object to approach or depart from them, do it by virtue of geometry and demonstration.

25. That one idea may suggest another to the mind, it will suffice that they have been observed to go together, without any demonstration of the necessity of their coexistence, or without so much as knowing what it is that makes them so to coexist. Of this there are innumerable instances of which no one can be ignorant.

26. Thus, greater confusion having been constantly attended with nearer distance, no sooner is the former id

perceived but it suggests the latter to our thoughts. And, if it had been the ordinary course of nature that the farther off an object were placed the more confused it should appear, it is certain the very same perception that now makes us think an object approaches would then have made us to imagine it went farther off—that perception, abstracting from custom and experience, being equally fitted to produce the idea of great distance, or small distance, or no distance at all.

27. *Thirdly*, an object being placed at the distance above specified, and brought nearer to the eye, we may nevertheless prevent, at least for some time, the appearance's growing more confused, by straining the eye. In which case that sensation supplies the place of confused vision, in aiding the mind to judge of the distance of the object; it being esteemed so much the nearer by how much the effort or straining of the eye in order to distinct vision is greater.

28. I have here set down those sensations or ideas that seem to be the constant and general occasions of introducing into the mind the different ideas of near distance. It is true, in most cases, that divers other circumstances contribute to frame our idea of distance, to wit, the particular number, size, kind, &c. of the things seen. Concerning which, as well as all other the forementioned occasions which suggest distance, I shall only observe, they have none of them, in their own nature, any relation or connexion with it : nor is it possible they should ever signify the various degrees thereof, otherwise than as by experience they have been found to be connected with them.

29. I shall proceed upon these principles to account for a phenomenon which has hitherto strangely puzzled the writers of optics, and is so far from being accounted for by any of their theories of vision, that it is, by their own confession, plainly repugnant to them ; and of consequence, if nothing else could be objected, were alone sufficient to bring their credit in question. The whole difficulty I shall lay before you in the words of the learned Doctor Barrow, with which he concludes his *Optic Lectures*.

" Hæc sunt, quæ circa partem opticæ præcipue mathematicam dicenda mihi suggessit meditatio. Circa reliquas (quæ φυσικώτεραι sunt, adeoque sepiuscule pro certis principiis

plausibiles conjecturas venditare necessum habent) nihil fere
quicquam admodum verisimile succurrit, a pervulgatis (ab iis,
inquam, quæ Keplerus, Scheinerus, Cartesius, et post illos alii
tradiderunt) alienum aut diversum. Atqui tacere malo, quam
toties oblatam cramben reponere. Proinde receptui cano ;
nec ita tamen ut prorsus discedam, anteaquam improbam
quandam difficultatem (pro sinceritate quam et vobis et veri-
tati debeo minime dissimulandam) in medium protulero, quæ
doctrinæ nostræ, hactenus inculcatæ, se objicit adversam, ab
ea saltem nullam admittit solutionem.   Illa, breviter, talis est.

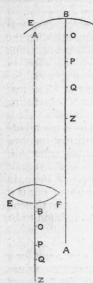

Lenti vel speculo cavo *E B F* expon-
atur punctum visibile *A*, ita distans, ut
radii ex *A* manantes ex inflectione versus
axem *A B* cogantur. Sitque radiationis
limes (seu puncti *A* imago, qualem supra
passim statuimus) punctum *Z*. Inter
hoc autem et inflectentis verticem
B uspiam positus concipiatur oculus.
Quæri jam potest, ubi loci debeat punctum *A* apparere ? Retrorsum ad punctum *Z* videri non fert natura (cum
omnis impressio sensum afficiens pro-
veniat a partibus *A*) ac experientia
reclamat.   Nostris autem e placitis
consequi videtur, ipsum ad partes an-
ticas apparens, ab intervallo longissime
dissito (quod et maximum sensibile
quodvis intervallum quodammodo ex-
superet), apparere. Cum enim quo
radiis minus divergentibus attingitur
objectum, eo (seclusis utique prænotionibus et præjudiciis) longius abesse
sentiatur ; et quod parallelos ad oculum
radios projicit, remotissime positum æstimetur : exigere ratio
videtur, ut quod convergentibus radiis apprehenditur, adhuc
magis, si fieri posset, quoad apparentiam elongetur. Quin et
circa casum hunc generatim inquiri possit, quidnam omnino
sit, quod apparentem puncti *A* locum determinet, faciatque
quod constanti ratione nunc propius, nunc remotius appareat?
Cui itidem dubio nihil quicquam ex hactenus dictorum ana-
logia responderi posse videtur, nisi debere punctum *A* perpetuo

longissime semotum videri. Verum experientia secus attestatur, illud pro diversa oculi inter puncta *B*, *Z*, positione varie distans, nunquam fere (si unquam) longinquius ipso *A* libere spectato, subinde vero multo propinquius adparere; quinimo, quo oculum appellentes radii magis convergunt, eo speciem objecti propius accedere. Nempe, si puncto *B* admoveatur oculus, suo (ad lentem) fere nativo in loco conspicitur punctum *A* (vel æque distans, ad speculum); ad *Q* reductus oculus ejusce speciem appropinquantem cernit; ad *P* adhuc vicinius ipsum existimat; ac ita sensim, donec alicubi tandem, velut ad *Q*, constituto oculo, objectum summe propinquum apparens in meram confusionem incipiat evanescere. Quæ sane cuncta rationibus atque decretis nostris repugnare videntur, aut cum iis saltem parum amice conspirant. Neque nostram tantum sententiam pulsat hoc experimentum, at ex æquo cæteras quas norim omnes : veterem imprimis ac vulgatam, nostræ præ reliquis affinem, ita convellere videtur, ut ejus vi coactus doctissimus A. Tacquetus isti principio (cui pene soli totam inædificaverat *Catoptricam* suam) ceu infido ac inconstanti renunciarit, adeoque suam ipse doctrinam labefactarit? id tamen, opinor, minime facturus, si rem totam inspexissit penitius, atque difficultatis fundum attigisset. Apud me vero non ita pollet hæc, nec eousque præpollebit ulla difficultas, ut ab iis quæ manifeste rationi consentanea video, discedam ; præsertim quum, ut hic accidit, ejusmodi difficultas in singularis cujuspiam casus disparitate fundetur. Nimirum in præsente casu peculiare quiddam, naturæ subtilitati involutum, delitescit, ægre fortassis, nisi perfectius explorato videndi modo, detegendum. Circa quod nil, fateor, hactenus excogitare potui, quod adblandiretur animo meo, nedum plane satisfaceret. Vobis itaque nodum hunc, utinam feliciore conatu, resolvendum committo."

In English as follows :

" I have here delivered what my thoughts have suggested to me concerning that part of optics which is more properly mathematical. As for the other parts of that science (which, being rather physical, do consequently abound with plausible conjectures instead of certain principles), there has in them scarce anything occurred to my observation different from what has been already said by Kepler, Scheinerus, Descartes, &c. And methinks I had better say nothing at all than repeat that which has been so often said by others. I think it therefore high time to take my leave of this subject. But, before I quit for good and all, the fair and ingenuous dealing that I owe both to you and to truth obligeth me to acquaint you with a certain untoward difficulty, which seems directly opposite to the doctrine I have been hitherto inculcating, at least admits of no solution from it. In short it is this.

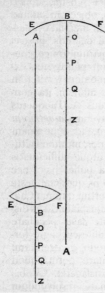

Before the double convex glass or concave speculum $E\,B\,F$, let the point A be placed at such a distance that the rays proceeding from A, after refraction or reflection, be brought to unite somewhere in the axis AB. And suppose the point of union (*i.e.* the image of the point A, as hath been already set forth) to be Z: between which and B, the vertex of the glass or speculum, conceive the eye to be anywhere placed. The question now is, where the point A ought to appear. Experience shews that it doth not appear behind at the point Z, and it were contrary to nature that it should; since all the impression which affects the sense comes from towards A. But, from our tenets it should seem to follow that it would appear before the eye at a vast distance off, so great as should in some sort surpass all sensible distance. For since, if we exclude all anticipations and prejudices, every object appears by so much the farther off, by how much the rays it sends to the eye are less diverging; and that object is thought to be most remote from which parallel rays proceed unto the eye; reason would make one think that object should appear at yet a greater distance which is seen by converging rays. Moreover, it may in general be asked concerning this case, what it is that determines the apparent place of the point A, and maketh it to appear after a constant manner, sometimes nearer, at other times farther off? To which doubt I see nothing that can be answered agreeable to the principles we have laid down, except only that the point *A* ought always to appear extremely remote. But, on the contrary, we are assured by experience, that the point *A* appears variously distant, according to the different situations of the eye between the points *B* and *Z*. And that it doth almost never (if at all) seem farther off than it would if it were beheld by the naked eye ; but, on the contrary, it doth sometimes appear much nearer. Nay, it is even certain that by how much the rays falling on the eye do more converge, by so much the nearer does the object seem to approach. For, the eye being placed close to the point *B*, the object *A* appears nearly in its own natural place, if the point *B* is taken in the glass, or at the same distance, if in the speculum. The eye being brought back to *O*, the object seems to draw near ; and, being come to *P*, it beholds it still nearer : and so on by little and little, till at length the eye being placed somewhere, suppose at *Q*, the object appearing extremely near begins to vanish into mere confusion. All which doth seem repugnant to our principles ; at least, not rightly to agree with them. Nor is our tenet alone struck at by this experiment, but likewise all others that ever came to my knowledge are every whit as much endangered by it. The ancient one especially (which is most commonly received, and comes nearest to mine) seems to be so effectually overthrown thereby that the most learned Tacquet has been forced to reject that principle, as false and uncertain, on which alone he had built almost his whole *Catoptrics*, and consequently, by taking away the foundation, hath himself pulled down the superstructure he had raised on it. Which, nevertheless, I do not believe he would have done, had he but considered the whole matter more thoroughly, and examined the difficulty to the bottom. But as for me, neither this nor any other difficulty shall have so great an influence on me, as to make me renounce that which I know to be manifestly agreeable to reason. Especially when, as it here falls out, the difficulty is founded in the peculiar nature of a certain odd and particular case. For, in the present case something peculiar lies hid, which, being involved in the subtilty of nature, will perhaps hardly be discovered till such time as the manner of vision is more perfectly made known. Concerning which, I must own I have hitherto been able to find out nothing that has the least show of probability, not to mention certainty. I shall therefore leave this knot to be untied by you, wishing you may have better success in it than I have had."

30. The ancient and received principle, which Dr. Barrow here mentions as the main foundation of Tacquet's Catoptrics, is, that every "visible point seen by reflection from a speculum shall appear placed at the intersection of the reflected ray and the perpendicular of incidence." Which intersection in the present case happening to be behind the eye, it greatly shakes the authority of that principle whereon the aforementioned author proceeds throughout his whole *Catoptrics* in determining the apparent place of objects seen by reflection from any kind of speculum.

31. Let us now see how this phenomenon agrees with our tenets. The eye, the nearer it is placed to the point B in the above figures, the more distinct is the appearance of the object : but, as it recedes to O, the appearance grows more confused ; and at P it sees the objects yet more confused ; and so on, till the eye, being brought back to Z, sees the object in the greatest confusion of all. Wherefore, by sect. 21, the object should seem to approach the eye gradually, as it recedes from the point B ; that is, at O it should (in consequence of the principle I have laid down in the aforesaid section) seem nearer than it did at B, and at P nearer than at O, and at Q nearer than at P, and so on, till it quite vanishes at Z. Which is the very matter of fact, as anyone that pleases may easily satisfy himself by experiment.

32. This case is much the same as if we should suppose an Englishman to meet a foreigner who used the same words with the English, but in a direct contrary signification. The Englishman would not fail to make a wrong judgment of the ideas annexed to those sounds, in the mind of him that used them. Just so in the present case, the object speaks (if I may so say) with words that the eye is well acquainted with, that is, confusions of appearance; but, whereas heretofore the greatest confusions were always wont to signify nearer distances, they have in this case a direct contrary signification, being connected with the greater distances. Whence it follows that the eye must unavoidably be mis-

taken, since it will take the confusions in the sense it has been used to, which is directly opposed to the true.

33. This phenomenon, as it entirely subverts the opinion of those who will have us judge of distance by lines and angles, on which supposition it is altogether inexplicable, so it seems to me no small confirmation of the truth of that principle whereby it is explained. But, in order to a more full explication of this point, and to show how far the hypothesis of the mind's judging by the various divergency of rays may be of use in determining the apparent place of an object, it will be necessary to premise some few things, which are already well known to those who have any skill in Dioptrics.

34. *First*, Any radiating point is then distinctly seen when the rays proceeding from it are, by the refractive power of the crystalline, accurately reunited in the retina or fund of the eye. But if they are reunited either before they arrive at the retina, or after they have passed it, then there is confused vision.

35. *Secondly*, Suppose, in the adjacent figures, $N\,P$ represent an eye duly framed, and retaining its natural figure. In fig. 1 the rays falling nearly parallel on the eye, are, by the crystalline $A\,B$, refracted, so as their focus, or point of union F, falls exactly on the retina. But, if the rays fall sensibly diverging on the eye, as in fig 2, then their focus falls beyond the retina; or, if the rays are made to converge by the lens $Q\,S$, before they come at the eye, as in fig. 3, their focus F will fall before the retina. In which two last cases it is evident, from the foregoing section, that the appearance of the point Z is confused. And, by how much the greater is the convergency or divergency of the rays falling on the pupil, by so much the farther will the point of their reunion be from the retina, either before or behind it, and consequently the point Z will appear by so much the more confused. And this, by the bye, may shew us the difference between confused and faint vision. Confused vision is, when the rays proceeding from each distinct point of the object are not accurately re-collected in one corresponding point on the retina, but take up some space thereon—so that rays from different points become mixed and confused together. This is opposed to a distinct vision,

and attends near objects. Faint vision is when, by reason
of the distance of the object, or grossness of the interjacent
medium, few rays arrive from the object to the eye. This is
opposed to vigorous or clear vision, and attends remote
objects. But to return.

36. The eye, or (to speak truly) the mind, perceiving only
the confusion itself, without ever considering the cause from
which it proceeds, doth constantly annex the same degree of

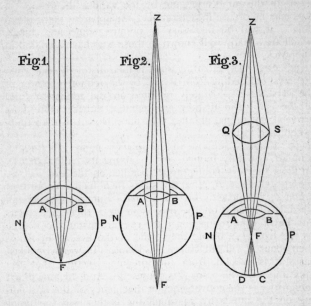

distance to the same degree of confusion. Whether that
confusion be occasioned by converging or by diverging rays
it matters not. Whence it follows that the eye, viewing the
object *Z* through the glass *Q S* (which by refraction causeth
the rays *Z Q, Z S*, &c. to converge), should judge it to be at
such a nearness, at which, if it were placed, it would radiate
on the eye, with rays diverging to that degree as would
produce the same confusion which is now produced by converging rays, *i.e.* would cover a portion of the retina equal to

D C. (Vide fig. 3, *sup.*) But then this must be understood (to use Dr. Barrow's phrase) " seclusis prænotionibus et præjudiciis," in case we abstract from all other circumstances of vision, such as the figure, size, faintness, &c., of the visible objects—all which do ordinarily concur to form our idea of distance, the mind having, by frequent experience, observed their several sorts or degrees to be connected with various distances.

37. It plainly follows from what hath been said, that a person perfectly purblind (*i.e.* that could not see an object distinctly but when placed close to his eye) would not make the same wrong judgment that others do in the forementioned case. For, to him, greater confusions constantly suggesting greater distances, he must, as he recedes from the glass, and the object grows more confused, judge it to be at a farther distance, contrary to what they do who have had the perception of the objects growing more confused connected with the idea of approach.

38. Hence also it doth appear, there may be good use of computation, by lines and angles, in optics ; not that the mind judgeth of distance immediately by them, but because it judgeth by somewhat which is connected with them, and to the determination whereof they may be subservient. Thus, the mind judging of the distance of an object by the confusedness of its appearance, and this confusedness being greater or lesser to the naked eye according as the object is seen by rays more or less diverging, it follows that a man may make use of the divergency of the rays, in computing the apparent distance, though not for its own sake, yet on account of the confusion with which it is connected. But, so it is, the confusion itself is entirely neglected by mathematicians, as having no necessary relation with distance, such as the greater or lesser angles of divergency are conceived to have. And these (especially for that they fall under mathematical computation) are alone regarded, in determining the apparent places of objects, as though they were the sole and immediate cause of the judgments the mind makes of distance. Whereas, in truth, they should not at all be regarded in themselves, or any otherwise than as they are supposed to be the cause of confused vision.

39. The not considering of this has been a fundamental

and perplexing oversight. For proof whereof, we need go no farther than the case before us. It having been observed that the most diverging rays brought into the mind the idea of nearest distance, and that still as the divergency decreased the distance increased, and it being thought the connexion between the various degrees of divergency and distance was immediate—this naturally leads one to conclude, from an ill-grounded analogy, that converging rays shall make an object appear at an immense distance, and that, as the convergency increases, the distance (if it were possible) should do so likewise. That this was the cause of Dr. Barrow's mistake is evident from his own words which we have quoted. Whereas, had the learned Doctor observed that diverging and converging rays, how opposite soever they may seem, do nevertheless agree in producing the same effect, to wit, confusedness of vision, greater degrees whereof are produced indifferently, either as the divergency or convergency of the rays increaseth; and that it is by this effect, which is the same in both, that either the divergency or convergency is perceived by the eye—I say, had he but considered this, it is certain he would have made a quite contrary judgment, and rightly concluded that those rays which fall on the eye with greater degrees of convergency should make the object from whence they proceed appear by so much the nearer. But it is plain it was impossible for any man to attain to a right notion of this matter, so long as he had regard only to lines and angles, and did not apprehend the true nature of vision, and how far it was of mathematical consideration.

40. Before we dismiss this subject, it is fit we take notice of a query relating thereto, proposed by the ingenious Mr. Molyneux, in his *Treatise of Dioptrics* (par. i. prop. 31. sect. 9.), where, speaking of the difficulty we have been explaining, he has these words : " And so he (*i.e.* Dr. Barrow) leaves this difficulty to the solution of others, which I (after so great an example) shall do likewise ; but with the resolution of the same admirable author, of not quitting the evident doctrine which we have before laid down, for determining the *locus objecti*, on account of being pressed by one difficulty, which seems inexplicable till a more intimate knowledge of the visive faculty be obtained by mortals. In the meantime

I propose it to the consideration of the ingenious, whether the *locus apparens* of an object placed as in this ninth section be not as much before the eye as the distinct base is behind the eye?" To which query we may venture to answer in the negative. For, in the present case, the rule for determining the distance of the distinct base, or respective focus from the glass is this: *As the difference between the distance of the object and focus is to the focus or focal length, so the distance of the object from the glass is to the distance of the respective focus or distinct base from the glass.* (Molyneux, *Dioptr.*, par. i. prop. 5.) Let us now suppose the object to be placed at the distance of the focal length, and one-half of the focal length from the glass, and the eye close to the glass. Hence it will follow, by the rule, that the distance of the distinct base behind the eye is double the true distance of the object before the eye. If, therefore, Mr. Molyneux's conjecture held good, it would follow that the eye should see the object twice as far off as it really is ; and in other cases at three or four times its due distance, or more. But this manifestly contradicts experience, the object never appearing, at farthest, beyond its due distance. Whatever, therefore, is built on this supposition (vide corol. i. prop. 57, ibid.) comes to the ground along with it.

41. From what hath been premised, it is a manifest consequence, that a man born blind, being made to see, would at first have no idea of distance by sight : the sun and stars, the remotest objects as well as the nearer, would all seem to be in his eye, or rather in his mind. The objects intromitted by sight would seem to him (as in truth they are) no other than a new set of thoughts or sensations, each whereof is as near to him as the perceptions of pain or pleasure, or the most inward passions of his soul. For, our judging objects perceived by sight to be at any distance, or without the mind, is (vide sect. xxviii.) entirely the effect of experience, which one in those circumstances could not yet have attained to.

42. It is indeed otherwise upon the common supposition— that men judge of distance by the angle of the optic axes, just as one in the dark, or a blind man by the angle comprehended by two sticks, one whereof he held in each hand. For, if this were true, it would follow that one blind from his

birth, being made to see, should stand in need of no new experience, in order to perceive distance by sight. But that this is false has, I think, been sufficiently demonstrated.

43. And perhaps, upon a strict inquiry, we shall not find that even those who from their birth have grown up in a continued habit of seeing are irrecoverably prejudiced on the other side, to wit, in thinking what they see to be at a distance from them. For, at this time it seems agreed on all hands, by those who have had any thoughts of that matter, that colours, which are the proper and immediate object of sight, are not without the mind.—But, then, it will be said, by sight we have also the ideas of extension, and figure, and motion ; all which may well be thought without and at some distance from the mind, though colour should not. In answer to this, I appeal to any man's experience, whether the visible extension of any object do not appear as near to him as the colour of that object ; nay, whether they do not both seem to be in the very same place. Is not the extension we see coloured, and is it possible for us, so much as in thought, to separate and abstract colour from extension ? Now, where the extension is, there surely is the figure, and there the motion too. I speak of those which are perceived by sight.

44. But for a fuller explication of this point, and to shew that the immediate objects of sight are not so much as the ideas or resemblances of things placed at a distance, it is requisite that we look nearer into the matter, and carefully observe what is meant in common discourse when one says, that which he sees is at a distance from him. Suppose, for example, that looking at the moon I should say it were fifty or sixty semidiameters of the earth distant from me. Let us see what moon this is spoken of. It is plain it cannot be the visible moon, or anything like the visible moon, or that which I see—which is only a round luminous plain, of about thirty visible points in diameter. For, in case I am carried from the place where I stand directly towards the moon, it is manifest the object varies still as I go on ; and, by the time that I am advanced fifty or sixty semidiameters of the earth, I shall be so far from being near a small, round, luminous flat that I shall perceive nothing like it—this object having long since disappeared, and, if I would recover it, it must be by

going back to the earth from whence I set out. Again, suppose I perceive by sight the faint and obscure idea of something, which I doubt whether it be a man, or a tree, or a tower, but judge it to be at the distance of about a mile. It is plain I cannot mean that what I see is a mile off, or that it is the image or likeness of anything which is a mile off; since that every step I take towards it the appearance alters, and from being obscure, small, and faint, grows clear, large, and vigorous. And when I come to the mile's end, that which I saw first is quite lost, neither do I find anything in the likeness of it.

45. In these and the like instances, the truth of the matter, I find, stands thus:—Having of a long time experienced certain ideas perceivable by touch—as distance, tangible figure, and solidity—to have been connected with certain ideas of sight, I do, upon perceiving these ideas of sight, forthwith conclude what tangible ideas are, by the wonted ordinary course of nature, like to follow. Looking at an object, I perceive a certain visible figure and colour, with some degree of faintness and other circumstances, which, from what I have formerly observed, determine me to think that if I advance forward so many paces or miles, I shall be affected with such and such ideas of touch. So that, in truth and strictness of speech I neither see distance itself, nor anything that I take to be at a distance. I say, neither distance nor things placed at a distance are themselves, or their ideas, truly perceived by sight. This I am persuaded of, as to what concerns myself. And I believe whoever will look narrowly into his own thoughts, and examine what he means by saying he sees this or that thing at a distance, will agree with me, that what he sees only suggests to his understanding that, after having passed a certain distance, to be measured by the motion of his body, which is perceivable by touch, he shall come to perceive such and such tangible ideas, which have been usually connected with such and such visible ideas. But, that one might be deceived by these suggestions of sense, and that there is no necessary connexion between visible and tangible ideas suggested by them, we need go no farther than the next looking-glass or picture to be convinced. Note that, when I speak of tangible ideas, I take the word idea for any the immediate object of sense, or understanding

—in which large signification it is commonly used by the moderns.

46. From what we have shown, it is a manifest consequence that the ideas of space, outness, and things placed at a distance are not, strictly speaking, the object of sight; they are not otherwise perceived by the eye than by the ear. Sitting in my study I hear a coach drive along the street; I look through the casement and see it; I walk out and enter into it. Thus, common speech would incline one to think I heard, saw, and touched the same thing, to wit, the coach. It is nevertheless certain the ideas intromitted by each sense are widely different, and distinct from each other; but, having been observed constantly to go together, they are spoken of as one and the same thing. By the variation of the noise, I perceive the different distances of the coach, and know that it approaches before I look out. Thus, by the ear I perceive distance just after the same manner as I do by the eye.

47. I do not nevertheless say I hear distance, in like manner as I say that I see it—the ideas perceived by hearing not being so apt to be confounded with the ideas of touch as those of sight are. So likewise a man is easily convinced that bodies and external things are not properly the object of hearing, but only sounds, by the mediation whereof the idea of this or that body, or distance, is suggested to his thoughts. But then one is with more difficulty brought to discern the difference there is betwixt the ideas of sight and touch: though it be certain, a man no more sees and feels the same thing, than he hears and feels the same thing.

48. One reason of which seems to be this. It is thought a great absurdity to imagine that one and the same thing should have any more than one extension and one figure. But, the extension and figure of a body being let into the mind two ways, and that indifferently, either by sight or touch, it seems to follow that we see the same extension and the same figure which we feel.

49. But, if we take a close and accurate view of the matter, it must be acknowledged that we never see and feel one and the same object. That which is seen is one thing, and that which is felt is another. If the visible figure and extension be not the same with the tangible figure and extension, we are not to infer that one and the same thing

has divers extensions. The true consequence is that the objects of sight and touch are two distinct things. It may perhaps require some thought rightly to conceive this distinction. And the difficulty seems not a little increased, because the combination of visible ideas hath constantly the same name as the combination of tangible ideas wherewith it is connected—which doth of necessity arise from the use and end of language.

50. In order, therefore, to treat accurately and unconfusedly of vision, we must bear in mind that there are two sorts of objects apprehended by the eye—the one primarily and immediately, the other secondarily and by intervention of the former. Those of the first sort neither are nor appear to be without the mind, or at any distance off. They may, indeed, grow greater or smaller, more confused, or more clear, or more faint. But they do not, cannot approach, or recede from us.[1] Whenever we say an object is at a distance, whenever we say it draws near, or goes farther off, we must always mean it of the latter sort, which properly belong to the touch, and are not so truly perceived as suggested by the eye, in like manner as thoughts by the ear.

51. No sooner do we hear the words of a familiar language pronounced in our ears but the ideas corresponding thereto present themselves to our minds : in the very same instant the sound and the meaning enter the understanding: so closely are they united that it is not in our power to keep out the one except we exclude the other also. We even act in all respects as if we heard the very thoughts themselves. So likewise the secondary objects, or those which are only suggested by sight, do often more strongly affect us, and are more regarded, than the proper objects of that sense ; along with which they enter into the mind, and with which they have a far more strict connexion than ideas have with words. Hence it is we find it so difficult to discriminate between the immediate and mediate objects of sight, and are so prone to attribute to the former what belongs only to the latter. They are, as it were, most closely twisted, blended, and incorporated together. And the prejudice is confirmed and riveted

---

[1] In all editions previous to the last (1732), this sentence read thus : "But they do not, cannot approach, or even seem to approach, or recede from us.

in our thoughts by a long tract of time, by the use of language, and want of reflection. However, I doubt not but anyone that shall attentively consider what we have already said, and shall say upon this subject before we have done (especially if he pursue it in his own thoughts), may be able to deliver himself from that prejudice. Sure I am, it is worth some attention to whoever would understand the true nature of vision.

52. I have now done with distance, and proceed to shew how it is that we perceive by sight the magnitude of objects. It is the opinion of some that we do it by angles, or by angles in conjunction with distance. But, neither angles nor distance being perceivable by sight, and the things we see being in truth at no distance from us, it follows that, as we have shewn lines and angles not to be the medium the mind makes use of in apprehending the apparent place, so neither are they the medium whereby it apprehends the apparent magnitude of objects.

53. It is well known that the same extension at a near distance shall subtend a greater angle, and at a farther distance a lesser angle. And by this principle (we are told) the mind estimates the magnitude of an object, comparing the angle under which it is seen with its distance, and thence inferring the magnitude thereof. What inclines men to this mistake (beside the humour of making one see by geometry) is, that the same perceptions or ideas which suggest distance do also suggest magnitude. But, if we examine it, we shall find they suggest the latter as immediately as the former. I say, they do not first suggest distance and then leave it to the judgment to use that as a medium whereby to collect the magnitude ; but they have as close and immediate a connexion with the magnitude as with the distance ; and suggest magnitude as independently of distance, as they do distance independently of magnitude. All which will be evident to whoever considers what has been already said and what follows.

54. It hath been shewn there are two sorts of objects apprehended by sight, each whereof has its distinct magnitude, or extension—the one, properly tangible, i.e., to be perceived and measured by touch, and not immediately falling under

the sense of seeing; the other, properly and immediately visible, by mediation of which the former is brought in view. Each of these magnitudes are greater or lesser, according as they contain in them more or fewer points, they being made up of points or minimums. For, whatever may be said of extension in abstract, it is certain sensible extension is not infinitely divisible. There is a *minimum tangibile*, and a *minimum visibile*, beyond which sense cannot perceive. This everyone's experience will inform him.

55. The magnitude of the object which exists without the mind, and is at a distance, continues always invariably the same: but, the visible object still changing as you approach to or recede from the tangible object, it hath no fixed and determinate greatness. Whenever therefore we speak of the magnitude of any thing, for instance a tree or a house, we must mean the tangible magnitude: otherwise there can be nothing steady and free from ambiguity spoken of it. Now, though the tangible and visible magnitude do in truth belong to two distinct objects, I shall nevertheless (especially since those objects are called by the same name, and are observed to coexist), to avoid tediousness and singularity of speech, sometimes speak of them as belonging to one and the same thing.

56. Now, in order to discover by what means the magnitude of tangible objects is perceived by sight, I need only reflect on what passes in my own mind, and observe what those things be which introduce the ideas of greater or lesser into my thoughts when I look on any object. And these I find to be, *first*, the magnitude or extension of a visible object, which, being immediately perceived by sight, is connected with that other which is tangible and placed at a distance: *secondly*, the confusion or distinctness: and *thirdly*, the vigorousness or faintness of the aforesaid visible appearance. *Cæteris paribus*, by how much the greater or lesser the visible object is, by so much the greater or lesser do I conclude the tangible object to be. But, be the idea immediately perceived by sight never so large, yet, if it be withal confused, I judge the magnitude of the thing to be but small. If it be distinct and clear, I judge it greater. And, if it be faint, I apprehend it to be yet greater. What is here meant by confusion and faintness has been explained in sect. 35.

57. Moreover, the judgments we make of greatness do, in like manner as those of distance, depend on the disposition of the eye ; also on the figure, number, and situation of intermediate objects, and other circumstances that have been observed to attend great or small tangible magnitudes. Thus, for instance, the very same quantity of visible extension which in the figure of a tower doth suggest the idea of great magnitude shall in the figure of a man suggest the idea of much smaller magnitude. That this is owing to the experience we have had of the usual bigness of a tower and a man, no one, I suppose, need be told.

58. It is also evident that confusion or faintness have no more a necessary connexion with little or great magnitude than they have with little or great distance. As they suggest the latter, so they suggest the former to our minds. And, by consequence, if it were not for experience, we should no more judge a faint or confused appearance to be connected with great or little magnitude than we should that it was connected with great or little distance.

59. Nor will it be found that great or small visible magnitude hath any necessary relation to great or small tangible magnitude—so that the one may certainly and infallibly be inferred from the other. But, before we come to the proof of this, it is fit we consider the difference there is betwixt the extension and figure which is the proper object of touch, and that other which is termed visible ; and how the former is principally, though not immediately, taken notice of when we look at any object. This has been before mentioned, but we shall here inquire into the cause thereof. We regard the objects that environ us in proportion as they are adapted to benefit or injure our own bodies, and thereby produce in our minds the sensations of pleasure or pain. Now, bodies operating on our organs by an immediate application, and the hurt and advantage arising therefrom depending altogether on the tangible, and not at all on the visible, qualities of any object—this is a plain reason why those should be regarded by us much more than these. And for this end the visive sense seems to have been bestowed on animals, to wit, that, by the perception of visible ideas (which in themselves are not capable of affecting or anywise altering the frame of their bodies), they may be able to foresee (from the experience they

have had what tangible ideas are connected with such and such visible ideas) the damage or benefit which is like to ensue upon the application of their own bodies to this or that body which is at a distance. Which foresight, how necessary it is to the preservation of an animal, everyone's experience can inform him. Hence it is that, when we look at an object, the tangible figure and extension thereof are principally attended to ; whilst there is small heed taken of the visible figure and magnitude, which, though more immediately perceived, do less sensibly affect us, and are not fitted to produce any alteration in our bodies.

60. That the matter of fact is true will be evident to any one who considers that a man placed at ten foot distance is thought as great as if he were placed at the distance only of five foot ; which is true, not with relation to the visible, but tangible greatness of the object : the visible magnitude being far greater at one station than it is at the other.

61. Inches, feet, &c., are settled, stated lengths, whereby we measure objects and estimate their magnitude. We say, for example, an object appears to be six inches, or six foot long. Now, that this cannot be meant of visible inches, &c., is evident, because a visible inch is itself no constant determinate magnitude, and cannot therefore serve to mark out and determine the magnitude of any other thing. Take an inch marked upon a ruler ; view it successively, at the distance of half a foot, a foot, a foot and a half, &c., from the eye : at each of which, and at all the intermediate distances, the inch shall have a different visible extension, *i.e.*, there shall be more or fewer points discerned in it. Now, I ask which of all these various extensions is that stated determinate one that is agreed on for a common measure of other magnitudes ? No reason can be assigned why we should pitch on one more than another. And, except there be some invariable determinate extension fixed on to be marked by the word inch, it is plain it can be used to little purpose ; and to say a thing contains this or that number of inches shall imply no more than that it is extended, without bringing any particular idea of that extension into the mind. Farther, an inch and a foot, from different distances, shall both exhibit the same visible magnitude, and yet at the same time you shall say that one seems several times greater than the other. From all which

it is manifest, that the judgments we make of the magnitude of objects by sight are altogether in reference to their tangible extension. Whenever we say an object is great or small, of this or that determinate measure, I say, it must be meant of the tangible and not the visible extension, which, though immediately perceived, is nevertheless little taken notice of.

62. Now, that there is no necessary connexion between these two distinct extensions is evident from hence—because our eyes might have been framed in such a manner as to be able to see nothing but what were less than the *minimum tangibile*. In which case it is not impossible we might have perceived all the immediate objects of sight the very same that we do now ; but unto those visible appearances there would not be connected those different tangible magnitudes that are now. Which shews the judgments we make of the magnitude of things placed at a distance, from the various greatness of the immediate objects of sight, do not arise from any essential or necessary, but only a customary, tie which has been observed betwixt them.

63. Moreover, it is not only certain that any idea of sight might not have been connected with this or that idea of touch we now observe to accompany it, but also that the greater visible magnitudes might have been connected with and introduced into our minds lesser tangible magnitudes, and the lesser visible magnitudes greater tangible magnitudes. Nay, that it actually is so, we have daily experience—that object which makes a strong and large appearance not seeming near so great as another the visible magnitude whereof is much less, but more faint, and the appearance upper, or which is the same thing, painted lower on the retina, which faintness and situation suggest both greater magnitude and greater distance.[1]

64. From which, and from sect. 57 and 58, it is manifest that, as we do not perceive the magnitude of objects immediately by sight, so neither do we perceive them by the mediation of anything which has a necessary connexion with them. Those ideas that now suggest unto us the various magnitudes of external objects before we touch them might possibly have suggested no such thing ; or they might have

[1] The last passage beginning "and the appearance upper" was added by Berkeley to the last (1732) edition.

signified them in a direct contrary manner, so that the very same ideas on the perception whereof we judge an object to be small might as well have served to make us conclude it great ;—those ideas being in their own nature equally fitted to bring into our minds the idea of small or great, or no size at all, of outward objects, just as the words of any language are in their own nature indifferent to signify this or that thing, or nothing at all.

65. As we see distance so we see magnitude. And we see both in the same way that we see shame or anger in the looks of a man. Those passions are themselves invisible ; they are nevertheless let in by the eye along with colours and altera- tions of countenance which are the immediate object of vision, and which signify them for no other reason than barely be- cause they have been observed to accompany them. With- out which experience we should no more have taken blushing for a sign of shame than of gladness.

66. We are nevertheless exceedingly prone to imagine those things which are perceived only by the mediation of others to be themselves the immediate objects of sight, or at least to have in their own nature a fitness to be suggested by them before ever they had been experienced to coexist with them. From which prejudice everyone perhaps will not find it easy to emancipate himself, by any the clearest convictions of reason. And there are some grounds to think that, if there was only one invariable and universal language in the world, and that men were born with the faculty of speaking it, it would be the opinion of many, that the ideas in other men's minds were properly perceived by the ear, or had at least a necessary and inseparable tie with the sounds that were affixed to them. All which seems to arise from want of a due application of our discerning faculty, thereby to discriminate between the ideas that are in our understandings, and con- sider them apart from each other ; which would preserve us from confounding those that are different, and make us see what ideas do, and what do not, include or imply this or that other idea.

67. There is a celebrated phenomenon the solution whereof I shall attempt to give, by the principles that have been laid down, in reference to the manner wherein we ap-

prehend by sight the magnitude of objects.—The apparent magnitude of the moon, when placed in the horizon, is much greater than when it is in the meridian, though the angle under which the diameter of the moon is seen be not observed greater in the former case than in the latter ; and the horizontal moon doth not constantly appear of the same bigness, but at some times seemeth far greater than at others.

68. Now, in order to explain the reason of the moon's appearing greater than ordinary in the horizon, it must be observed that the particles which compose our atmosphere do intercept the rays of light proceeding from any object to the eye ; and, by how much the greater is the portion of atmosphere interjacent between the object and the eye, by so much the more are the rays intercepted, and, by consequence, the appearance of the object rendered more faint—every object appearing more vigorous or more faint in proportion as it sendeth more or fewer rays into the eye. Now, between the eye and the moon when situated in the horizon there lies a far greater quantity of atmosphere than there does when the moon is in the meredian. Whence it comes to pass, that the appearance of the horizontal moon is fainter, and therefore, by sect. 56, it should be thought bigger in that situation than in the meridian, or in any other elevation above the horizon.

69. Farther, the air being variously impregnated, sometimes more and sometimes less, with vapours and exhalations fitted to retund and intercept the rays of light, it follows that the appearance of the horizontal moon hath not always an equal faintness, and, by consequence, that luminary, though in the very same situation, is at one time judged greater than at another.

70. That we have here given the true account of the phenomena of the horizontal moon, will, I suppose, be farther evident to anyone from the following considerations :—*First*, it is plain, that which in this case suggests the idea of greater magnitude, must be something which is itself perceived ; for, that which is unperceived cannot suggest to our perception any other thing. *Secondly*, it must be something that does not constantly remain the same, but is subject to some change or variation ; since the appearance of the horizontal

moon varies, being at one time greater than at another.[1] And yet, *thirdly*, it cannot be the visible figure or magnitude ; since that remains the same, or is rather lesser, by how much the moon is nearer to the horizon. It remains therefore, that the true cause is that affection or alteration of the visible appearance, which proceeds from the greater paucity of rays arriving at the eye, and which I term faintness : since this answers all the forementioned conditions, and I am not conscious of any other perception that doth.

71. Add to this that in misty weather it is a common observation, that the appearance of the horizontal moon is far larger than usual, which greatly conspires with and strengthens our opinion. Neither would it prove in the least irreconcilable with what we have said, if the horizontal moon should chance sometimes to seem enlarged beyond its usual extent, even in more serene weather. For, we must not only have regard to the mist which happens to be in the place where we stand ; we ought also to take into our thoughts the whole sum of vapours and exhalations which lie betwixt the eye and the moon : all which co-operating to render the appearance of the moon more faint, and thereby increase its magnitude, it may chance to appear greater than it usually does even in the horizontal position, at a time when, though there be no extraordinary fog or haziness just in the place where we stand, yet the air between the eye and the moon, taken altogether, may be loaded with a greater quantity of interspersed vapours and exhalations than at other times.

72. It may be objected that, in consequence of our principles, the interposition of a body in some degree opaque, which may intercept a great part of the rays of light, should render the appearance of the moon in the meridian as large as when it is viewed in the horizon. To which I answer, it is not faintness anyhow applied that suggests greater magnitude ; there being no necessary, but only an experimental connexion between those two things. It follows that the faintness which enlarges the appearance must be applied in

---

[1] The following passage was omitted from this place in the author's last revision : " *Thirdly*, it must not lie in the external circumjacent or intermediate objects, such as mountains, houses, fields, &c. ; because that when all those objects are excluded from sight the appearance is as great as ever." " *Thirdly* " in the following sentence was of course " *Fourthly*."

such sort, and with such circumstances, as have been observed to attend the vision of great magnitudes. When from a distance we behold great objects, the particles of the intermediate air and vapours, which are themselves unperceivable, do interrupt the rays of light, and thereby render the appearance less strong and vivid. Now, faintness of appearance caused in this sort hath been experienced to coexist with great magnitude. But when it is caused by the interposition of an opaque sensible body, this circumstance alters the case; so that a faint appearance this way caused does not suggest greater magnitude, because it hath not been experienced to coexist with it.

73. Faintness, as well as all other ideas or perceptions which suggest magnitude or distance, doth it in the same way that words suggest the notions to which they are annexed. Now, it is known a word pronounced with certain circumstances, or in a certain context with other words, hath not always the same import and signification that it hath when pronounced in some other circumstances, or different context of words. The very same visible appearance as to faintness and all other respects, if placed on high, shall not suggest the same magnitude that it would if it were seen at an equal distance on a level with the eye. The reason whereof is, that we are rarely accustomed to view objects at a great height; our concerns lie among things situated rather before than above us; and accordingly our eyes are not placed on the top of our heads, but in such a position as is most convenient for us to see distant objects standing in our way. And, this situation of them being a circumstance which usually attends the vision of distant objects, we may from hence account for (what is commonly observed) an object's appearing of different magnitude, even with respect to its horizontal extension, on the top of a steeple, *e.g.*, a hundred feet high, to one standing below, from what it would if placed at a hundred feet distance on a level with his eye. For, it hath been shewn that the judgment we make on the magnitude of a thing depends not on the visible appearance alone, but also on divers other circumstances, any one of which being omitted or varied may suffice to make some alteration in our judgment. Hence, the circumstance of viewing a distant object in such a situation as is usual, and suits with the ordinary posture of the head

and eyes being omitted, and instead thereof a different situation of the object, which requires a different posture of the head, taking place, it is not to be wondered at if the magnitude be judged different. But it will be demanded, why a high object should constantly appear less than an equidistant low object of the same dimensions ; for so it is observed to be. It may indeed be granted that the variation of some circumstances may vary the judgment made on the magnitude of high objects, which we are less used to look at ; but it does not hence appear why they should be judged less rather than greater? I answer, that in case the magnitude of distant objects was suggested by the extent of their visible appearance alone, and thought proportional thereto, it is certain they would then be judged much less than now they seem to be. (Vide sect. 79.) But, several circumstances concurring to form the judgment we make on the magnitude of distant objects, by means of which they appear far larger than others whose visible appearance hath an equal or even greater extension ; it follows that upon the change or omission of any of those circumstances which are wont to attend the vision of distant objects, and so come to influence the judgments made on their magnitude, they shall proportionably appear less than otherwise they would. For, any of those things that caused an object to be thought greater than in proportion to its visible extension being either omitted, or applied without the usual circumstances, the judgment depends more entirely on the visible extension, and consequently the object must be judged less. Thus, in the present case the situation of the thing seen being different from what it usually is in those objects we have occasion to view, and whose magnitude we observe, it follows that the very same object being a hundred feet high, should seem less than if it was a hundred feet off, on (or nearly on) a level with the eye. What has been here set forth seems to me to have no small share in contributing to magnify the appearance of the horizontal moon, and deserves not to be passed over in the explication of it.

74. If we attentively consider the phenomenon before us, we shall find the not discerning between the mediate and immediate objects of sight to be the chief cause of the difficulty that occurs in the explication of it. The magnitude of

the visible moon, or that which is the proper and immediate object of vision, is no greater when the moon is in the horizon than when it is in the meridian. How comes it, therefore, to seem greater in one situation than the other? What is it can put this cheat on the understanding? It has no other perception of the moon than what it gets by sight: and that which is seen is of the same extent—I say, the visible appearance hath the very same or rather a less magnitude, when the moon is viewed in the horizontal than when in the meridional position. And yet it is esteemed greater in the former than in the latter. Herein consists the difficulty, which doth vanish and admit of a most easy solution, if we consider that as the visible moon is not greater in the horizon than in the meridian, so neither is it thought to be so. It hath been already shewn that, in any act of vision, the visible object absolutely, or in itself, is little taken notice of —the mind still carrying its view from that to some tangible ideas, which have been observed to be connected with it, and by that means come to be suggested by it. So that when a thing is said to appear great or small, or whatever estimate be made of the magnitude of any thing, this is meant not of the visible but of the tangible object. This duly considered, it will be no hard matter to reconcile the seeming contradiction there is, that the moon should appear of a different bigness, the visible magnitude thereof remaining still the same. For, by sect. 56, the very same visible extension, with a different faintness, shall suggest a different tangible extension. When therefore the horizontal moon is said to appear greater than the meridional moon, this must be understood, not of a greater visible extension, but of a greater tangible or real extension, which, by reason of the more than ordinary faintness of the visible appearance, is suggested to the mind along with it.

75. Many attempts have been made by learned men to account for this appearance. Gassendus, Descartes, Hobbes, and several others have employed their thoughts on that subject; but how fruitless and unsatisfactory their endeavours have been is sufficiently shewn in the "Philosophical Transactions (Numb. 187, p. 314), where you may see their several opinions at large set forth and confuted, not without some surprise at the gross blunders that ingenious men have

been forced into by endeavouring to reconcile this appearance with the ordinary principles of optics. Since the writing of which there hath been published in the "Transactions" (Numb. 187, p. 323) another paper relating to the same affair, by the celebrated Dr. Wallis, wherein he attempts to account for that phenomenon, which, though it seems not to contain anything new, or different from what had been said before by others, I shall nevertheless consider in this place.

76. His opinion, in short, is this :—We judge not of the magnitude of an object by the visual angle alone, but by the visual angle in conjunction with the distance. Hence, though the angle remain the same, or even become less, yet, if withal the distance seem to have been increased, the object shall appear greater. Now, one way whereby we estimate the distance of anything is by the number and extent of the intermediate objects. When therefore the moon is seen in the horizon, the variety of fields, houses, &c., together with the large prospect of the wide extended land or sea that lies between the eye and the utmost limb of the horizon, suggest unto the mind the idea of greater distance, and consequently magnify the appearance. And this, according to Dr. Wallis, is the true account of the extraordinary largeness attributed by the mind to the horizontal moon, at a time when the angle subtended by its diameter is not one jot greater than it used to be.

77. With reference to this opinion, not to repeat what hath been already said concerning distance, I shall only observe, *first*, that if the prospect of interjacent objects be that which suggests the idea of farther distance, and this idea of farther distance be the cause that brings into the mind the idea of greater magnitude, it should hence follow that if one looked at the horizontal moon from behind a wall, it would appear no bigger than ordinary. For, in that case, the wall interposing cuts off all that prospect of sea and land, &c., which might otherwise increase the apparent distance, and thereby the apparent magnitude of the moon. Nor will it suffice to say, the memory doth even then suggest all that extent of land, &c., which lies within the horizon—which suggestion occasions a sudden judgment of sense, that the moon is farther off and larger than usual. For ask any man who

from such a station beholding the horizontal moon shall think her greater than usual, whether he hath at that time in his mind any idea of the intermediate objects, or long tract of land that lies between his eye and the extreme edge of the horizon? and whether it be that idea which is the cause of his making the aforementioned judgment? He will, without doubt, reply in the negative, and declare the horizontal moon shall appear greater than the meridional, though he never thinks of all or any of those things that lie between him and it.[1] *Secondly*, it seems impossible, by this hypothesis, to account for the moon's appearing, in the very same situation, at one time greater than at another; which, nevertheless, has been shewn to be very agreeable to the principles we have laid down, and receives a most easy and natural explication from them. [2]For the further clearing up of this point, it is to be observed that what we immediately and properly see are only lights and colours in sundry situations and shades, and degrees of faintness and clearness, confusion and distinctness. All which visible objects are only in the mind; nor do they suggest aught external, whether distance or magnitude, otherwise than by habitual connexion as words do things. We are also to remark, that beside the straining of the eyes, and beside the vivid and faint, the distinct and confused appearances (which, bearing some proportion to lines and angles, have been substituted instead of them in the foregoing part of this Treatise), there are other means which suggest both distance and magnitude— particularly the situation of visible points or objects, as upper or lower; the former suggesting a farther distance and greater magnitude, the latter a nearer distance and lesser magnitude—all which is an effect only of custom and experience, there being really nothing intermediate in the line of distance between the uppermost and the lowermost, which are both equidistant, or rather at no distance from the eye; as there is also nothing in upper or lower which by necessary

---

[1] The following passage was struck out from this place at the last revision: "And as for the absurdity of any idea's introducing into the mind another, whilst itself is not perceived, this hath already fallen under our observation, and is too evident to need any farther enlargement on it."

[2] The whole of the following passage up to the end of the section, was inserted in the last edition (1732).

connexion should suggest greater or lesser magnitude. Now, as these customary experimental means of suggesting distance do likewise suggest magnitude, so they suggest the one as immediately as the other. I say they do not (vide sect. 53) first suggest distance, and then leave the mind from thence to infer or compute magnitude, but suggest magnitude as immediately and directly as they suggest distance.

78. This phenomenon of the horizontal moon is a clear instance of the insufficiency of lines and angles for explaining the way wherein the mind perceives and estimates the magnitude of outward objects. There is, nevertheless, a use of computation by them—in order to determine the apparent magnitude of things, so far as they have a connexion with and are proportional to those other ideas or perceptions which are the true and immediate occasions that suggest to the mind the apparent magnitude of things. But this in general may, I think, be observed concerning mathematical computation in optics—that it can never be very precise and exact, since the judgments we make of the magnitude of external things do often depend on several circumstances which are not proportional to, or capable of being defined by lines and angles.

79. From what has been said, we may safely deduce this consequence, to wit, that a man born blind, and made to see, would, at first opening of his eyes, make a very different judgment of the magnitude of objects intromitted by them from what others do. He would not consider the ideas of sight with reference to, or as having any connexion with the ideas of touch. His view of them being entirely terminated within themselves, he can no otherwise judge them great or small than as they contain a greater or lesser number of visible points. Now, it being certain that any visible point can cover or exclude from view only one other visible point, it follows that whatever object intercepts the view of another hath an equal number of visible points with it; and, consequently, they shall both be thought by him to have the same magnitude. Hence, it is evident one in those circumstances would judge his thumb, with which he might hide a tower, or hinder its being seen, equal to that tower; or his hand, the interposition whereof might conceal the firmament

from his view, equal to the firmament: how great an inequality soever there may, in our apprehensions, seem to be betwixt those two things, because of the customary and close connexion that has grown up in our minds between the objects of sight and touch, whereby the very different and distinct ideas of those two senses are so blended and confounded together as to be mistaken for one and the same thing—out of which prejudice we cannot easily extricate ourselves.

80. For the better explaining the nature of vision, and setting the manner wherein we perceive magnitudes in a due light, I shall proceed to make some observations concerning matters relating thereto, whereof the want of reflection, and duly separating between tangible and visible ideas, is apt to create in us mistaken and confused notions. And, *first*, I shall observe, that the *minimum visibile* is exactly equal in all beings whatsoever that are endowed with the visive faculty. No exquisite formation of the eye, no peculiar sharpness of sight, can make it less in one creature than in another; for, it not being distinguishable into parts, nor in anywise consisting of them, it must necessarily be the same to all. For, suppose it otherwise, and that the *minimum visibile* of a mite, for instance, be less than the *minimum visibile* of a man; the latter therefore may, by detraction of some part, be made equal to the former. It doth therefore consist of parts, which is inconsistent with the notion of a *minimum visibile* or point.

81. It will, perhaps, be objected, that the *minimum visibile* of a man doth really and in itself contain parts whereby it surpasses that of a mite, though they are not perceivable by the man. To which I answer, the *minimum visibile* having (in like manner as all other the proper and immediate objects of sight) been shewn not to have any existence without the mind of him who sees it, it follows there cannot be any part of it that is not actually perceived and therefore visible. Now, for any object to contain several distinct visible parts, and at the same time to be a *minimum visibile*, is a manifest contradiction.

82. Of these visible points we see at all times an equal number. It is every whit as great when our view is con-

tracted and bounded by near objects as when it is extended
to larger and remoter ones. For, it being impossible that
one *minimum visibile* should obscure or keep out of sight
more than one other, it is a plain consequence that, when
my view is on all sides bounded by the walls of my study, I
see just as many visible points as I could in case that, by
the removal of the study-walls and all other obstructions, I
had a full prospect of the circumjacent fields, mountains, sea,
and open firmament. For, so long as I am shut up within
the walls, by their interposition every point of the external
objects is covered from my view. But, each point that is
seen being able to cover or exclude from sight one only other
corresponding point, it follows that, whilst my sight is confined to those narrow walls, I see as many points or *minima
visibilia* as I should were those walls away, by looking on all
the external objects whose prospect is intercepted by them.
Whenever, therefore, we are said to have a greater prospect
at one time than another, this must be understood with
relation, not to the proper and immediate, but the secondary
and mediate objects of vision—which, as hath been shewn,
do properly belong to the touch.

83. The visive faculty, considered with reference to its
immediate objects, may be found to labour of two defects.
First, in respect of the extent or number of visible points
that are at once perceivable by it, which is narrow and
limited to a certain degree. It can take in at one view but
a certain determinate number of *minima visibilia*, beyond
which it cannot extend its prospect. *Secondly*, our sight is
defective in that its view is not only narrow, but also for the
most part confused. Of those things that we take in at one
prospect, we can see but a few at once clearly and unconfusedly; and the more we fix our sight on any one object,
by so much the darker and more indistinct shall the rest
appear.

84. Corresponding to these two defects of sight, we may
imagine as many perfections, to wit, 1st., that of comprehending in one view a greater number of visible points; 2dly.,
of being able to view them all equally and at once, with the
utmost clearness and distinction. That those perfections are
not actually in some intelligences of a different order and
capacity from ours, it is impossible for us to know.

85. In neither of those two ways do microscopes contribute to the improvement of sight. For, when we look through a microscope, we neither see more visible points, nor are the collateral points more distinct than when we look with the naked eye at objects placed in a due distance. A microscope brings us, as it were, into a new world. It presents us with a new scene of visible objects, quite different from what we behold with the naked eye. But herein consists the most remarkable difference, to wit, that whereas the objects perceived by the eye alone have a certain connexion with tangible objects, whereby we are taught to foresee what will ensue upon the approach or application of distant objects to the parts of our own body, which much conduceth to its preservation ; there is not the like connexion between things tangible and those visible objects that are perceived by help of a fine microscope.

86. Hence, it is evident that, were our eyes turned into the nature of microscopes, we should not be much benefited by the change. We should be deprived of the forementioned advantage we at present receive by the visive faculty, and have left us only the empty amusement of seeing, without any other benefit arising from it. But, in that case, it will perhaps be said, our sight would be endued with a far greater sharpness and penetration than it now hath. But I would fain know wherein consists that sharpness which is esteemed so great an excellency of sight. It is certain, from what we have already shewn, that the *minimum visibile* is never greater or lesser, but in all cases constantly the same. And, in the case of microscopical eyes, I see only this difference, to wit, that upon the ceasing of a certain observable connexion betwixt the divers perceptions of sight and touch, which before enabled us to regulate our actions by the eye, it would now be rendered utterly unserviceable to that purpose.

87. Upon the whole it seems that, if we consider the use and end of sight, together with the present state and circumstances of our being, we shall not find any great cause to complain of any defect or imperfection in it, or easily conceive how it could be mended. With such admirable wisdom is that faculty contrived, both for the pleasure and convenience of life.

88. Having finished what I intended to say concerning the distance and magnitude of objects, I come now to treat of the manner wherein the mind perceives by sight their situation. Among the discoveries of the last age, it is reputed none of the least, that the manner of vision hath been more clearly explained than ever it had been before. There is, at this day, no one ignorant that the pictures of external objects are painted on the retina or fund of the eye; that we can see nothing which is not so painted ; and that, according as the picture is more distinct or confused, so also is the perception we have of the object. But then, in this explication of vision, there occurs one mighty difficulty—The objects are painted in an inverted order on the bottom of the eye : the upper part of any object being painted on the lower part of

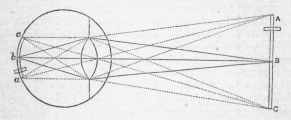

the eye, and the lower part of the object on the upper part of the eye ; and so also as to right and left. Since, therefore, the pictures are thus inverted, it is demanded how it comes to pass that we see the objects erect and in their natural posture ?

89. In answer to this difficulty, we are told that the mind, perceiving an impulse of a ray of light on the upper part of the eye, considers this ray as coming in a direct line from the lower part of the object ; and, in like manner, tracing the ray that strikes on the lower part of the eye, it is directed to the upper part of the object. Thus, in the adjacent figure, *C*, the lower point of the object *ABC*, is projected on *c* the upper part of the eye. So likewise, the highest point *A* is projected on *a* the lowest part of the eye ; which makes the representation *cba* inverted. But the mind, considering the stroke that is made on *c* as coming in the straight line *Cc* from the lower end of the object ; and the stroke or impulse

on *a*, as coming in the line *A a* from the upper end of the object, is directed to make a right judgment of the situation of the object *A B C*, notwithstanding the picture of it be inverted.   Moreover, this is illustrated by conceiving a blind man, who, holding in his hands two sticks that cross each other, doth with them touch the extremities of an object, placed in a perpendicular situation.   It is certain this man will judge that to be the upper part of the object which he touches with the stick held in the undermost hand, and that to be the lower part of the object which he touches with the stick in his uppermost hand.   This is the common explication of the erect appearance of objects, which is generally received and acquiesced in, being (as Mr. Molyneux tells us, *Diopt.* part ii. ch. vii. p. 289) 'allowed by all men as satisfactory.'

90. But this account to me does not seem in any degree true.   Did I perceive those impulses, decussations, and directions of the rays of light, in like manner as hath been set forth, then, indeed, it would not at first view be altogether void of probability.   And there might be some pretence for the comparison of the blind man and his cross sticks.   But the case is far otherwise.   I know very well that I perceive no such thing.   And, of consequence, I cannot thereby make an estimate of the situation of objects.   Moreover, I appeal to any one's experience, whether he be conscious to himself that he thinks on the intersection made by the radius pencils, or pursues the impulses they give in right lines, whenever he perceives by sight the position of any object?   To me it seems evident that crossing and tracing of the rays, &c., is never thought on by children, idiots, or, in truth, by any other, save only those who have applied themselves to the study of optics.   And for the mind to judge of the situation of objects by those things without perceiving them, or to perceive them without knowing it, take which you please, it is perfectly beyond my comprehension.   Add to this, that the explaining the manner of vision by the example of cross sticks, and hunting for the object along the axes of the radius pencils, doth suppose the proper objects of sight to be perceived at a distance from us, contrary to what hath been demonstrated.[1]

[1] The following passage appeared here in the first two editions, but

91. It remains, therefore, that we look for some other explication of this difficulty. And I believe it not impossible to find one, provided we examine it to the bottom, and carefully distinguish between the ideas of sight and touch; which cannot be too oft inculcated in treating of vision. But, more especially throughout the consideration of this affair, we ought to carry that distinction in our thoughts, for that from want of a right understanding thereof, the difficulty of explaining erect vision seems chiefly to arise.

92. In order to disentangle our minds from whatever prejudices we may entertain with relation to the subject in hand, nothing seems more apposite than the taking into our thoughts the case of one born blind, and afterwards, when grown up, made to see. And though perhaps it may not be a task altogether easy and familiar to us, to divest ourselves entirely of the experiences received from sight, so as to be able to put our thoughts exactly in the posture of such a one's: we must, nevertheless, as far as possible, endeavour to frame true conceptions of what might reasonably be supposed to pass in his mind.

93. It is certain that a man actually blind, and who had continued so from his birth, would, by the sense of feeling, attain to have ideas of upper and lower. By the motion of his hand, he might discern the situation of any tangible object placed within his reach. That part on which he felt himself supported, or towards which he perceived his body to gravitate, he would term "lower," and the contrary to this "upper;" and accordingly denominate whatsoever objects he touched.

94. But then, whatever judgments he makes concerning the situation of objects are confined to those only that are perceivable by touch. All those things that are intangible, and of a spiritual nature—his thoughts and desires, his passions, and in general all the modifications of his soul—to these he would never apply the terms upper and lower, except only in a metaphorical sense. He may perhaps, by

was omitted by the author from the last: "We may therefore venture to pronounce this opinion, concerning the way wherein the mind perceives the erect appearance of objects, to be of a piece with those other tenets of writers in optics, which in the foregoing parts of this treatise we have had occasion to examine and refute."

way of allusion, speak of high or low thoughts: but those terms, in their proper signification, would never be applied to anything that was not conceived to exist without the mind. For, a man born blind, and remaining in the same state, could mean nothing else by the words higher and lower than a greater or lesser distance from the earth—which distance he would measure by the motion or application of his hand, or some other part of his body. It is, therefore, evident that all those things which, in respect of each other, would by him be thought higher or lower, must be such as were conceived to exist without his mind, in the ambient space.

95. Whence it plainly follows, that such a one, if we suppose him made to see, would not at first sight think that anything he saw was high or low, erect or inverted. For, it hath been already demonstrated, in sect. 41, that he would not think the things he perceived by sight to be at any distance from him, or without his mind. The objects to which he had hitherto been used to apply the terms up and down, high and low, were such only as affected, or were some way perceived by his touch. But, the proper objects of vision make a new set of ideas, perfectly distinct and different from the former, and which can in no sort make themselves perceived by touch. There is, therefore, nothing at all that could induce him to think those terms applicable to them. Nor would he ever think it, till such time as he had observed their connexion with tangible objects, and the same prejudice began to insinuate itself into his understanding, which, from their infancy, had grown up in the understandings of other men.

96. To set this matter in a clearer light, I shall make use of an example. Suppose the above-mentioned blind person, by his touch, perceives a man to stand erect. Let us inquire into the manner of this. By the application of his hand to the several parts of a human body, he had perceived different tangible ideas, which being collected into sundry complex ones have distinct names annexed to them. Thus, one combination of a certain tangible figure, bulk, and consistency of parts is called the head; another the hand; a third the foot, and so of the rest—all which complex ideas could, in his understanding, be made up only of ideas perceivable by touch. He had also, by his touch, obtained an idea of

earth or ground, towards which he perceives the parts of his body to have a natural tendency.   Now, by "erect" nothing more being meant than that perpendicular position of a man wherein his feet are nearest to the earth : if the blind person, by moving his hand over the parts of the man who stands before him, do perceive the tangible ideas that compose the head to be farthest from, and those that compose the feet to be nearest to, that other combination of tangible ideas which he calls earth, he will denominate that man erect.   But, if we suppose him on a sudden to receive his sight, and that he behold a man standing before him, it is evident, in that case, he would neither judge the man he sees to be erect nor inverted ; for he, never having known those terms applied to any other save tangible things, or which existed in the space without him, and what he sees neither being tangible, nor perceived as existing without, he could not know that, in propriety of language, they were applicable to it.

97. Afterwards, when, upon turning his head or eyes up and down to the right and left, he shall observe the visible objects to change, and shall also attain to know that they are called by the same names, and connected with the objects perceived by touch ; then, indeed, he will come to speak of them and their situation in the same terms that he has been used to apply to tangible things : and those that he perceives by turning up his eyes he will call upper, and those that by turning down his eyes he will call lower.

98. And this seems to me the true reason why he should think those objects uppermost that are painted on the lower part of his eye.   For, by turning the eye up they shall be distinctly seen ; as likewise they that are painted on the highest part of the eye shall be distinctly seen by turning the eye down, and are for that reason esteemed lowest.   For, we have shewn that to the immediate objects of sight, considered in themselves, he would not attribute the terms high and low.   It must therefore be on account of some circumstances which are observed to attend them.   And these, it is plain, are the actions of turning the eye up and down, which suggest a very obvious reason why the mind should denominate the objects of sight accordingly high or low.   And, without this motion of the eye, this turning it up and down in order to discern different objects, doubtless

"erect," "inverse," and other the like terms relating to the position of tangible objects, would never have been transferred, or in any degree apprehended to belong to the ideas of sight—the mere act of seeing including nothing in it to that purpose; whereas the different situations of the eye naturally direct the mind to make a suitable judgment of the situation of objects intromitted by it.

99. Farther, when he has by experience learned the connexion there is between the several ideas of sight and touch, he will be able, by the perception he has of the situation of visible things in respect of one another, to make a sudden and true estimate of the situation of outward, tangible things corresponding to them. And thus it is he shall perceive by sight the situation of external objects, which do not properly fall under that sense.[1]

100. I know we are very prone to think that, if just made to see, we should judge of the situation of visible things as we do now. But, we are also as prone to think that, at first sight, we should in the same way apprehend the distance and magnitude of objects as we do now; which hath been shewn to be a false and groundless persuasion. And, for the like reasons, the same censure may be passed on the positive assurance that most men, before they have thought sufficiently of the matter, might have of their being able to determine by the eye, at first view, whether objects were erect or inverse.

101. It will perhaps be objected to our opinion, that a man, for instance, being thought erect when his feet are next the earth, and inverted when his head is next the earth, it doth hence follow that, by the mere act of vision, without any experience or altering the situation of the eye, we should have determined whether he were erect or inverted. For both the earth itself, and the limbs of the man who stands thereon, being equally perceived by sight, one cannot choose seeing what part of the man is nearest the earth, and what part farthest from it, *i.e.* whether he be erect or inverted.

102. To which I answer, the ideas which constitute the

---

[1] What Berkeley here supposes he was afterwards able to refer to actually in the "T. of V. Vindicated," namely, the Cheselden experiment, "Philosoph. Trans.," No. 402. Professor Fraser cites other instances in "Phil. Trans." for 1801, 1807, 1826, and in Nunneley's "The Organs of Vision" (1858).

tangible earth and man are entirely different from those which constitute the visible earth and man. Nor was it possible, by virtue of the visive faculty alone, without superadding any experience of touch, or altering the position of the eye, ever to have known, or so much as suspected, there had been any relation or connexion between them. Hence, a man at first view would not denominate anything he saw, "earth," or "head," or 'foot;" and consequently, he could not tell, by the mere act of vision, whether the head or feet were nearest the earth. Nor, indeed, would we have thereby any thought of earth or man, erect or inverse, at all—which will be made yet more evident, if we nicely observe, and make a particular comparison between, the ideas of both senses.

103. That which I see is only variety of light and colours. That which I feel is hard or soft, hot or cold, rough or smooth. What similitude, what connexion, have those ideas with these? Or, how is it possible that any one should see reason to give one and the same name to combinations of ideas so very different, before he had experienced their co-existence? We do not find there is any necessary connexion betwixt this or that tangible quality, and any colour whatso ever. And we may sometimes perceive colours, where there is nothing to be felt. All which doth make it manifest that no man, at first receiving of his sight, would know there was any agreement between this or that particular object of his sight and any object of touch he had been already acquainted with. The colours therefore of the head would to him no more suggest the idea of head than they would the idea or feet.

104. Farther, we have at large shewn (vide sect. 63 and 64) there is no discoverable necessary connexion between any given visible magnitude and any one particular tangible magnitude; but that it is entirely the result of custom and experience, and depends on foreign and accidental circum-stances, that we can, by the perception of visible extension, inform ourselves what may be the extension of any tangible object connected with it. Hence, it is certain, that neither the visible magnitude of head or foot would bring along with them into the mind, at first opening of the eyes, the respec-tive tangible magnitudes of those parts.

105. By the foregoing section, it is plain the visible figure

of any part of the body hath no necessary connexion with the tangible figure thereof, so as at first sight to suggest it to the mind. For, figure is the termination of magnitude. Whence it follows that no visible magnitude having in its own nature an aptness to suggest any one particular tangible magnitude, so neither can any visible figure be inseparably connected with its corresponding tangible figure, so as of itself, and in a way prior to experience, it might suggest it to the understanding. This will be farther evident, if we consider that what seems smooth and round to the touch may to sight, if viewed through a microscope, seem quite otherwise.

106. From all which, laid together and duly considered, we may clearly deduce this inference :—In the first act of vision, no idea entering by the eye would have a perceivable connexion with the ideas to which the names earth, man, head, foot, &c., were annexed in the understanding of a person blind from his birth ; so as in any sort to introduce them into his mind, or make themselves be called by the same names, and reputed the same things with them, as afterwards they come to be.

107. There doth, nevertheless, remain one difficulty, which to some may seem to press hard on our opinion, and deserve not to be passed over. For, though it be granted that neither the colour, size, nor figure of the visible feet have any necessary connexion with the ideas that compose the tangible feet, so as to bring them at first sight into my mind, or make me in danger of confounding them, before I had been used to and for some time experienced their connexion ; yet thus much seems undeniable, namely, that the number of the visible feet being the same with that of the tangible feet, I may from hence, without any experience of sight, reasonably conclude that they represent or are connected with the feet rather than the head. I say, it seems the idea of two visible feet will sooner suggest to the mind the idea of two tangible feet than of one head—so that the blind man, upon first reception of the visive faculty, might know which were the feet or two, and which the head or one.

108. In order to get clear of this seeming difficulty, we need only observe that diversity of visible objects does not necessarily infer diversity of tangible objects corresponding to them. A picture painted with great variety of colours

affects the touch in one uniform manner; it is therefore evident that I do not, by any necessary consecution, independent of experience, judge of the number of things tangible from the number of things visible. I should not therefore at first opening my eyes conclude that because I see two I shall feel two. How, therefore, can I, before experience teaches me, know that the visible legs, because two, are connected with the tangible legs; or the visible head, because one, is connected with the tangible head? The truth is, the things I see are so very different and heterogeneous from the things I feel that the perception of the one would never have suggested the other to my thoughts, or enabled me to pass the least judgment thereon, until I had experienced their connexion.

109. But, for a fuller illustration of this matter, it ought to be considered, that number (however some may reckon it amongst the primary qualities) is nothing fixed and settled, really existing in things themselves. It is entirely the creature of the mind, considering either a simple idea by itself, or any combination of simple ideas to which it gives one name, and so makes it pass for a unit. According as the mind variously combines its ideas, the unit varies; and as the unit, so the number, which is only a collection of units, doth also vary. We call a window one, a chimney one; and yet a house, in which there are many windows and many chimneys, has an equal right to be called one; and many houses go to the making of one city. In these and the like instances, it is evident the *unit* constantly relates to the particular draughts the mind makes of its ideas, to which it affixes names, and wherein it includes more or less, as best suits its own ends and purposes. Whatever therefore the mind considers as one, that is an unit. Every combination of ideas is considered as one thing by the mind, and in token thereof is marked by one name. Now, this naming and combining together of ideas is perfectly arbitrary, and done by the mind in such sort as experience shews it to be most convenient—without which our ideas had never been collected into such sundry distinct combinations as they now are.

110. Hence, it follows that a man born blind, and afterwards, when grown up, made to see, would not, in the first

act of vision, parcel out the ideas of sight into the same distinct collections that others do who have experienced which do regularly co-exist and are proper to be bundled up together under one name. He would not, for example, make into one complex idea, and thereby esteem and unite all those particular ideas which constitute the visible head or foot. For, there can be no reason assigned why he should do so, barely upon his seeing a man stand upright before him. There crowd into his mind the ideas which compose the visible man, in company with all the other ideas of sight perceived at the same time. But, all these ideas offered at once to his view he would not distribute into sundry distinct combinations, till such time as, by observing the motion of the parts of the man and other experiences, he comes to know which are to be separated and which to be collected together.

111. From what hath been premised, it is plain the objects of sight and touch make, if I may so say, two sets of ideas, which are widely different from each other. To objects of either kind we indifferently attribute the terms high and low, right and left, and such like, denoting the position or situation of things; but then we must well observe that the position of any object is determined with respect only to objects of the same sense. We say any object of touch is high or low, according as it is more or less distant from the tangible earth: and in like manner we denominate any object of sight high or low, in proportion as it is more or less distant from the visible earth. But, to define the situation of visible things with relation to the distance they bear from any tangible thing, or *vice versa*, this were absurd and perfectly unintelligible. For all visible things are equally in the mind, and take up no part of the external space; and consequently are equidistant from any tangible thing which exists without the mind.

112. Or rather, to speak truly, the proper objects of sight are at no distance, neither near nor far from any tangible thing. For, if we inquire narrowly into the matter, we shall find that those things only are compared together in respect of distance which exist after the same manner, or appertain unto the same sense. For, by the distance between any two points, nothing more is meant than the number of inter-

mediate points. If the given points are visible, the distance between them is marked out by the number of the interjacent visible points; if they are tangible, the distance between them is a line consisting of tangible points; but, if they are one tangible and the other visible, the distance between them doth neither consist of points perceivable by sight nor by touch, *i.e.* it is utterly inconceivable. This, perhaps, will not find an easy admission into all men's understanding. However, I should gladly be informed whether it be not true, by any one who will be at the pains to reflect a little, and apply it home to his thoughts.

113. The not observing what has been delivered in the two last sections, seems to have occasioned no small part of the difficulty that occurs in the business of direct appearances. The head, which is painted nearest the earth, seems to be farthest from it; and on the other hand, the feet, which are painted farthest from the earth, are thought nearest to it. Herein lies the difficulty, which vanishes if we express the thing more clearly and free from ambiguity, thus:—How comes it that, to the eye, the visible head, which is nearest the tangible earth, seems farthest from the earth; and the visible feet, which are farthest from the tangible earth, seem nearest the earth? The question being thus proposed, who sees not the difficulty is founded on a supposition that the eye or visive faculty, or rather the soul by means thereof, should judge of the situation of visible objects with reference to their distance from the tangible earth? Whereas, it is evident the tangible earth is not perceived by sight. And it hath been shewn, in the two last preceding sections, that the location of visible objects is determined only by the distance they bear from one another, and that it is nonsense to talk of distance, far or near, between a visible and tangible thing.

114. If we confine our thoughts to the proper objects of sight, the whole is plain and easy. The head is painted farthest from, and the feet nearest to, the visible earth; and so they appear to be. What is there strange or unaccountable in this? Let us suppose the pictures in the fund of the eye to be the immediate objects of sight. The consequence is that things should appear in the same posture they are painted in; and is it not so? The head which is

seen seems farthest from the earth which is seen ; and the feet which are seen seem nearest to the earth which is seen. And just so they are painted.

115. But, say you, the picture of the man is inverted, and yet the appearance is erect. I ask, what mean you by the picture of the man, or, which is the same thing, the visible man's being inverted ? You tell me it is inverted, because the heels are uppermost and the head undermost ? Explain me this. You say that by the head's being undermost, you mean that it is nearest to the earth ; and, by the heels being uppermost, that they are farthest from the earth. I ask again, what earth you mean ? You cannot mean the earth that is painted on the eye or the visible earth—for the picture of the head is farthest from the picture of the earth, and the picture of the feet nearest to the picture of the earth ; and accordingly the visible head is farthest from the visible earth, and the visible feet nearest to it. It remains, therefore, that you mean the tangible earth ; and so determine the situation of visible things with respect to tangible things —contrary to what hath been demonstrated in sect. 111 and 112. The two distinct provinces of sight and touch should be considered apart, and as though their objects had no intercourse, no manner of relation to one another, in point of distance or position.

116. Farther, what greatly contributes to make us mistake in this matter is that, when we think of the pictures in the fund of the eye, we imagine ourselves looking on the fund of another's eye, or another looking on the fund of our own eye, and beholding the pictures painted thereon. Suppose two eyes, A and B. A from some distance looking on the pictures in B sees them inverted, and for that reason concludes they are inverted in B. But this is wrong. There are projected in little on the bottom of A the images of the pictures of, suppose, man, earth, &c., which are painted on B. And, besides these, the eye B itself, and the objects which environ it, together with another earth, are projected in a larger size on A. Now, by the eye A these larger images are deemed the true objects, and the lesser only pictures in miniature. And it is with respect to those greater images that it determines the situation of the smaller images ; so that, comparing the little man with the great

earth, A judges him inverted, or that the feet are farthest from and the head nearest to the great earth. Whereas, if A compare the little man with the little earth, then he will appear erect, *i.e.* his head shall seem farthest from and his feet nearest to the little earth. But we must consider that B does not see two earths as A does. It sees only what is represented by the little pictures in A, and consequently shall judge the man erect. For, in truth, the man in B is not inverted, for there the feet are next the earth ; but it is the representation of it in A which is inverted, for there the head of the representation of the picture of the man in B is next the earth, and the feet farthest from the earth—meaning the earth which is without the representation of the pictures in B. For, if you take the little images of the pictures in B, and consider them by themselves, and with respect only to one another, they are all erect and in their natural posture.

117. Farther, there lies a mistake in our imagining that the pictures of external objects are painted on the bottom of the eye. It has been shewn there is no resemblance between the ideas of sight and things tangible. It hath likewise been demonstrated, that the proper objects of sight do not exist without the mind. Whence it clearly follows that the pictures painted on the bottom of the eye are not the pictures of external objects. Let any one consult his own thoughts, and then tell me, what affinity, what likeness, there is between that certain variety and disposition of colours which constitute the visible man, or picture of a man, and that other combination of far different ideas, sensible by touch, which compose the tangible man. But, if this be the case, how come they to be accounted pictures or images, since that supposes them to copy or represent some originals or other?

118. To which I answer—In the forementioned instance, the eye A takes the little images, included within the representation of the other eye B, to be pictures or copies, whereof the archetypes are not things existing without, but the larger pictures projected on its own fund ; and which by A are not thought pictures, but the originals or true things themselves. Though if we suppose a third eye C, from a due distance, to behold the fund of A, then indeed the

things projected thereon shall, to *C*, seem pictures or images, in the same sense that those projected on *B* do to *A*.

119. Rightly to conceive the business in hand, we must carefully distinguish between the ideas of sight and touch, between the visible and tangible eye ; for certainly on the tangible eye nothing either is or seems to be painted. Again, the visible eye, as well as all other visible objects, hath been shewn to exist only in the mind ; which, perceiving its own ideas, and comparing them together, does call some pictures in respect to others. What hath been said, being rightly comprehended and laid together, does, I think, afford a full and genuine explication of the erect appearance of objects—which phenomenon, I must confess, I do not see how it can be explained by any theories of vision hitherto made public.

120. In treating of these things, the use of language is apt to occasion some obscurity and confusion, and create in us wrong ideas. For, language being accommodated to the common notions and prejudices of men, it is scarce possible to deliver the naked and precise truth, without great circumlocution, impropriety, and (to an unwary reader) seeming contradictions. I do, therefore, once for all, desire whoever shall think it worth his while to understand what I have written concerning vision, that he would not stick in this or that phrase or manner of expression, but candidly collect my meaning from the whole sum and tenor of my discourse, and, laying aside the words as much as possible, consider the bare notions themselves, and then judge whether they are agreeable to truth and his own experience or no.

121. We have shewn the way wherein the mind, by mediation of visible ideas, doth perceive or apprehend the distance, magnitude, and situation of tangible objects. I come now to inquire more particularly concerning the difference between the ideas of sight and touch which are called by the same names, and see whether there be any idea common to both senses. From what we have at large set forth and demonstrated in the foregoing parts of this treatise, it is plain there is no one self-same numerical extension, perceived both by sight and touch ; but that the particular figures and extensions perceived by sight, however

they may be called by the same names, and reputed the same things with those perceived by touch, are nevertheless different, and have an existence very distinct and separate from them. So that the question is not now concerning the same numerical ideas, but whether there be any one and the same sort or species of ideas equally perceivable to both senses? or, in other words, whether extension, figure, and motion perceived by sight, are not specifically distinct from extension, figure, and motion perceived by touch?

122. But, before I come more particularly to discuss this matter, I find it proper to take into my thoughts extension in abstract. For of this there is much talk; and I am apt to think that when men speak of extension as being an idea common to two senses, it is with a secret supposition that we can single out extension from all other tangible and visible qualities, and form thereof an abstract idea, which idea they will have common both to sight and touch. We are therefore to understand by extension in abstract, an idea of extension—for instance, a line or surface entirely stripped of all other sensible qualities and circumstances that might determine it to any particular existence; it is neither black, nor white, nor red, nor hath it any colour at all, or any tangible quality whatsoever, and consequently it is of no finite determinate magnitude; for that which bounds or distinguishes one extension from another is some quality or circumstance wherein they disagree.

123. Now, I do not find that I can perceive, imagine, or anywise frame in my mind such an abstract idea as is here spoken of. A line or surface which is neither black, nor white, nor blue, nor yellow, &c.; nor long, nor short, nor rough, nor smooth, nor square, nor round, &c., is perfectly incomprehensible. This I am sure of as to myself; how far the faculties of other men may reach they best can tell.

124. It is commonly said that the object of geometry is abstract extension. But geometry contemplates figures: now, figure is the termination of magnitude; but we have shewn that extension in abstract hath no finite determinate magnitude; whence it clearly follows that it can have no figure, and consequently is not the object of geometry. It

is indeed a tenet, as well of the modern as the ancient philosophers, that all general truths are concerning universal abstract ideas; without which, we are told, there could be no science, no demonstration of any general proposition in geometry. But it were no hard matter, did I think it necessary to my present purpose, to shew that propositions and demonstrations in geometry might be universal, though they who make them never think of abstract general ideas of triangles or circles.

125. After reiterated endeavours to apprehend the general idea of a triangle, I have found it altogether incomprehensible. And surely, if any one were able to let that idea into my mind, it must be the author of the "Essay concerning Human Understanding": he, who has so far distinguished himself from the generality of writers, by the clearness and significancy of what he says. Let us therefore see how this celebrated author describes the general or abstract idea of a triangle. "It must be," says he, "neither oblique nor rectangle, neither equilateral, equicrural, nor scalenum; but all and none of these at once. In effect it is somewhat imperfect that cannot exist; an idea, wherein some parts of several different and inconsistent ideas are put together." ("Essay on Human Understanding," B. iv. ch. 7. s. 9.) This is the idea which he thinks needful for the enlargement of knowledge, which is the subject of mathematical demonstration, and without which we could never come to know any general proposition concerning triangles.[1] That author acknowledges it doth "require some pains and skill to form this general idea of a triangle." (*Ibid.*) But, had he called to mind what he says in another place, to wit, "that ideas of mixed modes wherein any inconsistent ideas are put together, cannot so much as exist in the mind, *i.e.* be conceived," (vide B. iii. ch. 10. s. 33, *ibid.*)—I say, had this occurred to his thoughts, it is not improbable he would have owned it above all the pains and skill he was master of, to form the above-mentioned idea of a triangle, which is made up of

---

[1] The following passage was omitted from this place in the last edition: "Sure I am, if this be the case, it is impossible for me to attain to know even the first elements of geometry: since I have not the faculty to frame in my mind such an idea as is here described."

manifest staring contradictions. That a man, who thought so much and so well, and laid so great a stress on clear and determinate ideas, should nevertheless talk at this rate, seems very surprising. But the wonder will lessen, if it be considered that the source whence this opinion flows is the prolific womb which has brought forth innumerable errors and difficulties, in all parts of philosophy, and in all the sciences. But this matter, taken in its full extent, were a subject too vast and comprehensive to be insisted on in this place.[1] And so much for extension in abstract.

126. Some, perhaps, may think pure space, vacuum, or trine dimension, to be equally the object of sight and touch. But, though we have a very great propension to think the ideas of outness and space to be the immediate object of sight, yet, if I mistake not, in the foregoing parts of this Essay, that hath been clearly demonstrated to be a mere delusion, arising from the quick and sudden suggestion of fancy, which so closely connects the idea of distance with those of sight, that we are apt to think it is itself a proper and immediate object of that sense, till reason corrects the mistake.

127. It having been shewn that there are no abstract ideas of figure, and that it is impossible for us, by any precision of thought, to frame an idea of extension separate from all other visible and tangible qualities, which shall be common both to sight and touch—the question now remaining is, whether the particular extensions, figures, and motions perceived by sight, be of the same kind with the particular extensions, figures, and motions perceived by touch? In answer to which I shall venture to lay down the following proposition :—*The extension, figures, and motions perceived by sight are specifically distinct from the ideas of touch, called by the same names; nor is there any such thing as one idea,*

---

[1] Between this sentence and the last phrase of the section stood, in the first two editions, the following paragraph : "I shall only observe that your metaphysicians and men of speculation seem to have faculties distinct from those of ordinary men, when they talk of general or abstracted triangles and circles, &c., and so peremptorily declare them to be the subject of all the eternal, immutable, universal truths in geometry."

or kind of idea, common to both senses. This proposition may, without much difficulty, be collected from what hath been said in several places of this Essay. But, because it seems so remote from, and contrary to the received notions and settled opinion of mankind, I shall attempt to demonstrate it more particularly and at large by the following arguments :—

128. When, upon perception of an idea, I range it under this or that sort, it is because it is perceived after the same manner, or because it has a likeness or conformity with, or affects me in the same way as the ideas of the sort I rank it under. In short, it must not be entirely new, but have something in it old and already perceived by me. It must, I say, have so much, at least, in common with the ideas I have before known and named, as to make me give it the same name with them. But, it has been, if I mistake not, clearly made out that a man born blind would not, at first reception of his sight, think the things he saw were of the same nature with the objects of touch, or had anything in common with them ; but that they were a new set of ideas, perceived in a new manner, and entirely different from all he had ever perceived before. So that he would not call them by the same name, nor repute them to be of the same sort, with anything he had hitherto known.[1]

129. *Secondly*, Light and colours are allowed by all to constitute a sort or species entirely different from the ideas of touch ; nor will any man, I presume, say they can make themselves perceived by that sense. But there is no other immediate object of sight besides light and colours. It is therefore a direct consequence, that there is no idea common to both senses.

130. It is a prevailing opinion, even amongst those who have thought and writ most accurately concerning our ideas, and the ways whereby they enter into the understanding, that something more is perceived by sight than barely light

---

[1] Here, in the first two editions, followed this passage : " And surely the judgment of such an unprejudiced person is more to be relied on in this case than the sentiments of the generality of men ; who, in this as in almost everything else, suffer themselves to be guided by custom, and the erroneous suggestions of prejudice, rather than reason and sedate reflexion."

and colours with their variations. Mr. Locke termeth sight
" the most comprehensive of all our senses, conveying to our
minds the ideas of light and colours, which are peculiar only
to that sense; and also the far different ideas of space, figure,
and motion." ("Essay on Human Understanding," B. ii.
ch. 9. s. 9.) Space or distance, we have shewn, is no
otherwise the object of sight than of hearing. (Vide sect.
46.) And, as for figure and extension, I leave it to anyone
that shall calmly attend to his own clear and distinct ideas
to decide whether he has any idea intromitted immediately
and properly by sight save only light and colours : or,
whether it be possible for him to frame in his mind a distinct
abstract idea of visible extension, or figure, exclusive of all
colour ; and, on the other hand, whether he can conceive
colour without visible extension ? For my own part, I must
confess, I am not able to attain so great a nicety of abstraction. I know very well that, in a strict sense, I see nothing
but light and colours, with their several shades and variations. He who beside these doth also perceive by sight
ideas far different and distinct from them, hath that faculty
in a degree more perfect and comprehensive than I can
pretend to. It must be owned, indeed, that, by the mediation of light and colours, other far different ideas are
suggested to my mind. But so they are by hearing, which,
besides sounds which are peculiar to that sense, doth, by
their mediation, suggest not only space, figure, and motion,
but also all other ideas whatsoever that can be signified by
words.

131. *Thirdly*, It is, I think, an axiom universally received,
that "quantities of the same kind may be added together
and make one entire sum." Mathematicians add lines together ; but they do not add a line to a solid, or conceive it
as making one sum with a surface. These three kinds of
quantity being thought incapable of any such mutual addition, and consequently of being compared together in the
several ways of proportion, are by them for that reason
esteemed entirely disparate and heterogeneous. Now let
anyone try in his thoughts to add a visible line or surface to
a tangible line or surface, so as to conceive them making one
continued sum or whole. He that can do this may think
them homogeneous ; but he that cannot must, by the fore-

going axiom, think them heterogeneous.[1] A blue and a red line I can conceive added together into one sum and making one continued line ; but, to make, in my thoughts, one continued line of a visible and tangible line added together, is, I find, a task far more difficult, and even insurmountable ; and I leave it to the reflection and experience of every particular person to determine for himself.

132. A farther confirmation of our tenet may be drawn from the solution of Mr. Molyneux's problem, published by Mr. Locke in his " Essay : " which I shall set down as it there lies, together with Mr. Locke's opinion of it :—
" Suppose a man born blind, and now adult, and taught by his touch to distinguish between a cube and a sphere of the same metal, and nighly of the same bigness, so as to tell when he felt one and the other, which is the cube, and which the sphere. Suppose then the cube and sphere placed on a table, and the blind man made to see : Quære, Whether by his sight, before he touched them, he could now distinguish, and tell, which is the globe, which the cube. To which the acute and judicious proposer answers : Not. For, though he has obtained the experience of how a globe, how a cube affects his touch ; yet he has not yet attained the experience, that what affects his touch so or so must affect his sight so or so : or that a protuberant angle in the cube, that pressed his hand unequally, shall appear to his eye as it doth in the cube. I agree with this thinking gentleman, whom I am proud to call my friend, in his answer to this his problem ; and am of opinion that the blind man, at first sight, would not be able with certainty to say, which was the globe, which the cube, whilst he only saw them."
(" Essay on Human Understanding," B. ii. ch. 9. s. 8.)

133. Now, if a square surface perceived by touch be of the same sort with a square surface perceived by sight, it is certain the blind man here mentioned might know a square surface as soon as he saw it. It is no more but introducing into his mind, by a new inlet, an idea he has been already well acquainted with. Since therefore he is supposed to have known by his touch that a cube is a body terminated by square surfaces ; and that a sphere is not terminated by

[1] In the first two editions here followed : " I acknowledge myself to be of the latter sort."

square surfaces—upon the supposition that a visible and
tangible square differ only *in numero*, it follows that he might
know, by the unerring mark of the square surfaces, which
was the cube, and which not, while he only saw them.   We
must therefore allow, either that visible extension and figures
are specially distinct from tangible extension and figures, or
else, that the solution of this problem, given by those two
thoughtful and ingenious men, is wrong.

134. Much more might be laid together in proof of the
proposition I have advanced.   But, what has been said is, if
I mistake not, sufficient to convince any one that shall yield
a reasonable attention.   And, as for those that will not be
at the pains of a little thought, no multiplication of words
will ever suffice to make them understand the truth, or
rightly conceive my meaning.

135. I cannot let go the above-mentioned problem without
some reflexion on it.   It hath been made evident that a
man blind from his birth would not, at first sight, denominate
anything he saw, by the names he had been used to appropriate to ideas of touch.   (Vide sect. 106.)   Cube, sphere,
table are words he has known applied to things perceivable
by touch, but to things perfectly intangible he never knew
them applied.   Those words, in their wonted application,
always marked out to his mind bodies or solid things which
were perceived by the resistance they gave.   But there is no
solidity, no resistance or protrusion, perceived by sight.   In
short, the ideas of sight are all new perceptions, to which
there be no names annexed in his mind ; he cannot therefore understand what is said to him concerning them.   And,
to ask of the two bodies he saw placed on the table, which
was the sphere, which the cube, were to him a question
downright bantering and unintelligible ; nothing he sees
being able to suggest to his thoughts the idea of body,
distance, or, in general, of anything he had already known.

136. It is a mistake to think the same thing affects both
sight and touch.   If the same angle or square which is the
object of touch be also the object of vision, what should
hinder the blind man, at first sight, from knowing it ?   For,
though the manner wherein it affects the sight be different
from that wherein it affected his touch, yet, there being,
beside this manner or circumstance, which is new and un-

known, the angle or figure, which is old and known, he cannot choose but discern it.

137. Visible figure and extension having been demonstrated to be of a nature entirely different and heterogeneous from tangible figure and extension, it remains that we inquire concerning motion. Now, that visible motion is not of the same sort with tangible motion seems to need no further proof; it being an evident corollary from what we have shewn concerning the difference there is betwixt visible and tangible extension. But, for a more full and express proof hereof, we need only observe that one who had not yet experienced vision would not at first sight know motion. Whence it clearly follows that motion perceivable by sight is of a sort distinct from motion perceivable by touch. The antecedent I prove thus—By touch he could not perceive any motion but what was up or down, to the right or left, nearer or farther from him; besides these, and their several varieties or complications, it is impossible he should have any idea of motion. He would not therefore think anything to be motion, or give the name motion to any idea, which he could not range under some or other of those particular kinds thereof. But, from sect. 95, it is plain that, by the mere act of vision, he could not know motion upwards or downwards, to the right or left, or in any other possible direction. From which I conclude, he would not know motion at all at first sight. As for the idea of motion in abstract, I shall not waste paper about it, but leave it to my reader to make the best he can of it. To me it is perfectly unintelligible.

138. The consideration of motion may furnish a new field for inquiry. But, since the manner wherein the mind apprehends by sight the motion of tangible objects, with the various degrees thereof, may be easily collected from what has been said concerning the manner wherein that sense doth suggest their various distances, magnitudes, and situations, I shall not enlarge any farther on this subject, but proceed to inquire what may be alleged, with greatest appearance of reason, against the proposition we have demonstrated to be true; for, where there is so much prejudice to be encountered, a bare and naked demonstration of the truth will scarce suffice. We must also satisfy

the scruples that men may start in favour of their preconceived notions, shew whence the mistake arises, how it came
to spread, and carefully disclose and root out those false
persuasions that an early prejudice might have implanted in
the mind.

139. *First*, therefore, it will be demanded how visible extension and figures come to be called by the same name
with tangible extension and figures, if they are not of the
same kind with them? It must be something more than
humour or accident that could occasion a custom so constant
and universal as this, which has obtained in all ages and
nations of the world, and amongst all ranks of men, the
learned as well as the illiterate.

140. To which I answer, we can no more argue a visible
and tangible square to be of the same species, from their
being called by the same name, than we can that a tangible
square, and the monosyllable consisting of six letters whereby it is marked, are of the same species, because they are
both called by the same name. It is customary to call
written words, and the things they signify, by the same name :
for, words not being regarded in their own nature, or otherwise than as they are marks of things, it had been superfluous, and beside the design of language, to have given
them names distinct from those of the things marked by
them. The same reason holds here also. Visible figures
are the marks of tangible figures ; and, from sect. 59, it is
plain that in themselves they are little regarded, or upon
any other score than for their connexion with tangible
figures, which by nature they are ordained to signify. And,
because this language of nature does not vary in different ages
or nations, hence it is that in all times and places visible
figures are called by the same names as the respective
tangible figures suggested by them ; and not because they
are alike, or of the same sort with them.

141. But, say you, surely a tangible square is liker to a
visible square than to a visible circle : it has four angles,
and as many sides ; so also has the visible square—but the
visible circle has no such thing, being bounded by one
uniform curve, without right lines or angles, which makes it
unfit to represent the tangible square, but very fit to represent
the tangible circle. Whence it clearly follows, that visible

figures are patterns of, or of the same species with, the respective tangible figures represented by them; that they are like unto them, and of their own nature fitted to represent them, as being of the same sort; and that they are in no respect arbitrary signs, as words.

142. I answer, it must be acknowledged the visible square is fitter than the visible circle to represent the tangible square, but then it is not because it is liker, or more of a species with it; but, because the visible square contains in it several distinct parts, whereby to mark the several distinct corresponding parts of a tangible square, whereas the visible circle doth not. The square perceived by touch hath four distinct equal sides, so also hath it four distinct equal angles. It is therefore necessary that the visible figure which shall be most proper to mark it contain four distinct equal parts, corresponding to the four sides of the tangible square; as likewise four other distinct and equal parts, whereby to denote the four equal angles of the tangible square. And accordingly we see the visible figures contain in them distinct visible parts, answering to the distinct tangible parts of the figures signified or suggested by them.

143. But, it will not hence follow that any visible figure is like unto or of the same species with its corresponding tangible figure, unless it be also shewn that not only the number, but also the kind of the parts be the same in both. To illustrate this, I observe that visible figures represent tangible figures much after the same manner that written words do sounds. Now, in this respect, words are not arbitrary; it not being indifferent what written word stands for any sound. But, it is requisite that each word contain in it as many distinct characters as there are variations in the sound it stands for. Thus, the single letter *a* is proper to mark one simple uniform sound; and the word *adultery* is accommodated to represent the sound annexed to it, in the formation whereof there being eight different collisions or modifications of the air by the organs of speech, each of which produces a difference of sound, it was fit the word representing it should consist of as many distinct characters, thereby to mark each particular difference or part of the whole sound. And yet nobody, I presume, will say the single letter *a*, or the word *adultery*, are alike unto or of the same species with

the respective sounds by them represented. It is indeed arbitrary that, in general, letters of any language represent sounds at all ; but, when that is once agreed, it is not arbitrary what combination of letters shall represent this or that particular sound. I leave this with the reader to pursue, and apply it in his own thoughts.

144. It must be confessed that we are not so apt to confound other signs with the things signified, or to think them of the same species, as we are visible and tangible ideas. But, a little consideration will shew us how this may well be, without our supposing them of a like nature. These signs are constant and universal ; their connexion with tangible ideas has been learnt at our first entrance into the world ; and ever since, almost every moment of our lives, it has been occurring to our thoughts, and fastening and striking deeper on our minds. When we observe that signs are variable, and of human institution; when we remember there was a time they were not connected in our minds with those things they now so readily suggest, but that their signification was learned by the slow steps of experience : this preserves us from confounding them. But, when we find the same signs suggest the same things all over the world ; when we know they are not of human institution, and cannot remember that we ever learned their signification, but think that at first sight they would have suggested to us the same things they do now : all this persuades us they are of the same species as the things respectively represented by them, and that it is by a natural resemblance they suggest them to our minds.

145. Add to this that whenever we make a nice survey of any object, successively directing the optic axis to each point thereof, there are certain lines and figures, described by the motion of the head or eye, which, being in truth perceived by feeling, do nevertheless so mix themselves, as it were, with the ideas of sight that we can scarce think but they appertain to that sense. Again, the ideas of sight enter into the mind several at once, more distinct and unmingled than is usual in the other senses beside the touch. Sounds, for example, perceived at the same instant, are apt to coalesce, if I may so say, into one sound : but we can perceive, at the same time, great variety of visible objects, very separate and distinct

from each other.   Now, tangible extension being made up of several distinct coexistent parts, we may hence gather another reason that may dispose us to imagine a likeness or analogy between the immediate objects of sight and touch. But nothing, certainly, doth more contribute to blend and confound them together, than the strict and close connexion they have with each other.   We cannot open our eyes but the ideas of distance, bodies, and tangible figures are suggested by them.   So swift, and sudden, and unperceived is the transit from visible to tangible ideas that we can scarce forbear thinking them equally the immediate object of vision.

146. The prejudice which is grounded on these, and whatever other causes may be assigned thereof, sticks so fast on our understandings, that it is impossible, without obstinate striving and labour of the mind, to get entirely clear of it. But then the reluctancy we find in rejecting any opinion can be no argument of its truth, to whoever considers what has been already shewn with regard to the prejudices we entertain concerning the distance, magnitude, and situation of objects; prejudices so familiar to our minds, so confirmed and inveterate, as they will hardly give way to the clearest demonstration.

147. Upon the whole, I think we may fairly conclude that the proper objects of vision constitute the universal language of nature, whereby we are instructed how to regulate our actions, in order to attain those things that are necessary to the preservation and well-being of our bodies, as also to avoid whatever may be hurtful and destructive of them.   It is by their information that we are principally guided in all the transactions and concerns of life.   And the manner wherein they signify and mark out unto us the objects which are at a distance is the same with that of languages and signs of human appointment; which do not suggest the things signified by any likeness or identity of nature, but only by an habitual connexion that experience has made us to observe between them.

148. Suppose one who had always continued blind be told by his guide that after he has advanced so many steps he shall come to the brink of a precipice, or be stopped by a wall; must not this to him seem very admirable and sur-

prising? He cannot conceive how it is possible for mortals to frame such predictions as these, which to him would seem as strange and unaccountable as prophecy does to others. Even they who are blessed with the visive faculty may (though familiarity make it less observed) find therein sufficient cause of admiration. The wonderful art and contrivance wherewith it is adjusted to those ends and purposes for which it was apparently designed; the vast extent, number, and variety of objects that are at once, with so much ease, and quickness, and pleasure, suggested by it—all these afford subject for much and pleasing speculation, and may, if anything, give us some glimmering analogous prænotion of things, that are placed beyond the certain discovery and comprehension of our present state.

149. I do not design to trouble myself much with drawing corollaries from the doctrine I have hitherto laid down. If it bears the test, others may, so far as they shall think convenient, employ their thoughts in extending it farther, and applying it to whatever purposes it may be subservient to. Only, I cannot forbear making some inquiry concerning the object of geometry, which the subject we have been upon does naturally lead one to. We have shewn there is no such idea as that of extension in abstract; and that there are two kinds of sensible extension and figures, which are entirely distinct and heterogeneous from each other. Now, it is natural to inquire which of these is the object of geometry.

150. Some things there are which, at first sight, incline one to think geometry conversant about visible extension. The constant use of the eyes, both in the practical and speculative parts of that science, doth very much induce us thereto. It would, without doubt, seem odd to a mathematician to go about to convince him the diagrams he saw upon paper were not the figures, or even the likeness of the figures, which make the subject of the demonstration—the contrary being held an unquestionable truth, not only by mathematicians, but also by those who apply themselves more particularly to the study of logic; I mean who consider the nature of science, certainty, and demonstration; it being by them assigned as one reason of the extraordinary clearness

and evidence of geometry, that in that science the reasonings are free from those inconveniences which attend the use of arbitrary signs, the very ideas themselves being copied out, and exposed to view upon paper. But, by the bye, how well this agrees with what they likewise assert of abstract ideas being the object of geometrical demonstration I leave to be considered.

151. To come to a resolution in this point, we need only observe what has been said in sect. 59, 60, 61, where it is shewn that visible extensions in themselves are little regarded, and have no settled determinate greatness, and that men measure altogether by the application of tangible extension to tangible extension. All which makes it evident that visible extension and figures are not the object of geometry.

152. It is therefore plain that visible figures are of the same use in geometry that words are. And the one may as well be accounted the object of that science as the other; neither of them being any otherwise concerned therein than as they represent or suggest to the mind the particular tangible figures connected with them. There is, indeed, this difference betwixt the signification of tangible figures by visible figures, and of ideas by words: that whereas the latter is variable and uncertain, depending altogether on the arbitrary appointment of men, the former is fixed, and immutably the same in all times and places. A visible square, for instance, suggests to the mind the same tangible figure in Europe that it doth in America. Hence it is, that the voice of nature, which speaks to our eyes, is not liable to that misinterpretation and ambiguity that languages of human contrivance are unavoidably subject to. From which may, in some measure, be derived that peculiar evidence and clearness of geometrical demonstrations.

153. Though what has been said may suffice to shew what ought to be determined with relation to the object of geometry, I shall, nevertheless, for the fuller illustration thereof, take into my thoughts the case of an intelligence or unbodied spirit, which is supposed to see perfectly well, *i.e.* to have a clear perception of the proper and immediate objects of sight, but to have no sense of touch. Whether there be any such being in nature or no, is beside my purpose to inquire; it suffices, that the supposition contains no contradiction in it.

Let us now examine what proficiency such a one may be able to make in geometry. Which speculation will lead us more clearly to see whether the ideas of sight can possibly be the object of that science.

154. *First*, then, it is certain the aforesaid intelligence could have no idea of a solid or quantity of three dimensions, which follows from its not having any idea of distance. We, indeed, are prone to think that we have by sight the ideas of space and solids; which arises from our imagining that we do, strictly speaking, see distance, and some parts of an object at a greater distance than others; which has been demonstrated to be the effect of the experience we have had what ideas of touch are connected with such and such ideas attending vision. But the intelligence here spoken of is supposed to have no experience of touch. He would not, therefore, judge as we do, nor have any idea of distance, out-ness, or profundity, nor consequently of space or body, either immediately or by suggestion. Whence it is plain he can have no notion of those parts of geometry which relate to the mensuration of solids, and their convex or concave surfaces, and contemplate the properties of lines generated by the section of a solid. The conceiving of any part whereof is beyond the reach of his faculties.

155. *Farther*, he cannot comprehend the manner wherein geometers describe a right line or circle; the rule and compass, with their use, being things of which it is impossible he should have any notion. Nor is it an easier matter for him to conceive the placing of one plane or angle on another, in order to prove their equality; since that supposes some idea of distance, or external space. All which makes it evident our pure intelligence could never attain to know so much as the first elements of plane geometry. And perhaps, upon a nice inquiry, it will be found he cannot even have an idea of plane figures any more than he can of solids; since some idea of distance is necessary to form the idea of a geometrical plane, as will appear to whoever shall reflect a little on it.

156. All that is properly perceived by the visive faculty amounts to no more than colours with their variations, and different proportions of light and shade; but the perpetual mutability and fleetingness of those immediate objects of sight render them incapable of being managed after the

manner of geometrical figures ; nor is it in any degree useful that they should. It is true there be divers of them perceived at once ; and more of some, and less of others : but accurately to compute their magnitude, and assign precise determinate proportions between things so variable and inconstant, if we suppose it possible to be done, must yet be a very trifling and insignificant labour.

157. I must confess, it seems to be the opinion of some very ingenious men that flat or plane figures are immediate objects of sight, though they acknowledge solids are not. And this opinion of theirs is grounded on what is observed in painting, wherein (say they) the ideas immediately imprinted in the mind are only of planes variously coloured, which, by a sudden act of the judgment, are changed into solids : but, with a little attention, we shall find the planes here mentioned as the immediate objects of sight are not visible but tangible planes. For, when we say that pictures are planes, we mean thereby that they appear to the touch smooth and uniform. But then this smoothness and uniformity, or, in other words, this planeness of the picture is not perceived immediately by vision ; for it appeareth to the eye various and multiform.

158 From all which we may conclude that planes are no more the immediate object of sight than solids. What we strictly see are not solids, nor yet planes variously coloured ; they are only diversity of colours. And some of hese suggest to the mind solids, and others plane figures ; just as they have been experienced to be connected with the one or the other : so that we see planes in the same way that we see solids ; both being equally suggested by the immediate objects of sight, which accordingly are themselves denominated planes and solids. But, though they are called by the same names with the things marked by them, they are, nevertheless, of a nature entirely different, as hath been demonstrated.

159. What has been said is, if I mistake not, sufficient to decide the question we proposed to examine, concerning the ability of a pure spirit, such as we have described, to know geometry. It is, indeed, no easy matter for us to enter precisely into the thoughts of such an intelligence ; because we cannot, without great pains, cleverly separate and disentangle

in our thoughts the proper objects of sight from those of touch which are connected with them. This, indeed, in a complete degree seems scarce possible to be performed; which will not seem strange to us, if we consider how hard it is for anyone to hear the words of his native language, which is familiar to him, pronounced in his ears without understanding them. Though he endeavour to disunite the meaning from the sound, it will nevertheless intrude into his thoughts, and he shall find it extreme difficult, if not impossible, to put himself exactly in the posture of a foreigner that never learnt the language, so as to be affected barely with the sounds themselves, and not perceive the signification annexed to them. By this time, I suppose, it is clear that neither abstract nor visible extension makes the object of geometry; the not discerning of which may, perhaps, have created some difficulty and useless labour in mathematics.[1]

[1] In the two editions previous to the last, the concluding sentence beginning "By this time" formed the first sentence of a section 160, which continued thus : " Sure I am that somewhat relating thereto has occurred to my thoughts, which, though after the most anxious and repeated examination I am forced to think it true, doth, nevertheless, seem so far out of the common road of geometry, that I know not whether it may not be thought presumption if I should make it public in an age wherein that science hath received such mighty improvements by new methods; great part whereof, as well as of the ancient discoveries, may perhaps lose their reputation, and much of that ardour with which men study the abstruse and fine geometry be abated, if what to me, and those few to whom I have imparted it, seems evidently true, should really prove to be so.

AN APPENDIX.[1]

THE censures which, I am informed, have been made on the foregoing Essay inclined me to think I had not been clear and express enough in some points; and, to prevent being misunderstood for the future, I was willing to make any necessary alterations or additions in what I had written. But that was impracticable, the present edition having been almost finished before I received this information. Wherefore, I think it proper to consider in this place the principal objections that are come to my notice.

In the *first* place, it is objected, that in the beginning of the Essay I argue either against all use of lines and angles in optics, and then what I say is false; or against those writers only who will have it that we can perceive by sense the optic axes, angles, &c., and then it is insignificant, this being an absurdity which no one ever held. To which I answer that I argue only against those who are of opinion that we perceive the distance of objects by lines and angles, or, as they term it, by a kind of innate geometry. And, to

show that this is not fighting with my own shadow, I shall here set down a passage from the celebrated Descartes:—

"Distantiam præterea discimus, per mutuam quandam conspirationem oculorum. Ut enim cæcus noster duo bacilla tenens, *A E* et *C E*, de quorum longitudine incertus, solumque intervallum manuum *A* et *C*, cum magnitudine angulorum *A C E*, et *C A E*

[1] This Appendix, first added to the second edition, was omitted from the third or last (1732).

exploratum habens, inde, ut ex Geometria quadam omnibus innata, scire potest ubi sit punctum *E*. Sic quum nostri oculi *R S T* et *r s t* ambo, vertuntur ad *X*, magnitudo lineæ *S s*, et angulorum *X S s* et *X s S*, certos nos reddunt ubi sit punctum *X*. Et idem opera alterutrius possumus indagare, loco illum movendo, ut si versus *X* illum semper dirigentes, primo sistamus in puncto *S*, et statim post in puncto *s*, hoc sufficiet ut magnitudo

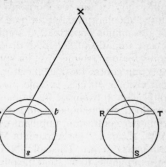

lineæ *S s*, et duorum angulorum *X S s* et *X s S* nostræ imaginationi simul occurrant, et distantiam puncti *X* nos edoceant: idque per actionem mentis, quæ licet simplex judicium esse videatur, ratiocinationem tamen quandam involutam habet, similem illi, qua Geometræ per duas stationes diversas, loca inaccessa dimetiuntur."

I might amass together citations from several authors to the same purpose, but, this being so clear in the point, and from an author of so great note, I shall not trouble the reader with any more. What I have said on this head was not for the sake of finding fault with other men; but, because I judged it necessary to demonstrate in the first place that we neither see distance immediately, nor yet perceive it by the mediation of anything that hath (as lines and angles) a necessary connexion with it. For on the demonstration of this point the whole theory depends.

Secondly, it is objected, that the explication I give of the appearance of the horizontal moon (which may also be applied to the sun) is the same that Gassendus had given before. I answer, there is, indeed, mention made of the grossness of the atmosphere in both, but then the methods wherein it is applied to solve the phenomenon are widely different, as will be evident to whoever shall compare what I have said on this subject with the following words of Gassendus :—

"Heinc dici posse videtur: solem humilem oculo spec-tatum ideo apparere majorem, quam dum altius egreditur, quia dum vicinus est horizonti prolixa est series vaporum, atque adeo corpusculorum quæ solis radios ita retundunt, ut oculus minus conniveat, et pupilla quasi umbrefacta longe magis amplificetur, quam dum sole multum elato rari vapores intercipiuntur, solque ipse ita splendescit, ut pupilla in ipsum spectans contractissima efficiatur. Nempe ex hoc esse videtur, cur visibilis species ex sole procedens, et per pupillam am-plificatam intromissa in retinam, ampliorem in illa sedem occupet, majoremque proinde creet solis apparentiam, quam dum per contractam pupillam eodem intromissa contendit." Vide *Epist.* 1. "De Apparente Magnitudine Solis Humilis et Sublimis," p. 6. This solution of Gassendus proceeds on a false principle, to wit, that the pupil's being enlarged augments the species or image on the fund of the eye.

Thirdly, against what is said in Sect. 80, it is objected, that the same thing which is so small as scarce to be dis-cerned by a man, may appear like a mountain to some small insect; from which it follows that the *minimum visibile* is not equal in respect of all creatures. I answer, if this objection be sounded to the bottom, it will be found to mean no more than that the same particle of matter which is marked to a man by one *minimum visibile*, exhibits to an insect a great number of *minima visibilia*. But this does not prove that one *minimum visibile* of the insect is not equal to one *minimum visibile* of the man. The not dis-tinguishing between the mediate and immediate objects of sight is, I suspect, a cause of misapprehension in this matter.

Some other misinterpretations and difficulties have been made, but, in the points they refer to, I have endeavoured to be so very plain, that I know not how to express myself more clearly. All I shall add is that, if they who are pleased to criticise on my Essay would but read the whole over with some attention, they might be the better able to comprehend my meaning, and consequently to judge of my mistakes.

₊˟ I am informed that, soon after the first edition of

this treatise, a man somewhere near London was made to see, who had been born blind and continued so for about twenty years. Such a one may be supposed a proper judge to decide how far some tenets laid down in several places of the foregoing Essay are agreeable to truth ; and if any curious person hath the opportunity of making proper interrogatories to him thereon, I should gladly see my notions either amended or confirmed by experience.

A TREATISE

CONCERNING

THE PRINCIPLES OF HUMAN KNOWLEDGE.

WHEREIN THE CHIEF CAUSES OF ERROR AND DIFFICULTY
IN THE SCIENCES WITH THE GROUNDS OF SCEPTIC-
ISM, ATHEISM, AND IRRELIGION, ARE
INQUIRED INTO.

First Printed in the Year 1710.

[THE "Treatise" was published at Dublin in 1710. The second and last edition, which appeared in the same volume with the third and last edition of "Hylas and Philonous" in 1734, was somewhat revised and enlarged. The text of 1734 is used in this edition. The Second Part, promised in the preface to "Hylas," was never completed, and the manuscript containing the fragment was lost in Italy, together with the materials collected for a work on the natural history of Sicily. The "Treatise" is an extension of the new Principles of the preceding Essay, and the two form the most ordered statement of Berkeley's philosophy. It may not be out of place to attempt here a brief indication of his doctrines of Vision and Matter. We see an object as we read a word. The vision immediately apprehends only the sensible conformation of the word, and from this, and past experience, we learn by a sort of induction, its ultimate significance. So with an object. What we *see* is a coloured "elevation" of the object—to borrow a term from Geometry—and we *unconsciously translate* this into the object itself, by what we have previously learned from touch and locomotion. Thus, in the apparently simple operation of seeing, we are receiving sight-impressions, and joining to these, remembered facts from our past experience.

The Treatise on Knowledge is an extension of this to all five senses. These, as Professor Fraser well calls them, are the "natural alphabet." From them are made up sense-impressions, and there must be *mind* to interpret these. Now Locke and others had divided the qualities of bodies into two species, the primary or essential, and the secondary or relative. It was, they taught, the latter that caused sense sense-impressions, while the former constituted "Absolute Matter"—unperceived and unperceivable—the source and cause of the secondary qualities. In this abstract Matter and its assumed powers, Berkeley found a subtle enemy to religion, and he fought it as such, denouncing it in addition as a fiction both contradictory and superfluous. Matter, he teaches, is utterly impotent: its supposed powers belong not to it, but to the perceiving mind; and if there must be a continued existence of sensible things, there must be, also, an Eternal Mind or God, in which they must be continually perceived; and so, in a letter to Sir John Percival, Berkeley explains the Mosaic story of the Creation by saying that, "the created things existed from all eternity in the Divine Intellect, and then became perceptible (*i.e.*, were *created*) in the manner and order as is described in Genesis." (Percival MSS.) Thus in his philosophical teaching there is always a religious purpose: for, considering Locke's "Eternal Mind," a sufficient explanation of the reality of the material world, he sought to banish the doctrine of a "pure unperceivable substance" both as unsound philosophy and as containing a subtle and certain invitation to an easy Materialism.]

A

TREATISE

Concerning the

PRINCIPLES

OF

Human Knowlege.

PART I.

Wherein the chief Causes of Error and Difficulty in the *Sciences*, with the Grounds of *Scepticism*, *Atheism*, and *Irreligion*, are inquir'd into.

By *George Berkeley*, M.A. Fellow of *Trinity-College*, *Dublin*.

DVBLIN:

Printed by Aaron Rhames, for Jeremy Pepyat, Bookseller in *Skinner-Row*, 1710.

A

TREATISE

Concerning the

PRINCIPLES

OF

Human Knowledge.

PART I.

Wherein the chief Causes of Error and Difficulty in the Sciences, with the Grounds of Scepticism, Atheism, and Irreligion, are inquir'd into.

By George Berkeley, M.A. Fellow of
Trinity-College, Dublin.

DUBLIN:

Printed by Aaron Rhames, for Jeremy
Pepyat, Bookseller in Skinner-Row, 1710.

---

[1] This dedication does not appear in the 1734 edition.

TO THE RIGHT HONOURABLE

THOMAS, EARL OF PEMBROKE, &c.

LORD OF THE SEALS, &c.

DEDICATION FROM LOCKE.

My Lord,

...

I am,

My Lord,

CHRISTCHURCH-KELLY

THE PREFACE.

WHAT I here make public has, after a long and scrupulous inquiry, seemed to me evidently true and not unuseful to be known—particularly to those who are tainted with Scepticism, or want a demonstration of the existence and immateriality of God, or the natural immortality of the soul. Whether it be so or no I am content the reader should impartially examine; since I do not think myself any farther concerned for the success of what I have written than as it is agreeable to truth. But, to the end this may not suffer, I make it my request that the reader suspend his judgment till he has once at least read the whole through with that degree of attention and thought which the subject-matter shall seem to deserve. For, as there are some passages that, taken by themselves, are very liable (nor could it be remedied) to gross misinterpretation, and to be charged with most absurd consequences, which, nevertheless, upon an entire perusal will appear not to follow from them; so likewise, though the whole should be read over, yet, if this be done transiently, it is very probable my sense may be mistaken; but to a thinking reader, I flatter myself it will be throughout clear and obvious. As for the characters of novelty and singularity which some of the following notions may seem to bear, it is, I hope, needless to make any apology on that account. He must surely be either very weak, or very little acquainted with the sciences, who shall reject a truth that is capable of demonstration, for no other reason but because it is newly known, and contrary to the prejudices of mankind. Thus much I thought fit to premise, in order to prevent, if possible, the hasty censures of a sort of men who are too apt to condemn an opinion before they rightly comprehend it.[1]

[1] This preface does not appear in the 1734 edition.

INTRODUCTION.

I.

PHILOSOPHY being nothing else but the study of wisdom and truth, it may with reason be expected that those who have spent most time and pains in it should enjoy a greater calm and serenity of mind, a greater clearness and evidence of knowledge, and be less disturbed with doubts and difficulties than other men. Yet so it is, we see the illiterate bulk of mankind that walk the high-road of plain common sense, and are governed by the dictates of nature, for the most part easy and undisturbed. To them nothing that is familiar appears unaccountable or difficult to comprehend. They complain not of any want of evidence in their senses, and are out of all danger of becoming Sceptics. But no sooner do we depart from sense and instinct to follow the light of a superior principle, to reason, meditate, and reflect on the nature of things, but a thousand scruples spring up in our minds concerning those things which before we seemed fully to comprehend. Prejudices and errors of sense do from all parts discover themselves to our view; and, endeavouring to correct these by reason, we are insensibly drawn into uncouth paradoxes, difficulties, and inconsistencies, which multiply and grow upon us as we advance in speculation, till at length, having wandered through many intricate mazes, we find ourselves just where we were, or, which is worse, sit down in a forlorn Scepticism.

2. The cause of this is thought to be the obscurity of things, or the natural weakness and imperfection of our understandings. It is said, the faculties we have are few, and those designed by nature for the support and comfort of life, and not to penetrate into the inward essence and constitution of things. Besides, the mind of man being finite, when it treats of things which partake of infinity, it is not to be

wondered at if it run into absurdities and contradictions, out of which it is impossible it should ever extricate itself, it being of the nature of infinite not to be comprehended by that which is finite.

3. But, perhaps, we may be too partial to ourselves in placing the fault originally in our faculties, and not rather in the wrong use we make of them. It is a hard thing to suppose that right deductions from true principles should ever end in consequences which cannot be maintained or made consistent. We should believe that God has dealt more bountifully with the sons of men than to give them a strong desire for that knowledge which he had placed quite out of their reach. This were not agreeable to the wonted indulgent methods of Providence, which, whatever appetites it may have implanted in the creatures, doth usually furnish them with such means as, if rightly made use of, will not fail to satisfy them. Upon the whole, I am inclined to think that the far greater part, if not all, of those difficulties which have hitherto amused philosophers, and blocked up the way to knowledge, are entirely owing to ourselves—that we have first raised a dust and then complain we cannot see.

4. My purpose therefore is, to try if I can discover what those Principles are which have introduced all that doubtfulness and uncertainty, those absurdities and contradictions, into the several sects of philosophy; insomuch that the wisest men have thought our ignorance incurable, conceiving it to arise from the natural dulness and limitation of our faculties. And surely it is a work well deserving our pains to make a strict inquiry concerning the First Principles of Human Knowledge, to sift and examine them on all sides, especially since there may be some grounds to suspect that those lets and difficulties, which stay and embarrass the mind in its search after truth, do not spring from any darkness and intricacy in the objects, or natural defect in the understanding, so much as from false Principles which have been insisted on, and might have been avoided.

5. How difficult and discouraging soever this attempt may seem, when I consider how many great and extraordinary men have gone before me in the like designs, yet I am not without some hopes—upon the consideration that the largest views are not always the clearest, and that he who

is short-sighted will be obliged to draw the object nearer, and may, perhaps, by a close and narrow survey, discern that which had escaped far better eyes.

6. In order to prepare the mind of the reader for the easier conceiving what follows, it is proper to premise somewhat, by way of Introduction, concerning the nature and abuse of Language. But the unravelling this matter leads me in some measure to anticipate my design, by taking notice of what seems to have had a chief part in rendering speculation intricate and perplexed, and to have occasioned innumerable errors and difficulties in almost all parts of knowledge. And that is the opinion that the mind hath a power of framing *abstract ideas* or notions of things. He who is not a perfect stranger to the writings and disputes of philosophers must needs acknowledge that no small part of them are spent about abstract ideas. These are in a more especial manner thought to be the object of those sciences which go by the name of Logic and Metaphysics, and of all that which passes under the notion of the most abstracted and sublime learning, in all which one shall scarce find any question handled in such a manner as does not suppose their existence in the mind, and that it is well acquainted with them.

7. It is agreed on all hands that the qualities or modes of things do never really exist each of them apart by itself, and separated from all others, but are mixed, as it were, and blended together, several in the same object. But, we are told, the mind being able to consider each quality singly, or abstracted from those other qualities with which it is united, does by that means frame to itself abstract ideas. For example, there is perceived by sight an object extended, coloured, and moved : this mixed or compound idea the mind resolving into its simple, constituent parts, and viewing each by itself, exclusive of the rest, does frame the abstract ideas of extension, colour, and motion. Not that it is possible for colour or motion to exist without extension ; but only that the mind can frame to itself by *abstraction* the idea of colour exclusive of extension, and of motion exclusive of both colour and extension.

8. Again, the mind having observed that in the particular

extensions perceived by sense there is something common and alike in all, and some other things peculiar, as this or that figure or magnitude, which distinguish them one from another ; it considers apart or singles out by itself that which is common, making thereof a most abstract idea of extension, which is neither line, surface, nor solid, nor has any figure or magnitude, but is an idea entirely prescinded from all these. So likewise the mind, by leaving out of the particular colours perceived by sense that which distinguishes them one from another, and retaining that only which is common to all, makes an idea of colour in abstract which is neither red, nor blue, nor white, nor any other determinate colour. And, in like manner, by considering motion abstractedly not only from the body moved, but likewise from the figure it describes, and all particular directions and velocities, the abstract idea of motion is framed ; which equally corresponds to all particular motions whatsoever that may be perceived by sense.

9. And as the mind frames to itself abstract ideas of qualities or modes, so does it, by the same precision or mental separation, attain abstract ideas of the more compounded beings which include several coexistent qualities. For example, the mind having observed that Peter, James, and John resemble each other in certain common agreements of shape and other qualities, leaves out of the complex or compounded idea it has of Peter, James, and any other particular man, that which is peculiar to each, retaining only what is common to all, and so makes an abstract idea wherein all the particulars equally partake—abstracting entirely from and cutting off all those circumstances and differences which might determine it to any particular existence. And after this manner it is said we come by the abstract idea of man, or, if you please, humanity, or human nature ; wherein it is true there is included colour, because there is no man but has some colour, but then it can be neither white, nor black, nor any particular colour, because there is no one particular colour wherein all men partake. So likewise there is included stature, but then it is neither tall stature, nor low stature, nor yet middle stature, but something abstracted from all these. And so of the rest. Moreover, their being a great variety of other creatures that partake in some parts, but not all, of the complex idea of man, the mind, leaving out those parts which

are peculiar to men, and retaining those only which are common to all the living creatures, frames the idea of *animal*, which abstracts not only from all particular men, but also all birds, beasts, fishes, and insects. The constituent parts of the abstract idea of animal are body, life, sense, and sponta-neous motion. By *body* is meant body without any particular shape or figure, there being no one shape or figure common to all animals, without covering, either of hair, or feathers, or scales, &c., nor yet naked : hair, feathers, scales, and naked-ness being the distinguishing properties of particular animals, and for that reason left out of the *abstract idea*. Upon the same account the spontaneous motion must be neither walking, nor flying, nor creeping ; it is nevertheless a motion, but what that motion is it is not easy to conceive.

10. Whether others have this wonderful faculty of ab-stracting their ideas, they best can tell : for myself,[1] I find indeed I have a faculty of imagining, or representing to myself, the ideas of those particular things I have per-ceived, and of variously compounding and dividing them. I can imagine a man with two heads, or the upper parts of a man joined to the body of a horse. I can consider the hand, the eye, the nose, each by itself abstracted or separated from the rest of the body. But then whatever hand or eye I imagine, it must have some particular shape and colour. Likewise the idea of man that I frame to myself must be either of a white, or a black, or a tawny, a straight, or a crooked, a tall, or a low, or a middle-sized man. I cannot by any effort of thought conceive the abstract idea above de-scribed. And it is equally impossible for me to form the abstract idea of motion distinct from the body moving, and which is neither swift nor slow, curvilinear nor rectilinear ; and the like may be said of all other abstract general ideas whatsoever. To be plain, I own myself able to abstract in one sense, as when I consider some particular parts or qualities separated from others, with which, though they are united in some object, yet it is possible they may really exist without them. But I deny that I can abstract from one another, or

---

[1] In the first edition (1710) this sentence read : " for myself, I dare be confident I have it not. I have indeed," &c.

conceive separately, those qualities which it is impossible should exist so separated; or that I can frame a general notion, by abstracting from particulars in the manner aforesaid—which last are the two proper acceptions of *abstraction*. And there are grounds to think most men will acknowledge themselves to be in my case. The generality of men which are simple and illiterate never pretend to *abstract notions*. It is said they are difficult and not to be attained without pains and study; we may therefore reasonably conclude that, if such there be, they are confined only to the learned.

11. I proceed to examine what can be alleged in defence of the doctrine of abstraction, and try if I can discover what it is that inclines the men of speculation to embrace an opinion so remote from common sense as that seems to be. There has been a late deservedly esteemed philosopher who, no doubt, has given it very much countenance, by seeming to think the having abstract general ideas is what puts the widest difference in point of understanding betwixt man and beast. "The having of general ideas," saith he, "is that which puts a perfect distinction betwixt man and brutes, and is an excellency which the faculties of brutes do by no means attain unto. For, it is evident we observe no foot-steps in them of making use of general signs for universal ideas; from which we have reason to imagine that they have not the faculty of abstracting, or making general ideas, since they have no use of words or any other general signs." And a little after. "Therefore, I think, we may suppose that it is in this that the species of brutes are discriminated from men, and it is that proper difference wherein they are wholly separated, and which at last widens to so wide a distance. For, if they have any ideas at all, and are not bare machines (as some would have them), we cannot deny them to have some reason. It seems as evident to me that they do, some of them, in certain instances reason as that they have sense; but it is only in particular ideas, just as they receive them from their senses. They are the best of them tied up within those narrow bounds, and have not (as I think) the faculty to enlarge them by any kind of abstraction."—"Essay on Human Understanding," B. ii. ch. 11. s. 10 and 11. I readily agree with this learned author, that the faculties of brutes can by no means attain to abstraction. But then if

this be made the distinguishing property of that sort of animals, I fear a great many of those that pass for men must be reckoned into their number. The reason that is here assigned why we have no grounds to think brutes have abstract general ideas is, that we observe in them no use of words or any other general signs; which is built on this supposition —that the making use of words implies the having general ideas. From which it follows that men who use language are able to abstract or generalize their ideas. That this is the sense and arguing of the author will further appear by his answering the question he in another place puts : "Since all things that exist are only particulars, how come we by general terms?" His answer is : "Words become general by being made the signs of general ideas."—"Essay on Human Understanding," B. iii. ch. 3. s. 6. But[1] it seems that a word becomes general by being made the sign, not of an abstract general idea, but of several particular ideas, any one of which it indifferently suggests to the mind. For example, when it is said "the change of motion is proportional to the impressed force," or that "whatever has extension is divisible," these propositions are to be understood of motion and extension in general ; and nevertheless it will not follow that they suggest to my thoughts an idea of motion without a body moved, or any determinate direction and velocity, or that I must conceive an abstract general idea of extension, which is neither line, surface, nor solid, neither great nor small, black, white, nor red, nor of any other determinate colour. It is only implied that whatever particular motion I consider, whether it be swift or slow, perpendicular, horizontal, or oblique, or in whatever object, the axiom concerning it holds equally true. As does the other of every particular extension, it matters not whether line, surface, or solid, whether of this or that magnitude or figure.

12. By observing how ideas become general we may the better judge how words are made so. And here it is to be noted that I do not deny absolutely there are general ideas, but only that there are any *abstract* general ideas ; for, in the passages we have quoted wherein there is mention of general ideas, it is always supposed that they are formed by abstrac-

---

[1] In the first edition this sentence began as follows: "To this I cannot assent being of opinion that a word becomes general," &c.

tion, after the manner set forth in sections 8 and 9. Now, if we will annex a meaning to our words, and speak only of what we can conceive, I believe we shall acknowledge that an idea which, considered in itself, is particular, becomes general by being made to represent or stand for all other particular ideas of the same sort. To make this plain by an example, suppose a geometrician is demonstrating the method of cutting a line in two equal parts. He draws, for instance, a black line of an inch in length: this, which in itself is a particular line, is nevertheless with regard to its signification general, since, as it is there used, it represents all particular lines whatsoever; so that what is demonstrated of it is demonstrated of all lines, or, in other words, of a line in general. And, as that particular line becomes general by being made a sign, so the name " line," which taken absolutely is particular, by being a sign is made general. And as the former owes its generality not to its being the sign of an abstract or general line, but of all particular right lines that may possibly exist, so the latter must be thought to derive its generality from the same cause, namely, the various particular lines which it indifferently denotes.

13. To give the reader a yet clearer view of the nature of abstract ideas, and the uses they are thought necessary to, I shall add one more passage out of the " Essay on Human Understanding," which is as follows: " *Abstract ideas* are not so obvious or easy to children or the yet unexercised mind as particular ones. If they seem so to grown men it is only because by constant and familiar use they are made so. For, when we nicely reflect upon them, we shall find that general ideas are fictions and contrivances of the mind, that carry difficulty with them, and do not so easily offer themselves as we are apt to imagine. For example, does it not require some pains and skill to form the general idea of a triangle (which is yet none of the most abstract, comprehensive, and difficult); for it must be neither oblique nor rectangle, neither equilateral, equicrural, nor scalenon, but *all and none* of these at once? In effect, it is something imperfect that cannot exist, an idea wherein some parts of several different and *inconsistent* ideas are put together. It is true the mind in this imperfect state has need of such ideas, and makes all the haste to them it can, for the con-

veniency of communication and enlargement of knowledge, to both which it is naturally very much inclined. But yet one has reason to suspect such ideas are marks of our imperfection. At least this is enough to show that the most abstract and general ideas are not those that the mind is first and most easily acquainted with, nor such as its earliest knowledge is conversant about."—B. iv. ch. 7. s. 9. If any man has the faculty of framing in his mind such an idea of a triangle as is here described, it is in vain to pretend to dispute him out of it, nor would I go about it. All I desire is that the reader would fully and certainly inform himself whether he has such an idea or no. And this, methinks, can be no hard task for anyone to perform. What more easy than for anyone to look a little into his own thoughts, and there try whether he has, or can attain to have, an idea that shall correspond with the description that is here given of the general idea of a triangle, which is "neither oblique nor rectangle, equilateral, equicrural nor scalenon, but all and none of these at once?"

14. Much is here said of the difficulty that abstract ideas carry with them, and the pains and skill requisite to the forming them. And it is on all hands agreed that there is need of great toil and labour of the mind, to emancipate our thoughts from particular objects, and raise them to those sublime speculations that are conversant about abstract ideas. From all which the natural consequence should seem to be, that so difficult a thing as the forming abstract ideas was not necessary for *communication*, which is so easy and familiar to all sorts of men. But, we are told, if they seem obvious and easy to grown men, it is only because by constant and familiar use they are made so. Now, I would fain know at what time it is men are employed in surmounting that difficulty, and furnishing themselves with those necessary helps for discourse. It cannot be when they are grown up, for then it seems they are not conscious of any such painstaking; it remains therefore to be the business of their childhood. And surely the great and multiplied labour of framing abstract notions will be found a hard task for that tender age. Is it not a hard thing to imagine that a couple of children cannot prate together of their sugar-plums and rattles and the rest of their little trinkets, till they have first

tacked together numberless inconsistencies, and so framed in their minds abstract general ideas, and annexed them to every common name they make use of?

15. Nor do I think them a whit more needful for the *enlargement of knowledge* than for *communication*. It is, I know, a point much insisted on, that all knowledge and demonstration are about universal notions, to which I fully agree : but then it doth not appear to me that those notions are formed by abstraction in the manner premised—*universality*, so far as I can comprehend, not consisting in the absolute, positive nature or conception of anything, but in the relation it bears to the particulars signified or represented by it ; by virtue whereof it is that things, names, or notions, being in their own nature *particular*, are rendered *universal*. Thus, when I demonstrate any proposition concerning triangles, it is to be supposed that I have in view the universal idea of a triangle ; which ought not to be understood as if I could frame an idea of a triangle which was neither equilateral, nor scalenon, nor equicrural ; but only that the particular triangle I consider, whether of this or that sort it matters not, doth equally stand for and represent all rectilinear triangles whatsoever, and is in that sense *universal*. All which seems very plain and not to include any difficulty in it.

16. But here it will be demanded, how we can know any proposition to be true of all particular triangles, except we have first seen it demonstrated of the abstract idea of a triangle which equally agrees to all? For, because a property may be demonstrated to agree to some one particular triangle, it will not thence follow that it equally belongs to any other triangle, which in all respects is not the same with it. For example, having demonstrated that the three angles of an isosceles rectangular triangle are equal to two right ones, I cannot therefore conclude this affection agrees to all other triangles which have neither a right angle nor two equal sides. It seems therefore that, to be certain this proposition is universally true, we must either make a particular demonstration for every particular triangle, which is impossible, or once for all demonstrate it of the abstract idea of a triangle, in which all the particulars do indifferently partake and by which they are all equally represented. To

which I answer, that, though the idea I have in view whilst
I make the demonstration be, for instance, that of an
isosceles rectangular triangle whose sides are of a determinate length, I may nevertheless be certain it extends to all
other rectilinear triangles, of what sort or bigness soever.
And that because neither the right angle, nor the equality,
nor determinate length of the sides are at all concerned in
the demonstration.   It is true the diagram I have in view
includes all these particulars, but then there is not the least
mention made of them in the proof of the proposition.   It
is not said the three angles are equal to two right ones,
because one of them is a right angle, or because the sides
comprehending it are of the same length. Which sufficiently
shows that the right angle might have been oblique, and the
sides unequal, and for all that the demonstration have held
good.   And for this reason it is that I conclude that to be
true of any obliquangular or scalenon which I had demonstrated of a particular right-angled equicrural triangle, and
not because I demonstrated the proposition of the abstract
idea of a triangle.   And here it must be acknowledged that
a man may consider a figure merely as triangular, without
attending to the particular qualities of the angles, or relations of the sides.   So far he may abstract ; but this will
never prove that he can frame an abstract, general, inconsistent idea of a triangle.   In like manner we may consider
Peter so far forth as man, or so far forth as animal,
without framing the forementioned abstract idea, either of
man or of animal, inasmuch as all that is perceived is not
considered.[1]

17. It were an endless as well as an useless thing to trace
the Schoolmen, those great masters of abstraction, through
all the manifold inextricable labyrinths of error and dispute
which their doctrine of abstract natures and notions seems to
have led them into.   What bickerings and controversies,
and what a learned dust have been raised about those
matters, and what mighty advantage has been from thence
derived to mankind, are things at this day too clearly known
to need being insisted on.   And it had been well if the ill
effects of that doctrine were confined to those only who

[1] The last three sentences, beginning "And here it must be acknowledged," were inserted in the last or 1734 edition.

make the most avowed profession of it. When men consider the great pains, industry, and parts that have for so many ages been laid out on the cultivation and advancement of the sciences, and that notwithstanding all this the far greater part of them remain full of darkness and uncertainty, and disputes that are like never to have an end, and even those that are thought to be supported by the most clear and cogent demonstrations contain in them paradoxes which are perfectly irreconcilable to the understandings of men, and that, taking all together, a very small portion of them does supply any real benefit to mankind, otherwise than by being an innocent diversion and amusement—I say, the consideration of all this is apt to throw them into a despondency and perfect contempt of all study. But this may perhaps cease upon a view of the false principles that have obtained in the world, amongst all which there is none, methinks, hath a more wide and extended sway over the thoughts of speculative men than this of *abstract* general ideas.

18. I come now to consider the *source* of this prevailing notion, and that seems to me to be language. And surely nothing of less extent than reason itself could have been the source of an opinion so universally received. The truth of this appears as from other reasons so also from the plain confession of the ablest patrons of abstract ideas, who acknowledge that they are made in order to naming ; from which it is a clear consequence that if there had been no such thing as speech or universal signs there never had been any thought of abstraction. See B. iii. ch. 6. s. 39, and elsewhere of the " Essay on Human Understanding." Let us examine the manner wherein words have contributed to the origin of that mistake.—First then, it is thought that every name has, or ought to have, one only precise and settled signification, which inclines men to think their are certain abstract, determinate ideas that constitute the true and only immediate signification of each general name ; and that it is by the mediation of these abstract ideas that a general name comes to signify any particular thing. Whereas, in truth, there is no such thing as one precise and definite signification annexed to any general name, they all signifying indifferently a great number of particular ideas. All which

doth evidently follow from what has been already said, and will clearly appear to anyone by a little reflexion. To this it will be objected that every name that has a definition is thereby restrained to one certain signification. For example, a triangle is defined to be "a plain surface comprehended by three right lines," by which that name is limited to denote one certain idea and no other. To which I answer, that in the definition it is not said whether the surface be great or small, black or white, nor whether the sides are long or short, equal or unequal, nor with what angles they are inclined to each other; in all which there may be great variety, and consequently there is no one settled idea which limits the signification of the word triangle. It is one thing for to keep a name constantly to the same definition, and another to make it stand everywhere for the same idea; the one is necessary, the other useless and impracticable.

19. But, to give a farther account how words came to produce the doctrine of abstract ideas, it must be observed that it is a received opinion that language has no other end but the communicating our ideas, and that every significant name stands for an idea. This being so, and it being withal certain that names which yet are not thought altogether insignificant do not always mark out particular conceivable ideas, it is straightway concluded that they stand for abstract notions. That there are many names in use amongst speculative men which do not always suggest to others determinate, particular ideas, or in truth anything at all, is what nobody will deny. And a little attention will discover that it is not necessary (even in the strictest reasonings) significant names which stand for ideas should, every time they are used, excite in the understanding the ideas they are made to stand for—in reading and discoursing, names being for the most part used as letters are in Algebra, in which, though a particular quantity be marked by each letter, yet to proceed right it is not requisite that in every step each letter suggest to your thoughts that particular quantity it was appointed to stand for.

20. Besides, the communicating of ideas marked by words is not the chief and only end of language, as is commonly supposed. There are other ends, as the raising of some passion, the exciting to or deterring from an action,

the putting the mind in some particular disposition—to
which the former is in many cases barely subservient, and
sometimes entirely omitted, when these can be obtained
without it, as I think does not unfrequently happen in the
familiar use of language. I entreat the reader to reflect
with himself, and see if it doth not often happen, either in
hearing or reading a discourse, that the passions of fear,
love, hatred, admiration, disdain, and the like, arise im
mediately in his mind upon the perception of certain words,
without any ideas coming between. At first, indeed, the
words might have occasioned ideas that were fitting to pro
duce those emotions; but, if I mistake not, it will be found
that, when language is once grown familiar, the hearing
of the sounds or sight of the characters is oft immediately
attended with those passions which at first were wont to be
produced by the intervention of ideas that are now quite
omitted. May we not, for example, be affected with the
promise of a *good thing*, though we have not an idea of what
it is? Or is not the being threatened with danger sufficient
to excite a dread, though we think not of any particular evil
likely to befal us, nor yet frame to ourselves an idea of
danger in abstract? If any one shall join ever so little
reflexion of his own to what has been said, I believe that it
will evidently appear to him that general names are often
used in the propriety of language without the speaker's
designing them for marks of ideas in his own, which he
would have them raise in the mind of the hearer. Even
proper names themselves do not seem always spoken with a
design to bring into our view the ideas of those individuals
that are supposed to be marked by them. For example
when a schoolman tells me " Aristotle hath said it," all
I conceive he means by it is to dispose me to embrace his
opinion with the deference and submission which custom has
annexed to that name. And this effect is often so instantly
produced in the minds of those who are accustomed to
resign their judgment to authority of that philosopher, as it
is impossible any idea either of his person, writings, or
reputation should go before.[1] Innumerable examples of
this kind may be given, but why should I insist on those

[1] Between this sentence and the next came in the first edition the
following passage : " So close and immediate a connexion may custom

ings which every one's experience will, I doubt not,
entifully suggest unto him?

21. We have, I think, shewn the impossibility of Abstract
Ideas. We have considered what has been said for them by
their ablest patrons; and endeavoured to shew they are of
no use for those ends to which they are thought necessary.
And lastly, we have traced them to the source from whence
they flow, which appears evidently to be language.—It
cannot be denied that words are of excellent use, in that by
their means all that stock of knowledge which has been
purchased by the joint labours of inquisitive men in all ages
and nations may be drawn into the view and made the
possession of one single person. But at the same time it
must be owned that most parts of knowledge have been
strangely perplexed and darkened by the abuse of words, and
general ways of speech wherein they are delivered. Since
therefore words are so apt to impose on the understanding,
whatever ideas I consider, I shall endeavour to take them
bare and naked into my view, keeping out of my thoughts,
so far as I am able, those names which long and constant
use hath so strictly united with them; from which I may
expect to derive the following advantages : [1]—

22. *First,* I shall be sure to get clear of all controversies
purely verbal—the springing up of which weeds in almost all
the sciences has been a main hindrance to the growth of true
and sound knowledge. *Secondly,* this seems to be a sure
way to extricate myself out of that fine and subtle net of
abstract ideas which has so miserably perplexed and entangled
the minds of men ; and that with this peculiar circumstance,
that by how much the finer and more curious was the wit of
any man, by so much the deeper was he likely to be ensnared

establish betwixt the very word Aristotle and the motions of assent and
reverence in the minds of some men."

[1] In the first edition the preceding passage read as follows : " But
most parts of knowledge have been so strangely perplexed and darkened
by the abuse of words, and general ways of speech wherein they are
delivered, that it may almost be made a question whether language has
contributed more to the hindrance or advancement of the sciences. Since
therefore words are so apt to impose on the understanding, I am resolved
in my inquiries to make as little use of them as possibly I can : whatever
ideas I consider," &c.

and faster held therein. *Thirdly*, so long as I confine m
thoughts to my own ideas divested of words, I do not se
how I can easily be mistaken. The objects I conside
I clearly and adequately know. I cannot be deceived i
thinking I have an idea which I have not. It is not possibl
for me to imagine that any of my own ideas are alik
or unlike that are not truly so. To discern the agreement
or disagreements there are between my ideas, to see wha
ideas are included in any compound idea and what not, ther
is nothing more requisite than an attentive perception o
what passes in my own understanding.

23. But the attainment of all these advantages doth pre
suppose an entire deliverance from the deception of words
which I dare hardly promise myself; so difficult a thing it i
to dissolve an union so early begun, and confirmed by so lon,
a habit as that betwixt words and ideas. Which difficult
seems to have been very much increased by the doctrine o
abstraction. For, so long as men thought abstract ideas wer
annexed to their words, it doth not seem strange that the
should use words for ideas—it being found an impracticabl
thing to lay aside the word, and retain the *abstract* idea i
the mind, which in itself was perfectly inconceivable. Thi
seems to me the principal cause why those men who have s
emphatically recommended to others the laying aside al
use of words in their meditations, and contemplating thei
bare ideas, have yet failed to perform it themselves. Of lat
many have been very sensible of the absurd opinions an
insignificant disputes which grow out of the abuse of words
And, in order to remedy these evils, they advise well, tha
we attend to the ideas signified, and draw off our attentio
from the words which signify them. But, how good soeve
this advice may be they have given others, it is plain the
could not have a due regard to it themselves, so long as the
thought the only immediate use of words was to signify ideas
and that the immediate signification of every general nam
was a determinate abstract idea.

24. But, these being known to be mistakes, a man ma
with greater ease prevent his being imposed on by words. H
that knows he has no other than *particular* ideas, will no
puzzle himself in vain to find out and conceive the *abstrac*
idea annexed to any name. And he that knows names do

not always stand for ideas will spare himself the labour of looking for ideas where there are none to be had. It were, therefore, to be wished that every one would use his utmost endeavours to obtain a clear view of the ideas he would consider, separating from them all that dress and incumbrance of words which so much contribute to blind the judgment and divide the attention. In vain do we extend our view into the heavens and pry into the entrails of the earth, in vain do we consult the writings of learned men and trace the dark footsteps of antiquity—we need only draw the curtain of words, to behold the fairest tree of knowledge, whose fruit is excellent, and within the reach of our hand.

25. Unless we take care to clear the First Principles of Knowledge from the embarras and delusion of words, we may make infinite reasonings upon them to no purpose ; we may draw consequences from consequences, and be never the wiser. The farther we go, we shall only lose ourselves the more irrecoverably, and be the deeper entangled in difficulties and mistakes. Whoever therefore designs to read the following sheets, I entreat him to make my words the occasion of his own thinking, and endeavour to attain the same train of thoughts in reading that I had in writing them. By this means it will be easy for him to discover the truth or falsity of what I say. He will be out of all danger of being deceived by my words, and I do not see how he can be led into an error by considering his own naked, undisguised ideas.

PRINCIPLES

HUMAN KNOWLEDGE.

PART I.[1]

I.

IT is evident to any one who takes a survey of the objects of human knowledge, that they are either ideas actually imprinted on the senses; or else such as are perceived by attending to the passions and operations of the mind; or lastly, ideas formed by help of memory and imagination— either compounding, dividing, or barely representing those originally perceived in the aforesaid ways. By sight I have the ideas of light and colours, with their several degrees and variations. By touch I perceive hard and soft, heat and cold, motion and resistance, and of all these more and less either as to quantity or degree. Smelling furnishes me with odours; the palate with tastes; and hearing conveys sounds to the mind in all their variety of tone and composition. And as several of these are observed to accompany each other, they come to be marked by one name, and so to be reputed as one thing. Thus, for example, a certain colour, taste, smell, figure and consistence having been observed to go together, are accounted one distinct thing, signified by the name *apple;* other collections of ideas constitute a stone, a tree, a book, and the like sensible things—which as they are

---

[1] Though omitted from the title-page of the second or 1734 edition, this acknowledgement of incompleteness was retained here. See also the Preface to "Hylas and Philonous."

pleasing or disagreeable excite the passions of love, hatred, joy, grief, and so forth.

2. But, besides all that endless variety of ideas or objects of knowledge, there is likewise something which knows or perceives them, and exercises divers operations, as willing, imagining, remembering, about them. This perceiving, active being is what I call *mind, spirit, soul,* or *myself.* By which words I do not denote any one of my ideas, but a thing entirely distinct from them, wherein they exist, or, which is the same thing, whereby they are perceived—for the existence of an idea consists in being perceived.

3. That neither our thoughts, nor passions, nor ideas formed by the imagination, exist without the mind, is what everybody will allow. And it seems no less evident that the various sensations or ideas imprinted on the sense, however blended or combined together (that is, whatever objects they compose), cannot exist otherwise than in a mind perceiving them.—I think an intuitive knowledge may be obtained of this by any one that shall attend to what is meant by the term *exist,* when applied to sensible things. The table I write on I say exists, that is, I see and feel it ; and if I were out of my study I should say it existed—meaning thereby that if I was in my study I might perceive it, or that some other spirit actually does perceive it. There was an odour, that is, it was smelt ; there was a sound, that is, it was heard ; a colour or figure, and it was perceived by sight or touch. This is all that I can understand by these and the like expressions. For as to what is said of the absolute existence of unthinking things without any relation to their being perceived, that seems perfectly unintelligible. Their *esse* is *percipi,* nor is it possible they should have any existence out of the minds or thinking things which perceive them.

4. It is indeed an opinion strangely prevailing amongst men, that houses, mountains, rivers, and in a word all sensible objects, have an existence, natural or real, distinct from their being perceived by the understanding. But, with how great an assurance and acquiescence soever this principle may be entertained in the world, yet whoever shall find in his heart

to call it in question may, if I mistake not, perceive it to involve a manifest contradiction. For, what are the forementioned objects but the things we perceive by sense? and what do we perceive besides our own ideas or sensations? and is it not plainly repugnant that any one of these, or any combination of them, should exist unperceived?

5. If we throughly examine this tenet it will, perhaps, be found at bottom to depend on the doctrine of *abstract ideas*. For can there be a nicer strain of abstraction than to distinguish the existence of sensible objects from their being perceived, so as to conceive them existing unperceived? Light and colours, heat and cold, extension and figures—in a word the things we see and feel—what are they but so many sensations, notions, ideas, or impressions on the sense? and is it possible to separate, even in thought, any of these from perception? For my part, I might as easily divide a thing from itself. I may, indeed, divide in my thoughts, or conceive apart from each other, those things which, perhaps, I never perceived by sense so divided. Thus, I imagine the trunk of a human body without the limbs, or conceive the smell of a rose without thinking on the rose itself. So far, I will not deny, I can abstract—if that may properly be called *abstraction* which extends only to the conceiving separately such objects as it is possible may really exist or be actually perceived asunder. But my conceiving or imagining power does not extend beyond the possibility of real existence or perception. Hence, as it is impossible for me to see or feel anything without an actual sensation of that thing, so is it impossible for me to conceive in my thoughts any sensible thing or object distinct from the sensation or perception of it.[1]

6. Some truths there are so near and obvious to the mind that a man need only open his eyes to see them. Such I take this important one to be, viz. that all the choir of heaven and furniture of the earth, in a word all those bodies which compose the mighty frame of the world, have not any subsistence without a mind, that their *being* is to be perceived or known; that consequently so long as they are not actually perceived by me, or do not exist in my mind or that

[1] In the first edition this additional sentence ended the section : "In truth, the object and the sensation are the same thing, and cannot therefore be abstracted from each other."

of any other created spirit, they must either have no existence at all, or else subsist in the mind of some Eternal Spirit—it being perfectly unintelligible, and involving all the absurdity of abstraction, to attribute to any single part of them an existence independent of a spirit. To be convinced of which, the reader need only reflect, and try to separate in his own thoughts the *being* of a sensible thing from its *being perceived*.[1]

7. From what has been said it follows there is not any other Substance than *Spirit*, or that which perceives. But, for the fuller proof of this point, let it be considered the sensible qualities are colour, figure, motion, smell, taste, &c., *i.e.* the ideas perceived by sense. Now, for an idea to exist in an unperceiving thing is a manifest contradiction, for to have an idea is all one as to perceive; that therefore wherein colour, figure, and the like qualities exist must perceive them; hence it is clear there can be no unthinking substance or *substratum* of those ideas.

8. But, say you, though the ideas themselves do not exist without the mind, yet there may be things like them, whereof they are copies or resemblances, which things exist without the mind in an unthinking substance. I answer, an idea can be like nothing but an idea; a colour or figure can be like nothing but another colour or figure. If we look but never so little into our thoughts, we shall find it impossible for us to conceive a likeness except only between our ideas. Again, I ask whether those supposed originals or external things, of which our ideas are the pictures or representations, be themselves perceivable or no? If they are, then they are ideas and we have gained our point; but if you say they are not, I appeal to any one whether it be sense to assert a colour is like something which is invisible; hard or soft, like something which is intangible; and so of the rest.

9. Some there are who make a distinction betwixt *primary* and *secondary* qualities. By the former they mean extension, figure, motion, rest, solidity or impenetrability, and number; by the latter they denote all other sensible qualities, as

[1] In the first edition this last sentence is not found, but in its place we have this: "To make this appear with all the light and evidence of an Axiom, it seems sufficient if I can but awaken the reflexion of the reader, that he may take an impartial view of his own meaning, and turn his thoughts upon the subject itself, free and disengaged from all embarras of words and prepossession in favour of received mistakes."

colours, sounds, tastes, and so forth. The ideas we have of these they acknowledge not to be the resemblances of anything existing without the mind, or unperceived, but they will have our ideas of the primary qualities to be patterns or images of things which exist without the mind, in an unthinking substance which they call Matter. By Matter, therefore, we are to understand an inert, senseless substance, in which extension, figure, and motion do actually subsist. But it is evident, from what we have already shewn, that extension, figure, and motion are only ideas existing in the mind, and that an idea can be like nothing but another idea, and that consequently neither they nor their archetypes can exist in an unperceiving substance. Hence, it is plain that the very notion of what is called *Matter* or *corporeal substance*, involves a contradiction in it.[1]

10. They who assert that figure, motion, and the rest of the primary or original qualities do exist without the mind in unthinking substances, do at the same time acknowledge that colours, sounds, heat, cold, and suchlike secondary qualities, do not—which they tell us are sensations existing in the mind alone, that depend on and are occasioned by the different size, texture, and motion of the minute particles of matter. This they take for an undoubted truth, which they can demonstrate beyond all exception. Now, if it be certain that those original qualities are inseparably united with the other sensible qualities, and not, even in thought, capable of being abstracted from them, it plainly follows that they exist only in the mind. But I desire any one to reflect and try whether he can, by any abstraction of thought, conceive the extension and motion of a body without all other sensible qualities. For my own part, I see evidently that it is not in my power to frame an idea of a body extended and moving, but I must withal give it some colour or other sensible quality which is acknowledged to exist only

---

[1] In the first edition this additional passage ended the section : "Insomuch that I should not think it necessary to spend more time in exposing its absurdity. But, because the tenet of the existence of Matter seems to have taken so deep a root in the minds of philosophers, and draws after it so many ill consequences, I choose rather to be thought prolix and tedious than omit anything that might conduce to the full discovery and extirpation of that prejudice."

in the mind. In short, extension, figure, and motion, abstracted from all other qualities, are inconceivable. Where therefore the other sensible qualities are, there must these be also, to wit, in the mind and nowhere else.

11. Again, *great* and *small*, *swift* and *slow*, are allowed to exist nowhere without the mind, being entirely relative, and changing as the frame or position of the organs of sense varies. The extension therefore which exists without the mind is neither great nor small, the motion neither swift nor slow, that is, they are nothing at all. But, say you, they are extension in general, and motion in general : thus we see how much the tenet of extended movable substances existing without the mind depends on that strange doctrine of *abstract ideas*. And here I cannot but remark how nearly the vague and indeterminate description of Matter or corporeal substance, which the modern philosophers are run into by their own principles, resembles that antiquated and so much ridiculed notion of *materia prima*, to be met with in Aristotle and his followers. Without extension solidity cannot be conceived ; since therefore it has been shewn that extension exists not in an unthinking substance, the same must also be true of solidity.

12. That number is entirely the creature of the mind, even though the other qualities be allowed to exist without, will be evident to whoever considers that the same thing bears a different denomination of number as the mind views it with different respects. Thus, the same extension is one, or three, or thirty-six, according as the mind considers it with reference to a yard, a foot, or an inch. Number is so visibly relative, and dependent on men's understanding, that it is strange to think how any one should give it an absolute existence without the mind. We say one book, one page, one line, &c. ; all these are equally units, though some contain several of the others. And in each instance, it is plain, the unit relates to some particular combination of ideas arbitrarily put together by the mind.

13. Unity I know some will have to be a simple or uncompounded idea, accompanying all other ideas into the mind. That I have any such idea answering the word *unity* I do not find ; and if I had, methinks I could not miss finding it : on the contrary, it should be the most familiar to my under-

standing, since it is said to accompany all other ideas, and to be perceived by all the ways of sensation and reflexion. To say no more, it is an *abstract idea*.

14. I shall farther add, that, after the same manner as modern philosophers prove certain sensible qualities to have no existence in Matter, or without the mind, the same thing may be likewise proved of all other sensible qualities what-soever. Thus, for instance, it is said that heat and cold are affections only of the mind, and not at all patterns of real beings, existing in the corporeal substances which excite them, for that the same body which appears cold to one hand seems warm to another. Now, why may we not as well argue that figure and extension are not patterns or resem-blances of qualities existing in Matter, because to the same eye at different stations, or eyes of a different texture at the same station, they appear various, and cannot therefore be the images of anything settled and determinate without the mind? Again, it is proved that sweetness is not really in the sapid thing, because the thing remaining unaltered the sweet-ness is changed into bitter, as in case of a fever or otherwise vitiated palate. Is it not as reasonable to say that motion is not without the mind, since if the succession of ideas in the mind become swifter, the motion, it is acknowledged, shall appear slower without any alteration in any external object? [1]

15. In short, let any one consider those arguments which are thought manifestly to prove that colours and taste exist only in the mind, and he shall find they may with equal force be brought to prove the same thing of extension, figure, and motion. Though it must be confessed this method of arguing does not so much prove that there is no extension or colour in an outward object, as that we do not know by sense which is the true extension or colour of the object. But the arguments foregoing plainly shew it to be impossible that any colour or extension at all, or other sensible quality whatso-ever, should exist in an unthinking subject without the mind, or in truth, that there should be any such thing as an out-ward object.

16. But let us examine a little the received opinion.—It is said extension is a mode or accident of Matter, and that

[1] In the first edition the closing phrase read thus: "without any external alteration."

Matter is the *substratum* that supports it.   Now I desire that you would explain to me what is meant by Matter's *supporting* extension.   Say you, I have no idea of Matter and therefore cannot explain it.   I answer, though you have no positive, yet, if you have any meaning at all, you must at least have a relative idea of Matter; though you know not what it is, yet you must be supposed to know what relation it bears to accidents, and what is meant by its supporting them.   It is evident " support " cannot here be taken in its usual or literal sense—as when we say that pillars support a building; in what sense therefore must it be taken?[1]

17. If we inquire into what the most accurate philosophers declare themselves to mean by *material substance*, we shall find them acknowledge they have no other meaning annexed to those sounds but the idea of Being in general, together with the relative notion of its supporting accidents.   The general idea of Being appeareth to me the most abstract and incomprehensible of all other; and as for its supporting accidents, this, as we have just now observed, cannot be understood in the common sense of those words; it must therefore be taken in some other sense, but what that is they do not explain.   So that when I consider the two parts or branches which make the signification of the words *material substance*, I am convinced there is no distinct meaning annexed to them.   But why should we trouble ourselves any farther, in discussing this material *substratum* or support of figure and motion, and other sensible qualities?   Does it not suppose they have an existence without the mind?   And is not this a direct repugnancy, and altogether inconceivable?

18. But, though it were possible that solid, figured, movable substances may exist without the mind, corresponding to the ideas we have of bodies, yet how is it possible for us to know this?   Either we must know it by sense or by reason. As for our senses, by them we have the knowledge only of our sensations, ideas, or those things that are immediately perceived by sense, call them what you will: but they do not inform us that things exist without the mind, or unperceived, like to those which are perceived.   This the materialists

---

[1] In the first edition this section ended with the following sentence : "For my part, I am not able to discover any sense at all that can be applicable to it."

themselves acknowledge. It remains therefore that if we have any knowledge at all of external things, it must be by reason, inferring their existence from what is immediately perceived by sense. But what reason can induce us to believe the existence of bodies without the mind, from what we perceive, since the very patrons of Matter themselves do not pretend there is any necessary connexion betwixt them and our ideas? I say it is granted on all hands (and what happens in dreams, phrensies, and the like, puts it beyond dispute) that it is possible we might be affected with all the ideas we have now, though there were no bodies existing without resembling them. Hence, it is evident the supposition of external bodies is not necessary for the producing our ideas; since it is granted they are produced sometimes, and might possibly be produced always in the same order, we see them in at present, without their concurrence.

19. But, though we might possibly have all our sensations without them, yet perhaps it may be thought easier to conceive and explain the manner of their production, by supposing external bodies in their likeness rather than otherwise; and so it might be at least probable there are such things as bodies that excite their ideas in our minds. But neither can this be said; for, though we give the materialists their external bodies, they by their own confession are never the nearer knowing how our ideas are produced; since they own themselves unable to comprehend in what manner body can act upon spirit, or how it is possible it should imprint any idea in the mind. Hence it is evident the production of ideas or sensations in our minds can be no reason why we should suppose Matter or corporeal substances, since that is acknowledged to remain equally inexplicable with or without this supposition. If therefore it were possible for bodies to exist without the mind, yet to hold they do so, must needs be a very precarious opinion; since it is to suppose, without any reason at all, that God has created innumerable beings that are entirely useless, and serve to no manner of purpose.

20. In short, if there were external bodies, it is impossible we should ever come to know it; and if there were not, we might have the very same reasons to think there were that we have now. Suppose—what no one can deny possible— an intelligence without the help of external bodies, to be

affected with the same train of sensations or ideas that you are, imprinted in the same order and with like vividness in his mind. I ask whether that intelligence hath not all the reason to believe the existence of corporeal substances, represented by his ideas, and exciting them in his mind, that you can possibly have for believing the same thing? Of this there can be no question—which one consideration were enough to make any reasonable person suspect the strength of whatever arguments he may think himself to have, for the existence of bodies without the mind.

21. Were it necessary to add any farther proof against the existence of Matter after what has been said, I could instance several of those errors and difficulties (not to mention impieties) which have sprung from that tenet. It has occasioned numberless controversies and disputes in philosophy, and not a few of far greater moment in religion. But I shall not enter into the detail of them in this place, as well because I think arguments *a posteriori* are unnecessary for confirming what has been, if I mistake not, sufficiently demonstrated *a priori*, as because I shall hereafter find occasion to speak somewhat of them.

22. I am afraid I have given cause to think I am needlessly prolix in handling this subject. For, to what purpose is it to dilate on that which may be demonstrated with the utmost evidence in a line or two, to any one that is capable of the least reflexion? It is but looking into your own thoughts, and so trying whether you can conceive it possible for a sound, or figure, or motion, or colour to exist without the mind or unperceived. This easy trial may perhaps make you see that what you contend for is a downright contradiction. Insomuch that I am content to put the whole upon this issue :—If you can but conceive it possible for one extended movable substance, or, in general, for any one idea, or anything like an idea, to exist otherwise than in a mind perceiving it, I shall readily give up the cause. And, as for all that compages of external bodies you contend for, I shall grant you its existence, though you cannot either give me any reason why you believe it exists, or assign any use to it when it is supposed to exist. I say, the bare possibility of your opinions being true shall pass for an argument that it is so.

23. But, say you, surely there is nothing easier than for me to imagine trees, for instance, in a park, or books existing in a closet, and nobody by to perceive them. I answer, you may so, there is no difficulty in it; but what is all this, I beseech you, more than framing in your mind certain ideas which you call books and trees, and at the same time omitting to frame the idea of any one that may perceive them? But do not you yourself perceive or think of them all the while? This therefore is nothing to the purpose: it only shews you have the power of imagining or forming ideas in your mind; but it does not shew that you can conceive it possible the objects of your thought may exist without the mind. To make out this, it is necessary that you conceive them existing unconceived or unthought of, which is a manifest repugnancy. When we do our utmost to conceive the existence of external bodies, we are all the while only contemplating our own ideas. But the mind taking no notice of itself, is deluded to think it can and does conceive bodies existing unthought of or without the mind, though at the same time they are apprehended by or exist in itself. A little attention will discover to any one the truth and evidence of what is here said, and make it unnecessary to insist on any other proofs against the existence of *material substance*.

24.[1] It is very obvious, upon the least inquiry into our thoughts, to know whether it be possible for us to understand what is meant by the *absolute existence of sensible objects in themselves, or without the mind*. To me it is evident those words mark out either a direct contradiction, or else nothing at all. And to convince others of this, I know no readier or fairer way than to entreat they would calmly attend to their own thoughts; and if by this attention the emptiness or repugnancy of those expressions does appear, surely nothing more is requisite for their conviction. It is on this therefore that I insist, to wit, that the absolute existence of unthinking things are words without a meaning, or which include a contradiction. This is what I repeat and inculcate, and earnestly recommend to the attentive thoughts of the reader.

[1] In the first edition this section began thus : " Could men but forbear to amuse themselves with words, we should, I believe, soon come to an agreement in this point. It is very obvious," &c.

25. All our ideas, sensations, or the things which we perceive, by whatsoever names they may be distinguished, are visibly inactive—there is nothing of power or agency included in them. So that one idea or object of thought cannot produce or make any alteration in another. To be satisfied of the truth of this, there is nothing else requisite but a bare observation of our ideas. For, since they and every part of them exist only in the mind, it follows that there is nothing in them but what is perceived: but whoever shall attend to his ideas, whether of sense or reflexion, will not perceive in them any power or activity; there is, therefore, no such thing contained in them. A little attention will discover to us that the very being of an idea implies passiveness and inertness in it, insomuch that it is impossible for an idea to do anything, or, strictly speaking, to be the cause of anything: neither can it be the resemblance or pattern of any active being, as is evident from sect. 8. Whence it plainly follows that extension, figure, and motion cannot be the cause of our sensations. To say, therefore, that these are the effects of powers resulting from the configuration, number, motion, and size of corpuscles, must certainly be false.

26. We perceive a continual succession of ideas, some are anew excited, others are changed or totally disappear. There is therefore some cause of these ideas, whereon they depend, and which produces and changes them. That this cause cannot be any quality or idea or combination of ideas, is clear from the preceding section. It must therefore be a substance; but it has been shewn that there is no corporeal or material substance: it remains therefore that the cause of ideas is an incorporeal active substance or Spirit.

27. A spirit is one simple, undivided, active being—as it perceives ideas it is called the *understanding*, and as it produces or otherwise operates about them it is called the *will*. Hence there can be no *idea* formed of a soul or spirit; for all ideas whatever, being passive and inert (Vide sect. 25), they cannot represent unto us, by way of image or likeness, that which acts. A little attention will make it plain to any one, that to have an idea which shall be like that active principle of motion and change of ideas is absolutely impossible. Such is the nature of *spirit*, or that which acts

that it cannot be of itself perceived, but only by the effects which it produceth. If any man shall doubt of the truth of what is here delivered, let him but reflect and try if he can frame the idea of any power or active being ; and whether he has ideas of two principal powers, marked by the names *will* and *understanding*, distinct from each other as well as from a third idea of Substance or Being in general, with a relative notion of its supporting or being the subject of the aforesaid powers—which is signified by the name *soul* or *spirit*. This is what some hold ; but, so far as I can see, the words *will*, *soul*, *spirit*, do not stand for different ideas, or, in truth, for any idea at all, but for something which is very different from ideas, and which, being an agent, cannot be like unto, or represented by, any idea whatsoever. Though it must be owned at the same time that we have some *notion* of soul, spirit, and the operations of the mind : such as willing, loving, hating—inasmuch as we know or understand the meaning of these words.[1]

28. I find I can excite ideas in my mind at pleasure, and vary and shift the scene as oft as I think fit. It is no more than willing, and straightway this or that idea arises in my fancy ; and by the same power it is obliterated and makes way for another. This making and unmaking of ideas doth very properly denominate the mind active. Thus much is certain and grounded on experience : but when we talk of unthinking agents, or of exciting ideas exclusive of volition, we only amuse ourselves with words.

29. But, whatever power I may have over my own thoughts, I find the ideas actually perceived by Sense have not a like dependence on my will. When in broad daylight I open my eyes, it is not in my power to choose whether I shall see no, or to determine what particular objects shall present themselves to my view ; and so likewise as to the hearing and other senses, the ideas imprinted on them are not creatures of my will. There is therefore some *other* Will or Spirit that produces them.

30. The ideas of Sense are more strong, lively, and distinct than those of the imagination ; they have likewise a

---

[1] The closing sentence of this section, "Though it must be owned," &c., was added to the last edition.

steadiness, order, and coherence, and are not excited at random, as those which are the effects of human wills often are, but in a regular train or series, the admirable connexion whereof sufficiently testifies the wisdom and benevolence of its Author. Now the set rules or established methods wherein the Mind we depend on excites in us the ideas of sense, are called the *laws of nature*; and these we learn by experience, which teaches us that such and such ideas are attended with such and such other ideas, in the ordinary course of things.

31. This gives us a sort of foresight which enables us to regulate our actions for the benefit of life. And without this we should be eternally at a loss; we could not know how to act anything that might procure us the least pleasure, or remove the least pain of sense. That food nourishes, sleep refreshes, and fire warms us; that to sow in the seed-time is the way to reap in the harvest; and in general that to obtain such or such ends, such or such means are conducive—all this we know, not by discovering any necessary connexion between our ideas, but only by the observation of the settled laws of nature, without which we should be all in uncertainty and confusion, and a grown man no more know how to manage himself in the affairs of life than an infant just born.

32. And yet this consistent uniform working, which so evidently displays the goodness and wisdom of that Governing Spirit whose Will constitutes the laws of nature, is so far from leading our thoughts to Him, that it rather sends them wandering after second causes. For, when we perceive certain ideas of Sense constantly followed by other ideas and we know this is not of our own doing, we forthwith attribute power and agency to the ideas themselves, and make one the cause of another, than which nothing can be more absurd and unintelligible. Thus, for example, having observed that when we perceive by sight a certain round luminous figure we at the same time perceive by touch the idea or sensation called heat, we do from thence conclude the sun to be the cause of heat. And in like manner perceiving the motion and collision of bodies to be attended with sound, we are inclined to think the latter an effect of the former.

33. The ideas imprinted on the Senses by the Author of nature are called *real things;* and those excited in the imagination being less regular, vivid, and constant, are more properly termed *ideas*, or *images of things*, which they copy and represent. But then our sensations, be they never so vivid and distinct, are nevertheless ideas, that is, they exist in the mind, or are perceived by it, as truly as the ideas of its own framing. The ideas of Sense are allowed to have more reality in them, that is, to be more strong, orderly, and coherent than the creatures of the mind ; but this is no argument that they exist without the mind. They are also less dependent on the spirit, or thinking substance which perceives them, in that they are excited by the will of another and more powerful spirit; yet still they are *ideas*, and certainly no idea, whether faint or strong, can exist otherwise than in a mind perceiving it.

34. Before we proceed any farther it is necessary we spend some time in answering objections which may probably be made against the principles we have hitherto laid down. In doing of which, if I seem too prolix to those of quick apprehensions, I hope it may be pardoned, since all men do not equally apprehend things of this nature, and I am willing to be understood by every one.

First, then, it will be objected that by the foregoing principles all that is real and substantial in nature is banished out of the world, and instead thereof a chimerical scheme of *ideas* takes place. All things that exist, exist only in the mind, that is, they are purely notional. What therefore becomes of the sun, moon, and stars ? What must we think of houses, rivers, mountains, trees, stones ; nay, even of our own bodies ? Are all these but so many chimeras and illusions on the fancy ? To all which, and whatever else of the same sort may be objected, I answer, that by the principles premised we are not deprived of any one thing in nature. Whatever we see, feel, hear, or anywise conceive or understand remains as secure as ever, and is as real as ever. There is a *rerum natura*, and the distinction between realities and chimeras retains its full force. This is evident from sect. 29, 30, and 33, where we have shewn what is meant by *real things*, in opposition to *chimeras* or ideas of our own framing; but then they both equally exist in the mind, and in that sense are alike *ideas*.

35. I do not argue against the existence of any one thing that we can apprehend either by sense or reflexion. That the things I see with my eyes and touch with my hands do exist, really exist, I make not the least question. The only thing whose existence we deny is that which *philosophers* call Matter or corporeal substance. And in doing of this there is no damage done to the rest of mankind, who, I dare say, will never miss it. The Atheist indeed will want the colour of an empty name to support his impiety; and the Philosophers may possibly find they have lost a great handle for trifling and disputation.[1]

36. If any man thinks this detracts from the existence or reality of things, he is very far from understanding what hath been premised in the plainest terms I could think of. Take here an abstract of what has been said:—There are spiritual substances, minds, or human souls, which will or excite ideas in themselves at pleasure; but these are faint, weak, and unsteady in respect of others they perceive by sense—which, being impressed upon them according to certain rules or laws of nature, speak themselves the effects of a mind more powerful and wise than human spirits. These latter are said to have more *reality* in them than the former;—by which is meant that they are more affecting, orderly, and distinct, and that they are not fictions of the mind perceiving them. And in this sense the sun that I see by day is the real sun, and that which I imagine by night is the idea of the former. In the sense here given of *reality* it is evident that every vegetable, star, mineral, and in general each part of the mundane system, is as much a *real being* by our principles as by any other. Whether others mean anything by the term *reality* different from what I do, I entreat them to look into their own thoughts and see.

37. It will be urged that thus much at least is true, to wit, that we take away all corporeal substance. To this my answer is, that if the word *substance* be taken in the vulgar sense—for a combination of sensible qualities, such as extension, solidity, weight, and the like—this we cannot be

---

[1] In the first edition this sentence follows: "But that is all the harm that I can see done."

ccused of taking away : but if it be taken in a philosophic
ense—for the support of accidents or qualities without the
mind—then indeed I acknowledge that we take it away, if
ne may be said to take away that which never had any
xistence, not even in the imagination.

38. But after all, say you, it sounds very harsh to say we
at and drink ideas, and are clothed with ideas. I acknowledge it does so—the word *idea* not being used in common
iscourse to signify the several combinations of sensible
ualities which are called *things ;* and it is certain that any
xpression which varies from the familiar use of language
ill seem harsh and ridiculous. But this doth not concern
ie truth of the proposition, which in other words is no more
ian to say, we are fed and clothed with those things which
e perceive immediately by our senses. The hardness or
oftness, the colour, taste, warmth, figure, and suchlike
ualities, which combined together constitute the several
orts of victuals and apparel, have been shewn to exist only
the mind that perceives them ; and this is all that is meant
calling them *ideas ;* which word if it was as ordinarily
sed as *thing,* would sound no harsher nor more ridiculous
an it. I am not for disputing about the propriety, but the
uth of the expression. If therefore you agree with me that
e eat and drink and are clad with the immediate objects of
nse, which cannot exist unperceived or without the mind,
shall readily grant it is more proper or conformable to
stom that they should be called things rather than ideas.

39. If it be demanded why I make use of the word *idea,*
d do not rather in compliance with custom call them
ings ; I answer, I do it for two reasons :—first, because the
rm *thing* in contradistinction to *idea,* is generally supposed
denote somewhat existing without the mind ; secondly,
cause *thing* hath a more comprehensive signification than
a, including spirit or thinking things as well as ideas.
nce therefore the objects of sense exist only in the mind,
d are withal thoughtless and inactive, I chose to mark
em by the word *idea,* which implies those properties.

40. But, say what we can, some one perhaps may be apt to
ly, he will still believe his senses, and never suffer any
guments, how plausible soever, to prevail over the certainty
them. Be it so ; assert the evidence of sense as high as

you please, we are willing to do the same. That what I see, hear, and feel doth exist, that is to say, is perceived by me, I no more doubt than I do of my own being. But I do not see how the testimony of sense can be alleged as a proof for the existence of anything which is not perceived by sense. We are not for having any man turn sceptic and disbelieve his senses; on the contrary, we give them all the stress and assurance imaginable; nor are there any principles more opposite to Scepticism than those we have laid down, as shall be hereafter clearly shewn.

41. *Secondly*, it will be objected that there is a great difference betwixt real fire for instance, and the idea of fire, betwixt dreaming or imagining oneself burnt, and actually being so: if you suspect it to be only the idea of fire which you see, do but put your hand into it and you will be convinced with a witness. This and the like may be urged in opposition to our tenets. To all which the answer is evident from what hath been already said; and I shall only add in this place, that if real fire be very different from the idea of fire, so also is the real pain that it occasions very different from the idea of the same pain, and yet nobody will pretend that real pain either is, or can possibly be, in an unperceiving thing, or without the mind, any more than its idea.

42. *Thirdly*, it will be objected that we see things actually without or at a distance from us, and which consequently do not exist in the mind; it being absurd that those things which are seen at the distance of several miles should be as near to us as our own thoughts. In answer to this, I desire it may be considered that in a dream we do oft perceive things as existing at a great distance off, and yet for all that, those things are acknowledged to have their existence only in the mind.

43. But, for the fuller clearing of this point, it may be worth while to consider how it is that we perceive distance and things placed at a distance by sight. For, that we should in truth see external space, and bodies actually existing in it, some nearer, others farther off, seems to carry with it some opposition to what hath been said of their existing nowhere without the mind. The consideration of this difficulty it was that gave birth to my " Essay towards a New

Theory of Vision," which was published not long since, wherein it is shewn that distance or outness is neither immediately of itself perceived by sight, nor yet apprehended or judged of by lines and angles, or anything that hath a necessary connexion with it ; but that it is only suggested to our thoughts by certain visible ideas and sensations attending vision, which in their own nature have no manner of similitude or relation either with distance or things placed at a distance ; but, by a connexion taught us by experience, they come to signify and suggest them to us, after the same manner that words of any language suggest the ideas they are made to stand for ; insomuch that a man born blind and afterwards made to see, would not, at first sight, think the things he saw to be without his mind, or at any distance from him.   See sect. 41 of the forementioned treatise.

44. The ideas of sight and touch make two species entirely distinct and heterogeneous.   The former are marks and prognostics of the latter.   That the proper objects of sight neither exist without the mind, nor are the images of external things, was shewn even in that treatise.   Though throughout the same the contrary be supposed true of tangible objects —not that to suppose that vulgar error was necessary for establishing the notion therein laid down, but because it was beside my purpose to examine and refute it in a discourse concerning *Vision*.   So that in strict truth the ideas of sight, when we apprehend by them distance and things placed at a distance, do not suggest or mark out to us things actually existing at a distance, but only admonish us what ideas of touch will be imprinted in our minds at such and such distances of time, and in consequence of such or such actions.   It is, I say, evident from what has been said in the foregoing parts of this Treatise, and in sect. 147 and elsewhere of the Essay concerning Vision, that visible ideas are the Language whereby the Governing Spirit on whom we depend informs us what tangible ideas he is about to imprint upon us, in case we excite this or that motion in our own bodies.   But for a fuller information in this point I refer to the Essay itself.

45. *Fourthly*, it will be objected that from the foregoing principles it follows things are every moment annihilated and

created anew. The objects of sense exist only when the
are perceived; the trees therefore are in the garden, or the
chairs in the parlour, no longer than while there is somebod
by to perceive them. Upon shutting my eyes all the furni
ture in the room is reduced to nothing, and barely upon
opening them it is again created. In answer to all which,
refer the reader to what has been said in sect. 3, 4, &c., and
desire he will consider whether he means anything by the
actual existence of an idea distinct from its being perceived
For my part, after the nicest inquiry I could make, I am no
able to discover that anything else is meant by those words
and I once more entreat the reader to sound his own
thoughts, and not suffer himself to be imposed on by words
If he can conceive it possible either for his ideas or thei
archetypes to exist without being perceived, then I give up
the cause; but if he cannot, he will acknowledge it is un
reasonable for him to stand up in defence of he knows no
what, and pretend to charge on me as an absurdity the no
assenting to those propositions which at bottom have no
meaning in them.

46. It will not be amiss to observe how far the received
principles of philosophy are themselves chargeable with those
pretended absurdities. It is thought strangely absurd tha
upon closing my eyelids all the visible objects around me
should be reduced to nothing; and yet is not this wha
philosophers commonly acknowledge, when they agree on al
hands that light and colours, which alone are the proper and
immediate objects of sight, are mere sensations that exist no
longer than they are perceived? Again, it may to some
perhaps seem very incredible that things should be every
moment creating, yet this very notion is commonly taught in
the schools. For the Schoolmen, though they acknowledge
the existence of Matter, and that the whole mundane fabric
is framed out of it, are nevertheless of opinion that it canno
subsist without the divine conservation, which by them is
expounded to be a continual creation.

47. Farther, a little thought will discover to us that though
we allow the existence of Matter or corporeal substance, yet
it will unavoidably follow, from the principles which are now
generally admitted, that the particular bodies, of what kind
soever, do none of them exist whilst they are not perceived

For, it is evident from sect. 11 and the following sections, that the Matter philosophers contend for is an incomprehensible somewhat, which hath none of those particular qualities whereby the bodies falling under our senses are distinguished one from another. But, to make this more plain, it must be remarked that the infinite divisibility of Matter is now universally allowed, at least by the most approved and considerable philosophers, who on the received principles demonstrate it beyond all exception. Hence, it follows there is an infinite number of parts in each particle of Matter which are not perceived by sense. The reason therefore that any particular body seems to be of a finite magnitude, or exhibits only a finite number of parts to sense, is, not because it contains no more, since in itself it contains an infinite number of parts, but because the sense is not acute enough to discern them. In proportion therefore as the sense is rendered more acute, it perceives a greater number of parts in the object, that is, the object appears greater, and its figure varies, those parts in its extremities which were before unperceivable appearing now to bound it in very different lines and angles from those perceived by an obtuser sense. And at length, after various changes of size and shape, when the sense becomes infinitely acute the body shall seem infinite. During all which there is no alteration in the body, but only in the sense. Each body therefore, considered in itself, is infinitely extended, and consequently void of all shape or figure. From which it follows that, though we should grant the existence of Matter to be never so certain, yet it is withal as certain, the materialists themselves are by their own principles forced to acknowledge, that neither the particular bodies perceived by sense, nor anything like them, exists without the mind. Matter, I say, and each particle thereof, is according to them infinite and shapeless, and it is the mind that frames all that variety of bodies which compose the visible world, any one whereof does not exist longer than it is perceived.

48. If we consider it, the objection proposed in sect. 45 will not be found reasonably charged on the principles we have premised, so as in truth to make any objection at all against our notions. For, though we hold indeed the objects of sense to be nothing else but ideas which

cannot exist unperceived; yet we may not hence conclude they have no existence except only while they are perceived by us, since there may be some other spirit that perceives them though we do not. Wherever bodies are said to have no existence without the mind, I would not be understood to mean this or that particular mind, but all minds whatsoever. It does not therefore follow from the foregoing principles that bodes are annihilated and created every moment, or exist not at all during the intervals between our perception of them.

49. *Fifthly*, it may perhaps be objected that if extension and figure exist only in the mind, it follows that the mind is extended and figured; since extension is a mode or attribute which (to speak with the schools) is predicated of the subject in which it exists. I answer, those qualities are in the mind only as they are perceived by it—that is, not by way of *mode* or *attribute*, but only by way of *idea*; and it no more follows the soul or mind is extended, because extension exists in it alone, than it does that it is red or blue, because those colours are on all hands acknowledged to exist in it, and nowhere else. As to what philosophers say of subject and mode, that seems very groundless and unintelligible. For instance, in this proposition "a die is hard, extended, and square," they will have it that the word *die* denotes a subject or substance, distinct from the hardness, extension, and figure which are predicated of it, and in which they exist. This I cannot comprehend: to me a die seems to be nothing distinct from those things which are termed its modes or accidents. And, to say a die is hard, extended, and square is not to attribute those qualities to a subject distinct from and supporting them, but only an explication of the meaning of the word *die*.

50. *Sixthly*, you will say there have been a great many things explained by matter and motion; take away these and you destroy the whole corpuscular philosophy, and undermine those mechanical principles which have been applied with so much success to account for the phenomena. In short, whatever advances have been made, either by ancient or modern philosophers, in the study of nature do all

proceed on the supposition that corporeal substance or Matter doth really exist. To this I answer that there is not any one phenomenon explained on that supposition which may not as well be explained without it, as might easily be made appear by an induction of particulars. To explain the phenomena, is all one as to shew why, upon such and such occasions, we are affected with such and such ideas. But how Matter should operate on a Spirit, or produce any idea in it, is what no philosopher will pretend to explain; it is therefore evident there can be no use of Matter in natural philosophy. Besides, they who attempt to account for things do it not by corporeal substance, but by figure, motion, and other qualities, which are in truth no more than mere ideas, and therefore cannot be the cause of anything, as hath been already shewn. See sect. 25.

51. *Seventhly*, it will upon this be demanded whether it does not seem absurd to take away natural causes, and ascribe everything to the immediate operation of Spirits? We must no longer say upon these principles that fire heats, or water cools, but that a Spirit heats, and so forth. Would not a man be deservedly laughed at, who should talk after this manner? I answer, he would so; in such things we ought to "think with the learned, and speak with the vulgar." They who to demonstration are convinced of the truth of the Copernican system do nevertheless say "the sun rises," "the sun sets," or "comes to the meridian;" and if they affected a contrary style in common talk it would without doubt appear very ridiculous. A little reflexion on what is here said will make it manifest that the common use of language would receive no manner of alteration or disturbance from the admission of our tenets.

52. In the ordinary affairs of life, any phrases may be retained, so long as they excite in us proper sentiments, or dispositions to act in such a manner as is necessary for our well-being, how false soever they may be if taken in a strict and speculative sense. Nay, this is unavoidable, since, propriety being regulated by custom, language is suited to the received opinions, which are not always the truest. Hence it is impossible, even in the most rigid, philosophic reasonings, so far to alter the bent and genius of the tongue we

speak, as never to give a handle for cavillers to pretend difficulties and inconsistencies. But, a fair and ingenuous reader will collect the sense from the scope and tenor and connexion of a discourse, making allowances for those inaccurate modes of speech which use has made inevitable.

53. As to the opinion that there are no Corporeal Causes, this has been heretofore maintained by some of the Schoolmen, as it is of late by others among the modern philosophers, who though they allow Matter to exist, yet will have God alone to be the immediate efficient cause of all things. These men saw that amongst all the objects of sense there was none which had any power or activity included in it ; and that by consequence this was likewise true of whatever bodies they supposed to exist without the mind, like unto the immediate objects of sense. But then, that they should suppose an innumerable multitude of created beings, which they acknowledge are not capable of producing any one effect in nature, and which therefore are made to no manner of purpose, since God might have done everything as well without them : this I say, though we should allow it possible, must yet be a very unaccountable and extravagant supposition.

54. In the *eighth* place, the universal concurrent assent of mankind may be thought by some an invincible argument in behalf of Matter, or the existence of external things. Must we suppose the whole world to be mistaken ? And if so, what cause can be assigned of so widespread and predominant an error ? I answer, first, that, upon a narrow inquiry, it will not perhaps be found so many as is imagined do really believe the existence of Matter or things without the mind. Strictly speaking, to believe that which involves a contradiction, or has no meaning in it, is impossible ; and whether the foregoing expressions are not of that sort, I refer it to the impartial examination of the reader. In one sense, indeed, men may be said to believe that Matter exists, that is, they act as if the immediate cause of their sensations, which affects them every moment, and is so nearly present to them, were some senseless unthinking being. But, that they should clearly apprehend any meaning marked by those words, and form thereof a settled speculative opinion, is what I am not able to conceive. This is not the only instance wherein men

impose upon themselves, by imagining they believe those propositions which they have often heard, though at bottom they have no meaning in them.

55. But secondly, though we should grant a notion to be never so universally and steadfastly adhered to, yet this is but a weak argument of its truth to whoever considers what a vast number of prejudices and false opinions are everywhere embraced with the utmost tenaciousness, by the unreflecting (which are the far greater) part of mankind. There was a time when the antipodes and motion of the earth were looked upon as monstrous absurdities even by men of learning : and if it be considered what a small proportion they bear to the rest of mankind, we shall find that at this day those notions have gained but a very inconsiderable footing in the world.

56. But it is demanded that we assign a cause of this prejudice, and account for its obtaining in the world. To this I answer, that men knowing they perceived several ideas, whereof they themselves were not the authors—as not being excited from within nor depending on the operation of their wills—this made them maintain those ideas, or objects of perception had an existence independent of and without the mind, without ever dreaming that a contradiction was involved in those words. But, philosophers having plainly seen that the immediate objects of perception do not exist without the mind, they in some degree corrected the mistake of the vulgar ; but at the same time run into another which seems no less absurd, to wit, that there are certain objects really existing without the mind, or having a subsistence distinct from being perceived, of which our ideas are only images or resemblances, imprinted by those objects on the mind. And this notion of the philosophers owes its origin to the same cause with the former, namely, their being conscious that they were not the authors of their own sensations, which they evidently knew were imprinted from without, and which therefore must have some cause distinct from the minds on which they are imprinted.

57. But why they should suppose the ideas of sense to be excited in us by things in their likeness, and not rather have recourse to *Spirit* which alone can act, may be accounted

for, first, because they were not aware of the repugnancy there is, as well in supposing things like unto our ideas existing without, as in attributing to them power or activity. Secondly, because the Supreme Spirit which excites those ideas in our minds, is not marked out and limited to our view by any particular finite collection of sensible ideas, as human agents are by their size, complexion, limbs, and motions. And thirdly, because His operations are regular and uniform. Whenever the course of nature is interrupted by a miracle, men are ready to own the presence of a superior agent. But, when we see things go on in the ordinary course they do not excite in us any reflexion ; their order and concatenation, though it be an argument of the greatest wisdom, power, and goodness in their creator, is yet so constant and familiar to us that we do not think them the immediate effects of a *Free Spirit ;* especially since inconsistency and mutability in acting, though it be an imperfection, is looked on as a mark of *freedom.*

58. *Tenthly,* it will be objected that the notions we advance are inconsistent with several sound truths in philosophy and mathematics. For example, the motion of the earth is now universally admitted by astronomers as a truth grounded on the clearest and most convincing reasons. But, on the foregoing principles, there can be no such thing. For, motion being only an idea, it follows that if it be not perceived it exists not : but the motion of the earth is not perceived by sense. I answer, that tenet, if rightly understood, will be found to agree with the principles we have premised ; for, the question whether the earth moves or no amounts in reality to no more than this, to wit, whether we have reason to conclude, from what has been observed by astronomers, that if we were placed in such and such circumstances, and such or such a position and distance both from the earth and sun, we should perceive the former to move among the choir of the planets, and appearing in all respects like one of them ; and this, by the established rules of nature which we have no reason to mistrust, is reasonably collected from the phenomena.

59. We may, from the experience we have had of the train and succession of ideas in our minds, often make, I

will not say uncertain conjectures, but sure and well-grounded predictions concerning the ideas we shall be affected with pursuant to a great train of actions, and be enabled to pass a right judgment of what would have appeared to us, in case we were placed in circumstances very different from those we are in at present. Herein consists the knowledge of nature, which may preserve its use and certainty very consistently with what hath been said. It will be easy to apply this to whatever objections of the like sort may be drawn from the magnitude of the stars, or any other discoveries in astronomy or nature.

60. In the *eleventh* place, it will be demanded to what purpose serves that curious organization of plants, and the animal mechanism in the parts of animals; might not vegetables grow, and shoot forth leaves and blossoms, and animals perform all their motions as well without as with all that variety of internal parts so elegantly contrived and put together; which, being ideas, have nothing powerful or operative in them, nor have any necessary connexion with the effects ascribed to them? If it be a Spirit that immediately produces every effect by a *fiat* or act of his will, we must think all that is fine and artificial in the works, whether of man or nature, to be made in vain. By this doctrine, though an artist hath made the spring and wheels, and every movement of a watch, and adjusted them in such a manner as he knew would produce the motions he designed, yet he must think all this done to no purpose, and that it is an Intelligence which directs the index, and points to the hour of the day. If so, why may not the Intelligence do it, without his being at the pains of making the movements and putting them together? Why does not an empty case serve as well as another? And how comes it to pass that whenever there is any fault in the going of a watch, there is some corresponding disorder to be found in the movements, which being mended by a skilful hand all is right again? The like may be said of all the clockwork of nature, great part whereof is so wonderfully fine and subtle as scarce to be discerned by the best microscope. In short, it will be asked, how, upon our principles, any tolerable account can be given, or any final cause assigned of an in-

numerable multitude of bodies and machines, framed with the most exquisite art, which in the common philosophy have very apposite uses assigned them, and serve to explain abundance of phenomena ?

61. To all which I answer, first, that though there were some difficulties relating to the administration of Providence, and the uses by it assigned to the several parts of nature, which I could not solve by the foregoing principles, yet this objection could be of small weight against the truth and certainty of those things which may be proved *a priori*, with the utmost evidence. Secondly, but neither are the received principles free from the like difficulties ; for, it may still be demanded to what end God should take those roundabout methods of effecting things by instruments and machines, which no one can deny might have been effected by the mere command of His will without all that apparatus : nay, if we narrowly consider it, we shall find the objection may be retorted with greater force on those who hold the existence of those machines without the mind ; for it has been made evident that solidity, bulk, figure, motion, and the like have no *activity* or *efficacy* in them, so as to be capable of producing any one effect in nature. See sect. 25. Whoever therefore supposes them to exist (allowing the supposition possible) when they are not perceived does it manifestly to no purpose ; since the only use that is assigned to them, as they exist unperceived, is that they produce those perceivable effects which in truth cannot be ascribed to anything but Spirit.

62. But, to come nigher the difficulty, it must be observed that though the fabrication of all those parts and organs be not absolutely necessary to the producing any effect, yet it is necessary to the producing of things in a constant regular way according to the laws of nature. There are certain general laws that run through the whole chain of natural effects : these are learned by the observation and study of nature, and are by men applied as well to the framing artificial things for the use and ornament of life as to the explaining the various phenomena—which explication consists only in shewing the conformity any particular phenomenon hath to the general laws of nature, or, which is the same thing, in discovering the *uniformity* there is in the pro-

duction of natural effects ; as will be evident to whoever
shall attend to the several instances wherein philosophers
pretend to account for appearances. That there is a great
and conspicuous use in these regular constant methods of
working observed by the Supreme Agent hath been shewn
in sect. 31. And it is no less visible that a particular size,
figure, motion, and disposition of parts are necessary, though
not absolutely to the producing any effect, yet to the producing it according to the standing mechanical laws of nature.
Thus, for instance, it cannot be denied that God, or the
Intelligence that sustains and rules the ordinary course of
things, might if He were minded to produce a miracle,
cause all the motions on the dial-plate of a watch, though
nobody had ever made the movements and put them in it :
but yet, if He will act agreeably to the rules of mechanism,
by Him for wise ends established and maintained in the
creation, it is necessary that those actions of the watchmaker,
whereby he makes the movements and rightly adjusts them,
precede the production of the aforesaid motions ; as also
that any disorder in them be attended with the perception of
some corresponding disorder in the movements, which being
once corrected all is right again.

63. It may indeed on some occasions be necessary that
the Author of nature display His overruling power in
producing some appearance out of the ordinary series of
things. Such exceptions from the general rules of nature
are proper to surprise and awe men into an acknowledgment
of the Divine Being; but then they are to be used but seldom,
otherwise there is a plain reason why they should fail of that
effect. Besides, God seems to choose the convincing our
reason of His attributes by the works of nature, which discover so much harmony and contrivance in their make, and
are such plain indications of wisdom and beneficence in their
Author, rather than to astonish us into a belief of His Being
by anomalous and surprising events.

64. To set this matter in a yet clearer light, I shall observe
that what has been objected in sect. 60 amounts in reality to
no more than this :—ideas are not anyhow and at random
produced, there being a certain order and connexion between
them, like to that of cause and effect : there are also several
combinations of them made in a very regular and artificial

manner, which seem like so many instruments in the hand of nature that, being hid as it were behind the scenes, have a secret operation in producing those appearances which are seen on the theatre of the world, being themselves discernible only to the curious eye of the philosopher. But, since one idea cannot be the cause of another, to what purpose is that connexion? And, since those instruments, being barely *inefficacious perceptions* in the mind, are not subservient to the production of natural effects, it is demanded why they are made; or, in other words, what reason can be assigned why God should make us, upon a close inspection into His works, behold so great variety of ideas so artfully laid together, and so much according to rule; it not being credible that He would be at the expense (if one may so speak) of all that art and regularity to no purpose.

65. To all which my answer is, first, that the connexion of ideas does not imply the relation of *cause* and *effect*, but only of a mark or *sign* with the thing *signified*. The fire which I see is not the cause of the pain I suffer upon my approaching it, but the mark that forewarns me of it. In like manner the noise that I hear is not the effect of this or that motion or collision of the ambient bodies, but the sign thereof. Secondly, the reason why ideas are formed into machines, that is, artificial and regular combinations, is the same with that for combining letters into words. That a few original ideas may be made to signify a great number of effects and actions, it is necessary they be variously combined together. And, to the end their use be permanent and universal, these combinations must be made by *rule*, and with *wise contrivance*. By this means abundance of information is conveyed unto us, concerning what we are to expect from such and such actions and what methods are proper to be taken for the exciting such and such ideas; which in effect is all that I conceive to be distinctly meant when it is said that, by discerning the figure, texture, and mechanism of the inward parts of bodies, whether natural or artificial, we may attain to know the several uses and properties depending thereon, or the nature of the thing.

66. Hence, it is evident that those things which, under the notion of a cause co-operating or concurring to the production of effects, are altogether inexplicable, and run us into great absurdities, may be very naturally explained, and

have a proper and obvious use assigned to them, when they are considered only as marks or signs for our information. And it is the searching after and endeavouring to understand those signs instituted by the Author of Nature,[1] that ought to be the employment of the natural philosopher; and not the pretending to explain things by corporeal causes, which doctrine seems to have too much estranged the minds of men from that active principle, that supreme and wise Spirit "in whom we live, move, and have our being."

67. In the *twelfth* place, it may perhaps be objected that —though it be clear from what has been said that there can be no such thing as an inert, senseless, extended, solid, figured, movable substance existing without the mind, such as philosophers describe Matter—yet, if any man shall leave out of his idea of *matter* the positive ideas of extension, figure, solidity and motion, and say that he means only by that word an inert, senseless substance, that exists without the mind or unperceived, which is the occasion of our ideas, or at the presence whereof God is pleased to excite ideas in us: it doth not appear but that Matter taken in this sense may possibly exist. In answer to which I say, first, that it seems no less absurd to suppose a substance without accidents, than it is to suppose accidents without a substance. But secondly, though we should grant this unknown substance may possibly exist, yet where can it be supposed to be? That it exists not in the mind is agreed; and that it exists not in place is no less certain—since all place or extension exists only in the mind, as hath been already proved. It remains therefore that it exists nowhere at all.

68. Let us examine a little the description that is here given us of *matter*. It neither acts, nor perceives, nor is perceived; for this is all that is meant by saying it is an inert, senseless, unknown substance; which is a definition entirely made up of negatives, excepting only the relative notion of its standing under or supporting. But then it must be observed that it supports nothing at all, and how nearly this comes to the description of a *nonentity* I desire may be considered. But, say you, it is the *unknown occasion*, at the

---

[1] In the first edition this phrase read thus : "this Language (if I may so call it) of the Author of Nature."

presence of which ideas are excited in us by the will of God. Now, I would fain know how anything can be present to us, which is neither perceivable by sense nor reflexion, nor capable of producing any idea in our minds, nor is at all extended, nor hath any form, nor exists in any place. The words "to be present," when thus applied, must needs be taken in some abstract and strange meaning, and which I am not able to comprehend.

69. Again, let us examine what is meant by *occasion*. So far as I can gather from the common use of language, that word signifies either the agent which produces any effect, or else something that is observed to accompany or go before it in the ordinary course of things. But, when it is applied to Matter as above described, it can be taken in neither of those senses; for Matter is said to be passive and inert, and so cannot be an agent or efficient cause. It is also unperceivable, as being devoid of all sensible qualities, and so cannot be the occasion of our perceptions in the latter sense: as when the burning my finger is said to be the occasion of the pain that attends it. What therefore can be meant by calling matter an *occasion*? This term is either used in no sense at all, or else in some very distant from its received signification.

70. You will perhaps say that Matter, though it be not perceived by us, is nevertheless perceived by God, to whom it is the occasion of exciting ideas in our minds. For, say you, since we observe our sensations to be imprinted in an orderly and constant manner, it is but reasonable to suppose there are certain constant and regular occasions of their being produced. That is to say, that there are certain permanent and distinct parcels of Matter, corresponding to our ideas, which, though they do not excite them in our minds, or anywise immediately affect us, as being altogether passive and unperceivable to us, they are nevertheless to God, by whom they are perceived, as it were so many occasions to remind Him when and what ideas to imprint on our minds: that so things may go on in a constant uniform manner

71. In answer to this, I observe that, as the notion of Matter is here stated, the question is no longer concerning the existence of a thing distinct from *Spirit* and *idea*, from perceiving and being perceived; but whether there are not certain ideas of I know not what sort, in the mind of God,

which are so many marks or notes that direct Him how to produce sensations in our minds in a constant and regular method—much after the same manner as a musician is directed by the notes of music to produce that harmonious train and composition of sound which is called a tune, though they who hear the music do not perceive the notes, and may be entirely ignorant of them. But, this notion of Matter [1] seems too extravagant to deserve a confutation. Besides, it is in effect no objection against what we have advanced, viz. that there is no senseless unperceived substance.

72. If we follow the light of reason, we shall, from the constant uniform method of our sensations, collect the goodness and wisdom of the Spirit who excites them in our minds; but this is all that I can see reasonably concluded from thence. To me, I say, it is evident that the being of a spirit infinitely wise, good, and powerful is abundantly sufficient to explain all the appearances of nature. But, as for *inert, senseless Matter*, nothing that I perceive has any the least connexion with it, or leads to the thoughts of it. And I would fain see any one explain any the meanest phenomenon in nature by it, or shew any manner of reason, though in the lowest rank of probability, that he can have for its existence, or even make any tolerable sense or meaning of that supposition. For, as to its being an occasion, we have, I think, evidently shewn that with regard to us it is no occasion. It remains therefore that it must be, if at all, the occasion to God of exciting ideas in us; and what this amounts to we have just now seen.

73. It is worth while to reflect a little on the motives which induced men to suppose the existence of *material substance ;* that so having observed the gradual ceasing and expiration of those motives or reasons, we may proportionably withdraw the assent that was grounded on them. First, therefore, it was thought that colour, figure, motion, and the rest of the sensible qualities or accidents, did really exist without the mind ; and for this reason it seemed needful to suppose some unthinking *substratum* or substance wherein they did exist, since they could not be conceived to exist

---

[1] In the first edition between "Matter" and "seems" occurred this parenthesis "(which after all is the only intelligible one that I can pick, from what is said of unknown Occasions)."

by themselves. Afterwards, in process of time, men being convinced that colours, sounds, and the rest of the sensible, secondary qualities had no existence without the mind, they stripped this *substratum* or material substance of those qualities, leaving only the primary ones, figure, motion, and suchlike, which they still conceived to exist without the mind, and consequently to stand in need of a material support. But, it having be shewn that none even of these can possibly exist therwise than in a Spirit or Mind which perceives them it follows that we have no longer any reason to suppose the being of Matter; nay, that it is utterly impossible there should be any such thing, so long as that word is taken to denote an *unthinking substratum* of qualities or accidents wherein they exist without the mind.

74. But though it be allowed by the materialists themselves that Matter was thought of only for the sake of supporting accidents, and, the reason entirely ceasing, one might expect the mind should naturally, and without any reluctance at all, quit the belief of what was solely grounded thereon: yet the prejudice is riveted so deeply in our thoughts, that we can scarce tell how to part with it, and are therefore inclined, since the *thing* itself is indefensible, at least to retain the *name*, which we apply to I know not what abstracted and indefinite notions of being, or occasion, though without any show of reason, at least so far as I can see. For, what is there on our part, or what do we perceive, amongst all the ideas, sensations, notions which are imprinted on our minds, either by sense or reflexion, from whence may be inferred the existence of an inert, thoughtless, unperceived occasion? and, on the other hand, on the part of an All-sufficient Spirit, what can there be that should make us believe or even suspect He is directed by an inert occasion to excite ideas in our minds?

75. It is a very extraordinary instance of the force of prejudice, and much to be lamented, that the mind of man retains so great a fondness, against all the evidence of reason, for a stupid thoughtless *somewhat*, by the interposition whereof it would as it were screen itself from the Providence of God, and remove it farther off from the affairs of the world. But, though we do the utmost we can to secure the belief of Matter, though, when reason forsakes

us, we endeavour to support our opinion on the bare possibility of the thing, and though we indulge ourselves in the full scope of an imagination not regulated by reason to make out that poor possibility, yet the upshot of all is, that there are certain *unknown Ideas* in the mind of God; for this, if anything, is all that I conceive to be meant by *occasion* with regard to God. And this at the bottom is no longer contending for the thing, but for the name.

76. Whether therefore there are such Ideas in the mind of God, and whether they may be called by the name *Matter*, I shall not dispute. But, if you stick to the notion of an unthinking substance or support of extension, motion, and other sensible qualities, then to me it is most evidently impossible there should be any such thing; since it is a plain repugnancy that those qualities should exist in or be supported by an unperceiving substance.

77. But, say you, though it be granted that there is no thoughtless support of extension and the other qualities or accidents which we perceive, yet there may perhaps be some inert, unperceiving substance or *substratum* of some other qualities, as incomprehensible to us as colours are to a man born blind, because we have not a sense adapted to them. But, if we had a new sense, we should possibly no more doubt of their existence than a blind man made to see does of the existence of light and colours. I answer, first, if what you mean by the word *Matter* be only the unknown support of unknown qualities, it is no matter whether there is such a thing or no, since it no way concerns us; and I do not see the advantage there is in disputing about what we know not *what*, and we know not *why*.

78. But, secondly, if we had a new sense it could only furnish us with new ideas or sensations; and then we should have the same reason against their existing in an unperceiving substance that has been already offered with relation to figure, motion, colour, and the like. Qualities, as hath been shewn, are nothing else but *sensations* or *ideas*, which exist only in a *mind* perceiving them; and this is true not only of the ideas we are acquainted with at present, but likewise of all possible ideas whatsoever.

79. But, you will insist, what if I have no reason to believe the existence of Matter? what if I cannot assign any

use to it or explain anything by it, or even conceive what is meant by that word? yet still it is no contradiction to say that Matter exists, and that this Matter is in general a *substance*, or *occasion of ideas;* though indeed to go about to unfold the meaning or adhere to any particular explication of those words may be attended with great difficulties. I answer, when words are used without a meaning, you may put them together as you please without danger of running into a contradiction. You may say, for example, that twice two is equal to seven, so long as you declare you do not take the words of that proposition in their usual acceptation but for marks of you know not what. And, by the same reason, you may say there is an inert thoughtless substance without accidents which is the occasion of our ideas. And we shall understand just as much by one proposition as the other.

✗ 80. In the *last* place, you will say, what if we give up the cause of material Substance, and stand to it that Matter is an unknown *somewhat*—neither substance nor accident, spirit nor idea, inert, thoughtless, indivisible, immovable, unextended, existing in no place? For, say you, whatever may be urged against *substance* or *occasion*, or any other positive or relative notion of Matter, hath no place at all, so long as this *negative* definition of Matter is adhered to. I answer, you may, if so it shall seem good, use the word "Matter" in the same sense as other men use "nothing," and so make those terms convertible in your style. For, after all, this is what appears to me to be the result of that definition, the parts whereof when I consider with attention, either collectively or separate from each other, I do not find that there is any kind of effect or impression made on my mind different from what is excited by the term *nothing*.

81. You will reply, perhaps, that in the foresaid definition is included what doth sufficiently distinguish it from no-thing—the positive abstract idea of *quiddity, entity*, or *existence*. I own, indeed, that those who pretend to the faculty of framing abstract general ideas do talk as if they had such an idea, which is, say they, the most abstract and general notion of all; that is, to me, the most incomprehensible of all others. That there are a great variety of spirits of different orders and capacities, whose faculties both in number

and extent are far exceeding those the Author of my being has bestowed on me, I see no reason to deny. And for me to pretend to determine by my own few, stinted, narrow inlets of perception, what ideas the inexhaustible power of the Supreme Spirit may imprint upon them were certainly the utmost folly and presumption—since there may be, for ought that I know, innumerable sorts of ideas or sensations, as different from one another, and from all that I have perceived, as colours are from sounds. But, how ready soever I may be to acknowledge the scantiness of my comprehension with regard to the endless variety of spirits and ideas that may possibly exist, yet for anyone to pretend to a notion of Entity or Existence, *abstracted* from *spirit* and *idea*, from perceived and being perceived, is, I suspect, a downright repugnancy and trifling with words.—It remains that we consider the objections which may possibly be made on the part of Religion.

82. Some there are who think that, though the arguments for the real existence of bodies which are drawn from Reason be allowed not to amount to demonstration, yet the Holy Scriptures are so clear in the point, as will sufficiently convince every good Christian that bodies do really exist, and are something more than mere ideas ; there being in Holy Writ innumerable facts related which evidently suppose the reality of timber and stone, mountains and rivers, and cities, and human bodies. To which I answer that no sort of writings whatever, sacred or profane, which use those and the like words in the vulgar acceptation, or so as to have a meaning in them, are in danger of having their truth called in question by our doctrine. That all those things do really exist, that there are bodies, even corporeal substances, when taken in the vulgar sense, has been shewn to be agreeable to our principles : and the difference betwixt *things* and *ideas*, *realities* and *chimeras*, has been distinctly explained. See sect. 29, 30, 33, 36, &c. And I do not think that either what philosophers call *Matter*, or the existence of objects without the mind, is anywhere mentioned in Scripture.

83. Again, whether there be or be not external things, it is agreed on all hands that the proper use of words is the marking our conceptions, or things only as they are known

and perceived by us; whence it plainly follows that in the tenets we have laid down there is nothing inconsistent with the right use and significancy of language, and that discourse, of what kind soever, so far as it is intelligible, remains undisturbed. But all this seems so manifest, from what has been set forth in the premises, that it is needless to insist any farther on it.

84. But, it will be urged that miracles do, at least, lose much of their stress and import by our principles. What must we think of Moses' rod? was it not *really* turned into a serpent; or was there only a change of *ideas* in the minds of the spectators? And, can it be supposed that our Saviour did no more at the marriage-feast in Cana than impose on the sight, and smell, and taste of the guests, so as to create in them the appearance or idea only of wine? The same may be said of other miracles; which, in consequence of the foregoing principles, must be looked upon only as so many cheats, or illusions of fancy. To this I reply, that the rod was changed into a real serpent, and the water into real wine. That this does not in the least contradict what I have elsewhere said will be evident from sect. 34 and 35. But this business of *real* and *imaginary* has been already so plainly and fully explained, and so often referred to, and the difficulties about it are so easily answered from what has gone before, that it were an affront to the reader's understanding to resume the explication of it in its place. I shall only observe that if at table all who were present should see, and smell, and taste, and drink wine, and find the effects of it, with me there could be no doubt of its reality; so that at bottom the scruple concerning real miracles has no place at all on ours, but only on the received principles, and consequently makes rather for than against what has been said.

85. Having done with the Objections, which I endeavoured to propose in the clearest light, and gave them all the force and weight I could, we proceed in the next place to take a view of our tenets in their Consequences. Some of these appear at first sight—as that several difficult and obscure questions, on which abundance of speculation has been thrown away, are entirely banished from philosophy. "Whether corporeal substance can think," "whether Matter

be infinitely divisible," and " how it operates on spirit "—
these and like inquiries have given infinite amusement to
philosophers in all ages ; but, depending on the existence of
Matter, they have no longer any place on our principles.
Many other advantages there are, as well with regard to
religion as the sciences, which it is easy for any one to
deduce from what has been premised ; but this will appear
more plainly in the sequel.

86. From the principles we have laid down it follows
human knowledge may naturally be reduced to two heads
—that of *ideas* and that of *spirits*. Of each of these I
shall treat in order.

And *first* as to ideas or unthinking things. Our knowledge of these hath been very much obscured and confounded,
and we have been led into very dangerous errors, by supposing a twofold existence of the objects of sense—the one
intelligible or in the mind, the other *real* and without the
mind ; whereby unthinking things are thought to have a
natural subsistence of their own distinct from being perceived
by spirits. This, which, if I mistake not, hath been shewn
to be a most groundless and absurd notion, is the very root of
Scepticism ; for, so long as men thought that real things
subsisted without the mind, and that their knowledge was
only so far forth *real* as it was conformable to *real things*, it
follows they could not be certain that they had any real
knowledge at all. For how can it be known that the things
which are perceived are conformable to those which are not
perceived, or exist without the mind ?

87. Colour, figure, motion, extension, and the like, considered only as so many *sensations* in the mind, are perfectly
known, there being nothing in them which is not perceived.
But, if they are looked on as notes or images, referred to
things or *archetypes* existing without the mind, then are we
involved all in scepticism. We see only the appearances,
and not the real qualities of things. What may be the
extension, figure, or motion of anything really and absolutely,
or in itself, it is impossible for us to know, but only the
proportion or relation they bear to our senses. Things
remaining the same, our ideas vary, and which of them, or
even whether any of them at all, represent the true quality

really existing in the thing, it is out of our reach to determine. So that, for aught we know, all we see, hear, and
feel, may be only phantom and vain chimera, and not at all
agree with the real things existing in *rerum natura*. All this
scepticism [1] follows from our supposing a difference between
things and *ideas*, and that the former have a subsistence
without the mind or unperceived. It were easy to dilate on
this subject, and show how the arguments urged by sceptics
in all ages depend on the supposition of external objects.

88. So long as we attribute a real existence to unthinking
things, distinct from their being perceived, it is not only impossible for us to know with evidence the nature of any real
unthinking being, but even that it exists. Hence it is that
we see philosophers distrust their senses, and doubt of the
existence of heaven and earth, of everything they see or feel,
even of their own bodies. And, after all their labour and
struggle of thought, they are forced to own we cannot attain
to any self-evident or demonstrative knowledge of the existence of sensible things. But, all this doubtfulness, which so
bewilders and confounds the mind and makes philosophy
ridiculous in the eyes of the world, vanishes if we annex a
meaning to our words, and not amuse ourselves with the
terms "absolute," "external," "exist," and such like, signifying we know not what. I can as well doubt of my own
being as of the being of those things which I actually perceive
by sense; it being a manifest contradiction that any sensible
object should be immediately perceived by sight or touch,
and at the same time have no existence in nature, since the
very *existence* of an unthinking being consists in *being perceived*.

89. Nothing seems of more importance towards erecting a
firm system of sound and real knowledge, which may be
proof against the assaults of Scepticism, than to lay the beginning in a distinct explication of what is meant by *thing*,
reality, *existence*; for in vain shall we dispute concerning the
real existence of things, or pretend to any knowledge thereof,
so long as we have not fixed the meaning of those words.
Thing or *Being* is the most general name of all; it comprehends under it two kinds entirely distinct and heterogeneous, and which have nothing common but the name,
viz. *spirits* and *ideas*. The former are active, indivisible

[1] " Sceptical cant " in the first edition.

substances: the latter are inert, fleeting, dependent beings, which subsist not by themselves, but are supported by, or exist in minds or spiritual substances.[1] We comprehend our own existence by inward feeling or reflexion, and that of other spirits by reason. We may be said to have some knowledge or notion of our own minds, of spirits and active beings, whereof in a strict sense we have not ideas. In like manner, we know and have a notion of relations between things or ideas—which relations are distinct from the ideas or things related, inasmuch as the latter may be perceived by us without our perceiving the former. To me it seems that *ideas*, *spirits*, and *relations* are all in their respective kinds the object of human knowledge and subject of discourse; and that the term *idea* would be improperly extended to signify everything we know or have any notion of.

90. Ideas imprinted on the senses are real things, or do really exist; this we do not deny, but we deny they can subsist without the minds which perceive them, or that they are resemblances of any archetypes existing without the mind; since the very being of a sensation or idea consists in being perceived, and an idea can be like nothing but an idea. Again, the things perceived by sense may be termed *external*, with regard to their origin—in that they are not generated from within by the mind itself, but imprinted by a Spirit distinct from that which perceives them. Sensible objects may likewise be said to be "without the mind" in another sense, namely when they exist in some other mind; thus, when I shut my eyes, the things I saw may still exist, but it must be in another mind.

91. It were a mistake to think that what is here said derogates in the least from the reality of things. It is acknowledged, on the received principles, that extension, motion, and in a word all sensible qualities have need of a support, as not being able to subsist by themselves. But the objects perceived by sense are allowed to be nothing but combinations of those qualities, and consequently cannot subsist by themselves. Thus far it is agreed on all hands. So

---

[1] In the first edition this last sentence ended the section and read thus: "The former are *active*, *indivisible*, *incorruptible*, substances: the latter are *inert*, *fleeting*, *perishable passions* or *dependent beings* . . . spiritual substances."

that in denying the things perceived by sense an existence independent of a substance or support wherein they may exist, we detract nothing from the received opinion of their *reality*, and are guilty of no innovation in that respect. All the difference is that, according to us, the unthinking beings perceived by sense have no existence distinct from being perceived, and cannot therefore exist in any other substance than those unextended indivisible substances or *spirits* which act and think and perceive them; whereas philosophers vulgarly hold that the sensible qualities do exist in an inert, extended, unperceiving substance which they call *Matter*, to which they attribute a natural subsistence, exterior to all thinking beings, or distinct from being perceived by any mind whatsoever, even the eternal mind of the Creator, wherein they suppose only ideas of the corporeal substances created by Him: if indeed they allow them to be at all created.

92. For, as we have shewn the doctrine of Matter or corporeal substance to have been the main pillar and support of Scepticism, so likewise upon the same foundation have been raised all the impious schemes of Atheism and Irreligion. Nay, so great a difficulty has it been thought to conceive Matter produced out of nothing, that the most celebrated among the ancient philosophers, even of those who maintained the being of a God, have thought Matter to be uncreated and coeternal with Him. How great a friend *material substance* has been to Atheists in all ages were needless to relate. All their monstrous systems have so visible and necessary a dependence on it that, when this corner-stone is once removed, the whole fabric cannot choose but fall to the ground, insomuch that it is no longer worth while to bestow a particular consideration on the absurdities of every wretched sect of Atheists.

93. That impious and profane persons should readily fall in with those systems which favour their inclinations, by deriding immaterial substance, and supposing the soul to be divisible and subject to corruption as the body; which exclude all freedom, intelligence, and design from the formation of things, and instead thereof make a self-existent, stupid, unthinking substance the root and origin of all beings; that they should hearken to those who deny a Pro-

vidence, or inspection of a Superior Mind over the affairs oi the world, attributing the whole series of events either to blind chance or fatal necessity arising from the impulse of one body on another—all this is very natural. And, on the other hand, when men of better principles observe the enemies of religion lay so great a stress on *unthinking Matter*, and all of them use so much industry and artifice to reduce everything to it, methinks they should rejoice to see them deprived of their grand support, and driven from that only fortress, without which your Epicureans, Hobbists, and the like, have not even the shadow of a pretence, but become the most cheap and easy triumph in the world.

94. The existence of Matter, or bodies unperceived, has not only been the main support of Atheists and Fatalists, but on the same principle doth Idolatry likewise in all its various forms depend. Did men but consider that the sun, moon, and stars, and every other object of the senses are only so many sensations in their minds, which have no other existence but barely being perceived, doubtless they would never fall down and worship their own *ideas*, but rather address their homage to that ETERNAL INVISIBLE MIND which produces and sustains all things.

95. The same absurd principle, by mingling itself with the articles of our faith, has occasioned no small difficulties to Christians. For example, about the Resurrection, how many scruples and objections have been raised by Socinians and others? But do not the most plausible of them depend on the supposition that a body is denominated the *same*, with regard not to the form or that which is perceived by sense, but the material substance, which remains the same under several forms? Take away this *material substance*, about the identity whereof all the dispute is, and mean by *body* what every plain ordinary person means by that word, to wit, that which is immediately seen and felt, which is only a combination of sensible qualities or ideas, and then their most unanswerable objections come to nothing.

96. Matter being once expelled out of nature drags with it so many sceptical and impious notions, such an incredible number of disputes and puzzling questions, which have been thorns in the sides of divines as well as philosophers, and made so much fruitless work for mankind, that if the arguments

we have produced against it are not found equal to demonstration (as to me they evidently seem), yet I am sure all friends to knowledge, peace, and religion have reason to wish they were.

97. Beside the external existence of the objects of perception, another great source of errors and difficulties with regard to ideal knowledge is the doctrine of *abstract ideas*, such as it hath been set forth in the Introduction. The plainest things in the world, those we are most intimately acquainted with and perfectly know, when they are considered in an abstract way, appear strangely difficult and incomprehensible. Time, place, and motion, taken in particular or concrete, are what everybody knows; but, having passed through the hands of a metaphysician, they become too abstract and fine to be apprehended by men of ordinary sense. Bid your servant meet you at such a *time* in such a *place*, and he shall never stay to deliberate on the meaning of those words; in conceiving that particular time and place, or the motion by which he is to get thither, he finds not the least difficulty. But if *time* be taken exclusive of all those particular actions and ideas that diversify the day, merely for the continuation of existence or duration in abstract, then it will perhaps gravel even a philosopher to comprehend it.

98. For my own part, whenever I attempt to frame a simple idea of *time*, abstracted from the succession of ideas in my mind, which flows uniformly and is participated by all beings, I am lost and embrangled in inextricable difficulties. I have no notion of it at all, only I hear others say it is infinitely divisible, and speak of it in such a manner as leads me to entertain odd thoughts of my existence; since that doctrine lays one under an absolute necessity of thinking, either that he passes away innumerable ages without a thought, or else that he is annihilated every moment of his life, both which seem equally absurd. Time therefore being nothing, abstracted from the succession of ideas in our minds, it follows that the duration of any finite spirit must be estimated by the number of ideas or actions succeeding each other in that same spirit or mind. Hence, it is a plain consequence that the soul always thinks; and in truth whoever shall go about to divide in his thoughts, or abstract the *existence* of a spirit from its *cogitation*, will, I believe, find it no easy task.

99. So likewise when we attempt to abstract extension and motion from all other qualities, and consider them by themselves, we presently lose sight of them, and run into great extravagances.[1] All which depend on a twofold abstraction ; first, it is supposed that extension, for example, may be abstracted from all other sensible qualities ; and secondly, that the entity of extension may be abstracted from its being perceived. But, whoever shall reflect, and take care to understand what he says, will, if I mistake not, acknowledge that all sensible qualities are alike *sensations* and alike *real ;* that where the extension is, there is the colour too, *i.e.* in his mind, and that their archetypes can exist only in some other *mind ;* and that the objects of sense are nothing but those sensations combined, blended, or (if one may so speak) concreted together ; none of all which can be supposed to exist unperceived.[2]

100. What it is for a man to be happy, or an object good, every one may think he knows. But to frame an abstract idea of happiness, prescinded from all particular pleasure, or of goodness from everything that is good, this is what few can pretend to. So likewise a man may be just and virtuous without having precise ideas of justice and virtue. The opinion that those and the like words stand for general notions, abstracted from all particular persons and actions, seems to have rendered morality very difficult, and the study thereof of small use to mankind. And in effect[3] the doctrine of *abstraction* has not a little contributed towards spoiling the most useful parts of knowledge.

101. The two great provinces of speculative science con-

---

[1] Here in the first edition followed this sentence : " Hence spring those odd paradoxes, that the 'fire is not hot,' nor 'the wall white,' &c., or that heat and colour are in the objects nothing but figure and motion."

[2] Here in the first edition followed this sentence : " And that consequently the wall is as truly white as it is extended, and in the same sense."

[3] In the first edition this passage read as follows: "And in effect one may make a great progress in school-ethics without ever being the wiser or better man for it, or knowing how to behave himself in the affairs of life more to the advantage of himself or his neighbours than he did before. This hint may suffice to let any one see the doctrine of *abstraction*," &c.

versant about ideas received from sense, are Natural Philosophy and Mathematics ; with regard to each of these I
shall make some observations.   And first I shall say somewhat of Natural Philosophy.   On this subject it is that the
sceptics triumph.   All that stock of arguments they produce to
depreciate our faculties and make mankind appear ignorant
and low, are drawn principally from this head, namely, that we
are under an invincible blindness as to the *true* and *real*
nature of things.   This they exaggerate, and love to enlarge
on.   We are miserably bantered, say they, by our senses, and
amused only with the outside and show of things.   The real
essence, the internal qualities and constitution of every the
meanest object, is hid from our view ; something there is in
every drop of water, every grain of sand, which it is beyond
the power of human understanding to fathom or comprehend.
But, it is evident from what has been shewn that all this
complaint is groundless, and that we are influenced by false
principles to that degree as to mistrust our senses, and think
we know nothing of those things which we perfectly comprehend.

102. One great inducement to our pronouncing ourselves
ignorant of the nature of things is the current opinion that
everything includes within itself the cause of its properties ;
or that there is in each object an inward essence which is the
source whence its discernible qualities flow, and whereon
they depend.   Some have pretended to account for appearances by occult qualities, but of late they are mostly resolved
into mechanical causes, to wit, the figure, motion, weight, and
suchlike qualities, of insensible particles ; whereas, in truth,
there is no other agent or efficient cause than *spirit*, it being
evident that motion, as well as all other *ideas*, is perfectly
inert.   See sect. 25.   Hence, to endeavour to explain the
production of colours or sounds, by figure, motion, magnitude and the like, must needs be labour in vain.   And accordingly we see the attempts of that kind are not at all satisfactory.   Which may be said in general of those instances
wherein one idea or quality is assigned for the cause of
another.   I need not say how many hypotheses and speculations are left out, and how much the study of nature is
abridged by this doctrine.

103. The great mechanical principle now in vogue is

attraction. That a stone falls to the earth, or the sea swells towards the moon, may to some appear sufficiently explained thereby. But how are we enlightened by being told this is done by attraction? Is it that that word signifies the manner of the tendency, and that it is by the mutual drawing of bodies instead of their being impelled or protruded towards each other? But, nothing is determined of the manner or action, and it may as truly (for aught we know) be termed "impulse," or "protrusion," as "attraction." Again, the parts of steel we see cohere firmly together, and this also is accounted for by attraction; but, in this as in the other instances, I do not perceive that anything is signified besides the effect itself; for as to the manner of the action whereby it is produced, or the cause which produces it, these are not so much as aimed at.

104. Indeed, if we take a view of the several phenomena, and compare them together, we may observe some likeness and conformity between them. For example, in the falling of a stone to the ground, in the rising of the sea towards the moon, in cohesion, crystallization, &c., there is something alike, namely, a union or mutual approach of bodies. So that any one of these or the like phenomena may not seem strange or surprising to a man who has nicely observed and compared the effects of nature. For that only is thought so which is uncommon, or a thing by itself, and out of the ordinary course of our observation. That bodies should tend towards the centre of the earth is not thought strange, because it is what we perceive every moment of our lives. But, that they should have a like gravitation towards the centre of the moon may seem odd and unaccountable to most men, because it is discerned only in the tides. But a philosopher, whose thoughts take in a larger compass of nature, having observed a certain similitude of appearances, as well in the heavens as the earth, that argue innumerable bodies to have a mutual tendency towards each other, which he denotes by the general name "attraction," whatever can be reduced to that he thinks justly accounted for. Thus he explains the tides by the attraction of the terraqueous globe towards the moon, which to him does not appear odd or anomalous, but only a particular example of a general rule or law of nature.

105. If therefore we consider the difference there is be-

twixt natural philosophers and other men, with regard to their knowledge of the phenomena, we shall find it consists not in an exacter knowledge of the efficient cause that pro-. duces them—for that can be no other than the *will of a spirit*—but only in a greater largeness of comprehension, whereby analogies, harmonies, and agreements are discovered in the works of nature, and the particular effects explained, that is, reduced to general rules, see sect. 62, which rules, grounded on the analogy and uniformness observed in the production of natural effects, are most agreeable and sought after by the mind; for that they extend our prospect beyond what is present and near to us, and enable us to make very probable conjectures touching things that may have happened at very great distances of time and place, as well as to predict things to come; which sort of endeavour towards omniscience is much affected by the mind.

106. But we should proceed warily in such things, for we are apt to lay too great a stress on analogies, and, to the prejudice of truth, humour that eagerness of the mind whereby it is carried to extend its knowledge into general theorems. For example, gravitation or mutual attraction, because it appears in many instances, some are straightway for pronouncing it *universal;* and that to attract and be attracted by every other body is an essential quality inherent in all bodies whatsoever. Whereas it is evident the fixed stars have no such tendency towards each other; and, so far is that gravitation from being *essential* to bodies that in some instances a quite contrary principle seems to shew itself; as in the perpendicular growth of plants, and the elasticity of the air. There is nothing necessary or essential in the case, but it depends entirely on the will of the Governing Spirit, who causes certain bodies to cleave together or tend towards each other according to various laws, whilst He keeps others at a fixed distance; and to some He gives a quite contrary tendency to fly asunder just as He sees convenient.

107. After what has been premised, I think we may lay down the following conclusions. First, it is plain philosophers amuse themselves in vain, when they inquire for any natural efficient cause, distinct from a *mind* or *spirit* Secondly, considering the whole creation is the workmanship of a *wise and good Agent*, it should seem to become philo-

sophers to employ their thoughts (contrary to what some hold) about the final causes of things ;[1] and I confess I see no reason why pointing out the various ends to which natural things are adapted, and for which they were originally with unspeakable wisdom contrived, should not be thought one good way of accounting for them, and altogether worthy a philosopher.   Thirdly, from what has been premised no reason can be drawn why the history of nature should not still be studied, and observations and experiments made, which, that they are of use to mankind, and enable us to draw any general conclusions, is not the result of any immutable habitudes or relations between things themselves, but only of God's goodness and kindness to men in the administration of the world.   See sect. 30 and 31.   Fourthly, by a diligent observation of the phenomena within our view, we may discover the general laws of nature, and from them deduce the other phenomena ; I do not say *demonstrate*, for all deductions of that kind depend on a supposition that the Author of nature always operates uniformly, and in a constant observance of those rules we take for principles : which we cannot evidently know.

108.[2] Those men who frame general rules from the phenomena, and afterwards derive the phenomena from those rules, seem to consider signs rather than causes.   A man may well understand natural signs without knowing their analogy, or being able to say by what rule a thing is so or so.   And, as it is very possible to write improperly, through too strict an observance of general grammar rules ; so, in arguing from general laws of nature, it is not impossible we may extend the analogy too far, and by that means run into mistakes.

109. As in reading other books a wise man will choose to fix

[1] This following passage was omitted from here in the last edition : "for, besides that this would prove a very pleasing entertainment to the mind, it might be of great advantage, in that it not only discovers to us the attributes of the Creator, but may also direct us in several instances to the proper uses and applications of things."

[2] Sect. 108 in the first edition began thus : " It appears from sect. 66, &c. that the steady consistent methods of nature may not unfitly be styled the Language of its Author, whereby He discovers His attributes to our view and directs us how to act for the convenience and felicity of life.   And to me those men," &c.

his thoughts on the sense and apply it to use, rather than lay them out in grammatical remarks on the language ; so, in perusing the volume of nature, it seems beneath the dignity of the mind to affect an exactness in reducing each particular phenomenon to general rules, or shewing how it follows from them. We should propose to ourselves nobler views, namely, to recreate and exalt the mind with a prospect of the beauty, order, extent, and variety of natural things : hence, by proper inferences, to enlarge our notions of the grandeur, wisdom, and beneficence of the Creator; and lastly, to make the several parts of the creation, so far as in us lies, subservient to the ends they were designed for, God's glory, and the sustentation and comfort of ourselves and fellow-creatures.

110.[1] The best key for the aforesaid analogy or natural Science will be easily acknowledged to be a certain celebrated Treatise of *Mechanics*. In the entrance of which justly admired treatise, Time, Space, and Motion are distinguished into *absolute* and *relative*, *true* and *apparent*, *mathematical* and *vulgar;* which distinction, as it is at large explained by the author, does suppose those quantities to have an existence without the mind; and that they are ordinarily conceived with relation to sensible things, to which never-theless in their own nature they bear no relation at all.

111. As for *Time*, as it is there taken in an absolute or abstracted sense, for the duration or perseverance of the existence of things, I have nothing more to add concerning it after what has been already said on that subject. Sect. 97 and 98. For the rest, this celebrated author holds there is an *absolute Space*, which, being unperceivable to sense, remains in itself similar and immovable ; and relative space

---

[1] Section 110 in the first edition began as follows : "The best grammar of the kind we are speaking of will be easily acknowledged to be a treatise of *Mechanics*, demonstrated and applied to nature by a philosopher of a neighbouring nation whom all the world admire. I shall not take upon me to make remarks on the performance of that extraordinary person : only some things he has advanced so directly opposite to the doctrine we have hitherto laid down, that we should be wanting in the regard due to the authority of so great a man did we not take some notice of them. In the entrance," &c. As the first edition appeared in Dublin, Newton is spoken of as belonging to a "neighbouring nation."

to be the measure thereof, which, being movable and defined by its situation in respect of sensible bodies, is vulgarly taken for immovable space. *Place* he defines to be that part of space which is occupied by any body ; and according as the space is absolute or relative so also is the place. *Absolute Motion* is said to be the translation of a body from absolute place to absolute place, as relative motion is from one relative place to another. And, because the parts of absolute space do not fall under our senses, instead of them we are obliged to use their sensible measures, and so define both place and motion with respect to bodies which we regard as immovable. But, it is said in philosophical matters we must abstract from our senses, since it may be that none of those bodies which seem to be quiescent are truly so, and the same thing which is moved relatively may be really at rest ; as likewise one and the same body may be in relative rest and motion, or even moved with contrary relative motions at the same time, according as its place is variously defined. All which ambiguity is to be found in the apparent motions, but not at all in the true or absolute, which should therefore be alone regarded in philosophy. And the true we are told are distinguished from apparent or relative motions by the following properties.—First, in true or absolute motion all parts which preserve the same position with respect of the whole, partake of the motions of the whole. Secondly, the place being moved, that which is placed therein is also moved ; so that a body moving in a place which is in motion doth participate the motion of its place. Thirdly, true motion is never generated or changed otherwise than by force impressed on the body itself. Fourthly, true motion is always changed by force impressed on the body moved. Fifthly, in circular motion barely relative there is no centrifugal force, which, nevertheless, in that which is true or absolute, is proportional to the quantity of motion.

112. But, notwithstanding what has been said, I must confess it does not appear to me that there can be any motion other than *relative ;* so that to conceive motion there must be at least conceived two bodies, whereof the distance or position in regard to each other is varied. Hence, if there was one only body in being it could not possibly be moved. This

seems evident, in that the idea I have of motion doth necessarily include relation.[1]

113. But, though in every motion it be necessary to conceive more bodies than one, yet it may be that one only is moved, namely, that on which the force causing the change in the distance or situation of the bodies, is impressed. For however some may define relative motion, so as to term that body *moved* which changes its distance from some other body,[2] whether the force or action causing that change were impressed on it or no, yet as relative motion is that which is perceived by sense, and regarded in the ordinary affairs of life, it should seem that every man of common sense knows what it is as well as the best philosopher. Now, I ask any one whether, in his sense of motion as he walks along the streets, the stones he passes over may be said to *move*, because they change distance with his feet? To me it appears that though motion includes a relation of one thing to another, yet it is not necessary that each term of the relation be denominated from it. As a man may think of somewhat which does not think, so a body may be moved to or from another body which is not therefore itself in motion.[3]

114. As the place happens to be variously defined, the motion which is related to it varies. A man in a ship may be said to be quiescent with relation to the sides of the vessel, and yet move with relation to the land. Or he may move eastward in respect of the one, and westward in respect of the other. In the common affairs of life men never go beyond the earth to define the place of any body; and what is quiescent in respect of that is accounted *absolutely* to be so. But philosophers, who have a greater extent of thought, and juster notions of the system of things, discover even the earth itself to be moved. In order therefore to fix their notions they seem to conceive the corporeal world as finite, and the utmost unmoved walls or shell thereof to be the place

---

[1] In the first edition this followed: "Whether others can conceive it otherwise, a little attention may satisfy them."

[2] In the first edition: "whether the force causing that change were impressed on it or no, yet I cannot assent to this; for, since we are told relative motion," &c.

[3] In the first edition the section closed with this passage: "I mean relative motion, for other I am not able to conceive."

whereby they estimate true motions. If we sound our own conceptions, I believe we may find all the absolute motion we can frame an idea of to be at bottom no other than relative motion thus defined. For, as hath been already observed, absolute motion, exclusive of all external relation, is incomprehensible; and to this kind of relative motion all the above-mentioned properties, causes, and effects ascribed to absolute motion will, if I mistake not, be found to agree. As to what is said of the centrifugal force, that it does not at all belong to circular relative motion, I do not see how this follows from the experiment which is brought to prove it. See *Philosophiae Naturalis Principia Mathematica, in Schol. Def. VIII.* For the water in the vessel at that time wherein it is said to have the greatest relative circular motion, hath, I think, no motion at all; as is plain from the foregoing section.

115. For, to denominate a body *moved* it is requisite, first, that it change its distance or situation with regard to some other body; and secondly, that the force occasioning that change be applied to it. If either of these be wanting, I do not think that, agreeably to the sense of mankind, or the propriety of language, a body can be said to be in motion. I grant indeed that it is possible for us to think a body which we see change its distance from some other to be moved, though it have no force applied to it (in which sense there may be apparent motion), but then it is because the force causing the change of distance is imagined by us to be applied or impressed on that body thought to move; which indeed shews we are capable of mistaking a thing to be in motion which is not, and that is all.[1]

116. From what has been said it follows that the philosophic consideration of motion does not imply the being of an

[1] In the first edition the section continued: "which is not, but does not prove that, in the common acceptation of motion, a body is moved merely because it changes distance from another; since as soon as we are undeceived, and find that the moving force was not communicated to it, we no longer hold it to be moved. So, on the other hand, when only one body (the parts whereof preserve a given position between themselves) is imaged to exist, some there are who think that it can be moved all manner of ways, though without any change of distance or situation to any other bodies; which we should not deny if they meant only that it might have an impressed force, which, upon the bare creation

absolute Space, distinct from that which is perceived by sense and related to bodies ; which that it cannot exist without the mind is clear upon the same principles that demonstrate the like of all other objects of sense. And perhaps, if we inquire narrowly, we shall find we cannot even frame an idea of *pure Space* exclusive of all body. This I must confess seems impossible, as being a most abstract idea. When I excite a motion in some part of my body, if it be free or without resistance, I say there is *Space ;* but if I find a resistance, then I say there is *Body :* and in proportion as the resistance to motion is lesser or greater, I say the space is more or less *pure.* So that when I speak of pure or empty space, it is not to be supposed that the word "space" stands for an idea distinct from or conceivable without body and motion—though indeed we are apt to think every noun substantive stands for a distinct idea that may be separated from all others ; which has occasioned infinite mistakes. When, therefore, supposing all the world to be annihilated besides my own body, I say there still remains *pure Space*, thereby nothing else is meant but only that I conceive it possible for the limbs of my body to be moved on all sides without the least resistance ; but if that too were annihilated then there could be no motion, and consequently no Space. Some, perhaps, may think the sense of seeing doth furnish them with the idea of pure space ; but it is plain from what we have elsewhere shewn, that the ideas of space and distance are not obtained by that sense. See the Essay concerning Vision.

117. What is here laid down seems to put an end to all those disputes and difficulties that have sprung up amongst the learned concerning the nature of *pure Space.* But the chief advantage arising from it is that we are freed from that dangerous dilemma, to which several who have employed their thoughts on that subject imagine themselves reduced, to wit, of thinking either that Real Space is God, or else that there is something beside God which is eternal, uncreated, infinite, indivisible, immutable. Both which may justly be

of other bodies, would produce a motion of some certain quantity and determination. But that an actual motion (distinct from the impressed force or power productive of change of place in case there were bodies present whereby to define it) can exist in such a single body, I must confess I am not able to comprehend."

thought pernicious and absurd notions. It is certain that not a few divines, as well as philosophers of great note, have, from the difficulty they found in conceiving either limits or annihilation of space, concluded it must be divine. And some of late have set themselves particularly to shew the incommunicable attributes of God agree to it. Which doctrine, how unworthy soever it may seem of the Divine Nature, yet I do not see how we can get clear of it, so long as we adhere to the received opinions.

118. Hitherto of Natural Philosophy: we come now to make some inquiry concerning that other great branch of speculative knowledge, to wit, Mathematics. These, how celebrated soever they may be for their clearness and certainty of demonstration, which is hardly anywhere else to be found, cannot nevertheless be supposed altogether free from mistakes, if in their principles there lurks some secret error which is common to the professors of those sciences with the rest of mankind. Mathematicians, though they deduce their theorems from a great height of evidence, yet their first principles are limited by the consideration of quantity: and they do not descend into any inquiry concerning those transcendental maxims which influence all the particular sciences, each part whereof, Mathematics not excepted, does consequently participate of the errors involved in them. That the principles laid down by mathematicians are true, and their way of deduction from those principles clear and incontestible, we do not deny; but, we hold there may be certain erroneous maxims of greater extent than the object of Mathematics, and for that reason not expressly mentioned, though tacitly supposed throughout the whole progress of that science; and that the ill effects of those secret unexamined errors are diffused through all the branches thereof. To be plain, we suspect the mathematicians are as well as other men concerned in the errors arising from the doctrine of abstract general ideas, and the existence of objects without the mind.

119. Arithmetic has been thought to have for its object abstract ideas of *Number;* of which to understand the properties and mutual habitudes, is supposed no mean part of speculative knowledge. The opinion of the pure and in-

tellectual nature of numbers in abstract has made them in esteem with those philosophers who seem to have affected an uncommon fineness and elevation of thought. It hath set a price on the most trifling numerical speculations which in practice are of no use, but serve only for amusement; and hath therefore so far infected the minds of some, that they have dreamed of mighty mysteries involved in numbers, and attempted the explication of natural things by them. But, if we inquire into our own thoughts, and consider what has been premised, we may perhaps entertain a low opinion of those high flights and abstractions, and look on all inquiries, about numbers only as so many *difficiles nugæ*, so far as they are not subservient to practice, and promote the benefit of life.

120. Unity in abstract we have before considered in sect. 13, from which and what has been said in the Introduction, it plainly follows there is not any such idea. But, number being defined a " collection of units," we may conclude that, if there be no such thing as unity or unit in abstract, there are no ideas of number in abstract denoted by the numeral names and figures. The theories therefore in Arithmetic, if they are abstracted from the names and figures, as likewise from all use and practice, as well as from the particular things numbered, can be supposed to have nothing at all for their object; hence we may see how entirely the science of numbers is subordinate to practice, and how jejune and trifling it becomes when considered as a matter of mere speculation.

121. However, since there may be some who, deluded by the specious show of discovering abstracted verities, waste their time in arithmetical theorems and problems which have not any use, it will not be amiss if we more fully consider and expose the vanity of that pretence; and this will plainly appear by taking a view of Arithmetic in its infancy, and observing what it was that originally put men on the study of that science, and to what scope they directed it. It is natural to think that at first, men, for ease of memory and help of computation, made use of counters, or in writing of single strokes, points, or the like, each whereof was made to signify an unit, *i.e.* some one thing of whatever kind they had occasion to reckon. Afterwards they found out the more compendious ways of making one character stand in place of

several strokes or points. And, lastly, the notation of the Arabians or Indians came into use, wherein, by the repetition of a few characters or figures, and varying the signification of each figure according to the place it obtains, all numbers may be most aptly expressed; which seems to have been done in imitation of language, so that an exact analogy is observed betwixt the notation by figures and names, the nine simple figures answering the nine first numeral names and places in the former, corresponding to denominations in the latter. And agreeably to those conditions of the simple and local value of figures, were contrived methods of finding, from the given figures or marks of the parts, what figures and how placed are proper to denote the whole, or *vice versa*. And having found the sought figures, the same rule or analogy being observed throughout, it is easy to read them into words; and so the number becomes perfectly known. For then the number of any particular things is said to be known, when we know the name or figures (with their due arrangement) that according to the standing analogy belong to them. For, these signs being known, we can by the operations of arithmetic know the signs of any part of the particular sums signified by them; and, thus computing in signs (because of the connexion established betwixt them and the distinct multitudes of things whereof one is taken for an unit), we may be able rightly to sum up, divide, and proportion the things themselves that we intend to number.

122. In Arithmetic, therefore, we regard not the *things* but the *signs*, which nevertheless are not regarded for their own sake, but because they direct us how to act with relation to things, and dispose rightly of them. Now, agreeably to what we have before observed of words in general (sect. 19, Introd.) it happens here likewise that abstract ideas are thought to be signified by numeral names or characters, while they do not suggest ideas of particular things to our minds. I shall not at present enter into a more particular dissertation on this subject, but only observe that it is evident from what has been said, those things which pass for abstract truths and theorems concerning numbers, are in reality conversant about no object distinct from particular numerable things, except only names and characters, which originally came to be considered on no other account but

their being signs, or capable to represent aptly whatever particular things men had need to compute. Whence it follows that to study them for their own sake would be just as wise, and to as good purpose as if a man, neglecting the true use or original intention and subserviency of language, should spend his time in impertinent criticisms upon words, or reasonings and controversies purely verbal.

123. From numbers we proceed to speak of *Extension*, which, considered as relative,[1] is the object of Geometry. The *infinite* divisibility of *finite* extension, though it is not expressly laid down either as an axiom or theorem in the elements of that science, yet is throughout the same everywhere supposed and thought to have so inseparable and essential a connexion with the principles and demonstrations in Geometry, that mathematicians never admit it into doubt, or make the least question of it. And, as this notion is the source from whence do spring all those amusing geometrical paradoxes which have such a direct repugnancy to the plain common sense of mankind, and are admitted with so much reluctance into a mind not yet debauched by learning; so is it the principal occasion of all that nice and extreme subtilty which renders the study of Mathematics so difficult and tedious. Hence, if we can make it appear that no finite extension contains innumerable parts, or is infinitely divisible, it follows that we shall at once clear the science of Geometry from a great number of difficulties and contradictions which have ever been esteemed a reproach to human reason, and withal make the attainment thereof a business of much less time and pains than it hitherto has been.

124. Every particular finite extension which may possibly be the object of our thought is an *idea* existing only in the mind, and consequently each part thereof must be perceived. If, therefore, I cannot perceive innumerable parts in any finite extension that I consider, it is certain they are not contained in it; but, it is evident that I cannot distinguish innumerable parts in any particular line, surface, or solid, which I either perceive by sense, or figure to myself in my mind: wherefore I conclude they are not contained in it. Nothing can be plainer to me than that the extensions I

[1] The words "considered as relative" were added to the last edition.

have in view are no other than my own ideas; and it is no less plain that I cannot resolve any one of my ideas into an infinite number of other ideas, that is, that they are not infinitely divisible. If by finite extension be meant something distinct from a finite idea, I declare I do not know what that is, and so cannot affirm or deny anything of it. But if the terms "extension," "parts," &c., are taken in any sense conceivable, that is, for ideas, then to say a finite quantity or extension consists of parts infinite in number is so manifest a contradiction, that every one at first sight acknowledges it to be so; and it is impossible it should ever gain the assent of any reasonable creature who is not brought to it by gentle and slow degrees, as a converted Gentile to the belief of transubstantiation. Ancient and rooted prejudices do often pass into principles; and those propositions which once obtain the force and credit of a *principle*, are not only themselves, but likewise whatever is deducible from them, thought privileged from all examination. And there is no absurdity so gross, which, by this means, the mind of man may not be prepared to swallow.

125. He whose understanding is prepossessed with the doctrine of abstract general ideas may be persuaded that (whatever be thought of the ideas of sense) extension in *abstract* is infinitely divisible. And one who thinks the objects of sense exist without the mind will perhaps in virtue thereof be brought to admit that a line but an inch long may contain innumerable parts—really existing, though too small to be discerned. These errors are grafted as well in the minds of geometricians as of other men, and have a like influence on their reasonings; and it were no difficult thing to shew how the arguments from Geometry made use of to support the infinite divisibility of extension are bottomed on them.[1] At present we shall only observe in general whence it is the mathematicians are all so fond and tenacious of that doctrine.

126. It hath been observed in another place that the theorems and demonstrations in Geometry are conversant about universal ideas (sect. 15. Introd.); where it is explained in what sense this ought to be understood, to wit,

[1] Here came in the first edition : "But this, if it be thought necessary, we may hereafter find a proper place to treat of in a particular manner."

the particular lines and figures included in the diagram are supposed to stand for innumerable others of different sizes; or, in other words, the geometer considers them abstracting from their magnitude—which does not imply that he forms an abstract idea, but only that he cares not what the particular magnitude is, whether great or small, but looks on that as a thing indifferent to the demonstration. Hence it follows that a line in the scheme but an inch long must be spoken of as though it contained ten thousand parts, since it is regarded not in itself, but as it is universal; and it is universal only in its signification, whereby it represents innumerable lines greater than itself, in which may be distinguished ten thousand parts or more, though there may not be above an inch in it. After this manner, the properties of the lines signified are (by a very usual figure) transferred to the sign, and thence, through mistake, thought to appertain to it considered in its own nature.

127. Because there is no number of parts so great but it is possible there may be a line containing more, the inch-line is said to contain parts more than any assignable number; which is true, not of the inch taken absolutely, but only for the things signified by it. But men, not retaining that distinction in their thoughts, slide into a belief that the small particular line described on paper contains in itself parts innumerable. There is no such thing as the ten thousandth part of an inch; but there is of a mile or diameter of the earth, which may be signified by that inch. When therefore I delineate a triangle on paper, and take one side not above an inch, for example, in length to be the radius, this I consider as divided into 10,000 or 100,000 parts or more; for, though the ten thousandth part of that line considered in itself is nothing at all, and consequently may be neglected without any error or inconveniency, yet these described lines, being only marks standing for greater quantities, whereof it may be the ten thousandth part is very considerable, it follows that, to prevent notable errors in practice, the radius must be taken of 10,000 parts or more.

128. From what has been said the reason is plain why, to the end any theorem become universal in its use, it is necessary we speak of the lines described on paper as though they contained parts which really they do not. In doing of

which, if we examine the matter thoroughly, we shall perhaps discover that we cannot conceive an inch itself as consisting of, or being divisible into, a thousand parts, but only
some other line which is far greater than an inch, and
represented by it; and that when we say a line is infinitely
divisible, we must mean[1] a line which is infinitely great.
What we have here observed seems to be the chief cause
why, to suppose the infinite divisibility of finite extension
has been thought necessary in geometry.

129. The several absurdities and contradictions which
flowed from this false principle might, one would think, have
been esteemed so many demonstrations against it. But, by
I know not what logic, it is held that proofs *a posteriori* are
not to be admitted against propositions relating to infinity,
as though it were not impossible even for an infinite mind
to reconcile contradictions; or as if anything absurd and
repugnant could have a necessary connexion with truth or
flow from it. But, whoever considers the weakness of this
pretence will think it was contrived on purpose to humour the
laziness of the mind which had rather acquiesce in an indolent
scepticism than be at the pains to go through with a severe
examination of those principles it has ever embraced for true.

130. Of late the speculations about Infinites have run so
high, and grown to such strange notions, as have occasioned
no small scruples and disputes among the geometers of the
present age. Some there are of great note who, not content
with holding that finite lines may be divided into an infinite
number of parts, do yet farther maintain that each of those
infinitesimals is itself subdivisible into an infinity of other
parts or infinitesimals of a second order, and so on *ad
infinitum*. These, I say, assert there are infinitesimals of
infinitesimals of infinitesimals, without ever coming to an
end: so that according to them an inch does not barely
contain an infinite number of parts, but an infinity of an
infinity of an infinity *ad infinitum* of parts. Others there be
who hold all orders of infinitesimals below the first to be
nothing at all; thinking it with good reason absurd to
imagine there is any positive quantity or part of extension
which, though multiplied infinitely, can never equal the

---

[1] In the first edition: "we mean (if we mean anything) a line which
is," &c.

smallest given extension. And yet on the other hand it seems no less absurd to think the square, cube, or other power of a positive real root, should itself be nothing at all; which they who hold infinitesimals of the first order, denying all of the subsequent orders, are obliged to maintain.

131. Have we not therefore reason to conclude they are *both* in the wrong, and that there is in effect no such thing as parts infinitely small, or an infinite number of parts contained in any finite quantity? But you will say that if this doctrine obtains it will follow the very foundations of Geometry are destroyed, and those great men who have raised that science to so astonishing a height, have been all the while building a castle in the air. To this it may be replied that whatever is useful in geometry, and promotes the benefit of human life, does still remain firm and unshaken on our principles; that science considered as practical will rather receive advantage than any prejudice from what has been said. But to set this in a due light [1] may be the subject of a distinct inquiry. For the rest, though it should follow that some of the more intricate and subtle parts of Speculative Mathematics may be pared off without any prejudice to truth, yet I do not see what damage will be thence derived to mankind. On the contrary, I think it were highly to be wished that men of great abilities and obstinate application would draw off their thoughts from those amusements, and employ them in the study of such things as lie nearer the concerns of life, or have a more direct influence on the manners.

132. If it be said that several theorems undoubtedly true are discovered by methods in which infinitesimals are made use of, which could never have been if their existence included a contradiction in it; I answer that upon a thorough examination it will not be found that in any instance it is necessary to make use of or conceive infinitesimal parts of finite lines, or even quantities less than the *minimum sensibile;* nay, it will be evident this is never done, it being impossible. [2]

---

[1] Here followed in the first edition : "and show how lines and figures may be measured, and their properties investigated, without supposing finite extension to be infinitely divisible, may be the proper business of another place. For the rest," &c.

[2] In the first edition there followed this closing passage : "And,

133. By what we have premised, it is plain that very numerous and important errors have taken their rise from those false Principles which were impugned in the foregoing parts of this treatise; and the opposites of those erroneous tenets at the same time appear to be most fruitful Principles, from whence do flow innumerable consequences highly advantageous to true philosophy, as well as to religion. Particularly *Matter*, or *the absolute existence of corporeal objects*, hath been shewn to be that wherein the most avowed and pernicious enemies of all knowledge, whether human or divine, have ever placed their chief strength and confidence. And surely, if by distinguishing the real existence of unthinking things from their being perceived, and allowing them a subsistence of their own out of the minds of spirits, no one thing is explained in nature, but on the contrary a great many inexplicable difficulties arise; if the supposition of Matter is barely precarious, as not being grounded on so much as one single reason; if its consequences cannot endure the light of examination and free inquiry, but screen themselves under the dark and general pretence of "infinites being incomprehensible;" if withal the removal of this *Matter* be not attended with the least evil consequence; if it be not even missed in the world, but everything as well, nay much easier conceived without it; if, lastly, both Sceptics and Atheists are for ever silenced upon supposing only spirits and ideas, and this scheme of things is perfectly agreeable both to Reason and Religion: methinks we may expect it should be admitted and firmly embraced, though it were proposed only as an *hypothesis*, and the existence of Matter had been allowed possible, which yet I think we have evidently demonstrated that it is not.

134. True it is that, in consequence of the foregoing principles, several disputes and speculations which are esteemed

whatever mathematicians may think of fluxions, or the differential calculus and the like, a little reflexion will shew them that, in working by those methods, they do not conceive or imagine lines or surfaces less than what are perceivable to sense. They may indeed call those little and almost insensible quantities infinitesimals, or infinitesimals of infinitesimals, if they please; but at bottom this is all, they being in truth finite; nor does the solution of problems require the supposing any other. But this will be more clearly made out hereafter."

no mean parts of learning, are rejected as useless.[1] But, how great a prejudice soever against our notions this may give to those who have already been deeply engaged, and made large advances in studies of that nature, yet by others we hope it will not be thought any just ground of dislike to the principles and tenets herein laid down, that they abridge the labour of study, and make human sciences far more clear, compendious, and attainable than they were before.

135. Having despatched what we intended to say concerning the knowledge of IDEAS, the method we proposed leads us in the next place to treat of SPIRITS—with regard to which, perhaps, human knowledge is not so deficient as is vulgarly imagined. The great reason that is assigned for our being thought ignorant of the nature of spirits is our not having an *idea* of it. But, surely it ought not to be looked on as a defect in a human understanding that it does not perceive the idea of spirit, if it is manifestly impossible there should be any such idea. And this if I mistake not has been demonstrated in section 27 ; to which I shall here add that a spirit has been shewn to be the only substance or support wherein unthinking beings or ideas can exist ; but that this *substance* which supports or perceives ideas should itself be an idea or like an idea is evidently absurd.

136. It will perhaps be said that we want a sense (as some have imagined) proper to know substances withal, which, if we had, we might know our own soul as we do a triangle. To this I answer, that, in case we had a new sense bestowed upon us, we could only receive thereby some new sensations or ideas of sense. But I believe nobody will say that what he means by the terms *soul* and *substance* is only some particular sort of idea or sensation. We may therefore infer that, all things duly considered, it is not more reasonable to think our faculties defective, in that they do not furnish us with an idea of spirit or active thinking substance, than it would be if we should blame them for not being able to comprehend a *round square*.

137. From the opinion that spirits are to be known after

---

[1] In the first edition: "useless and in effect conversant about nothing at all."

the manner of an idea or sensation have risen many absurd and heterodox tenets, and much scepticism about the nature of the soul. It is even probable that this opinion may have produced a doubt in some whether they had any soul at all distinct from their body, since upon inquiry they could not find they had an idea of it. That an *idea* which is inactive, and the existence whereof consists in being perceived, should be the image or likeness of an agent subsisting by itself, seems to need no other refutation than barely attending to what is meant by those words. But, perhaps you will say that though an idea cannot resemble a spirit in its thinking, acting, or subsisting by itself, yet it may in some other respects ; and it is not necessary that an idea or image be in all respects like the original.

138. I answer, if it does not in those mentioned, it is impossible it should represent it in any other thing. Do but leave out the power of willing, thinking, and perceiving ideas, and there remains nothing else wherein the idea can be like a spirit. For, by the word *spirit* we mean only that which thinks, wills, and perceives ; this, and this alone, constitutes the signification of that term. If therefore it is impossible that any degree of those powers should be represented in an idea,[1] it is evident there can be no idea of a spirit.

139. But it will be objected that, if there is no idea signified by the terms *soul*, *spirit*, and *substance*, they are wholly insignificant, or have no meaning in them. I answer, those words do mean or signify a real thing, which is neither an idea nor like an idea, but that which perceives ideas, and wills, and reasons about them. What I am myself, that which I denote by the term *I*, is the same with what is meant by *soul* or *spiritual substance*.[2] If it be said that this is only quarrelling at a word, and that, since the immediate significations of other names are by common consent called *ideas*, no reason can be assigned why that which is signified by the name *spirit* or *soul* may not partake in the same appellation. I answer, all the unthinking objects of the mind

---

[1] In the first edition here and below was "idea *or notion.*" See section 142 for Berkeley's definition of a notion.

[2] In the first edition this passage here appeared : "But if I should say that *I* was nothing, or that *I* was an idea or notion, nothing could be more evidently absurd than either of these propositions."

agree in that they are entirely passive, and their existence consists only in being perceived; whereas a soul or spirit is an active being, whose existence consists, not in being perceived, but in perceiving ideas and thinking. It is therefore necessary, in order to prevent equivocation and confounding natures perfectly disagreeing and unlike, that we distinguish between *spirit* and *idea*. See sect. 27.

140. In a large sense indeed, we may be said to have an idea or rather a notion of *spirit;*[1] that is, we understand the meaning of the word, otherwise we could not affirm or deny anything of it. Moreover, as we conceive the ideas that are in the minds of other spirits by means of our own, which we suppose to be resemblances of them; so we know other spirits by means of our own soul, which in that sense is the image or idea of them; it having a like respect to other spirits that blueness or heat by me perceived has to those ideas perceived by another.

141.[2] It must not be supposed that they who assert the natural immortality of the soul are of opinion that it is absolutely incapable of annihilation even by the infinite power of the Creator who first gave it being, but only that it is not liable to be broken or dissolved by the ordinary laws of nature or motion. They indeed who hold the soul of man to be only a thin vital flame, or system of animal spirits, make it perishing and corruptible as the body; since there is nothing more easily dissipated than such a being, which it is naturally impossible should survive the ruin of the tabernacle wherein it is inclosed. And this notion has been greedily embraced and cherished by the worst part of mankind, as the most effectual antidote against all impressions of virtue and religion. But it has been made evident that bodies, of what frame or texture soever, are barely passive ideas in the mind, which is more distant and heterogeneous from them than light is from darkness. We have shewn that the soul is indivisible, incorporeal, unextended, and it is consequently incorrup-

---

[1] The words "or rather a notion" were inserted in the second edition. See section 142.

[2] In the first edition section 141 began with this passage: "The *natural immortality of the soul* is a necessary consequence of the foregoing doctrine. But before we attempt to prove this, it is fit that we explain the meaning of that tenet. It must not be supposed," &c.

tible.   Nothing can be plainer than that the motions, changes, decays, and dissolutions which we hourly see befall natural bodies (and which is what we mean by the *course of nature*) cannot possibly affect an active, simple, uncompounded substance : such a being therefore is indissoluble by the force of nature ; that is to say, "the soul of man is naturally immortal."

142. After what has been said, it is, I suppose, plain that our souls are not to be known in the same manner as senseless, inactive objects, or by way of *idea*. *Spirits* and *ideas* are things so wholly different, that when we say "they exist," "they are known," or the like, these words must be thought to signify anything common to both natures.   There is nothing alike or common in them : and to expect that by any multiplication or enlargement of our faculties we may be enabled to know a spirit as we do a triangle, seems as absurd as if we should hope to see a sound.   This is inculcated because I imagine it may be of moment towards clearing several important questions, and preventing some very dangerous errors concerning the nature of the soul.[1]   We may not, I think, strictly be said to have an *idea* of an active being, or of an action, although we may be said to have a *notion* of them. I have some knowledge or notion of my mind, and its acts about ideas, inasmuch as I know or understand what is meant by these words.   What I know, that I have some notion of.   I will not say that the terms *idea* and *notion* may not be used convertibly, if the world will have it so ; but yet it conduceth to clearness and propriety that we distinguish things very different by different names.   It is also to be remarked that, all relations including an act of the mind, we cannot so properly be said to have an idea, but rather a notion of the relations and habitudes between things.   But if, in the modern way, the word *idea* is extended to spirits, and relations, and acts, this is, after all, an affair of verbal concern.

143. It will not be amiss to add, that the doctrine of *abstract ideas* has had no small share in rendering those sciences intricate and obscure which are particularly conversant about spiritual things.   Men have imagined they could

---

[1] From this point to the end of the section is matter inserted in the second edition.

frame abstract notions of the powers and acts of the mind, and consider them prescinded as well from the mind or spirit itself, as from their respective objects and effects. Hence a great number of dark and ambiguous terms, presumed to stand for abstract notions, have been introduced into metaphysics and morality, and from these have grown infinite distractions and disputes amongst the learned.

144. But, nothing seems more to have contributed towards engaging men in controversies and mistakes with regard to the nature and operations of the mind, than the being used to speak of those things in terms borrowed from sensible ideas. For example, the will is termed the *motion* of the soul : this infuses a belief that the mind of man is as a ball in motion, impelled and determined by the objects of sense, as necessarily as that is by the stroke of a racket. Hence arise endless scruples and errors of dangerous consequence in morality. All which, I doubt not, may be cleared, and truth appear plain, uniform, and consistent, could but philosophers be prevailed on to retire into themselves, and attentively consider their own meaning.[1]

145. From what has been said, it is plain that we cannot know the existence of other spirits otherwise than by their operations, or the ideas by them excited in us. I perceive several motions, changes, and combinations of ideas, that inform me there are certain particular agents, like myself, which accompany them and concur in their production. Hence, the knowledge I have of other spirits is not immediate, as is the knowledge of my ideas ; but depending on the intervention of ideas, by me referred to agents or spirits distinct from myself, as effects or concomitant signs.

146. But, though there be some things which convince us human agents are concerned in producing them ; yet it is evident to every one that those things which are called the Works of Nature, that is, the far greater part of the ideas or sensations perceived by us, are not produced by, or dependent on, the wills of men. There is therefore some other

---

[1] This appears in the first edition as follows : " could but philosophers be prevailed on to depart from some received prejudices and modes of speech, and retire into themselves, and attentively consider their own meaning. But the difficulties arising on this head demand a more particular disquisition than suits with the design of this treatise."

Spirit that causes them ; since it is repugnant that they should subsist by themselves. See sect. 29. But, if we attentively consider the constant regularity, order, and concatenation of natural things, the surprising magnificence, beauty, and perfection of the larger, and the exquisite contrivance of the smaller parts of the creation, together with the exact harmony and correspondence of the whole, but above all the never-enough-admired laws of pain and pleasure, and the instincts or natural inclinations, appetites, and passions of animals ; I say if we consider all these things, and at the same time attend to the meaning and import of the attributes One, Eternal, Infinitely Wise, Good, and Perfect, we shall clearly perceive that they belong to the aforesaid Spirit, " who works all in all," and " by whom all things consist."

147. Hence, it is evident that God is known as certainly and immediately as any other mind or spirit whatsoever distinct from ourselves. We may even assert that the existence of God is far more evidently perceived than the existence of men ; because the effects of nature are infinitely more numerous and considerable than those ascribed to human agents. There is not any one mark that denotes a man, or effect produced by him, which does not more strongly evince the being of that Spirit who is the Author of Nature. For, it is evident that in affecting other persons the will of man has no other object than barely the motion of the limbs of his body ; but that such a motion should be attended by, or excite any idea in the mind of another, depends wholly on the will of the Creator. He alone it is who, " upholding all things by the word of His power," maintains that intercourse between spirits whereby they are able to perceive the existence of each other. And yet this pure and clear light which enlightens every one is itself invisible.[1]

148. It seems to be a general pretence of the unthinking herd that they cannot *see* God. Could we but see Him, say they, as we see a man, we should believe that He is, and believing obey His commands. But alas, we need only open our eyes to see the Sovereign Lord of all things, with a more full and clear view than we do any one of our fellow-creatures. Not that I imagine we see God (as some will have it) by a

---

[1] First edition: "invisible to the greatest part of mankind."

direct and immediate view; or see corporeal things, not by themselves, but by seeing that which represents them in the essence of God, which doctrine is, I must confess, to me incomprehensible. But I shall explain my meaning:—A human spirit or person is not perceived by sense, as not being an idea; when therefore we see the colour, size, figure, and motions of a man, we perceive only certain sensations or ideas excited in our own minds; and these being exhibited to our view in sundry distinct collections, serve to mark out unto us the existence of finite and created spirits like ourselves. Hence it is plain we do not see a man—if by *man* is meant that which lives, moves, perceives, and thinks as we do—but only such a certain collection of ideas as directs us to think there is a distinct principle of thought and motion, like to ourselves, accompanying and represented by it. And after the same manner we see God; all the difference is that, whereas some one finite and narrow assemblage of ideas denotes a particular human mind, whithersoever we direct our view, we do at all times and in all places perceive manifest tokens of the Divinity: everything we see, hear, feel, or anywise perceive by sense, being a sign or effect of the power of God; as is our perception of those very motions which are produced by men.

149. It is therefore plain that nothing can be more evident to any one that is capable of the least reflexion than the existence of God, or a Spirit who is intimately present to our minds, producing in them all that variety of ideas or sensations which continually affect us, on whom we have an absolute and entire dependence, in short " in whom we live, and move, and have our being." That the discovery of this great truth, which lies so near and obvious to the mind, should be attained to by the reason of so very few, is a sad instance of the stupidity and inattention of men, who, though they are surrounded with such clear manifestations of the Deity, are yet so little affected by them that they seem, as it were, blinded with excess of light.

150. But you will say, Hath Nature no share in the production of natural things, and must they be all ascribed to the immediate and sole operation of God? I answer, if by *Nature* is meant only the visible *series* of effects or sensations imprinted on our minds, according to certain fixed

and general laws, then it is plain that Nature, taken in this sense, cannot produce anything at all. But, if by *Nature* is meant some being distinct from God, as well as from the laws of nature, and things perceived by sense, I must confess that word is to me an empty sound without any intelligible meaning annexed to it. Nature, in this acceptation, is a vain chimera, introduced by those heathens who had not just notions of the omnipresence and infinite perfection of God. But, it is more unaccountable that it should be received among Christians, professing belief in the Holy Scriptures, which constantly ascribe those effects to the immediate hand of God that heathen philosophers are wont to impute to Nature. "The Lord He causeth the vapours to ascend; He maketh lightnings with rain; He bringeth forth the wind out of his treasures." Jerem. x. 13. "He turneth the shadow of death into the morning, and maketh the day dark with night." Amos v. 8. "He visiteth the earth, and maketh it soft with showers: He blesseth the springing thereof, and crowneth the year with His goodness; so that the pastures are clothed with flocks, and the valleys are covered over with corn." See Psalm lxv. But, notwithstanding that this is the constant language of Scripture, yet we have I know not what aversion from believing that God concerns Himself so nearly in our affairs. Fain would we suppose Him at a great distance off, and substitute some blind unthinking deputy in His stead, though (if we may believe Saint Paul) "He be not far from every one of us."

151. It will, I doubt not, be objected that the slow and gradual methods observed in the production of natural things do not seem to have for their cause the immediate hand of an Almighty Agent. Besides, monsters, untimely births, fruits blasted in the blossom, rains falling in desert places, miseries incident to human life, and the like, are so many arguments that the whole frame of nature is not immediately actuated and superintended by a Spirit of infinite wisdom and goodness. But the answer to this objection is in a good measure plain from sect. 62; it being visible that the aforesaid methods of nature are absolutely necessary, in order to working by the most simple and general rules, and after a steady and consistent manner; which argues

both the wisdom and goodness of God.[1] Such is the arti-ficial contrivance of this mighty machine of nature that, whilst its motions and various phenomena strike on our senses, the hand which actuates the whole is itself unper-ceivable to men of flesh and blood. "Verily" (saith the prophet) "thou art a God that hidest thyself." Isaiah xlv. 15. But, though the Lord conceal Himself from the eyes of the sensual and lazy, who will not be at the least expense of thought, yet to an unbiassed and attentive mind nothing can be more plainly legible than the intimate presence of an All-wise Spirit, who fashions, regulates, and sustains the whole system of beings. It is clear, from what we have elsewhere observed, that the operating according to general and stated laws is so necessary for our guidance in the affairs of life, and letting us into the secret of nature, that without it all reach and compass of thought, all human sagacity and design, could serve to no manner of purpose; it were even impossible there should be any such faculties or powers in the mind. See sect. 31. Which one consideration abundantly out-balances whatever particular inconveniences may thence arise.

152. We should further consider that the very blemishes and defects of nature are not without their use, in that they make an agreeable sort of variety, and augment the beauty of the rest of the creation, as shades in a picture serve to set off the brighter and more enlightened parts. We would likewise do well to examine whether our taxing the waste of seeds and embryos, and accidental destruction of plants and animals, before they come to full maturity, as an imprudence in the Author of nature, be not the effect of prejudice contracted by our familiarity with impotent and saving mortals. In man indeed a thrifty management of those things which he cannot procure without much pains and industry may be esteemed wisdom. But, we must not imagine that the inexplicably fine machine of an animal or vegetable costs the great Creator any more pains or trouble in its production than a pebble does; nothing being more

---

[1] In the first edition the following sentence appeared here : "For, it doth hence follow that the finger of God is not so conspicuous to the resolved and careless sinner, which gives him an opportunity to harden in his impiety and grow ripe for vengeance. (Vide sect. 57.)"

evident than that an Omnipotent Spirit can indifferently produce everything by a mere *fiat* or act of his will. Hence, it is plain that the splendid profusion of natural things should not be interpreted weakness or prodigality in the agent who produces them, but rather be looked on as an argument of the riches of his power.

153. As for the mixture of pain or uneasiness which is in the world, pursuant to the general laws of nature, and the actions of finite, imperfect spirits, this, in the state we are in at present, is indispensably necessary to our well-being. But our prospects are too narrow. We take, for instance, the idea of some one particular pain into our thoughts, and account it *evil;* whereas, if we enlarge our view, so as to comprehend the various ends, connexions, and dependencies of things, on what occasions and in what proportions we are affected with pain and pleasure, the nature of human freedom, and the design with which we are put into the world ; we shall be forced to acknowledge that those particular things which, considered in themselves, appear to be evil, have the nature of good, when considered as linked with the whole system of beings.

154. From what has been said, it will be manifest to any considering person, that it is merely for want of attention and comprehensiveness of mind that there are any favourers of Atheism or the Manichean Heresy to be found. Little and unreflecting souls may indeed burlesque the works of Providence the beauty and order whereof they have not capacity, or will not be at the pains, to comprehend ; but those who are masters of any justness and extent of thought, and are withal used to reflect, can never sufficiently admire the divine traces of Wisdom and Goodness that shine throughout the Economy of Nature. But what truth is there which shineth so strongly on the mind that by an aversion of thought, a wilful shutting of the eyes, we may not escape seeing it ?[1] Is it therefore to be wondered at, if the generality of men, who are ever intent on business or pleasure, and little used to fix or open the eye of their mind, should not have all that conviction and evidence of the Being of God which might be expected in reasonable creatures ?

[1] In the first edition : "seeing it, at least with a full and direct view?"

155. We should rather wonder that men can be found so stupid as to neglect, than that neglecting they should be unconvinced of such an evident and momentous truth. And yet it is to be feared that too many of parts and leisure, who live in Christian countries, are, merely through a supine and dreadful negligence, sunk into Atheism.[1] Since it is downright impossible that a soul pierced and enlightened with a thorough sense of the omnipresence, holiness, and justice of that Almighty Spirit should persist in a remorseless violation of His laws. We ought, therefore, earnestly to meditate and dwell on those important points; that so we may attain conviction without all scruple " that the eyes of the Lord are in every place beholding the evil and the good; that He is with us and keepeth us in all places whither we go, and giveth us bread to eat and raiment to put on ;" that He is present and conscious to our innermost thoughts; and that we have a most absolute and immediate dependence on Him. A clear view of which great truths cannot choose but fill our hearts with an awful circumspection and holy fear, which is the strongest incentive to *Virtue*, and the best guard against *Vice*.

156. For, after all, what deserves the first place in our studies is the consideration of GOD and our DUTY; which to promote, as it was the main drift and design of my labours, so shall I esteem them altogether useless and ineffectual if, by what I have said, I cannot inspire my readers with a pious sense of the Presence of God ; and, having shewn the falseness or vanity of those barren speculations which make the chief employment of learned men, the better dispose them to reverence and embrace the salutary truths of the Gospel, which to know and to practice is the highest perfection of human nature.

---

[1] In the first edition: " sunk into a sort of Demy-Atheism. They cannot say there is not a God, but neither are they convinced that there is. For what else can it be but some lurking infidelity, some secret misgivings of mind with regard to the existence and attributes of God, which permits sinners to grow and harden in impiety? Since it is downright," &c.

PASSIVE OBEDIENCE:

OR,

THE CHRISTIAN DOCTRINE OF NOT RESISTING THE SUPREME POWER, PROVED AND VINDICATED,

UPON

THE PRINCIPLES OF THE LAW OF NATURE, IN A DISCOURSE DELIVERED AT THE COLLEGE-CHAPEL,

1712.

[THIS, the first of Berkeley's politico-ethical tracts, appeared in 1712. A second edition followed in the same year. The last edition corrected by the author appeared in 1713 and the text of that year is used in this reprint. Strange to say a report of these Sermons caused Lord Galway to accuse Berkeley to the King, of *Jacobitism*. The " Discourse concerning Obedience " referred to in the Author's note to sect. 48 was written by Matthew Tindal, one of the Deists. " The Rights of the Christian Church addressed," &c., was published in 1706. See also sects. 2 and 5 of the "Theory of Vision Vindicated " for other references to Tindal.]

Paſsive Obedience,

OR, THE

Chriſtian Doctrine

Of Not Reſiſting the

SUPREME POWER,

Proved and Vindicated upon the

PRINCIPLES

OF THE

LAW of NATURE.

In a DISCOURSE Deliver'd
at the *College-Chapel.*

By *GEORGE BERKELEY*, M.A Fellow
of *Trinity-College, Dublin*

Noc vero aut per Senatum aut per Populum ſolvi hac
lege *poſſumus.*   Cicero Fragment. de Repub.

LONDON:
Printed for H. Clements, at the *Half-Moon*
in St. *Paul's* Church-Yard 1712

TO THE READER.

THAT an absolute passive obedience ought not to be paid any civil power, but that submission to government should be measured and limited by the public good of the society; and that therefore subjects may lawfully resist the supreme authority, in those cases where the public good shall plainly seem to require it; nay, that it is their duty to do so, inasmuch as they are all under an indispensable obligation to promote the common interest:—these and the like notions, which I cannot help thinking pernicious to mankind, and repugnant to right reason, having of late years been industriously cultivated, and set in the most advantageous lights by men of parts and learning, it seemed necessary to arm the youth of our University against them, and take care they go into the world well principled;—I do not mean obstinately prejudiced in favour of a party, but, from an early acquaintance with their duty, and the clear rational grounds of it, determined to such practices as may speak them good Christians and loyal subjects.

In this view, I made three Discourses not many months since in the College-chapel,[1] which some who heard them thought it might be of use to make more public: and, indeed, the false accounts that are gone abroad concerning them have made it necessary. Accordingly, I now send them into the world under the form of one entire Discourse.

To conclude: as in writing these thoughts it was my endeavour to preserve that cool and impartial temper which becomes every sincere inquirer after truth, so I heartily wish they may be read with the same disposition.

[1] Trinity College, Dublin.

PASSIVE OBEDIENCE.

ROMANS, chap. xiii. ver. 2.

"Whosoever resisteth the Power, resisteth the ordinance of God."

1.

IT is not my design to inquire into the particular nature of the government and constitution of these kingdoms; much less to pretend to determine concerning the merits of the different parties now reigning in the state. Those topics I profess to lie out of my sphere, and they will probably be thought by most men improper to be treated of in an audience almost wholly made up of young persons, set apart from the business and noise of the world, for their more convenient instruction in learning and piety. But surely it is in no respect unsuitable to the circumstances of this place to inculcate and explain every branch of the Law of Nature; or those virtues and duties which are equally binding in every kingdom or society of men under heaven; and of this kind I take to be that Christian Duty of not resisting the supreme Power implied in my text—"Whosoever resisteth the Power, resisteth the ordinance of God."

In treating on which words I shall observe the following method:—

2. First, I shall endeavour to prove that there is an absolute unlimited non-resistance or passive obedience due to the supreme civil power, wherever placed in any nation.

Secondly, I shall inquire into the grounds and reasons of the contrary opinion.

Thirdly, I shall consider the objections drawn from the pretended consequences of non-resistance to the supreme power.

In handling these points I intend not to build on the authority of Holy Scripture, but altogether on the principles of Reason common to all mankind ; and that, because there are some very rational and learned men, who, being verily persuaded an absolute passive subjection to any earthly power is repugnant to right Reason, can never bring themselves to admit such an interpretation of Holy Scripture (however natural and obvious from the words) as shall make that a part of Christian religion which seems to them in itself manifestly absurd, and destructive of the original inherent rights of human nature.

3. I do not mean to treat of that submission which men are, either in duty or prudence, obliged to pay inferior or executive powers ; neither shall I consider where or in what persons the supreme or legislative power is lodged in this or that government.   Only thus much I shall take for granted— that there is in every civil community, somewhere or other, placed a supreme power of making laws, and enforcing the observation of them.   The fulfilling of those laws, either by a punctual performance of what is enjoined in them, or, if that be inconsistent with reason or conscience, by a patient submission to whatever penalties the supreme power hath annexed to the neglect or transgression of them, is termed *loyalty ;* as, on the other hand, the making use of force and open violence, either to withstand the execution of the laws, or ward off the penalties appointed by the supreme power, is properly named *rebellion*.

Now, to make it evident that every degree of rebellion is criminal in the subject, I shall, in the first place, endeavour to prove that loyalty is a natural or moral duty; and disloyalty, or rebellion, in the most strict and proper sense, a vice or breach of the law of nature.   And, secondly, I propose to show that the prohibitions of vice, or negative precepts of the law of nature, as, "Thou shalt not commit adultery, Thou shalt not forswear thyself, Thou shalt not resist the supreme power," and the like, ought to be taken in a most absolute, necessary, and immutable sense : insomuch that the attainment of the greatest good, or deliverance from the greatest evil, that can befal any man or number of men in this life, may not justify the least violation of them.

First then, I am to show that loyalty is a Moral Duty, and disloyalty or rebellion, in the most strict and proper sense, a Vice, or breach of the Law of Nature.

4. Though it be a point agreed amongst all wise men, that there are certain moral rules or laws of nature, which carry with them an eternal and indispensable obligation; yet, concerning the proper methods for discovering those laws, and distinguishing them from others dependent on the humour and discretion of men, there are various opinions. Some direct us to look for them in the Divine Ideas; others in the natural inscriptions on the mind: some derive them from the authority of learned men, and the universal agreement and consent of nations. Lastly, others hold that they are only to be discovered by the deductions of reason. The three first methods must be acknowledged to labour under great difficulties; and the last has not, that I know, been anywhere distinctly explained, or treated of so fully as the importance of the subject doth deserve.

I hope therefore it will be pardoned, if, in a discourse of passive obedience, in order to lay the foundation of that duty the deeper, we make some inquiry into the origin, nature, and obligation of Moral Duties in general, and the criterions whereby they are to be known.

5. Self-love being a principle of all others the most universal, and the most deeply engraven in our hearts, it is natural for us to regard things as they are fitted to augment or impair our own happiness; and accordingly we denominate them *good* or *evil*. Our judgment is ever employed in distinguishing between these two, and it is the whole business of our lives to endeavour, by a proper application of our faculties, to procure the one and avoid the other. At our first coming into the world, we are entirely guided by the impressions of sense; sensible pleasure being the infallible characteristic of present good, as pain is of evil. But, by degrees, as we grow up in our acquaintance with

the nature of things, experience informs us that present good is afterwards often attended with a greater evil; and, on the other side, that present evil is not less frequently the occasion of procuring to us a greater future good. Besides, as the nobler faculties of the human soul begin to display themselves, they discover to us goods far more excellent than those which affect the senses. Hence an alteration is wrought in our judgments; we no longer comply with the first solicitations of sense, but stay to consider the remote consequences of an action, what good may be hoped, or what evil feared from it, according to the wonted course of things. This obliges us frequently to overlook present momentary enjoyments, when they come in competition with greater and more lasting goods, though too far off, or of too refined a nature to affect our senses.

6. But, as the whole earth, and the entire duration of those perishing things contained in it is altogether inconsiderable, or, in the prophet's expressive style, "less than nothing" in respect of Eternity, who sees not that every reasonable man ought so to frame his actions as that they may most effectually contribute to promote his eternal interest? And, since it is a truth evident by the light of nature, that there is a sovereign omniscient Spirit, who alone can make us for ever happy, or for ever miserable; it plainly follows that a conformity to His will, and not any prospect of temporal advantage, is the sole rule whereby every man who acts up to the principles of Reason must govern and square his actions. The same conclusion doth likewise evidently result from the relation which God bears to his creatures. God alone is maker and preserver of all things. He is, therefore, with the most undoubted right, the great legislator of the world; and mankind are, by all the ties of duty, no less than interest, bound to obey His laws.

7. Hence we should above all things endeavour to trace out the Divine will, or the general design of Providence with regard to mankind, and the methods most directly tending to the accomplishment of that design; and this seems the genuine and proper way for discovering the laws of nature. For, laws being rules directive of our actions to the end intended by the legislator, in order to attain the knowledge of God's laws, we ought first to inquire what that end is which

He designs should be carried on by human actions.   Now as God is a being of infinite goodness, it is plain the end He proposes is good.   But, God enjoying in Himself all possible perfection, it follows that it is not His own good, but that of His creatures.   Again, the moral actions of men are entirely terminated within themselves, so as to have no influence on the other orders of intelligences or reasonable creatures; the end therefore to be procured by them can be no other than the good of men.   But, as nothing in a natural state can entitle one man more than another to the favour of God, except only moral goodness; which, consisting in a conformity to the laws of God, doth presuppose the being of such laws, and law ever supposing an end, to which it guides our actions; it follows that, antecedent to the end proposed by God, no distinction can be conceived between men; that end therefore itself, or general design of Providence, is not determined or limited by any respect of persons.   It is not therefore the private good of this or that man, nation, or age, but the general well-being of all men, of all nations, of all ages of the world, which God designs should be procured by the concurring actions of each individual.

Having thus discovered the great end to which all moral obligations are subordinate, it remains that we inquire what methods are necessary for the obtaining that end.

8.   The well-being of mankind must necessarily be carried on in one of these two ways :—either, first, without the injunction of any certain universal rules of morality, only by obliging every one, upon each particular occasion, to consult the public good, and always to do that which to him shall seem, in the present time and circumstances, most to conduce to it.   Or, secondly, by enjoining the observation of some determinate, established laws, which, if universally practised, have, from the nature of things, an essential fitness to procure the well-being of mankind; though, in their particular application, they are sometimes, through untoward accidents, and the perverse irregularity of human wills, the occasions of great sufferings and misfortunes, it may be, to very many good men.

Against the former of these methods there lie several strong objections.   For brevity I shall mention only two :—

9. First, it will thence follow that the best men, for want of judgment, and the wisest, for want of knowing all the hidden circumstances and consequences of an action, may very often be at a loss how to behave themselves ;—which they would not be, in case they judged of each action by comparing it with some particular precept, rather than by examining the good or evil which in that single instance it tends to procure : it being far more easy to judge with certainty, whether such or such an action be a transgression of this or that precept, than whether it will be attended with more good or ill consequences. In short, to calculate the events of each particular action is impossible ; and, though it were not, would yet take up too much time to be of use in the affairs of life.

Secondly, if that method be observed, it will follow that we can have no sure standard to which, comparing the actions of another, we may pronounce them good or bad, virtues or vices. For, since the measure and rule of every good man's actions is supposed to be nothing else but his own private disinterested opinion of what makes most for the public good at that juncture ; and, since this opinion must unavoidably in different men, from their particular views and circumstances, be very different : it is impossible to know, whether any one instance of parricide or perjury, for example, be criminal. The man may have had his reasons for it, and that which in me would have been a heinous sin may be in him a duty. Every man's particular rule is buried in his own breast, invisible to all but himself, who therefore can only tell whether he observes it or no. And, since that rule is fitted to particular occasions, it must ever change as they do : hence it is not only various in different men, but in one and the same man at different times.

10. From all which it follows, there can be no harmony or agreement between the actions of good men : no apparent steadiness or consistency of one man with himself, no adhering to principles : the best actions may be condemned, and the most villainous meet with applause. In a word, there ensues the most horrible confusion of vice and virtue, sin and duty, that can possibly be imagined. It follows there-fore, that the great end to which God requires the con-currence of human actions must of necessity be carried on

by the second method proposed, namely, the observation of certain, universal, determinate rules or moral precepts, which, in their own nature, have a necessary tendency to promote the well-being of the sum of mankind, taking in all nations and ages, from the beginning to the end of the world.

11. Hence, upon an equal comprehensive survey of the general nature, the passions, interests, and mutual respects of mankind; whatsoever practical proposition doth to right reason evidently appear to have a necessary connexion with the universal well-being included in it is to be looked upon as enjoined by the will of God. For, he that willeth the end doth will the necessary means conducive to that end; but it hath been shewn that God willeth the universal well-being of mankind should be promoted by the concurrence of each particular person; therefore, every such practical proposition necessarily tending thereto is to be esteemed a decree of God, and is consequently a law to man.

12. These propositions are called *laws of nature*, because they are universal, and do not derive their obligation from any civil sanction, but immediately from the Author of nature himself. They are said to be *stamped on the mind*, to be *engraven on the tables of the heart*, because they are well known to mankind, and suggested and inculcated by conscience. Lastly, they are termed *eternal rules of reason*, because they necessarily result from the nature of things, and may be demonstrated by the infallible deductions of reason.

13. And, notwithstanding that these rules are too often, either by the unhappy concurrence of events, or more especially by the wickedness of perverse men who will not conform to them, made accidental causes of misery to those good men who do, yet this doth not vacate their obligation: they are ever to be esteemed the fixed unalterable standards of moral good and evil; no private interest, no love of friends, no regard to the public good, should make us depart from them. Hence, when any doubt arises concerning the morality of an action, it is plain this cannot be determined by computing the public good which in that particular case it is attended with, but only by comparing it with the Eternal Law of Reason. He who squares his actions by this rule can never do amiss, though thereby he should bring himself

to poverty, death, or disgrace : no, not though he should involve his family, his friends, his country, in all those evils which are accounted the greatest and most insupportable to human nature. Tenderness and benevolence of temper are often motives to the best and greatest actions ; but we must not make them the sole rule of our actions: they are passions rooted in our nature, and, like all other passions, must be restrained and kept under, otherwise they may possibly betray us into as great enormities as any other unbridled lust. Nay, they are more dangerous than other passions, insomuch as they are more plausible, and apt to dazzle and corrupt the mind with the appearance of goodness and generosity.

14. For the illustration of what has been said, it will not be amiss, if from the moral we turn our eyes on the natural world. *Homo ortus est* (says Balbus in Cicero[1]) *ad mundum contemplandum, et imitandum.* And, surely, it is not possible for free intellectual agents to propose a nobler pattern for their imitation than Nature, which is nothing else but a series of free actions produced by the best and wisest Agent. But, it is evident that those actions are not adapted to particular views, but all conformed to certain general rules, which, being collected from observation, are by philosophers termed laws of nature. And these indeed are excellently suited to promote the general well-being of the creation : but, what from casual combinations of events, and what from the voluntary motions of animals, it often falls out, that the natural good not only of private men but of entire cities and nations would be better promoted by a particular suspension, or contradiction, than an exact observation of those laws. Yet, for all that, nature still takes its course ; nay, it is plain that plagues, famines, inundations, earthquakes, with an infinite variety of pains and sorrows—in a word, all kinds of calamities public and private, do arise from a uniform steady observation of those General Laws, which are once established by the Author of nature, and which He will not change or deviate from upon any of those accounts, how wise or benevolent soever it may be thought by foolish men to do so. As for the miracles recorded in Scripture, they

"De Natura Deorum," lib. ii., § 37.—AUTHOR.

were always wrought for confirmation of some doctrine or mission from God, and not for the sake of the particular natural goods, as health or life, which some men might have reaped from them. From all which it seems sufficiently plain that we cannot be at a loss which way to determine, in case we think God's own methods the properest to obtain His ends, and that it is our duty to copy after them, so far as the frailty of our nature will permit.

15. Thus far in general, of the nature and necessity of Moral Rules, and the criterion or mark whereby they may be known.

As for the particulars, from the foregoing discourse, the principal of them may without much difficulty be deduced. It hath been shewn that the Law of Nature is a system of such rules or precepts as that, if they be all of them, at all times, in all places, and by all men observed, they will necessarily promote the well-being of mankind, so far as it is attainable by human actions. Now, let any one who hath the use of reason take but an impartial survey of the general frame and circumstances of human nature, and it will appear plainly to him that the constant observation of truth, for instance, of justice, and chastity hath necessary connexion with their universal well-being ; that, therefore, they are to be esteemed virtues or duties ; and that "Thou shalt not forswear thyself," "Thou shalt not commit adultery," "Thou shalt not steal," are so many unalterable moral rules, which to violate in the least degree is vice or sin. I say, the agreement of these particular practical propositions with the definition or criterion premised doth so clearly result from the nature of things that it were a needless digression, in this place, to enlarge upon it.

And, from the same principle, by the very same reasoning, it follows that Loyalty is a moral virtue, and "Thou shalt not resist the supreme power" a rule or law of nature, the least breach whereof hath the inherent stain of moral turpitude.

16. The miseries inseparable from a state of anarchy are easily imagined. So insufficient is the wit or strength of any single man, either to avert the evils, or procure the blessings of life, and so apt are the wills of different persons to contradict and thwart each other, that it is absolutely necessary

several independent powers be combined together, under the direction (if I may so speak) of one and the same will—I mean the law of the society. Without this there is no politeness, no order, no peace, among men, but the world is one great heap of misery and confusion; the strong as well as the weak, the wise as well as the foolish, standing on all sides exposed to all those calamities which man can be liable to in a state where he has no other security than the not being possessed of any thing which may raise envy or desire in another. A state by so much more ineligible than that of brutes as a reasonable creature hath a greater reflexion and foresight of miseries than they. From all which it plainly follows, that loyalty, or submission to the supreme civil authority, hath, if universally practised in conjunction with all other virtues, a necessary connexion with the well-being of the whole sum of mankind; and, by consequence, if the criterion we have laid down be true, it is, strictly speaking, a moral duty, or branch of natural religion. And, therefore, the least degree of rebellion is, with the utmost strictness and propriety, a sin: not only in Christians, but also in those who have the light of reason alone for their guide. Nay, upon a thorough and impartial view, this submission will, I think, appear one of the very first and fundamental laws of nature; inasmuch as it is civil government which ordains and marks out the various relations between men, and regulates property, thereby giving scope and laying a foundation for the exercise to all other duties. And, in truth, whoever considers the condition of man will scarce conceive it possible that the practice of any one moral virtue should obtain, in the naked, forlorn state of nature.

17. But, since it must be confessed that in all cases our actions come not within the direction of certain fixed moral rules, it may possibly be still questioned, whether obedience to the supreme power be not one of those exempted cases, and consequently to be regulated by the prudence and discretion of every single person rather than adjusted to the rule of absolute non-resistance. I shall therefore endeavour to make it yet more plain, that "Thou shalt not resist the supreme power" is an undoubted precept of morality; as will appear from the following considerations :—

First, then, submission to government is a point important

enough to be established by a moral rule. Things of insignificant and trifling concern are, for that very reason, exempted from the rules of morality. But government, on which so much depend the peace, order, and well-being, of mankind, cannot surely be thought of too small importance to be secured and guarded by a moral rule. Government, I say, which is itself the principal source under heaven of those particular advantages for the procurement and conservation whereof several unquestionable moral rules were prescribed to men.

18. Secondly, obedience to government is a case universal enough to fall under the direction of a law of nature. Numberless rules there may be for regulating affairs of great concernment, at certain junctures, and to some particular persons or societies, which, notwithstanding, are not to be esteemed moral or natural laws, but may be either totally abrogated or dispensed with; because the private ends they were intended to promote respect only some particular persons, as engaged in relations not founded in the general nature of man, who, on various occasions, and in different postures of things, may prosecute their own designs by different measures, as in human prudence shall seem convenient. But what relation is there more extensive and universal than that of subject and law? This is confined to no particular age or climate, but universally obtains, at all times, and in all places, wherever men live in a state exalted above that of brutes. It is, therefore, evident that the rule forbidding resistance to the law or supreme power is not, upon pretence of any defect in point of universality, to be excluded from the number of the laws of nature.

19. Thirdly, there is another consideration which confirms the necessity of admitting this rule for a moral or natural law: namely, because the case it regards is of too nice and difficult a nature to be left to the judgment and determination of each private person. Some cases there are so plain and obvious to judge of that they may safely be trusted to the prudence of every reasonable man. But in all instances to determine, whether a civil law is fitted to promote the public interest; or whether submission or resistance will prove most advantageous in the consequence; or when it is that the general good of a nation may require an alteration of

government, either in its form, or in the hands which ad-
minister it : these are points too arduous and intricate, and
which require too great a degree of parts, leisure, and liberal
education, as well as disinterestedness and thorough knowledge in the particular state of a kingdom, for every subject
to take upon him the determination of them.   From which
it follows that, upon this account also, non-resistance, which,
in the main, nobody can deny to be a most profitable and
wholesome duty, ought not to be limited by the judgment of
private persons to particular occasions, but esteemed a most
sacred law of nature.

20. The foregoing arguments do, I think, make it manifest,
that the precept against rebellion is on a level with other
moral rules.   Which will yet further appear from this fourth
and last consideration.   It cannot be denied that right reason
doth require some common stated rule or measure, whereby
subjects ought to shape their submission to the supreme
power ; since any clashing or disagreement in this point must
unavoidably tend to weaken and dissolve the society.   And
it is unavoidable that there should be great clashing, where it
is left to the breast of each individual to suit his fancy with a
different measure of obedience.   But this common stated
measure must be either the general precept forbidding resistance, or else the public good of the whole nation ; which last,
though it is allowed to be in itself something certain and determinate, yet, forasmuch as men can regulate their conduct
only by what appears to them, whether in truth it be what it
appears or no ; and, since the prospects men form to themselves of a country's public good are commonly as various as
its landscapes, which meet the eye in several situations : it
clearly follows, that to make the public good the rule of
obedience is, in effect, not to establish any determinate,
agreed, common measure of loyalty, but to leave every subject to the guidance of his own particular mutable fancy.

21. From all which arguments and considerations it is a
most evident conclusion, that the law prohibiting rebellion is
in strict truth a law of nature, universal reason, and morality.
But to this it will perhaps be objected by some that, whatever
may be concluded with regard to resistance from the tedious
deductions of reason, yet there is I know not what turpitude
and deformity in some actions, which at first blush shews

them to be vicious; but they, not finding themselves struck with such a sensible and immediate horror at the thought of rebellion, cannot think it on a level with other crimes against nature. To which I answer:—that it is true, there are certain natural antipathies implanted in the soul, which are ever the most lasting and insurmountable; but, as custom is a second nature, whatever aversions are from our early childhood continually infused into the mind give it so deep a stain as is scarce to be distinguished from natural complexion. And, as it doth hence follow, that to make all the inward horrors of soul pass for infallible marks of sin were the way to establish error and superstition in the world; so, on the other hand, to suppose all actions lawful which are unattended with those starts of nature would prove of the last dangerous consequence to virtue and morality. For, these pertaining to us as men, we must not be directed in respect of them by any emotion in our blood and spirits, but by the dictates of sober and impartial reason. And, if there be any who find they have a less abhorrence of rebellion than of other villanies, all that can be inferred from it is, that this part of their duty was not so much reflected on, or so early and frequently inculcated into their hearts, as it ought to have been. Since without question there are other men who have as thorough an aversion for that as for any other crime.[1]

22. Again, it will probably be objected that submission to government differs from moral duties in that it is founded in a contract, which, upon the violation of its conditions, doth of course become void, and in such case rebellion is lawful: it hath not therefore the nature of a sin or crime, which is in itself absolutely unlawful, and must be committed on no pretext whatsoever.—Now, passing over all inquiry and dispute, concerning the first obscure rise of government, I observe its being founded on a contract may be understood in a twofold sense:—either, first, that several independent persons, finding the insufferable inconvenience of a state of anarchy, where

---

[1] "Il disoit ordinairement qu'il avoit un aussi grand éloignement pour ce péché là que pour assassiner le monde, ou pour voler sur les grands chemins, et qu'enfin il n'y avoit rien qui fut plus contraire à son naturel." He (Mr. Pascal) used to say he had as great an abhorrence of rebellion as of murder, or robbing on the way, and that there was nothing more shocking to his nature.—Vide *M. Pascal*, p. 44.—AUTHOR.

every one was governed by his own will, consented and agreed together to pay an absolute submission to the decrees of some certain legislative ; which, though sometimes they may bear hard on the subject, yet must surely prove easier to be governed by than the violent humours and unsteady opposite wills of a multitude of savages. And, in case we admit such a compact to have been the original foundation of civil government, it must even on that supposition be held sacred and inviolable.

23. Or, secondly, it is meant that subjects have contracted with their respective sovereigns or legislators to pay, not an absolute, but conditional and limited, submission to their laws, that is, upon condition, and so far forth, as the observation of them shall contribute to the public good : reserving still to themselves a right of superintending the laws, and judging whether they are fitted to promote the public good or no ; and (in case they or any of them think it needful) of resisting the higher powers, and changing the whole frame of government by force : which is a right that all mankind, whether single persons or societies, have over those that are deputed by them. But, in this sense, a contract cannot be admitted for the ground and measure of civil obedience, except one of these two things be clearly shewn :—either, first, that such a contract is an express known part of the fundamental constitution of a nation, equally allowed and unquestioned by all as the common law of the land ; or, secondly, if it be not express, that it is at least necessarily implied in the very nature or notion of civil polity, which supposes it is a thing manifestly absurd, that a number of men should be obliged to live under an unlimited subjection to civil law, rather than continue wild and independent of each other. But to me it seems most evident that neither of those points will ever be proved.

24. And till they are proved beyond all contradiction, the doctrine built upon them ought to be rejected with detestation. Since, to represent the higher powers as deputies of the people manifestly tends to diminish that awe and reverence which all good men should have for the laws and government of their country. And to speak of a conditioned, limited loyalty, and I know not what vague and undetermined contracts, is a most effectual means to loosen the

bands of civil society; than which nothing can be of more mischievous consequence to mankind. But, after all, if there be any man who either cannot or will not see the absurdity and perniciousness of those notions, he would, I doubt not, be convinced with a witness, in case they should once become current, and every private man take it in his head to believe them true, and put them in practice.

25. But there still remains an objection which hath the appearance of some strength against what has been said. Namely, that, whereas civil polity is a thing entirely of human institution, it seems contrary to reason to make submission to it part of the law of nature, and not rather of the civil law. For, how can it be imagined that nature should dictate or prescribe a natural law about a thing which depends on the arbitrary humour of men, not only as to its kind or form, which is very various and mutable, but even as to its existence; there being no where to be found a civil government set up by nature. In answer to this, I observe, first, that most moral precepts do presuppose some voluntary actions, or pacts of men, and are nevertheless esteemed laws of nature. Property is assigned, the signification of words ascertained, and matrimony contracted by the agreement and consent of mankind; and, for all that, it is not doubted whether theft, falsehood, and adultery be prohibited by the law of nature. Loyalty, therefore, though it should suppose and be the result of human institutions, may, for all that, be of natural obligation.—I say, secondly, that, notwithstanding particular societies are formed by men, and are not in all places alike, as things esteemed natural are wont to be, yet there is implanted in mankind a natural tendency or disposition to a social life. I call it *natural*, because it is universal, and because it necessarily results from the differences which distinguish man from beast; the peculiar wants, appetites, faculties, and capacities of man being exactly calculated and framed for such a state, insomuch that without it it is impossible he should live in a condition in any degree suitable to his nature. And, since the bond and cement of society is a submission to its laws, it plainly follows that this duty hath an equal right with any other to be thought a law of nature. And surely that precept which enjoins obedience to civil laws cannot itself, with any propriety, be accounted

I. T

a civil law ; it must therefore either have no obligation at all on the conscience, or, if it hath, it must be derived from the universal voice of nature and reason.

26. And thus the first point proposed seems clearly made out :—namely, that Loyalty is a virtue or moral duty ; and Disloyalty or Rebellion, in the most strict and proper sense, a vice or crime against the law of nature. We are now come to the second point, which was to shew that the prohibitions of vice, or negative precepts of morality, are to be taken in a most absolute, necessary, and immutable sense ; insomuch that the attainment of the greatest good, or deliverance from the greatest evil, that can befal any man or number of men in this life may not justify the least violation of them. But, in the first place, I shall explain the reason of distinguishing between positive and negative precepts, the latter only being included in this general proposition. Now, the ground of that distinction may be resolved into this : namely, that very often, either through the difficulty or number of moral actions, or their inconsistence with each other, it is not possible for one man to perform several of them at the same time ; whereas it is plainly consistent and possible that any man should, at the same time, abstain from all manner of positive actions whatsoever. Hence it comes to pass that prohibitions or negative precepts must by every one, in all times and places, be all actually observed : whereas those which enjoin the doing of an action allow room for human prudence and discretion in the execution of them : it for the most part depending on various accidental circumstances ; all which ought to be considered, and care taken that duties of less moment do not interfere with, and hinder the fulfilling of those which are more important. And, for this reason, if not the positive laws themselves, at least the exercise of them, admits of suspension, limitation, and diversity of degrees. As to the indispensableness of the negative precepts of the law of nature, I shall in its proof offer two arguments ; the first from the nature of the thing, and the second from the imitation of God in His government of the world.

27. First, then, from the nature of the thing it hath been already shewn that the great end of morality can never be carried on, by leaving each particular person to promote the public good in such a manner as he shall think most con-

venient, without prescribing certain determinate universal rules, to be the common measure of moral actions. And, if we allow the necessity of these, and at the same time think it lawful to transgress them whenever the public good shall seem to require it, what is this but in words indeed to enjoin the observation of moral rules, but in effect to leave every one to be guided by his own judgment ? than which nothing can be imagined more pernicious and destructive to mankind, as hath been already proved. Secondly, this same point may be collected from the example set us by the Author of nature, who, as we have above observed, acts according to certain fixed laws, which He will not transgress upon the account of accidental evils arising from them. Suppose a prince on whose life the welfare of a kingdom depends to fall down a precipice, we have no reason to think that the universal law of gravitation would be suspended in that case. The like may be said of all other laws of nature, which we do not find to admit of exceptions on particular accounts.

28. And as, without such a steadiness in nature, we should soon, instead of this beautiful frame, see nothing but a disorderly and confused chaos ; so, if once it become current that the moral actions of men are not to be guided by certain definite inviolable rules, there will be no longer found that beauty, order, and agreement in the system of rational beings, or moral world, which will then be all covered over with darkness and violence. It is true, he who stands close to a palace can hardly make a right judgment of the architecture and symmetry of its several parts, the nearer ever appearing disproportionably great. And, if we have a mind to take a fair prospect of the order and general well-being which the inflexible laws of nature and morality derive on the world, we must, if I may so say, go out of it, and imagine ourselves to be distant spectators of all that is transacted and contained in it ; otherwise we are sure to be deceived by the too near view of the little present interests of ourselves, our friends, or our country.

The right understanding of what hath been said will, I think, afford a clear solution to the following difficulties :—

29. First, it may perhaps seem to some that, in consequence of the foregoing doctrine, men will be left to their own private judgments as much as ever. For, first, the very

being of the laws of nature ; secondly, the criterion whereby to know them ; and, thirdly, the agreement of any particular precept with that criterion are all to be discovered by reason and argumentation, in which every man doth necessarily judge for himself : hence, upon that supposition, there is place for as great confusion, unsteadiness, and contrariety of opinions and actions as upon any other.   I answer, that however men may differ as to what were most proper and beneficial to the public to be done or omitted on particular occasions, when they have for the most part narrow and interested views ; yet, in general conclusions, drawn from an equal and enlarged view of things, it is not possible there should be so great, if any, disagreement at all amongst candid rational inquirers after truth.

30. Secondly, the most plausible pretence of all against the doctrine we have premised concerning a rigid indispensable observation of moral rules is that which is founded on the consideration of the public weal.   For, since the common good of mankind is confessedly the end which God requires should be promoted by the free actions of men, it may seem to follow that all good men ought ever to have this in view, as the great mark to which all their endeavours should be directed ; if, therefore, in any particular case, a strict keeping to the moral rule shall prove manifestly inconsistent with the public good, it may be thought agreeable to the will of God that in that case the rule does not restrain an honest disinterested person, from acting for that end to which the rule itself was ordained.   For, it is an axiom that "the end is more excellent than the means," which, deriving their goodness from the end, may not come in competition with it.

31. In answer to this, let it be observed, that nothing is a law merely because it conduceth to the public good, but because it is decreed by the will of God, which alone can give the sanction of a law of nature to any precept ; neither is any thing, how expedient or plausible soever, to be esteemed lawful on any other account than its being coincident with, or not repugnant to the laws promulgated by the voice of nature and reason.   It must indeed be allowed that the rational deduction of those laws is founded in the intrinsic tendency they have to promote the well-being of mankind, on condition they are universally and constantly observed.

But, though it afterwards come to pass that they accidentally fail of that end, or even promote the contrary, they are nevertheless binding, as hath been already proved. In short, that whole difficulty may be resolved by the following distinction. —In framing the general laws of nature, it is granted we must be entirely guided by the public good of mankind, but not in the ordinary moral actions of our lives. Such a rule, if universally observed, hath, from the nature of things, a necessary fitness to promote the general well-being of mankind: therefore it is a law of nature. This is good reasoning. But if we should say, such an action doth in this instance produce much good, and no harm to mankind; therefore it is lawful: this were wrong. The rule is framed with respect to the good of mankind; but our practice must be always shaped immediately by the rule. They who think the public good of a nation to be the sole measure of the obedience due to the civil power seem not to have considered this distinction.

32. If it be said that some negative precepts, *e.g.*, "Thou shalt not kill," do admit of limitation, since otherwise it were unlawful for the magistrate, for a soldier in a battle, or a man in his own defence, to kill another :—I answer, when a duty is expressed in too general terms, as in this instance, in order to a distinct declaration of it, either those terms may be changed for others of a more limited sense, as *kill* for *murder*, or else, from the general proposition remaining in its full latitude, exceptions may be made of those precise cases which, not agreeing with the notion of murder, are not prohibited by the law of nature. In the former case there is a limitation ; but it is only of the signification of a single term too general and improper, by substituting another more proper and particular in its place. In the latter case there are exceptions ; but then they are not from the law of nature, but from a more general proposition which, besides that law, includes somewhat more, which must be taken away in order to leave the law by itself clear and determinate. From neither of which concessions will it follow that any negative law of nature is limited to those cases only where its particular application promotes the public good, or admits all other cases to be excepted from it wherein its being actually observed produceth harm to the public. But of this I shall have occasion to say more in the sequel.

I have now done with the first head, which was to shew that there is an absolute, unlimited, passive obedience due to the supreme power, wherever placed in any nation; and come to inquire into the grounds and reasons of the contrary opinion : which was the second thing proposed.

33. One great principle which the pleaders for resistance make the ground-work of their doctrine is, that the law of self-preservation is prior to all other engagements, being the very first and fundamental law of nature.   Hence, say they, subjects are obliged by nature, and it is their duty, to resist the cruel attempts of tyrants, however authorised by unjust and bloody laws, which are nothing else but the decrees of men, and consequently must give way to those of God or nature.   But, perhaps if we narrowly examine this notion, it will not be found so just and clear as some men may imagine, or, indeed, as at first sight it seems to be.   For, we ought to distinguish between a twofold signification of the terms *law of nature ;* which words do either denote a rule or precept for the direction of the voluntary actions of reasonable agents, and in that sense they imply a duty ; or else they are used to signify any general rule which we observe to obtain in the works of nature, independent of the wills of men ; in which sense no duty is implied.   And, in this last acceptation, I grant it is a general law of nature, that in every animal there be implanted a desire of self-preservation, which, though it is the earliest, the deepest, and most lasting of all, whether natural or acquired appetites, yet cannot with any propriety be termed a moral duty.   But if, in the former sense of the words, they mean that self-preservation is the first and most fundamental law of nature, which therefore must take place of all other natural or moral duties, I think that assertion to be manifestly false ; for this plain reason, because it would thence follow, a man may lawfully commit any sin whatsoever to preserve his life, than which nothing can be more absurd.

34. It cannot indeed be denied that the law of nature restrains us from doing those things which may injure the life of any man, and consequently our own.   But, notwithstanding all that is said of the obligativeness and priority of the law of self-preservation, yet, for aught I can see, there is no

particular law which obliges any man to prefer his own temporal good, not even life itself, to that of another man, much less to the observation of any one moral duty. This is what we are too ready to perform of our own accord; and there is more need of a law to curb and restrain than there is of one to excite and inflame our self-love.

35. But, secondly, though we should grant the duty of self-preservation to be the first and most necessary of all the positive or affirmative laws of nature; yet, forasmuch as it is a maxim allowed by all moralists, that "evil is never to be committed, to the end good may come of it," it will thence plainly follow that no negative precept ought to be transgressed for the sake of observing a positive one; and therefore, since we have shewn, "Thou shalt not resist the supreme power," to be a negative law of nature, it is a necessary consequence that it may not be transgressed under pretence of fulfilling the positive duty of self-preservation.

36. A second erroneous ground of our adversaries, whereon they lay a main stress, is that they hold the public good of a particular nation to be the measure of the obedience due from the subject to the civil power, which therefore may be resisted whensoever the public good shall verily seem to require it. But this point hath been already considered; and in truth it can give small difficulty to whoever understands loyalty to be on the same foot with other moral duties enjoined in negative precepts, all which, though equally calculated to promote the general well-being, may not nevertheless be limited or suspended under pretext of giving way to the end, as is plain from what hath been premised on that subject.

37. A third reason which they insist on is to this effect:— All civil authority or right is derived originally from the people; but nobody can transfer that to another which he hath not himself; therefore, since no man hath an absolute unlimited right over his own life, the subject cannot transfer such a right to the prince (or supreme power), who consequently hath no such unlimited right to dispose of the lives of his subjects. In case, therefore, a subject resist his prince, who, acting according to law, maketh an unjust, though legal, attempt on his life, he does him no wrong; since wrong it is not, to prevent another from seizing what he hath no right

to : whence it would seem to follow that, agreeably to reason, the prince, or supreme power, wheresoever placed, may be resisted. Having thus endeavoured to state their argument in its clearest light, I make this answer :—First, it is granted, no civil power hath an unlimited right to dispose of the life of any man. Secondly, in case one man resist another invading that which he hath no right to, it is granted he doth him no wrong. But, in the third place, I deny that it doth thence follow, the supreme power may consonantly to reason be resisted ; because that, although such resistance wronged not the prince or supreme power wheresoever placed, yet it were injurious to the author of nature, and a violation of his law, which reason obligeth us to transgress upon no account whatsoever, as hath been demonstrated.

38. A fourth mistake or prejudice which influenceth the impugners of non-resistance arises from the natural dread of slavery, chains, and fetters, which inspires them with an aversion for any thing, which even metaphorically comes under those denominations. Hence they cry out against us that we would deprive them of their natural freedom, that we are making chains for mankind, that we are for enslaving them, and the like. But, how harsh soever the sentence may appear, yet it is most true, that our appetites, even the most natural, as of ease, plenty, or life itself, must be chained and fettered by the laws of nature and reason. This slavery, if they will call it so, or subjection of our passions to the immutable decrees of reason, though it may be galling to the sensual part or the beast, yet sure I am it addeth much to the dignity of that which is peculiarly human in our composition. This leads me to the fifth fundamental error :—

39. Namely, the mistaking the object of passive obedience. We should consider that when a subject endures the insolence and oppression of one or more magistrates, armed with the supreme civil power, the object of his submission is, in strict truth, nothing else but right reason, which is the voice of the Author of nature. Think not we are so senseless as to imagine tyrants cast in a better mould than other men : no, they are the worst and vilest of men, and for their own sakes have not the least right to our obedience. But the laws of God and nature must be obeyed, and our

obedience to them is never more acceptable and sincere than when it exposeth us to temporal calamities.

40. A sixth false ground of persuasion to those we argue against is their not distinguishing between the natures of positive and negative duties. For, say they, since our active obedience to the supreme civil power is acknowledged to be limited, why may not our duty of non-resistance be thought so too? The answer is plain; because positive and negative moral precepts are not of the same nature—the former admitting such limitations and exceptions as the latter are on no account liable to, as hath been already proved. It is very possible that a man, in obeying the commands of his lawful governors, might transgress some law of God contrary to them; which it is not possible for him to do merely by a patient suffering and non-resistance for conscience sake. And this furnishes such a satisfactory and obvious solution of the fore-mentioned difficulty that I am not a little surprised to see it insisted on, by men, otherwise, of good sense and reason. And so much for the grounds and reasons of the adversaries of non-resistance.

I now proceed to the third and last thing proposed, namely, the consideration of the objections drawn from the pretended consequences of non-resistance.

41. First, then, it will be objected that, in consequence of that notion, we must believe that God hath, in several instances, laid the innocent part of mankind under an unavoidable necessity of enduring the greatest sufferings and hardships without any remedy; which is plainly inconsistent with the Divine wisdom and goodness: and therefore the principle from whence that consequence flows, ought not to be admitted as a law of God or nature. In answer to which I observe, we must carefully distinguish between the necessary and accidental consequences of a moral law. The former kind are those which the law is in its own nature calculated to produce, and which have an inseparable connexion with the observation of it; and indeed, if these are bad, we may justly conclude the law to be so too, and consequently not from God. But the accidental consequences of a law have no intrinsic natural connexion with, nor do they strictly

speaking flow from its observation, but are the genuine result of something foreign and circumstantial, which happens to be joined with it. And these accidental consequences of a very good law may nevertheless be very bad; which badness of theirs is to be charged on their own proper and necessary cause, and not on the law, which hath no essential tendency to produce them. Now, though it must be granted that a lawgiver infinitely wise and good will constitute such laws for the regulation of human actions as have in their own nature a necessary inherent aptness to promote the common good of all mankind, and that in the greatest degree that the present circumstances and capacities of human nature will admit, yet we deny that the wisdom and goodness of the lawgiver are concerned, or may be called in question, on account of the particular evils which arise, necessarily and properly, from the transgression of some one or more good laws, and but accidentally from the observation of others. But it is plain that the several calamities and devastations which oppressive governments bring on the world are not the genuine necessary effects of the law that enjoineth a passive subjection to the supreme power, neither are they included in the primary intention thereof, but spring from avarice, ambition, cruelty, revenge, and the like inordinate affections and vices raging in the breasts of governors. They may not therefore argue a defect of wisdom or goodness in God's law, but of righteousness in men.

42. Such is the present state of things, so irregular are the wills, and so unrestrained the passions, of men, that we every day see manifest breaches and violations of the laws of nature, which, being always committed in favour of the wicked, must surely be sometimes attended with heavy disadvantages and miseries on the part of those who by a firm adhesion to His laws endeavour to approve themselves in the eyes of their Creator. There are in short no rules of morality, not excepting the best, but what may subject good men to great sufferings and hardships; which necessarily follows from the wickedness of those they have to deal with, and but accidentally from those good rules. And as, on the one hand, it was inconsistent with the wisdom of God, by suffering a retaliation of fraud, perjury, or the like, on the head of offenders, to punish one transgression by another:

so, on the other hand, it were inconsistent with His justice to leave the good and innocent a hopeless sacrifice to the wicked. God therefore hath appointed a day of retribution in another life, and in this we have His grace and a good conscience for our support. We should not therefore repine at the Divine laws, or shew a frowardness or impatience of those transient sufferings they accidentally expose us to, which, however grating to flesh and blood, will yet seem of small moment, if we compare the littleness and fleetingness of this present world with the glory and eternity of the next.

43. From what hath been said, I think it is plain that the premised doctrine of non-resistance were safe, though the evils incurred thereby should be allowed never so great. But perhaps, upon a strict examination, they will be found much less than by many they are thought to be. The mischievous effects which are charged on that doctrine may be reduced to these two points :—First, that it is an encouragement for all governors to become tyrants, by the prospect it gives them of impunity or non-resistance. Secondly, that it renders the oppression and cruelty of those who are tyrants more insupportable and violent, by cutting off all oppositions and consequently all means of redress. I shall consider each of these distinctly.—As to the first point, either you will suppose the governors to be good or ill men. If they are good, there is no fear of their becoming tyrants. And if they are ill men, that is, such as postpone the observation of God's laws to the satisfying of their own lusts, then it can be no security to them that others will rigidly observe those moral precepts which they find themselves so prone to transgress.

44. It is indeed a breach of the law of nature for a subject, though under the greatest and most unjust sufferings, to lift up his hand against the supreme power. But it is a more heinous and inexcusable violation of it for the persons invested with the supreme power to use that power to the ruin and destruction of the people committed to their charge. What encouragement therefore can any man have to think that others will not be pushed on by the strong implanted appetite of self-preservation, to commit a crime, when he himself commits a more brutish and unnatural crime, perhaps

without any provocation at all? Or is it to be imagined that they who daily break God's laws, for the sake of some little profit or transient pleasure, will not be tempted, by the love of property, liberty, or life itself, to transgress that single precept which forbids resistance to the supreme power?

45. But it will be demanded—To what purpose then is this duty of non-resistance preached, and proved, and recommended to our practice, if, in all likelihood, when things come to an extremity, men will never observe it? I answer, to the very same purpose that any other duty is preached. For, what duty is there which many, too many, upon some consideration or other, may not be prevailed on to transgress? Moralists and divines do not preach the duties of nature and religion with a view of gaining mankind to a perfect observation of them; that they know is not to be done. But, however, our pains are answered, if we can make men less sinners than otherwise they would be; if, by opposing the force of duty to that of present interest and passion, we can get the better of some temptations, and balance others, while the greatest still remain invincible.

46. But, granting those who are invested with the supreme power to have all imaginable security that no cruel and barbarous treatment whatever could provoke their subjects to rebellion, yet I believe it may be justly questioned, whether such security would tempt them to more or greater acts of cruelty than jealousy, distrust, suspicion, and revenge may do in a state less secure. And so far in consideration of the first point, namely, that the doctrine of non-resistance is an encouragement for governors to become tyrants.

47. The second mischievous effects it was charged with is, that it renders the oppression and cruelty of those who are tyrants more insupportable and violent, by cutting off all opposition, and consequently all means of redress. But, if things are rightly considered, it will appear that redressing the evils of government by force is at best a very hazardous attempt, and what often puts the public in a worse state than it was before. For, either you suppose the power of the rebels to be but small, and easily crushed, and then this is apt to inspire the governors with confidence and cruelty. Or, in case you suppose it more considerable, so as to be a match for the supreme power supported by the public

treasure, forts, and armies, and that the whole nation is engaged in a civil war;—the certain effects of this are, rapine, bloodshed, misery, and confusion to all orders and parties o men, greater and more insupportable by far than are known under any the most absolute and severe tyranny upon earth. And it may be that, after much mutual slaughter, the rebellious party may prevail. And if they do prevail to destroy the government in being, it may be they will substitute a better in its place, or change it into better hands. And may not this come to pass without the expense, and toil, and blood of war? Is not the heart of a prince in the hand of God? May He not therefore give him a right sense of his duty, or may He not call him out of the world by sickness, accident, or the hand of some desperate ruffian, and send a better in his stead? When I speak as of a monarchy, I would be understood to mean all sorts of government, wheresoever the supreme power is lodged. Upon the whole, I think we may close with the heathen philosopher, who thought it the part of a wise man never to attempt the change of government by force, when it could not be mended without the slaughter and banishment of his countrymen: but to sit still, and pray for better times.[1] For, this way may do, and the other may not do; there is uncertainty in both courses. The difference is that in the way of rebellion we are sure to increase the public calamities, for a time at least, though we are not sure of lessening them for the future.

48. But, though it should be acknowledged that, in the main, submission and patience ought to be recommended, yet, men will be still apt to demand, whether extraordinary cases may not require extraordinary measures; and therefore, in case the oppression be insupportable, and the prospect of deliverance sure, whether rebellion may not be allowed of? I answer, by no means. Perjury, or breach of faith, may, in some possible cases, bring great advantage to a nation, by freeing it from conditions inconsistent with its liberty and public welfare. So likewise may adultery, by procuring a domestic heir, prevent a kingdom's falling into the hands of a foreign power, which would in all probability prove its ruin. Yet, will any man say, the extraordinary

---

[1] Plato, in Epist. vii.—AUTHOR.

nature of those cases can take away the guilt of perjury and adultery?[1] This is what I will not suppose. But it hath been shewn, that rebellion is as truly a crime against nature and reason as either of the foregoing; it may not therefore be justified upon any account whatever, any more than they.

49. What! must we then submit our necks to the sword? and is there no help, no refuge, against extreme tyranny established by law? In answer to this I say, in the first place, it is not to be feared that men in their wits should seek the destruction of their people, by such cruel and unnatural decrees as some are forward to suppose. I say, secondly, that, in case they should, yet most certainly the subordinate magistrates may not, nay, they ought not, in obedience to those decrees, to act any thing contrary to the express laws of God. And, perhaps, all things considered, it will be thought that representing this limitation of their active obedience, by the laws of God or nature, as a duty to the ministers of the supreme power, may prove in those extravagant supposed cases no less effectual for the peace and safety of a nation than preaching up the power of resistance to the people.

50. Further, it will probably be objected as an absurdity in the doctrine of passive obedience, that it enjoineth sub-

---

[1] [The following note was added to the third or 1713 edition. The author of the condemned book was Matthew Tindal.] When I wrote this, I could not think any man would avow the justifying those crimes on any pretext: but I since find that an author (supposed the same who published the book entitled, "The Rights of the Christian Church") in a "Discourse concerning Obedience to the Supreme Powers," printed with three other discourses at London, in the year 1709, chap. iv. p. 28, speaking wholly of Divine laws, is not ashamed to assert, "There is no law which wholly relates to man but ceases to oblige, if, upon the infinite variety of circumstances attending human affairs, it happens to be contrary to the good of man." So that, according to this writer, parricide, incest, or breach of faith become innocent things, if, in the infinite variety of circumstances, they should happen to promote (or be thought by any private person to promote) the public good. After what has been already said, I hope I need not be at any pains to convince the reader of the absurdity and perniciousness of this notion. I shall only observe, that it appears the author was led into it by a more than ordinary aversion to passive obedience, which put him upon measuring or limiting that duty, and, with equal reason, all others, by the public good, to the entire unhinging of all order and morality among men. And it must be owned the transition was very natural.—AUTHOR.

jects a blind implicit submission to the decrees of other men; which is unbecoming the dignity and freedom of reasonable agents; who indeed ought to pay obedience to their superiors, but it should be a rational obedience, such as arises from a knowledge of the equity of their laws, and the tendency they have to promote the public good. To which I answer, that it is not likely a government should suffer much for want of having its laws inspected and amended by those who are not legally entitled to a share in the management of affairs of that nature. And it must be confessed the bulk of mankind are by their circumstances and occupations so far unqualified to judge of such matters, that they must necessarily pay an implicit deference to some or other; and to whom so properly as to those invested with the supreme power?

51. There is another objection against absolute submission, which I should not have mentioned but that I find it insisted on by men of so great note as Grotius and Puffendorf, who think our non-resistance should be measured by the intention of those who first framed the society. Now, say they, if we suppose the question put to them, whether they meant to lay every subject under the necessity of choosing death, rather than in any case to resist the cruelty of his superiors, it cannot be imagined they would answer in the affirmative. For, this were to put themselves in a worse condition than that which they endeavoured to avoid by entering into society. For, although they were before obnoxious to the injuries of many, they had nevertheless the power of resisting them. But now they are bound, without any opposition at all, to endure the greatest injuries from those whom they have armed with their own strength. Which is by so much worse than the former state, as the undergoing an execution is worse than the hazard of a battle. But (passing by all other exceptions which this method of arguing may be liable to), it is evident that a man had better be exposed to the absolute irresistible decrees, even of one single person, whose own and posterity's true interest it is to preserve him in peace and plenty, and protect him from the

---

[1] Grotius "De Jure Belli et Pacis," lib. I., cap. iv., sect. 7; et Puffendorf "De Jure Naturæ et Gentium," lib. VII., cap. vii., sect. 7. —AUTHOR.

injuries of all mankind beside, than remain an open prey to
the rage and avarice of every wicked man upon earth, who
either exceeds him in strength, or takes him at an advantage.
The truth of this is confirmed, as well by the constant experience of the far greater part of the world, as by what we
have already observed concerning anarchy, and the inconsistence of such a state with that manner of life which human
nature requires. Hence it is plain the objection last mentioned is built on a false supposition; viz. That men, by
quitting the natural state of anarchy for that of absolute non-
resisting obedience to government, would put themselves in
a worse condition than they were in before.

52. The last objection I shall take notice of is, that, in pursuance of the premised doctrine, where no exceptions, no
limitations, are to be allowed of, it should seem to follow men
were bound to submit without making any opposition to
usurpers, or even madmen, possessed of the supreme
authority. Which is a notion so absurd, and repugnant to
common sense, that the foundation on which it is built may
justly be called in question. Now, in order to clear this
point, I observe the limitation of moral duties may be understood in a twofold sense—either, first, as a distinction applied
to the terms of a proposition, whereby that which was expressed before too generally is limited to a particular acceptation; and this, in truth, is not so properly limiting the
duty as defining it. Or, secondly, it may be understood as a
suspending the observation of a duty for avoiding some extraordinary inconvenience, and thereby confining it to certain
occasions. And in this last sense only, we have shewn
negative duties not to admit of limitation. Having premised
this remark, I make the following answer to the objection :—
namely, that by virtue of the duty of non-resistance we are
not obliged to submit the disposal of our lives and fortunes
to the discretion either of madmen, or of all those who by
craft or violence invade the supreme power ; because the object of the submission enjoined subjects by the law of nature
is, from the reason of the thing, manifestly limited so as to
exclude both the one and the other. Which I shall not go
about to prove, because I believe nobody has denied it. Nor
doth the annexing such limits to the object of our obedience
at all limit the duty itself, in the sense we except against.

53.[1] In morality the eternal rules of action have the same immutable universal truth with propositions in geometry. Neither of them depends on circumstances or accidents, being at all times, and in all places, without limitation or exception, true. "Thou shalt not resist the supreme civil power" is no less constant and unalterable a rule, for modelling the behaviour of a subject toward the government, than "multiply the height by half the base" is for measuring a triangle. And, as it would not be thought to detract from the universality of this mathematical rule that it did not exactly measure a field which was not an exact triangle, so ought it not to be thought an argument against the universality of the rule prescribing passive obedience that it does not reach a man's practice in all cases where a government is unhinged, or the supreme power disputed. There must be a triangle, and you must use your senses to know this, before there is room for applying your mathematical rule. And there must be a civil government, and you must know in whose hands it is lodged, before the moral precept takes place. But, where the supreme power is ascertained, we should no more doubt of our submission to it, than we would doubt of the way to measure a figure we know to be a triangle.

54. In the various changes and fluctuations of government, it is impossible to prevent that controversies should sometimes arise concerning the seat of the supreme power. And in such cases subjects cannot be denied the liberty of judging for themselves, or of taking part with some, and opposing others, according to the best of their judgments; all which is consistent with an exact observation of their duty, so long as, when the constitution is clear in the point, and the object of their submission undoubted, no pretext of interest, friends, or the public good, can make them depart from it. In short, it is acknowledged that the precept enjoining non-resistance is limited to particular objects, but not to particular occasions. And in this it is like all other moral negative duties, which, considered as general propositions, do admit of limitations and restrictions, in order to a distinct definition of the duty; but what is once known to be a duty of that sort

[1] The whole of this significant section was added to the author's last (1713) edition.

I.   U

can never become otherwise by any good or ill effect, circumstance, or event whatsoever.   And in truth if it were not
so, if there were no general inflexible rules, but all negative
as well as positive duties might be dispensed with, and warpt
to serve particular interests and occasions, there were an end
of all morality.

55. It is therefore evident that, as the observation of any
other negative moral law is not to be limited to those instances
only where it may produce good effects, so neither is the observation of non-resistance limited in such sort as that any
man may lawfully transgress it, whensoever in his judgment
the public good of his particular country shall require it.
And it is with regard to this limitation by the effects that I
speak of non-resistance as an absolute, unconditioned, unlimited duty.   Which must inevitably be granted, unless one
of these three things can be proved :—either, first, that non-
resistance is no moral duty : or, secondly, that other negative
moral duties are limited by the effects : or, lastly, that there is
something peculiar in the nature of non-resistance, which necessarily subjects it to such a limitation as no other negative
moral duty can admit.   The contrary to each of which points,
if I mistake not, hath been clearly made out.

56. I have now briefly gone through the objections drawn
from the consequences of non-resistance, which was the last
general head I proposed to treat of.   In handling this and
the other points, I have endeavoured to be as full and clear
as the usual length of these discourses would permit, and
throughout to consider the argument with the same indiffer-
ence as I should any other part of general knowledge, being
verily persuaded that men as Christians are obliged to the
practice of no one moral duty which may not abide the
severest test of Reason.

THREE DIALOGUES

HYLAS AND PHILONOUS.

THE DESIGN OF WHICH IS PLAINLY TO DEMONSTRATE
THE REALITY AND PERFECTION OF

HUMAN KNOWLEDGE,

THE INCORPOREAL NATURE OF THE

SOUL,

AND THE IMMEDIATE PROVIDENCE OF A

DEITY:

IN OPPOSITION TO

SCEPTICS AND ATHEISTS.

ALSO TO OPEN A METHOD FOR RENDERING THE SCIENCES MORE
EASY, USEFUL, AND COMPENDIOUS.

FIRST PRINTED IN THE YEAR 1713.

[THE Essay on Vision and the Treatise on Knowledge had been generally mis-conceived and objected to ; and Berkeley resolved on a new work in which objections could be cited and answers given. With impeccable instinct he threw his work into the form of the Platonic dialogue, personifying the doctrines of his opponents as "Hylas" the stickler for "Matter," and his own teachings as "Philonous" the "lover of good sense." It was the earliest work of his to be first published in London. It appeared in 1713 and was reprinted in 1725. The third and last edition was slightly revised, and appeared in 1734 with the last edition of the "Principles of Human Knowledge." The text of the "Dialogues" here given is that of 1734, with the exception that the Preface, deleted then, is now restored. Mr. Gosse has said very justly "the abstruse nature of his contributions to literature have unduly concealed the fact that Berkeley is one of the most exquisite of all writers of English prose ;" and if any proof of this be needed it will be found written in these dialogues.]

THREE
DIALOGUES
BETWEEN
Hylas and *Philonous*.

The Defign of which

Is plainly to demonſtrate the Reality and
Perfection of Humane Knowlege, the Incorporeal Nature of the Soul, and the Immediate Providence of a DEITY:

In Oppoſition to

SCEPTICS and *ATHEISTS*

ALSO,

To open a METHOD for rendering the
SCIENCES more eaſy, uſeful, and
compendious.

By *George Berkeley*, M. A.
Fellow of *Trinity*-College,
Dublin.

LONDON:
Printed by G. *James*, for HENRY CLEMENTS,
at the *Half-Moon*, in S. *Paul's* Church-
yard. MDCCXIII.

TO THE RIGHT HONOURABLE

THE

LORD BERKELEY OF STRATTON,

MASTER OF THE ROLLS IN THE KINGDOM OF IRELAND,
CHANCELLOR OF THE DUCHY OF LANCASTER, AND
ONE OF THE LORDS OF HER MAJESTY'S MOST
HONOURABLE PRIVY COUNCIL.

My Lord,

The virtue, learning, and good sense which are acknowledged to distinguish your character, would tempt me to indulge myself the pleasure men naturally take in giving applause to those whom they esteem and honour: and it should seem of importance to the subjects of Great Britain that they knew the eminent share you enjoy in the favour of your sovereign, and the honours she has conferred upon you, have not been owing to any application from your lordship, but entirely to her majesty's own thought, arising from a sense of your personal merit, and an inclination to reward it. But, as your name is prefixed to this treatise with an intention to do honour to myself alone, I shall only say that I am encouraged by the favour you have treated me with, to address these papers to your lordship. And I was the more ambitious of doing this, because a Philosophical Treatise could not so properly be addressed to any one as to a person of your lordship's character, who, to your other valuable distinctions, have added the knowledge and relish of Philosophy.

I am, with the greatest respect,

My Lord,

Your lordship's most obedient and

most humble servant,

GEORGE BERKELEY.[1]

[1] This dedication does not appear in the third edition, 1734.

THE PREFACE.[1]

THOUGH it seems the general opinion of the world, no less than the design of nature and providence, that the end of speculation be Practice, or the improvement and regulation of our lives and actions; yet those who are most addicted to speculative studies, seem as generally of another mind. And, indeed, if we consider the pains that have been taken to perplex the plainest things—that distrust of the senses, those doubts and scruples, those abstractions and refinements that occur in the very entrance of the sciences; it will not seem strange that men of leisure and curiosity should lay themselves out in fruitless disquisitions, without descending to the practical parts of life, or informing themselves in the more necessary and important parts of knowledge.

Upon the common principles of philosophers, we are not assured of the existence of things from their being perceived. And we are taught to distinguish their real nature from that which falls under our senses. Hence arise Scepticism and Paradoxes. It is not enough that we see and feel, that we taste and smell a thing : its true nature, its absolute external entity, is still concealed. For, though it be the fiction of our own brain, we have made it inaccessible to all our faculties. Sense is fallacious, reason defective. We spend our lives in doubting of those things which other men evidently know, and believing those things which they laugh at and despise.

In order, therefore, to divert the busy mind of man from vain researches, it seemed necessary to inquire into the source of its perplexities; and, if possible, to lay down such

---

[1] The Preface is here included, though omitted by the author at his last revision (1734).

Principles as, by an easy solution of them, together with their own native evidence, may at once recommend themselves for genuine to the mind, and rescue it from those endless pursuits it is engaged in. Which with a plain demonstration of the Immediate Providence of an all-seeing God, and the natural Immortality of the soul, should seem the readiest preparation, as well as the strongest motive, to the study and practice of virtue.

This design I proposed in the First Part of a treatise concerning *Principles of Human Knowledge*, published in the year 1710. But, before I proceed to publish the Second Part, I thought it requisite to treat more clearly and fully of certain Principles laid down in the First, and to place them in a new light. Which is the business of the following *Dialogues*.

In this treatise, which does not presuppose in the reader any knowledge of what was contained in the former, it has been my aim to introduce the notions I advance into the mind in the most easy and familiar manner ; especially because they carry with them a great opposition to the prejudices of philosophers, which have so far prevailed against the common sense and natural notions of mankind.

If the principles which I here endeavour to propagate are admitted for true, the consequences which, I think, evidently flow from thence are, that Atheism and Scepticism will be utterly destroyed, many intricate points made plain, great difficulties solved, several useless parts of science retrenched, speculation referred to practice, and men reduced from paradoxes to common sense.

And, although it may, perhaps, seem an uneasy reflexion to some that, when they have taken a circuit through so many refined and unvulgar notions, they should at last come to think like other men ; yet, methinks, this return to the simple dictates of nature, after having wandered through the wild mazes of philosophy, is not unpleasant. It is like coming home from a long voyage : a man reflects with pleasure on the many difficulties and perplexities he has passed through, sets his heart at ease, and enjoys himself with more satisfaction for the future.

As it was my intention to convince Sceptics and Infidels by reason, so it has been my endeavour strictly to observe the most rigid laws of reasoning. And, to an impartial reader, I hope it will be manifest that the sublime notion of a Gôd, and the comfortable expectation of Immorality, do naturally arise from a close and methodical application of thought—whatever may be the result of that loose, rambling way, not altogether improperly termed Free-thinking, by certain libertines in thought, who can no more endure the restraints of logic than those of religion or government.

It will perhaps be objected to my design that, so far as it tends to ease the mind of difficult and useless inquiries, it can affect only a few speculative persons ; but, if by their speculations rightly placed, the study of morality and the law of nature were brought more into fashion among men of parts and genius, the discouragements that draw to Scepticism removed, the measures of right and wrong accurately defined, and the principles of Natural Religion reduced into regular systems, as artfully disposed and clearly connected as those of some other sciences : there are grounds to think these effects would not only have a gradual influence in repairing the too much defaced sense of virtue in the world ; but also, by showing that such parts of revelation as lie within the reach of human inquiry are most agreeable to right reason, would dispose all prudent, unprejudiced persons to a modest and wary treatment of those sacred mysteries which are above the comprehension of our faculties.

It remains that I desire the reader to withhold his censure of these *Dialogues* till he has read them through. Otherwise he may lay them aside, in a mistake of their design, or on account of difficulties or objections which he would find answered in the sequel. A treatise of this nature would require to be once read over coherently, in order to comprehend its design, the proofs, solution of difficulties, and the connexion and disposition of its parts. If it be thought to deserve a second reading, this, I imagine, will make the entire scheme very plain ; especially if recourse be had to an Essay I wrote some years since upon *Vision*, and the Treatise concerning the *Principles of Human Knowledge*—wherein divers notions advanced in these *Dialogues* are farther pursued, or placed in different lights, and other points handled which naturally tend to confirm and illustrate them.

THREE DIALOGUES

BETWEEN HYLAS AND PHILONOUS, IN OPPOSI-
TION TO SCEPTICS AND ATHEISTS.

THE FIRST DIALOGUE.

Philonous.

GOOD morrow, *Hylas:* I did not expect to find you
abroad so early.

Hyl. It is indeed something unusual; but my thoughts
were so taken up with a subject I was discoursing of last
night, that finding I could not sleep, I resolved to rise and
take a turn in the garden.

Phil. It happened well, to let you see what innocent and
agreeable pleasures you lose every morning. Can there be
a pleasanter time of the day, or a more delightful season of
the year? That purple sky, those wild but sweet notes of
birds, the fragrant bloom upon the trees and flowers, the
gentle influence of the rising sun, these and a thousand
nameless beauties of nature inspire the soul with secret
transports; its faculties too being at this time fresh and
lively, are fit for these meditations, which the solitude of a
garden and tranquillity of the morning naturally dispose us
to. But I am afraid I interrupt your thoughts: for you
seemed very intent on something.

Hyl. It is true, I was, and shall be obliged to you if you
will permit me to go on in the same vein; not that I would
by any means deprive mysef of your company, for my
thoughts always flow more easily in conversation with a
friend, than when I am alone: but my request is, that you
would suffer me to impart my reflexions to you.

Phil. With all my heart, it is what I should have requested myself if you had not prevented me.

Hyl. I was considering the odd fate of those men who have in all ages, through an affectation of being distinguished from the vulgar, or some unaccountable turn of thought, pretended either to believe nothing at all, or to believe the most extravagant things in the world. This however might be borne, if their paradoxes and scepticism did not draw after them some consequences of general disadvantage to mankind. But the mischief lieth here; that when men of less leisure see them who are supposed to have spent their whole time in the pursuits of knowledge professing an entire ignorance of all things, or advancing such notions as are repugnant to plain and commonly received principles, they will be tempted to entertain suspicions concerning the most important truths, which they had hitherto held sacred and unquestionable.

Phil. I entirely agree with you, as to the ill tendency of the affected doubts of some philosophers, and fantastical conceits of others. I am even so far gone of late in this way of thinking, that I have quitted several of the sublime notions I had got in their schools for vulgar opinions. And I give it you on my word, since this revolt from metaphysical notions, to the plain dictates of nature and common sense, I find my understanding strangely enlightened, so that I can now easily comprehend a great many things which before were all mystery and riddle.

Hyl. I am glad to find there was nothing in the accounts I heard of you.

Phil. Pray, what were those?

Hyl. You were represented in last night's conversation, as one who maintained the most extravagant opinion that ever entered into the mind of man, to wit, that there is no such thing as *material substance* in the world.

Phil. That there is no such thing as what Philosophers call *material substance*, I am seriously persuaded: but, if I were made to see anything absurd or sceptical in this, I should then have the same reason to renounce this that I imagine I have now to reject the contrary opinion.

Hyl. What! can anything be more fantastical, more repugnant to common sense, or a more manifest piece of Scepticism, than to believe there is no such thing as *matter*?

Phil. Softly, good *Hylas*. What if it should prove, that you, who hold there is, are, by virtue of that opinion, a greater sceptic, and maintain more paradoxes and repugnances to common sense, than I who believe no such thing?

Hyl. You may as soon persuade me, the part is greater than the whole, as that, in order to avoid absurdity and Scepticism, I should ever be obliged to give up my opinion in this point.

Phil. Well then, are you content to admit that opinion for true, which, upon examination, shall appear most agreeable to common sense, and remote from Scepticism?

Hyl. With all my heart. Since you are for raising disputes about the plainest things in nature, I am content for once to hear what you have to say.

Phil. Pray, *Hylas*, what do you mean by a *sceptic*?

Hyl. I mean what all men mean, one that doubts of everything.

Phil. He then who entertains no doubt concerning some particular point, with regard to that point cannot be thought a sceptic.

Hyl. I agree with you.

Phil. Whether doth doubting consist in embracing the affirmative or negative side of a question?

Hyl. In neither; for whoever understands English cannot but know that *doubting* signifies a suspense between both.

Phil. He then that denieth any point, can no more be said to doubt of it, than he who affirmeth it with the same degree of assurance.

Hyl. True.

Phil. And, consequently, for such his denial is no more to be esteemed a sceptic than the other.

Hyl. I acknowledge it.

Phil. How cometh it to pass then, *Hylas*, that you pronounce me a *sceptic*, because I deny what you affirm, to wit, the existence of Matter? Since, for aught you can tell, I am as peremptory in my denial, as you in your affirmation.

Hyl. Hold, *Philonous*, I have been a little out in my definition; but every false step a man makes in discourse is not to be insisted on. I said indeed that a *sceptic* was one who doubted of everything; but I should have added, or who denies the reality and truth of things.

Phil. What things? Do you mean the principles and theorems of sciences? But these you know are universal intellectual notions, and consequently independent of Matter; the denial therefore of this doth not imply the denying them.

Hyl. I grant it. But are there no other things? What think you of distrusting the senses, of denying the real existence of sensible things, or pretending to know nothing of them. Is not this sufficient to denominate a man a *sceptic*?

Phil. Shall we therefore examine which of us it is that denies the reality of sensible things, or professes the greatest ignorance of them; since, if I take you rightly, he is to be esteemed the greatest *sceptic*?

Hyl. That is what I desire.

Phil. What mean you by Sensible Things?

Hyl. Those things which are perceived by the senses. Can you imagine that I mean anything else?

Phil. Pardon me, *Hylas*, if I am desirous clearly to apprehend your notions, since this may much shorten our inquiry. Suffer me then to ask you this farther question. Are those things only perceived by the senses which are perceived immediately? Or, may those things properly be said to be *sensible* which are perceived mediately, or not without the intervention of others?

Hyl. I do not sufficiently understand you.

Phil. In reading a book, what I immediately perceive are the letters, but mediately, or by means of these, are suggested to my mind the notions of God, virtue, truth, &c. Now, that the letters are truly sensible things, or perceived by sense, there is no doubt: but I would know whether you take the things suggested by them to be so too.

Hyl. No, certainly; it were absurd to think *God* or *virtue* sensible things, though they may be signified and suggested to the mind by sensible marks, with which they have an arbitrary connexion.

Phil. It seems then, that by *sensible things* you mean those only which can be perceived *immediately* by sense?

Hyl. Right.

Phil. Doth it not follow from this, that though I see one part of the sky red, and another blue, and that my reason doth thence evidently conclude there must be some cause of that diversity of colours, yet that cause cannot be said to be a sensible thing, or perceived by the sense of seeing?

Hyl. It doth.

Phil. In like manner, though I hear variety of sounds, yet I cannot be said to hear the causes of those sounds?

Hyl. You cannot.

Phil. And when by my touch I perceive a thing to be hot and heavy, I cannot say, with any truth or propriety, that I feel the cause of its heat or weight?

Hyl. To prevent any more questions of this kind, I tell you once for all, that by *sensible things* I mean those only which are perceived by sense, and that in truth the senses perceive nothing which they do not perceive immediately: for they make no inferences. The deducing therefore of causes or occasions from effects and appearances, which alone are perceived by sense, entirely relates to reason.

Phil. This point then is agreed between us—that *sensible things are those only which are immediately perceived by sense.* You will farther inform me, whether we immediately perceive by sight anything beside light, and colours, and figures; or by hearing, anything but sounds; by the palate, anything beside tastes; by the smell, beside odours; or by the touch, more than tangible qualities.

Hyl. We do not.

Phil. It seems, therefore, that if you take away all sensible qualities, there remains nothing sensible?

Hyl. I grant it.

Phil. Sensible things therefore are nothing else but so many sensible qualities, or combinations of sensible qualities?

Hyl. Nothing else.

Phil. *Heat* then is a sensible thing?

Hyl. Certainly.

Phil. Doth the reality of sensible things consist in being perceived? or, is it something distinct from their being perceived, and that bears no relation to the mind?

Hyl. To *exist* is one thing, and to be *perceived* is another.

I.   X

Phil. I speak with regard to sensible things only: and of these I ask, whether by their real existence you mean a subsistence exterior to the mind, and distinct from their being perceived?

Hyl. I mean a real absolute being, distinct from, and without any relation to their being perceived.

Phil. Heat therefore, if it be allowed a real being, must exist without the mind?

Hyl. It must.

Phil. Tell me, *Hylas*, is this real existence equally compatible to all degrees of heat, which we perceive; or is there any reason why we should attribute it to some, and deny it to others? and if there be, pray let me know that reason.

Hyl. Whatever degree of heat we perceive by sense, we may be sure the same exists in the object that occasions it.

Phil. What! the greatest as well as the least?

Hyl. I tell you, the reason is plainly the same in respect of both: they are both perceived by sense; nay, the greater degree of heat is more sensibly perceived; and consequently, if there is any difference, we are more certain of its real existence than we can be of the reality of a lesser degree.

Phil. But is not the most vehement and intense degree of heat a very great pain?

Hyl. No one can deny it.

Phil. And is any unperceiving thing capable of pain or pleasure?

Hyl. No certainly.

Phil. Is your material substance a senseless being, or a being endowed with sense and perception?

Hyl. It is senseless without doubt.

Phil. It cannot therefore be the subject of pain?

Hyl. By no means.

Phil. Nor consequently of the greatest heat perceived by sense, since you acknowledge this to be no small pain?

Hyl. I grant it.

Phil. What shall we say then of your external object; is it a material Substance, or no?

Hyl. It is a material substance with the sensible qualities inhering in it.

Phil. How then can a great heat exist in it, since you own it cannot in a material substance ? I desire you would clear this point.

Hyl. Hold, *Philonous*, I fear I was out in yielding intense heat to be a pain. It should seem rather, that pain is something distinct from heat, and the consequence or effect of it.

Phil. Upon putting your hand near the fire, do you perceive one simple uniform sensation, or two distinct sensations ?

Hyl. But one simple sensation.

Phil. Is not the heat immediately perceived ?

Hyl. It is.

Phil. And the pain ?

Hyl. True.

Phil. Seeing therefore they are both immediately perceived at the same time, and the fire affects you only with one simple, or uncompounded idea, it follows that this same simple idea is both the intense heat immediately perceived, and the pain ; and, consequently, that the intense heat immediately perceived, is nothing distinct from a particular sort of pain.

Hyl. It seems so.

Phil. Again, try in your thoughts, *Hylas*, if you can conceive a vehement sensation to be without pain or pleasure.

Hyl. I cannot.

Phil. Or can you frame to yourself an idea of sensible pain or pleasure in general, abstracted from every particular idea of heat, cold, tastes, smells, &c. ?

Hyl. I do not find that I can.

Phil. Doth it not therefore follow, that sensible pain is nothing distinct from those sensations or ideas, in an intense degree ?

Hyl. It is undeniable ; and, to speak the truth, I begin to suspect a very great heat cannot exist but in a mind perceiving it.

Phil. What ! are you then in that *sceptical* state of suspense, between affirming and denying ?

Hyl. I think I may be positive in the point. A very violent and painful heat cannot exist without the mind.

Phil. It hath not therefore, according to you, any real being ?

Hyl. I own it.

Phil. Is it therefore certain, that there is no body in nature really hot ?

Hyl. I have not denied there is any real heat in bodies. I only say, there is no such thing as an intense real heat.

Phil. But, did you not say before that all degrees of heat were equally real ; or, if there was any difference, that the greater were more undoubtedly real than the lesser ?

Hyl. True : but it was because I did not then consider the ground there is for distinguishing between them, which I now plainly see. And it is this :—because intense heat is nothing else but a particular kind of painful sensation ; and pain cannot exist but in a perceiving being ; it follows that no intense heat can really exist in an unperceiving corporeal substance. But this is no reason why we should deny heat in an inferior degree to exist in such a substance.

Phil. But how shall we be able to discern those degrees of heat which exist only in the mind from those which exist without it ?

Hyl. That is no difficult matter. You know the least pain cannot exist unperceived ; whatever, therefore, degree of heat is a pain exists only in the mind. But, as for all other degrees of heat, nothing obliges us to think the same of them.

Phil. I think you granted before that no unperceiving being was capable of pleasure, any more than of pain.

Hyl. I did.

Phil. And is not warmth, or a more gentle degree of heat than what causes uneasiness, a pleasure ?

Hyl. What then ?

Phil. Consequently, it cannot exist without the mind in an unperceiving substance, or body.

Hyl. So it seems.

Phil. Since, therefore, as well those degrees of heat that are not painful, as those that are, can exist only in a thinking substance ; may we not conclude that external bodies are absolutely incapable of any degree of heat whatsoever ?

Hyl. On second thoughts, I do not think it is so evident that warmth is a pleasure, as that a great degree of heat is a pain.

Phil. I do not pretend that warmth is as great a pleasure

as heat is a pain. But, if you grant it to be even a small pleasure, it serves to make good my conclusion.

Hyl. I could rather call it an *indolence.* It seems to be nothing more than a privation of both pain and pleasure. And that such a quality or state as this may agree to an unthinking substance, I hope you will not deny.

Phil. If you are resolved to maintain that warmth, or a gentle degree of heat, is no pleasure, I know not how to convince you otherwise, than by appealing to your own sense. But what think you of cold?

Hyl. The same that I do of heat. An intense degree of cold is a pain; for to feel a very great cold, is to perceive a great uneasiness: it cannot therefore exist without the mind; but a lesser degree of cold may, as well as a lesser degree of heat.

Phil. Those bodies, therefore, upon whose application to our own, we perceive a moderate degree of heat, must be concluded to have a moderate degree of heat or warmth in them; and those, upon whose application we feel a like degree of cold, must be thought to have cold in them.

Hyl. They must.

Phil. Can any doctrine be true that necessarily leads a man into an absurdity?

Hyl. Without doubt it cannot.

Phil. Is it not an absurdity to think that the same thing should be at the same time both cold and warm?

Hyl. It is.

Phil. Suppose now, one of your hands hot, and the other cold, and that they are both at once put into the same vessel of water, in an intermediate state; will not the water seem cold to one hand, and warm to the other?

Hyl. It will.

Phil. Ought we not therefore, by your principles, to conclude it is really both cold and warm at the same time, that is, according to your own concession, to believe an absurdity?

Hyl. I confess it seems so.

Phil. Consequently, the principles themselves are false, since you have granted that no true principle leads to an absurdity.

Hyl. But, after all, can anything be more absurd than to say, *there is no heat in the fire?*

Phil. To make the point still clearer ; tell me whether, in two cases, exactly alike, we ought not to make the same judgment ?

Hyl. We ought.

Phil. When a pin pricks your finger, doth it not rend and divide the fibres of your flesh ?

Hyl. It doth.

Phil. And when a coal burns your finger, doth it any more ?

Hyl. It doth not.

Phil. Since, therefore, you neither judge the sensation itself occasioned by the pin, nor anything like it to be in the pin ; you should not, conformably to what you have now granted, judge the sensation occasioned by the fire, or anything like it, to be in the fire.

Hyl. Well, since it must be so, I am content to yield this point, and acknowledge that heat and cold are only sensations existing in our minds. But there still remain qualities enough to secure the reality of external things.

Phil. But what will you say, *Hylas,* if it shall appear that the case is the same with regard to all other sensible qualities, and that they can no more be supposed to exist without the mind, than heat and cold ?

Hyl. Then indeed you will have done something to the purpose ; but that is what I despair of seeing proved.

Phil. Let us examine them in order. What think you of *tastes*—do they exist without the mind, or no ?

Hyl. Can any man in his senses doubt whether sugar is sweet, or wormwood bitter ?

Phil. Inform me, *Hylas.* Is a sweet taste a particular kind of pleasure or pleasant sensation, or is it not ?

Hyl. It is.

Phil. And is not bitterness some kind of uneasiness or pain ?

Hyl. I grant it.

Phil. If therefore sugar and wormwood are unthinking corporeal substances existing without the mind, how can sweetness and bitterness, that is, pleasure and pain, agree to hem ?

Hyl. Hold, *Philonous,* I now see what it was deluded me all this time. You asked whether heat and cold, sweetness and bitterness, were not particular sorts of pleasure and pain ; to which I answered simply, that they were.   Whereas I should have thus distinguished :—those qualities, as perceived by us, are pleasures or pains ; but not as existing in the external objects.   We must not therefore conclude absolutely, that there is no heat in the fire, or sweetness in the sugar, but only that heat or sweetness, as perceived by us, are not in the fire or sugar.   What say you to this ?

Phil. I say it is nothing to the purpose.   Our discourse proceeded altogether concerning sensible things, which you defined to be, *the things we immediately perceive by our senses.* Whatever other qualities, therefore, you speak of, as distinct from these, I know nothing of them, neither do they at all belong to the point of dispute.   You may, indeed, pretend to have discovered certain qualities which you do not perceive, and assert those insensible qualities exist in fire and sugar.   But what use can be made of this to your present purpose, I am at a loss to conceive.   Tell me then once more, do you acknowledge that heat and cold, sweetness and bitterness (meaning those qualities which are perceived by the senses), do not exist without the mind ?

Hyl. I see it is to no purpose to hold out, so I give up the cause as to those mentioned qualities.   Though I profess it sounds oddly, to say that sugar is not sweet.

Phil. But, for your farther satisfaction, take this along with you : that which at other times seem sweet, shall, to a distempered palate, appear bitter.   And, nothing can be plainer than that divers persons perceive different tastes in the same food ; since that which one man delights in, another abhors. And how could this be, if the taste was something really inherent in the food ?

Hyl. I acknowledge I know not how.

Phil. In the next place, *odours* are to be considered.   And, with regard to these, I would fain know whether what has been said of tastes doth not exactly agree to them ?   Are they not so many pleasing or displeasing sensations ?

Hyl. They are.

Phil. Can you then conceive it possible that they should exist in an unperceiving thing ?

Hyl. I cannot.

Phil. Or, can you imagine that filth and ordure affect those brute animals that feed on them out of choice, with the same smells which we perceive in them?

Hyl. By no means.

Phil. May we not therefore conclude of smells, as of the other forementioned qualities, that they cannot exist in any but a perceiving substance or mind.

Hyl. I think so.

Phil. Then as to *sounds*, what must we think of them : are they accidents really inherent in external bodies, or not?

Hyl. That they inhere not in the sonorous bodies is plain from hence ; because a bell struck in the exhausted receiver of an air-pump sends forth no sound. The air, therefore, must be thought the subject of sound.

Phil. What reason is there for that, *Hylas?*

Hyl. Because, when any motion is raised in the air, we perceive a sound greater or lesser, according to the air's motion ; but without some motion in the air, we never hear any sound at all.

Phil. And granting that we never hear a sound but when some motion is produced in the air, yet I do not see how you can infer from thence, that the sound itself is in the air.

Hyl. It is this very motion in the external air that produces in the mind the sensation of *sound*. For, striking on the drum of the ear, it causeth a vibration, which by the auditory nerves being communicated to the brain, the soul is thereupon affected with the sensation called *sound*.

Phil. What ! is sound then a sensation?

Hyl. I tell you, as perceived by us, it is a particular sensation in the mind.

Phil. And can any sensation exist without the mind?

Hyl. No, certainly.

Phil. How then can sound, being a sensation, exist in the air, if by the *air* you mean a senseless substance existing without the mind?

Hyl. You must distinguish, *Philonous*, between sound as it is perceived by us, and as it is in itself ; or (which is the same thing) between the sound we immediately perceive, and that which exists without us. The former, indeed, is a particular kind of sensation, but the latter is merely a vibrative or undulatory motion in the air.

Phil. I thought I had already obviated that distinction, by the answer I gave when you were applying it in a like case before. But, to say no more of that, are you sure then that sound is really nothing but motion?

Hyl. I am.

Phil. Whatever therefore agrees to real sound, may with truth be attributed to motion?

Hyl. It may.

Phil. It is then good sense to speak of *motion* as of a thing that is *loud, sweet, acute, or grave.*

Hyl. I see you are resolved not to understand me. Is it not evident those accidents or modes belong only to sensible sound, or *sound* in the common acceptation of the word, but not to *sound* in the real and philosophic sense; which, as I just now told you, is nothing but a certain motion of the air?

Phil. It seems then there are two sorts of sound—the one vulgar, or that which is heard, the other philosophical and real?

Hyl. Even so.

Phil. And the latter consists in motion?

Hyl. I told you so before.

Phil. Tell me, *Hylas,* to which of the senses, think you, the idea of motion belongs? to the hearing?

Hyl. No, certainly; but to the sight and touch.

Phil. It should follow then, that, according to you, real sounds may possibly been *seen* or *felt,* but never *heard.*

Hyl. Look you, *Philonous,* you may, if you please, make a jest of my opinion, but that will not alter the truth of things. I own, indeed, the inferences you draw me into, sound something oddly; but common language, you know, is framed by, and for the use of the vulgar: we must not therefore wonder, if expressions adapted to exact philosophic notions seem uncouth and out of the way.

Phil. Is it come to that? I assure you, I imagine myself to have gained no small point, since you make so light of parting from common phrases and opinions; it being a main part of our inquiry, to examine whose notions are widest of the common road, and most repugnant to the general sense of the world. But, can you think it no more than a philosophical paradox, to say that *real sounds are never heard,* and that the idea of them is obtained by some other sense? And is there nothing in this contrary to nature and the truth of things?

Hyl. To deal ingenuously, I do not like it. And, after the concessions already made, I had as well grant that sounds too have no real being without the mind.

Phil. And I hope you will make no difficulty to acknowledge the same of *colours*.

Hyl. Pardon me : the case of colours is very different. Can anything be plainer than that we see them on the objects ?

Phil. The objects you speak of are, I suppose, corporeal Substances existing without the mind ?

Hyl. They are.

Phil. And have true and real colours inhering in them ?

Hyl. Each visible object hath that colour which we see in it.

Phil. How ! is there anything visible but what we perceive by sight ?

Hyl. There is not.

Phil. And do we perceive anything by sense which we do not perceive immediately ?

Hyl. How often must I be obliged to repeat the same thing ? I tell you, we do not.

Phil. Have patience, good *Hylas ;* and tell me once more, whether there is anything immediately perceived by the senses, except sensible qualities. I know you asserted there was not ; but I would now be informed, whether you still persist in the same opinion.

Hyl. I do.

Phil. Pray, is your corporeal substance either a sensible quality, or made up of sensible qualities ?

Hyl. What a question that is ! who ever thought it was ?

Phil. My reason for asking was, because in saying, *each visible object hath that colour which we see in it,* you make visible objects to be corporeal substances ; which implies either that corporeal substances are sensible qualities, or else that there is something beside sensible qualities perceived by sight : but, as this point was formerly agreed between us, and is still maintained by you, it is a clear consequence, that your corporeal substance is nothing distinct from sensible qualities.

Hyl. You may draw as many absurd consequences as you please, and endeavour to perplex the plainest things ; but you shall never persuade me out of my senses. I clearly understand my own meaning.

Phil. I wish you would make me understand it too. But,

since you are unwilling to have your notion of corporeal substance examined, I shall urge that point no farther. Only be pleased to let me know, whether the same colours which we see exist in external bodies, or some other.

Hyl. The very same.

Phil. What! are then the beautiful red and purple we see on yonder clouds really in them? Or do you imagine they have in themselves any other form than that of a dark mist or vapour?

Hyl. I must own, *Philonous*, those colours are not really in the clouds as they seem to be at this distance. They are only apparent colours.

Phil. Apparent call you them? how shall we distinguish these apparent colours from real?

Hyl. Very easily. Those are to be thought apparent which, appearing only at a distance, vanish upon a nearer approach.

Phil. And those, I suppose, are to be thought real which are discovered by the most near and exact survey.

Hyl. Right.

Phil. Is the nearest and exactest survey made by the help of a microscope, or by the naked eye?

Hyl. By a microscope, doubtless.

Phil. But a microscope often discovers colours in an object different from those perceived by the unassisted sight. And, in case we had microscopes magnifying to any assigned degree, it is certain that no object whatsoever, viewed through them, would appear in the same colour which it exhibits to the naked eye.

Hyl. And what will you conclude from all this? You cannot argue that there are really and naturally no colours on objects: because by artificial managements they may be altered, or made to vanish.

Phil. I think it may evidently be concluded from your own concessions, that all the colours we see with our naked eyes are only apparent as those on the clouds, since they vanish upon a more close and accurate inspection which is afforded us by a microscope. Then, as to what you say by way of prevention: I ask you whether the real and natural state of an object is better discovered by a very sharp and piercing sight, or by one which is less sharp?

Hyl. By the former without doubt.

Phil. Is it not plain from *Dioptrics* that microscopes make the sight more penetrating, and represent objects as they would appear to the eye in case it were naturally endowed with a most exquisite sharpness?

Hyl. It is.

Phil. Consequently the microscopical representation is to be thought that which best sets forth the real nature of the thing, or what it is in itself. The colours, therefore, by it perceived are more genuine and real than those perceived otherwise.

Hyl. I confess there is something in what you say.

Phil. Besides, it is not only possible but manifest, that there actually are animals whose eyes are by nature framed to perceive those things which by reason of their minuteness escape our sight. What think you of those inconceivably small animals perceived by glasses? must we suppose they are all stark blind? Or, in case they see, can it be imagined their sight hath not the same use in preserving their bodies from injuries, which appears in that of all other animals? And if it hath, is it not evident they must see particles less than their own bodies, which will present them with a far different view in each object from that which strikes our senses? Even our own eyes do not always represent objects to us after the same manner. In the *jaundice* every one knows that all things seem yellow. Is it not therefore highly probable those animals in whose eyes we discern a very different texture from that of ours, and whose bodies abound with different humours, do not see the same colours in every object that we do? From all which, should it not seem to follow that all colours are equally apparent, and that none of those which we perceive are really inherent in any outward object?

Hyl. It should.

Phil. The point will be past all doubt, if you consider that, in case colours were real properties or affections inherent in external bodies, they could admit of no alteration without some change wrought in the very bodies themselves: but, is it not evident from what hath been said that, upon the use of microscopes, upon a change happening in the humours of the eye, or a variation of distance, without any manner of real alteration in the thing itself, the colours of any object are either changed, or totally disappear? Nay, all other circumstances remaining the same, change but the situation of some objects, and they shall present different colours to the eye. The same thing happens upon viewing an object in various degrees of light. And what is more known than that the same bodies appear differently coloured by candle-light from what they do in the open day? Add to these the experiment of a prism which, separating the heterogeneous rays of light, alters the colour of any object, and will cause the whitest to appear of a deep blue or red to the naked eye. And now tell me whether you are still of opinion that every body hath its true real colour inhering in it; and, if you think it hath, I would fain know farther from you, what certain distance and position of the object, what peculiar texture and formation of the eye, what degree or kind of light is necessary for ascertaining that true colour, and distinguishing it from apparent ones.

Hyl. I own myself entirely satisfied, that they are all equally apparent, and that there is no such thing as colour really inhering in external bodies, but that it is altogether in the light. And what confirms me in this opinion is that in proportion to the light colours are still more or less vivid; and if there be no light, then are there no colours perceived. Besides, allowing there are colours on external objects, yet, how is it possible for us to perceive them? For no external body affects the mind, unless it acts first on our organs of sense. But the only action of bodies is motion; and motion cannot be communicated otherwise than by impulse. A distant object therefore cannot act on the eye, nor consequently make itself or its properties perceivable to the soul. Whence it plainly follows that it is immediately some contiguous substance, which, operating on the eye, occasions a perception of colours: and such is light.

Phil. How! is light then a substance?

Hyl. I tell you, *Philonous*, external light is nothing but a thin fluid substance, whose minute particles being agitated with a brisk motion, and in various manners reflected from the different surfaces of outward objects to the eyes, communicate different motions to the optic nerves; which, being propagated to the brain, cause therein various impressions;

and these are attended with the sensations of red, blue, yellow, &c.

Phil. It seems then the light doth no more than shake the optic nerves.

Hyl. Nothing else.

Phil. And, consequent to each particular motion of the nerves, the mind is affected with a sensation, which is some particular colour.

Hyl. Right.

Phil. And these sensations have no existence without the mind.

Hyl. They have not.

Phil. How then do you affirm that colours are in the light; since by *light* you understand a corporeal substance external to the mind?

Hyl. Light and colours, as immediately perceived by us, I grant cannot exist without the mind. But, in themselves they are only the motions and configurations of certain insensible particles of matter.

Phil. Colours then, in the vulger sense, or taken for the immediate objects of sight, cannot agree to any but a perceiving substance.

Hyl. That is what I say.

Phil. Well then, since you give up the point as to those sensible qualities which are alone thought colours by all mankind beside, you may hold what you please with regard to those invisible ones of the philosophers. It is not my business to dispute about them; only I would advise you to bethink yourself, whether, considering the inquiry we are upon, it be prudent for you to affirm—*the red and blue which we see are not real colours, but certain unknown motions and figures, which no man ever did or can see, are truly so.* Are not these shocking notions, and are not they subject to as many ridiculous inferences, as those you were obliged to renounce before in the case of sounds?

Hyl. I frankly own, *Philonous*, that it is in vain to stand out any longer. Colours, sounds, tastes, in a word all those termed *secondary qualities*, have certainly no existence without the mind. But, by this acknowledgment I must not be supposed to derogate anything from the reality of Matter or external objects; seeing it is no more than several philosophers maintain, who nevertheless are the farthest imaginable from denying Matter. For the clearer understanding of this, you must know sensible qualities are by philosophers divided into *primary* and *secondary*. The former are Extension, Figure, Solidity, Gravity, Motion, and Rest. And these they hold exist really in bodies. The latter are those above enumerated; or, briefly, all sensible qualities beside the Primary, which they assert are only so many sensations or ideas existing nowhere but in the mind. But all this, I doubt not, you are apprised of. For my part, I have been a long time sensible there was such an opinion current among philosophers, but was never thoroughly convinced of its truth until now.

Phil. You are still then of opinion that *extension* and *figures* are inherent in external unthinking substances?

Hyl. I am.

Phil. But what if the same arguments which are brought against Secondary Qualities will hold good against these also?

Hyl. Why then I shall be obliged to think, they too exist only in the mind.

Phil. Is it your opinion the very figure and extension which you perceive by sense exist in the outward object or material substance?

Hyl. It is.

Phil. Have all other animals as good grounds to think the same of the figure and extension which they see and feel?

Hyl. Without doubt, if they have any thought at all.

Phil. Answer me, *Hylas.* Think you the senses were bestowed upon all animals for their preservation and well-being in life? or were they given to men alone for this end?

Hyl. I make no question but they have the same use in all other animals.

Phil. If so, is it not necessary they should be enabled by them to perceive their own limbs, and those bodies which are capable of harming them?

Hyl. Certainly.

Phil. A mite therefore must be supposed to see his own foot, and things equal or even less than it, as bodies of some considerable dimension; though at the same time they appear to you scarce discernible, or at best as so many visible points?

Hyl. I cannot deny it.

Phil. And to creatures less than the mite they will seem yet larger?

Hyl. They will.

Phil. Insomuch that what you can hardly discern will to another extremely minute animal appear as some huge mountain?

Hyl. All this I grant.

Phil. Can one and the same thing be at the same time in itself of different dimensions?

Hyl. That were absurd to imagine.

Phil. But, from what you have laid down it follows that both the extension by you perceived, and that perceived by the mite itself, as likewise all those perceived by lesser animals, are each of them the true extension of the mite's foot; that is to say, by your own principles you are led into an absurdity.

Hyl. There seems to be some difficulty in the point.

Phil. Again, have you not acknowledged that no real inherent property of any object can be changed without some change in the thing itself?

Hyl. I have.

Phil. But, as we approach to or recede from an object, the visible extension varies, being at one distance ten or a hundred times greater than at another. Doth it not therefore follow from hence likewise that it is not really inherent in the object?

Hyl. I own I am at a loss what to think?

Phil. Your judgment will soon be determined, if you will venture to think as freely concerning this quality as you have done concerning the rest. Was it not admitted as a good argument, that neither heat nor cold was in the water, because it seemed warm to one hand and cold to the other?

Hyl. It was.

Phil. Is it not the very same reasoning to conclude, there is no extension or figure in an object, because to one eye it shall seem little, smooth, and round, when at the same time it appears to the other, great, uneven, and angular?

Hyl. The very same.   But does this latter fact ever happen ?

Phil. You may at any time make the experiment, by looking with one eye bare, and with the other through a microscope.

Hyl. I know not how to maintain it, and yet I am loath to give up *extension*, I see so many odd consequences following upon such a concession.

Phil. Odd, say you ?   After the concessions already made, I hope you will stick at nothing for its oddness.[1]   But, on the other hand, should it not seem very odd, if the general reasoning which includes all other sensible qualities did not also include extension ?   If it be allowed that no idea nor anything like an idea can exist in an unperceiving substance, then surely it follows that no figure or mode of extension, which we can either perceive or imagine, or have any idea of, can be really inherent in Matter ; not to mention the peculiar difficulty there must be in conceiving a material substance, prior to and distinct from extension, to be the *substratum* of extension.   Be the sensible quality what it will—figure, or sound, or colour ; it seems alike impossible it should subsist in that which doth not perceive it.

Hyl. I give up the point for the present, reserving still a right to retract my opinion, in case I shall hereafter discover any false step in my progress to it.

Phil. That is a right you cannot be denied.   Figures and extension being despatched, we proceed next to *motion*. Can a real motion in any external body be at the same time both very swift and very slow ?

Hyl. It cannot.

Phil. Is not the motion of a body swift in a reciprocal proportion to the time it takes up in describing any given space ?   Thus a body that describes a mile in an hour moves three times faster than it would in case it described only a mile in three hours.

Hyl. I agree with you.

Phil. And is not time measured by the succession of ideas in our minds ?

Hyl. It is.

---

[1] This speech of Philonous ended here in the first and second editions.

Phil. And is it not possible ideas should succeed one another twice as fast in your mind as they do in mine, or in that of some spirit of another kind?

Hyl. I own it.

Phil. Consequently, the same body may to another seem to perform its motion over any space in half the time that it doth to you. And the same reasoning will hold as to any other proportion : that is to say, according to your principles (since the motions perceived are both really in the object) it is possible one and the same body shall be really moved the same way at once, both very swift and very slow. How is this consistent either with common sense, or with what you just now granted?

Hyl. I have nothing to say to it.

Phil. Then as for *solidity ;* either you do not mean any sensible quality by that word, and so it is beside our inquiry: or if you do, it must be either hardness or resistance. But both the one and the other are plainly relative to our senses : it being evident that what seems hard to one animal may appear soft to another, who hath greater force and firmness of limbs. Nor is it less plain that the resistance I feel is not in the body.

Hyl. I own the very sensation of resistance, which is all you immediately perceive, is not in the *body ;* but the cause of that sensation is.

Phil. But the causes of our sensations are not things immediately perceived, and therefore not sensible. This point I thought had been already determined.

Hyl. I own it was ; but you will pardon me if I seem a little embarrassed : I know not how to quit my old notions.

Phil. To help you out, do but consider that if *extension* be once acknowledged to have no existence without the mind, the same must necessarily be granted of motion, solidity, and gravity—since they all evidently suppose extension. It is therefore superfluous to inquire particularly concerning each of them. In denying extension, you have denied them all to have any real existence.

Hyl. I wonder, *Philonous*, if what you say be true, why those philosophers who deny the Secondary Qualities any real existence, should yet attribute it to the Primary. If there is no difference between them, how can this be accounted for?

Phil. It is not my business to account for every opinion of the philosophers. But, among other reasons which may be assigned for this, it seems probable that pleasure and pain being rather annexed to the former than the latter may be one. Heat and cold, tastes and smells, have something more vividly pleasing or disagreeable than the ideas of extension, figure, and motion affect us with. And, it being too visibly absurd to hold that pain or pleasure can be in an unperceiving Substance, men are more easily weaned from believing the external existence of the Secondary than the Primary Qualities. You will be satisfied there is something in this, if you recollect the difference you made between an intense and more moderate degree of heat ; allowing the one a real existence, while you denied it to the other. But, after all, there is no rational ground for that distinction ; for, surely an indifferent sensation is as truly *a sensation* as one more pleasing or painful; and consequently should not any more than they be supposed to exist in an unthinking subject.

Hyl. It is just come into my head, *Philonous,* that I have somewhere heard of a distinction between absolute and sensible extension. Now, though it be acknowledged that *great* and *small,* consisting merely in the relation which other extended beings have to the parts of our own bodies, do not really inhere in the Substances themselves ; yet nothing obliges us to hold the same with regard to *absolute extension,* which is something abstracted from *great* and *small,* from this or that particular magnitude or figure. So likewise as to motion ; *swift* and *slow* are altogether relative to the succession of ideas in our own minds. But, it doth not follow, because those modifications of motion exist not without the mind, that therefore absolute motion abstracted from them doth not.

Phil. Pray what is it that distinguishes one motion, or one part of extension, from another ? Is it not something sensible, as some degree of swiftness or slowness, some certain magnitude or figure peculiar to each ?

Hyl. I think so.

Phil. These qualities, therefore, stripped of all sensible properties, are without all specific and numerical differences, as the schools call them.

Hyl. They are.

Phil. That is to say, they are extension in general, and motion in general.

Hyl. Let it be so.

Phil. But it is a universally received maxim that *Everything which exists is particular.* How then can motion in general, or extension in general, exist in any corporeal Substance?

Hyl. I will take time to solve your difficulty.

Phil. But I think the point may be speedily decided. Without doubt you can tell whether you are able to frame this or that idea. Now I am content to put our dispute on this issue. If you can frame in your thoughts a distinct abstract idea of motion or extension; divested of all those sensible modes, as swift and slow, great and small, round and square, and the like, which are acknowledged to exist only in the mind, I will then yield the point you contend for. But, if you cannot, it will be unreasonable on your side to insist any longer upon what you have no notion of.

Hyl. To confess ingenuously, I cannot.

Phil. Can you even separate the ideas of extension and motion from the ideas of all those qualities which they who make the distinction term *secondary?*

Hyl. What ! is it not an easy matter to consider extension and motion by themselves, abstracted from all other sensible qualities? Pray how do the mathematicians treat of them?

Phil. I acknowledge, *Hylas*, it is not difficult to form general propositions and reasonings about those qualities, without mentioning any other; and, in this sense, to consider or treat of them abstractedly. But, how doth it follow that, because I can pronounce that word *motion* by itself, I can form the idea of it in my mind exclusive of body? Or, because theorems may be made of extension and figures, without any mention of *great* or *small*, or any other sensible mode or quality, that therefore it is possible such an abstract idea of extension, without any particular size or figure, or sensible quality, should be distinctly formed, and apprehended by the mind? Mathematicians treat of quantity,

without regarding what other sensible qualities it is attended
with, as being altogether indifferent to their demonstrations.
But, when laying aside the words, they contemplate the bare
ideas, I believe you will find, they are not the pure abstracted
ideas of extension.

Hyl. But what say you to *pure intellect?*   May not abstracted idea be framed by that faculty?

Phil. Since I cannot frame abstract ideas at all, it is plain
I cannot frame them by the help of *pure intellect;* whatsoever faculty you understand by those words.   Besides, not
to inquire into the nature of pure intellect and its spiritual
objects, as *virtue, reason, God,* or the like, thus much seems
manifest, that sensible things are only to be perceived by
sense, or represented by the imagination.   Figures, therefore,
and extension, being originally perceived by sense, do not
belong to pure intellect: but, for your farther satisfaction,
try if you can frame the idea of any figure, abstracted
from all particularities of size, or even from other sensible
qualities.

Hyl. Let me think a little——I do not find that I can.

Phil. And can you think it possible that should really
exist in nature which implies a repugnancy in its conception?

Hyl. By no means.

Phil. Since therefore it is impossible even for the mind to
disunite the ideas of extension and motion from all other
sensible qualities, doth it not follow, that where the one exist
there necessarily the other exist likewise?

Hyl. It should seem so.

Phil. Consequently, the very same arguments which you
admitted as conclusive against the Secondary Qualities are,
without any farther application of force, against the Primary
too.   Besides, if you will trust your senses, is it not plain all
sensible qualities coexist, or to them appear as being in
the same place?   Do they ever represent a motion, or
figure, as being divested of all other visible and tangible
qualities?

Hyl. You need say no more on this head.   I am free to
own, if there be no secret error or oversight in our proceed-
ings hitherto, that all sensible qualities are alike to be
denied existence without the mind.   But, my fear is that

I have been too liberal in my former concessions, or overlooked some fallacy or other. In short, I did not take time to think.

Phil. For that matter, *Hylas*, you may take what time you please in reviewing the progress of our inquiry, You are at liberty to recover any slips you might have made, or offer whatever you have omitted which makes for your first opinion.

Hyl. One great oversight I take to be this—that I did not sufficiently distinguish the *object* from the *sensation*. Now, though this latter may not exist without the mind, yet it will not thence follow that the former cannot.

Phil. What object do you mean? The object of the senses?

Hyl. The same.

Phil. It is then immediately perceived?

Hyl. Right.

Phil. Make me to understand the difference between what is immediately perceived, and a sensation.

Hyl. The sensation I take to be an act of the mind perceiving; besides which, there is something perceived; and this I call the *object*. For example, there is red and yellow on that tulip. But then the act of perceiving those colours is in me only, and not in the tulip.

Phil. What tulip do you speak of? Is it that which you see?

Hyl. The same.

Phil. And what do you see besides colour, figure, and extension?

Hyl. Nothing.

Phil. What you would say then is that the red and yellow are coexistent with the extension; is it not?

Hyl. That is not all; I would say they have a real existence without the mind, in some unthinking substance.

Phil. That the colours are really in the tulip which I see is manifest. Neither can it be denied that this tulip may exist independent of your mind or mine; but, that any immediate object of the senses—that is, any idea, or combination of ideas—should exist in an unthinking substance, or exterior to all minds, is in itself an evident contradiction. Nor can I imagine how this follows from what you said just now, to wit, that the red and yellow were on the tulip *you saw*, since you do not pretend to *see* that unthinking substance.

Hyl. You have an artful way, *Philonous*, of diverting our inquiry from the subject.

Phil. I see you have no mind to be pressed that way. To return then to your distinction between *sensation* and *object*; if I take you right, you distinguish in every perception two things, the one an action of the mind, the other not.

Hyl. True.

Phil. And this action cannot exist in, or belong to, any unthinking thing; but, whatever beside is implied in a perception may?

Hyl. That is my meaning.

Phil. So that if there was a perception without any act of the mind, it were possible such a perception should exist in an unthinking substance?

Hyl. I grant it. But it is impossible there should be such a perception.

Phil. When is the mind said to be active?

Hyl. When it produces, puts an end to, or changes, anything.

Phil. Can the mind produce, discontinue, or change anything, but by an act of the will?

Hyl. It cannot.

Phil. The mind therefore is to be accounted *active* in its perceptions so far forth as *volition* is included in them?

Hyl. It is.

Phil. In plucking this flower I am active; because I do it by the motion of my hand, which was consequent upon my volition; so likewise in applying it to my nose. But is either of these smelling?

Hyl. No.

Phil. I act too in drawing the air through my nose; because my breathing so rather than otherwise is the effect of my volition. But neither can this be called *smelling:* for, if it were, I should smell every time I breathed in that manner?

Hyl. True.

Phil. Smelling then is somewhat consequent to all this?

Hyl. It is.

Phil. But I do not find my will concerned any farther. Whatever more there is—as that I perceive such a particular smell, or any smell at all—this is independent of my will, and therein I am altogether passive. Do you find it otherwise with you, *Hylas?*

Hyl. No, the very same.

Phil. Then, as to seeing, is it not in your power to open your eyes, or keep them shut; to turn them this or that way?

Hyl. Without doubt.

Phil. But, doth it in like manner depend on your will that in looking on this flower you perceive *white* rather than any other colour? Or, directing your open eyes towards yonder part of the heaven, can you avoid seeing the sun? Or is light or darkness the effect of your volition?

Hyl. No certainly.

Phil. You are then in these respects altogether passive?

Hyl. I am.

Phil. Tell me now, whether *seeing* consists in perceiving light and colours, or in opening and turning the eyes?

Hyl. Without doubt, in the former.

Phil. Since therefore you are in the very perception of light and colours altogether passive, what is become of that action you were speaking of as an ingredient in every sensation? And, doth it not follow from your own concessions, that the perception of light and colours, including no action in it, may exist in an unperceiving substance? And is not this a plain contradiction?

Hyl. I know not what to think of it.

Phil. Besides, since you distinguish the *active* and *passive* in every perception, you must do it in that of pain. But how is it possible that pain, be it as little active as you please, should exist in an unperceiving substance? In short, do but consider the point, and then confess ingenuously, whether light and colours, tastes, sounds, &c., are not all equally passions or sensations in the soul. You may indeed call them *external objects*, and give them in words what subsistence you please. But, examine your own thoughts, and then tell me whether it be not as I say?

Hyl. I acknowledge, *Philonous*, that, upon a fair observation of what passes in my mind, I can discover nothing else but that I am a thinking being, affected with variety of sensations ; neither is it possible to conceive how a sensation should exist in an unperceiving substance. But then, on the other hand, when I look on sensible things in a different view, considering them as so many modes and qualities, I find it necessary to suppose a material *substratum*, without which they cannot be conceived to exist.

Phil. Material substratum call you it? Pray, by which of your senses came you acquainted with that being?

Hyl. It is not itself sensible ; its modes and qualities only being perceived by the senses.

Phil. I presume then it was by reflexion and reason you obtained the idea of it?

Hyl. I do not pretend to any proper positive idea of it. However, I conclude it exists, because qualities cannot be conceived to exist without a support.

Phil. It seems then you have only a relative notion of it, or that you conceive it not otherwise than by conceiving the relation it bears to sensible qualities?

Hyl. Right.

Phil. Be pleased therefore to let me know wherein that relation consists.

Hyl. Is it not sufficiently expressed in the term *substratum* or *substance?*

Phil. If so, the word *substratum* should import that it is spread under the sensible qualities or accidents?

Hyl. True.

Phil. And consequently under extension?

Hyl. I own it.

Phil. It is therefore somewhat in its own nature entirely distinct from extension?

Hyl. I tell you, extension is only a mode, and Matter is something that supports modes. And is it not evident the thing supported is different from the thing supporting?

Phil. So that something distinct from, and exclusive of, extension is supposed to be the *substratum* of extension?

Hyl. Just so.

Phil. Answer me, *Hylas.* Can a thing be spread without extension? or is not the idea of extension necessarily included in *spreading?*

Hyl. It is.

Phil. Whatsoever therefore you suppose spread under anything must have in itself an extension distinct from the extension of that thing under which it is spread?

Hyl. It must.

Phil. Consequently, every corporeal substance being the *substratum* of extension must have in itself another extension, by which it is qualified to be a *substratum:* and so on to infinity? And I ask whether this be not absurd in itself, and repugnant to what you granted just now, to wit, that the *substratum* was something distinct from and exclusive of extension?

Hyl. Aye, but, *Philonous*, you take me wrong. I do not mean that Matter is *spread* in a gross literal sense under extension. The word *substratum* is used only to express in general the same thing with *substance*.

Phil. Well then, let us examine the relation implied in the term *substance*. Is it not that it stands under accidents?

Hyl. The very same.

Phil. But, that one thing may stand under or support another, must it not be extended?

Hyl. It must.

Phil. Is not therefore this supposition liable to the same absurdity with the former?

Hyl. You still take things in a strict literal sense; that is not fair, *Philonous*.

Phil. I am not for imposing any sense on your words: you are at liberty to explain them as you please. Only, I beseech you, make me understand something by them. You tell me Matter supports or stands under accidents. How! is it as your legs support your body?

Hyl. No; that is the literal sense.

Phil. Pray let me know any sense, literal or not literal, that you understand it in. . . . How long must I wait for an answer, *Hylas?*

Hyl. I declare I know not what to say. I once thought I understood well enough what was meant by Matter's supporting accidents. But now, the more I think on it the less can I comprehend it; in short I find that I know nothing of it.

Phil. It seems then you have no idea at all, neither relative nor positive, of Matter; you know neither what it is in itself, nor what relation it bears to accidents?

Hyl. I acknowledge it.

Phil. And yet you asserted that you could not conceive how qualities or accidents should really exist, without conceiving at the same time a material support of them?

Hyl. I did.

Phil. That is to say, when you conceive the real existence of qualities, you do withal conceive something which you cannot conceive?

Hyl. It was wrong I own. But still I fear there is some fallacy or other. Pray what think you of this? It is just come into my head that the ground of all our mistake lies in your treating of each quality by itself. Now, I grant that each quality cannot singly subsist without the mind. Colour cannot without extension, neither can figure without some other sensible quality. But, as the several qualities united or blended together form entire sensible things, nothing hinders why such things may not be supposed to exist without the mind.

Phil. Either, *Hylas*, you are jesting, or have a very bad memory. Though indeed we went through all the qualities by name one after another; yet my arguments, or rather your concessions, nowhere tended to prove that the Secondary Qualities did not subsist each alone by itself; but, that they were not *at all* without the mind. Indeed, in treating of figure and motion we concluded they could not exist without the mind, because it was impossible even in thought to separate them from all secondary qualities, so as to conceive them existing by themselves. But then this was not the only argument made use of upon that occasion. But (to pass by all that hath been hitherto said, and reckon it for nothing, if you will have it so) I am content to put the whole upon this issue. If you can conceive it possible for any mixture or combination of qualities, or any sensible object whatever, to exist without the mind, then I will grant it actually to be so.

Hyl. If it comes to that the point will soon be decided. What more easy than to conceive a tree or house existing by itself, independent of, and unperceived by, any mind whatsoever? I do at this present time conceive them existing after that manner.

Phil. How say you, *Hylas*, can you see a thing which is at the same time unseen ?

Hyl. No, that were a contradiction.

Phil. Is it not as great a contradiction to talk of *conceiving* a thing which is *unconceived* ?

Hyl. It is.

Phil. The tree or house therefore which you think of is conceived by you ?

Hyl. How should it be otherwise ?

Phil. And what is conceived is surely in the mind ?

Hyl. Without question, that which is conceived is in the mind.

Phil. How then came you to say, you conceived a house or tree existing independent and out of all minds whatsoever?

Hyl. That was I own an oversight ; but stay, let me consider what led me into it.—It is a pleasant mistake enough. As I was thinking of a tree in a solitary place where no one was present to see it, methought that was to conceive a tree as existing unperceived or unthought of—not considering that I myself conceived it all the while. But now I plainly see that all I can do is to frame ideas in my own mind.   I may indeed conceive in my own thoughts the idea of a tree, or a house, or a mountain, but that is all. And this is far from proving that I can conceive them *existing out of the minds of all Spirits.*

Phil. You acknowledge then that you cannot possibly conceive how any one corporeal sensible thing should exist otherwise than in a mind ?

Hyl. I do.

Phil. And yet you will earnestly contend for the truth of that which you cannot so much as conceive ?

Hyl. I profess I know not what to think ; but still there are some scruples remain with me. Is it not certain I *see* things at a distance?   Do we not perceive the stars and moon, for example, to be a great way off ? Is not this, I say, manifest to the senses ?

Phil. Do you not in a dream too perceive those or the like objects ?

Hyl. I do.

Phil. And have they not then the same appearance of being distant ?

Hyl. They have.

Phil. But you do not thence conclude the apparitions in a dream to be without the mind ?

Hyl. By no means.

Phil. You ought not therefore to conclude that sensible objects are without the mind, from their appearance or manner wherein they are perceived.

Hyl. I acknowledge it. But doth not my sense deceive me in those cases ?

Phil. By no means. The idea or thing which you immediately perceive, neither sense nor reason informs you that it actually exists without the mind. By sense you only know that you are affected with such certain sensations of light and colours, &c. And these you will not say are without the mind.

Hyl. True : but, beside all that, do you not think the sight suggests something of *outness* or *distance* ?

Phil. Upon approaching a distant object, do the visible size and figure change perpetually, or do they appear the same at all distances ?

Hyl. They are in a continual change.

Phil. Sight therefore doth not suggest or any way inform you that the visible object you immediately perceive exists at a distance,[1] or will be perceived when you advance farther onward ; there being a continued series of visible objects succeeding each other during the whole time of your approach.

Hyl. It doth not ; but still I know, upon seeing an object, what object I shall perceive after having passed over a certain distance : no matter whether it be exactly the same or no : there is still something of distance suggested in the case.

Phil. Good *Hylas*, do but reflect a little on the point, and then tell me whether there be any more in it than this :— From the ideas you actually perceive by sight, you have by experience learned to collect what other ideas you will (according to the standing order of nature) be affected with, after such a certain succession of time and motion.

Hyl. Upon the whole, I take it to be nothing else.

---

[1] See the " Essay towards a New Theory of Vision," and its " Vindication."—AUTHOR, 1734.

Phil. Now, is it not plain that if we suppose a man born blind was on a sudden made to see, he could at first have no experience of what may be suggested by sight?

Hyl. It is.

Phil. He would not then, according to you, have any notion of distance annexed to the things he saw; but would take them for a new set of sensations existing only in his mind?

Hyl. It is undeniable.

Phil. But, to make it still more plain : is not *distance* a line turned endwise to the eye?

Hyl. It is.

Phil. And can a line so situated be perceived by sight?

Hyl. It cannot.

Phil. Doth it not therefore follow that distance is not properly and immediately perceived by sight?

Hyl. It should seem so.

Phil. Again, is it your opinion that colours are at a distance?

Hyl. It must be acknowledged they are only in the mind.

Phil. But do not colours appear to the eye as coexisting in the same place with extension and figures?

Hyl. They do.

Phil. How can you then conclude from sight that figures exist without, when you acknowledge colours do not; the sensible appearance being the very same with regard to both?

Hyl. I know not what to answer.

Phil. But, allowing that distance was truly and immediately perceived by the mind, yet it would not thence follow it existed out of the mind. For, whatever is immediately perceived is an idea : and can any *idea* exist out of the mind?

Hyl. To suppose that were absurd : but, inform me, *Philonous*, can we perceive or know nothing beside our ideas?

Phil. As for the rational deducing of causes from effects, that is beside our inquiry. And, by the senses you can best tell whether you perceive anything which is not immediately perceived. And I ask you, whether the things immediately

perceived are other than your own sensations or ideas? You
have indeed more than once, in the course of this conversation, declared yourself on those points; but you seem, by
this last question, to have departed from what you then
thought.

Hyl. To speak the truth, *Philonous*, I think there are two
kinds of objects :—the one perceived immediately, which are
likewise called *ideas ;* the other are real things or external
objects, perceived by the mediation of ideas, which are their
images and representations. Now, I own ideas do not exist
without the mind ; but the latter sort of objects do. I am
sorry I did not think of this distinction sooner; it would
probably have cut short your discourse.

Phil. Are those external objects perceived by sense, or by
some other faculty?

Hyl. They are perceived by sense.

Phil. How! is there anything perceived by sense which is
not immediately perceived?

Hyl. Yes, *Philonous*, in some sort there is. For example,
when I look on a picture or statue of Julius Cæsar, I may be
said after a manner to perceive him (though not immediately)
by my senses.

Phil. It seems then you will have our ideas, which alone
are immediately perceived, to be pictures of external things :
and that these also are perceived by sense, inasmuch as they
have a conformity or resemblance to our ideas?

Hyl. That is my meaning.

Phil. And, in the same way that Julius Cæsar, in himself
invisible, is nevertheless perceived by sight; real things, in
themselves imperceptible, are perceived by sense.

Hyl. In the very same.

Phil. Tell me, *Hylas*, when you behold the picture of
Julius Cæsar, do you see with your eyes any more than some
colours and figures, with a certain symmetry and composition
of the whole?

Hyl. Nothing else.

Phil. And would not a man who had never known anything of Julius Cæsar see as much?

Hyl. He would.

Phil. Consequently he hath his sight, and the use of it, in
as a perfect a degree as you?

Hyl. I agree with you.

Phil. Whence comes it then that your thoughts are directed to the Roman emperor, and his are not? This cannot proceed from the sensations or ideas of sense by you then perceived; since you acknowledge you have no advantage over him in that respect. It should seem therefore to proceed from reason and memory: should it not?

Hyl. It should.

Phil. Consequently, it will not follow from that instance that anything is perceived by sense which is not immediately perceived. Though I grant we may, in one acceptation, be said to perceive sensible things mediately by sense—that is, when, from a frequently perceived connexion, the immediate perception of ideas by one sense suggests to the mind others, perhaps belonging to another sense, which are wont to be connected with them. For instance, when I hear a coach drive along the streets, immediately I perceive only the sound; but, from the experience I have had that such a sound is connected with a coach, I am said to hear the coach. It is nevertheless evident that, in truth and strictness, nothing can be *heard* but *sound;* and the coach is not then properly perceived by sense, but suggested from experience. So likewise when we are said to see a red-hot bar of iron; the solidity and heat of the iron are not the objects of sight, but suggested to the imagination by the colour and figure which are properly perceived by that sense. In short, those things alone are actually and strictly perceived by any sense, which would have been perceived in case that same sense had then been first conferred on us. As for other things, it is plain they are only suggested to the mind by experience, grounded on former perceptions. But, to return to your comparison of Cæsar's picture, it is plain, if you keep to that, you must hold the real things or archetypes of our ideas are not perceived by sense, but by some internal faculty of the soul, as reason or memory. I would therefore fain know what arguments you can draw from reason for the existence of what you call *real things* or *material objects.* Or, whether you remember to have seen them formerly as they are in themselves; or, if you have heard or read of any one that did.

Hyl. I see, *Philonous,* you are disposed to raillery; but that will never convince me.

Phil. My aim is only to learn from you the way to come at the knowledge of *material beings.* Whatever we perceive is perceived immediately or mediately: by sense, or by reason and reflexion. But, as you have excluded sense, pray shew me what reason you have to believe their existence; or what *medium* you can possibly make use of to prove it, either to mine or your own understanding.

Hyl. To deal ingenuously, *Philonous,* now I consider the point, I do not find I can give you any good reason for it. But, thus much seems pretty plain, that it is at least possible such things may really exist. And, as long as there is no absurdity in supposing them, I am resolved to believe as I did, till you bring good reasons to the contrary.

Phil. What ! is it come to this, that you only believe the existence of material objects, and that your belief is founded barely on the possibility of its being true? Then you will have me bring reasons against it : though another would think it reasonable the proof should lie on him who holds the affirmative. And, after all, this very point which you are now resolved to maintain, without any reason, is in effect what you have more than once during this discourse seen good reason to give up. But, to pass over all this ; if I understand you rightly, you say our ideas do not exist without the mind ; but that they are copies, images, or representations, of certain originals that do ?

Hyl. You take me right.

Phil. They are then like external things ?

Hyl. They are.

Phil. Have those things a stable and permanent nature, independent of our senses ; or are they in a perpetual change, upon our producing any motions in our bodies, suspending, exerting, or altering, our faculties or organs of sense ?

Hyl. Real things, it is plain, have a fixed and real nature, which remains the same notwithstanding any change in our senses, or in the posture and motion of our bodies ; which indeed may affect the ideas in our minds, but it were absurd to think they had the same effect on things existing without the mind.

Phil. How then is it possible that things perpetually fleeting and variable as our ideas should be copies or images of anything fixed and constant ? Or, in other words, since all sensible qualities, as size, figure, colour, &c., that is, our ideas, are continually changing upon every alteration in the distance, medium, or instruments of sensation ; how can any determinate material objects be properly represented or painted forth by several distinct things, each of which is so different from and unlike the rest ? Or, if you say it resembles some one only of our ideas, how shall we be able to distinguish the true copy from all the false ones ?

Hyl. I profess, *Philonous*, I am at a loss. I know not what to say to this.

Phil. But neither is this all. Which are material objects in themselves—perceptible or imperceptible ?

Hyl. Properly and immediately nothing can be perceived but ideas. All material things, therefore, are in themselves insensible, and to be perceived only by our ideas.

Phil. Ideas then are sensible, and their archetypes or originals insensible ?

Hyl. Right.

Phil. But how can that which is sensible be like that which is insensible ? Can a real thing, in itself *invisible*, be like a *colour ;* or a real thing, which is not *audible*, be like a *sound ?* In a word, can anything be like a sensation or idea, but another sensation or idea ?

Hyl. I must own, I think not.

Phil. Is it possible there should be any doubt on the point ? Do you not perfectly know your own ideas ?

Hyl. I know them perfectly ; since what I do not perceive or know can be no part of my idea.

Phil. Consider, therefore, and examine them, and then tell me if there be anything in them which can exist without the mind ? or if you can conceive anything like them existing without the mind ?

Hyl. Upon inquiry, I find it is impossible for me to conceive or understand how anything but an idea can be like an idea. And it is most evident that *no idea can exist without the mind*.

Phil. You are therefore, by your principles, forced to deny the reality of sensible things ; since you made it to consist in an absolute existence exterior to the mind. That is to say, you are a downright sceptic. So I have gained my point, which was to shew your principles led to Scepticism.

Hyl. For the present I am, if not entirely convinced, at least silenced.

Phil. I would fain know what more you would require in order to a perfect conviction. Have you not had the liberty of explaining yourself all manner of ways? Were any little slips in discourse laid hold and insisted on? Or were you not allowed to retract or reinforce anything you had offered, as best served your purpose? Hath not everything you could say been heard and examined with all the fairness imaginable? In a word, have you not in every point been convinced out of your own mouth? and, if you can at present discover any flaw in any of your former concessions, or think of any remaining subterfuge, any new distinction, colour, or comment whatsoever, why do you not produce it?

Hyl. A little patience, *Philonous.* I am at present so amazed to see myself ensnared, and as it were imprisoned in the labyrinths you have drawn me into, that on the sudden it cannot be expected I should find my way out. You must give me time to look about me and recollect myself.

Phil. Hark; is not this the college bell?

Hyl. It rings for prayers.

Phil. We will go in then, if you please, and meet here again to-morrow morning. In the meantime, you may employ your thoughts on this morning's discourse, and try if you can find any fallacy in it, or invent any new means to extricate yourself.

Hyl. Agreed.

THE SECOND DIALOGUE.

Hylas.

I BEG your pardon, *Philonous*, for not meeting you sooner. All this morning my head was so filled with our late conversation that I had not leisure to think of the time of the day, or indeed of anything else.

Philonous. I am glad you were so intent upon it, in hopes if there were any mistakes in your concessions, or fallacies in my reasonings from them, you will now discover them to me.

Hyl. I assure you I have done nothing ever since I saw you but search after mistakes and fallacies, and, with that view, have minutely examined the whole series of yesterday's discourse : but all in vain, for the notions it led me into, upon review, appear still more clear and evident ; and, the more I consider them, the more irresistibly do they force my assent.

Phil. And is not this, think you, a sign that they are genuine, that they proceed from nature, and are conformable to right reason? Truth and beauty are in this alike, that the strictest survey sets them both off to advantage ; while the false lustre of error and disguise cannot endure being reviewed, or too nearly inspected.

Hyl. I own there is a great deal in what you say. Nor can any one be more entirely satisfied of the truth of those odd consequences, so long as I have in view the reasonings that lead to them. But, when these are out of my thoughts, there seems, on the other hand, something so satisfactory, so natural and intelligible, in the modern way of explaining things that, I profess, I know not how to reject it.

Phil. I know not what way you mean.

Hyl. I mean the way of accounting for our sensations or ideas.

Phil. How is that?

Hyl. It is supposed the soul makes her residence in some part of the brain, from which the nerves take their rise, and are thence extended to all parts of the body; and that outward objects, by the different impressions they make on the organs of sense, communicate certain vibrative motions to the nerves; and these being filled with spirits propagate them to the brain or seat of the soul, which, according to the various impressions or traces thereby made in the brain, is variously affected with ideas.

Phil. And call you this an explication of the manner whereby we are affected with ideas?

Hyl. Why not, *Philonous;* have you anything to object against it?

Phil. I would first know whether I rightly understand your hypothesis. You make certain traces in the brain to be the causes or occasions of our ideas. Pray tell me whether by the *brain* you mean any sensible thing.

Hyl. What else think you I could mean?

Phil. Sensible things are all immediately perceivable; and those things which are immediately perceivable are ideas; and these exist only in the mind. Thus much you have, if I mistake not, long since agreed to.

Hyl. I do not deny it.

Phil. The brain therefore you speak of, being a sensible thing, exists only in the mind. Now, I would fain know whether you think it reasonable to suppose that one idea or thing existing in the mind occasions all other ideas. And, if you think so, pray how do you account for the origin of that primary idea or brain itself?

Hyl. I do not explain the origin of our ideas by that brain which is perceivable to sense, this being itself only a combination of sensible ideas, but by another which I imagine.

Phil. But are not things imagined as truly *in the mind as* things perceived?

Hyl. I must confess they are.

Phil. It comes, therefore, to the same thing; and you have been all this while accounting for ideas by certain motions or impressions of the brain, that is, by some alterations in an idea, whether sensible or imaginable it matters not.

Hyl. I begin to suspect my hypothesis.

Phil. Besides spirits, all that we know or conceive are our own ideas. When, therefore, you say all ideas are occasioned by impressions in the brain, do you conceive this brain or no? If you do, then you talk of ideas imprinted in an idea causing that same idea, which is absurd. If you do not conceive it, you talk unintelligibly, instead of forming a reasonable hypothesis.

Hyl. I now clearly see it was a mere dream. There is nothing in it.

Phil. You need not be much concerned at it; for after all, this way of explaining things, as you called it, could never have satisfied any reasonable man. What connexion is there between a motion in the nerves, and the sensations of sound or colour in the mind? Or how is it possible these should be the effect of that?

Hyl. But I could never think it had so little in it as now it seems to have.

Phil. Well then, are you at length satisfied that no sensible things have a real existence; and that you are in truth an arrant *sceptic?*

Hyl. It is too plain to be denied.

Phil. Look! are not the fields covered with a delightful verdure? Is there not something in the woods and groves, in the rivers and clear springs, that soothes, that delights, that transports the soul? At the prospect of the wide and deep ocean, or some huge mountain whose top is lost in the clouds, or of an old gloomy forest, are not our minds filled with a pleasing horror? Even in rocks and deserts is there not an agreeable wildness? How sincere a pleasure is it to behold the natural beauties of the earth! To preserve and renew our relish for them, is not the veil of night alternately drawn over her face, and doth she not change her dress with the seasons? How aptly are the elements disposed! What variety and use in the meanest productions of nature! What delicacy, what beauty, what contrivance, in animal and vegetable bodies! How exquisitely are all things suited, as well to their particular ends, as to constitute opposite parts of the whole! And, while they mutually aid and support, do they not also set off and illustrate each other? Raise now your thought from this ball of earth to all those glorious luminaries that adorn the high arch of heaven. The motion and situation of the planets, are they not admirable for use and order? Were those (miscalled *erratic*) globes ever known to stray, in their repeated journeys through the pathless void? Do they not measure areas round the sun ever proportioned to the times? So fixed, so immutable are the laws by which the unseen Author of nature actuates the universe. How vivid and radiant is the lustre of the fixed stars! How magnificent and rich that negligent profusion with which they appear to be scattered throughout the whole azure vault! Yet, if you take the telescope, it brings into your sight a new host of stars that escape the naked eye. Here they seem contiguous and minute, but to a nearer view immense orbs of light at various distances, far sunk in the abyss of space. Now you must call imagination to your aid. The feeble narrow sense cannot descry innumerable worlds revolving round the central fires; and in those worlds the energy of an all-perfect Mind displayed in endless forms. But, neither sense nor imagination are big enough to comprehend the boundless extent, with all its glittering furniture. Though the labouring mind exert and strain each power to its utmost reach, there still stands out ungrasped a surplusage immeasurable. Yet all the vast bodies that compose this mighty frame, how distant and remote soever, are by some secret mechanism, some Divine art and force, linked in a mutual dependence and intercourse with each other, even with this earth, which was almost slipt from my thoughts and lost in the crowd of worlds. Is not the whole system immense, beautiful, glorious beyond expression and beyond thought! What treatment, then, do those philosophers deserve, who would deprive these noble and delightful scenes of all reality? How should those Principles be entertained that lead us to think all the visible beauty of the creation a false imaginary glare? To be plain, can you expect this Scepticism of yours will not be thought extravagantly absurd by all men of sense?

Hyl. Other men may think as they please; but for your part you have nothing to reproach me with. My comfort is, your are as much a sceptic as I am.

Phil. There, *Hylas*, I must beg leave to differ from you.

Hyl. What! have you all along agreed to the premises, and do you now deny the conclusion, and leave me to maintain those paradoxes by myself which you led me into? This surely is not fair.

Phil. I deny that I agreed with you in those notions that led to Scepticism. You indeed said the *reality* of sensible things consisted in an *absolute existence* out of the minds of spirits, or distinct from their being perceived. And, pursuant to this notion of reality, you are obliged to deny sensible things any real existence : that is, according to your own definition, you profess yourself a sceptic. But I neither said nor thought the reality of sensible things was to be defined after that manner. To me it is evident, for the reasons you allow of, that sensible things cannot exist otherwise than in a mind or spirit. Whence I conclude, not that they have no real existence, but that, seeing they depend not on my thought, and have an existence distinct from being perceived by me, *there must be some other mind wherein they exist.* As sure, therefore, as the sensible world really exists, so sure is there an infinite omnipresent Spirit, who contains and supports it.

Hyl. What ! this is no more than I and all Christians hold ; nay, and all others too who believe there is a God, and that He knows and comprehends all things.

Phil. Aye, but here lies the difference. Men commonly believe that all things are known or perceived by God, because they believe the being of a God ; whereas I, on the other side, immediately and necessarily conclude the being of a God, because all sensible things must be perceived by him.

Hyl. But so long as we all believe the same thing, what matter is it how we come by that belief ?

Phil. But neither do we agree in the same opinion. For philosophers, though they acknowledge all corporeal beings to be perceived by God, yet they attribute to them an absolute subsistence distinct from their being perceived by any mind whatever, which I do not. Besides, is there no difference between saying, *There is a God, therefore He perceives all things ;* and saying, *Sensible things do really exist ; and, if they really exist, they are necessarily perceived by an infinite mind : therefore there is an infinite mind, or God ?* This furnishes you with a direct and immediate demonstration, from a most evident principle, of the *being of a God*. Divines and philosophers had proved beyond all controversy, from the beauty and usefulness of the several parts of the creation, that it was the workmanship of God. But that—setting aside all help of astronomy and natural philosophy, all contemplation of the contrivance, order and adjustment of things—an infinite mind should be necessarily inferred from the bare *existence* of the sensible world, is an advantage to them only who have made this easy reflexion, that the sensible world is that which we perceive by our several senses ; and that nothing is perceived by the senses beside ideas ; and that no idea or archetype of an idea can exist otherwise than in a mind. You may now, without any laborious search into the sciences, without any subtlety of reason, or tedious length of discourse, oppose and baffle the most strenuous advocate for Atheism ; those miserable refuges, whether in an eternal succession of unthinking causes and effects, or in a fortuitous concourse of atoms ; those wild imaginations of Vanini, Hobbes, and Spinoza : in a word, the whole system of Atheism, is it not entirely overthrown, by this single reflexion on the repugnancy included in supposing the whole, or any part, even the most rude and shapeless, of the visible world, to exist without a mind ? Let any one of those abettors of impiety but look into his own thoughts, and there try if he can conceive how so much as a rock, a desert, a chaos, or confused jumble of atoms ; how anything at all, either sensible or imaginable, can exist independent of a mind, and he need go no farther to be convinced of his folly. Can anything be fairer than to put a dispute on such an issue, and leave it to a man himself to see if he can conceive, even in thought, what he holds to be true in fact, and from a notional to allow it a real existence.

Hyl. It cannot be denied there is something highly serviceable to religion in what you advance. But do you not think it looks very like a notion entertained by some eminent moderns, of *seeing all things in God ?*

Phil. I would gladly know that opinion : pray explain it to me.

Hyl. They conceive that the soul, being immaterial, is incapable of being united with material things, so as to perceive them in themselves ; but that she perceives them by her union with the substance of God, which, being spiritual, is therefore purely intelligible, or capable of being the immediate object of a spirit's thought. Besides, the Divine essence contains in it perfections correspondent to each created being ; and which are, for that reason, proper to exhibit or represent them to the mind.

Phil. I do not understand how our ideas, which are things altogether passive and inert, can be the essence, or any part (or like any part) of the essence or substance of God, who is an impassive, indivisible, purely active being. Many more difficulties and objections there are which occur at first view against this hypothesis ; but I shall only add that it is liable to all the absurdities of the common hypothesis, in making a created world exist otherwise than in the mind of a Spirit. Beside all which it hath this peculiar to itself ; that it makes that material world serve to no purpose. And, if it pass for a good argument against other hypotheses in the sciences that they suppose nature or the Divine wisdom to make something in vain, or do that by tedious roundabout methods which might have been performed in a much more easy and compendious way, what shall we think of that hypothesis which supposes the whole world made in vain ?

Hyl. But what say you, are not you too of opinion that we see all things in God ? If I mistake not, what you advance comes near it.

Phil. Few men think, yet all will have opinions. Hence men's opinions are superficial and confused. It is nothing strange that tenets, which in themselves are ever so different should nevertheless be confounded with each other by those who do not consider them attentively. I shall not therefore be surprised if some men imagine that I run into the enthusiasm of Malebranche ; though in truth I am very remote from it. He builds on the most abstract general ideas, which I entirely disclaim. He asserts an absolute external world, which I deny. He maintains that we are deceived by our senses, and know not the real natures or the true forms and figures of extended beings ; of all which I hold the direct contrary. So that upon the whole there are no principles more fundamentally opposite than his and mine. It must be owned that,[1] I entirely agree with what

---

[1] This speech began here in the first and second editions.

the holy Scripture saith, "That in God we live and move and have our being." But that we see things in His essence, after the manner above set forth, I am far from believing. Take here in brief my meaning.—It is evident that the things I perceive are my own ideas, and that no idea can exist unless it be in a mind. Nor is it less plain that these ideas or things by me perceived, either themselves or their arche-types, exist independently of my mind; since I know my-self not to be their author, it being out of my power to determine at pleasure what particular ideas I shall be affected with upon opening my eyes or ears. They must therefore exist in some other mind, whose will it is they should be exhibited to me. The things, I say, immediately perceived are ideas or sensations, call them which you will. But how can any idea or sensation exist in, or be pro-duced by, anything but a mind or spirit? This indeed is inconceivable; and to assert that which is inconceivable is to talk nonsense : is it not?

Hyl. Without doubt.

Phil. But, on the other hand, it is very conceivable that they should exist in and be produced by a Spirit; since this is no more than I daily experience in myself, inasmuch as I perceive numberless ideas; and, by an act of my will, can form a great variety of them, and raise them up in my imagin-ation : though, it must be confessed, these creatures of the fancy are not altogether so distinct, so strong, vivid, and permanent, as those perceived by my senses, which latter are called *real things*. From all which I conclude, *there is a Mind which affects me every moment with all the sensible impressions I perceive.* And, from the variety, order, and manner of these, I conclude the Author of them to be *wise, powerful, and good, beyond comprehension.* Mark it well; I do not say, I see things by perceiving that which represents them in the intelligible Substance of God. This I do not understand; but I say, the things by me perceived are known by the understanding, and produced by the will of an infinite Spirit. And is not all this most plain and evident? Is there any more in it than what a little observation of our own minds, and that which passeth in them, not only enableth us to conceive, but also obligeth us to acknowledge?

Hyl. I think I understand you very clearly; and own the

proof you give of a Deity seems no less evident than surprising. But, allowing that God is the supreme and universal
Cause of all things, yet, may there not be still a third nature
besides Spirits and Ideas? May we not admit a subordinate
and limited cause of our ideas? In a word, may there not
for all that be *Matter?*

Phil. How often must I inculcate the same thing? You
allow the things immediately perceived by sense to exist nowhere without the mind; but there is nothing perceived by
sense which is not perceived immediately : therefore there
is nothing sensible that exists without the mind. The
Matter, therefore, which you still insist on is something intelligible, I suppose; something that may be discovered by
reason, and not by sense.

Hyl. You are in the right.

Phil. Pray let me know what reasoning your belief of
Matter is grounded on; and what this Matter is in your
present sense of it.

Hyl. I find myself affected with various ideas, whereof I
know I am not the cause; neither are they the cause of
themselves, or of one another, or capable of subsisting by
themselves, as being altogether inactive, fleeting, dependent
beings. They have therefore some cause distinct from me
and them : of which I pretend to know no more than that
it is *the cause of my ideas.* And this thing, whatever it be, I
call Matter.

Phil. Tell me, *Hylas,* hath every one a liberty to change
the current proper signification attached to a common name
in any language? For example, suppose a traveller should
tell you that in a certain country men pass unhurt through
the fire ; and, upon explaining himself, you found he meant
by the word *fire* that which others call *water:* or, if he
should assert that there are trees that walk upon two legs,
meaning men by the term *trees.* Would you think this
reasonable?

Hyl. No, I should think it very absurd. Common custom
is the standard of propriety in language. And for any man
to affect speaking improperly is to pervert the use of speech,
and can never serve to a better purpose than to protract and
multiply disputes where there is no difference in opinion.

Phil. And doth not *Matter,* in the common current

acceptation of the word, signify an extended, solid, movable unthinking, inactive Substance?

Hyl. It doth.

Phil. And, hath it not been made evident that no such substance can possibly exist? And, though it should be allowed to exist, yet how can that which is *inactive* be a *cause;* or that which is *unthinking* be a *cause of thought?* You may, indeed, if you please, annex to the word *Matter* a contrary meaning to what is vulgarly received; and tell me you understand by it an unextended, thinking, active being, which is the cause of our ideas. But what else is this than to play with words, and run into that very fault you just now condemned with so much reason? I do by no means find fault with your reasoning, in that you collect a cause from the *phenomena:* but I deny that the cause deducible by reason can properly be termed Matter.

Hyl. There is indeed something in what you say. But I am afraid you do not thoroughly comprehend my meaning. I would by no means be thought to deny that God, or an infinite Spirit, is the Supreme Cause of all things. All I contend for is, that, subordinate to the Supreme Agent, there is a cause of a limited and inferior nature, which concurs in the production of our ideas, not by any act of will or spiritual efficiency, but by that kind, of action which belongs to Matter, viz. *motion.*

Phil. I find you are at every turn relapsing into your old exploded conceit, of a movable, and consequently an extended, substance existing without the mind. What! have you already forgotten you were convinced, or are you willing I should repeat what has been said on that head? In truth this is not fair dealing in you, still to suppose the being of that which you have so often acknowledged to have no being. But, not to insist farther on what has been so largely handled, I ask whether all your ideas are not perfectly passive and inert, including nothing of action in them.

Hyl. They are.

Phil. And are sensible qualities anything else but ideas?

Hyl. How often have I acknowledged that they are not.

Phil. But is not motion a sensible quality?

Hyl. It is.

Phil. Consequently it is no action?

Hyl. I agree with you. And indeed it is very plain that when I stir my finger it remains passive ; but my will which produced the motion is active.

Phil. Now, I desire to know, in the first place, whether, motion being allowed to be no action, you can conceive any action besides volition : and, in the second place, whether to say something and conceive nothing be not to talk nonsense : and, lastly, whether, having considered the premises, you do not perceive that to suppose any efficient or active cause of our ideas, other than *Spirit*, is highly absurd and unreasonable ?

Hyl. I give up the point entirely. But, though Matter may not be a cause, yet what hinders its being an *instrument* subservient to the supreme Agent in the production of our ideas ?

Phil. An instrument say you ; pray what may be the figure, springs, wheels, and motions, of that instrument ?

Hyl. Those I pretend to determine nothing of, both the substance and its qualities being entirely unknown to me.

Phil. What ! You are then of opinion it is made up of unknown parts, that it hath unknown motions, and an unknown shape ?

Hyl. I do not believe that it hath any figure or motion at all, being already convinced, that no sensible qualities can exist in an unperceiving substance.

Phil. But what notion is it possible to frame of an instrument void of all sensible qualities, even extension itself ?

Hyl. I do not pretend to have any notion of it.

Phil. And what reason have you to think this unknown, this inconceivable Somewhat doth exist ? Is it that you imagine God cannot act as well without it ; or that you find by experience the use of some such thing, when you form ideas in your own mind ?

Hyl. You are always teasing me for reasons of my belief. Pray what reasons have you not to believe it ?

Phil. It is to me a sufficient reason not to believe the existence of anything, if I see no reason for believing it. But, not to insist on reasons for believing, you will not so much as let me know what it is you would have me believe ; since you say you have no manner of notion of it. After all, let me entreat you to consider whether it be like a philosopher, or even like a man of common sense, to pretend to believe you know not what, and you know not why.

Hyl. Hold, *Philonous.* When I tell you matter is an *instrument,* I do not mean altogether nothing. It is true, I know not the particular kind of instrument; but, however, I have some notion of *instrument in general,* which I apply to it.

Phil. But what if it should prove that there is something, even in the most general notion of *instrument,* as taken in a distinct sense from *cause,* which makes the use of it inconsistent with the Divine attributes?

Hyl. Make that appear and I shall give up the point.

Phil. What mean you by the general nature or notion of *instrument?*

Hyl. That which is common to all particular instruments composeth the general notion.

Phil. Is it not common to all instruments, that they are applied to the doing those things only which cannot be performed by the mere act of our wills? Thus, for instance, I never use an instrument to move my finger, because it is done by a volition. But I should use one if I were to remove part of a rock, or tear up a tree by the roots. Are you of the same mind? Or, can you shew any example where an instrument is made use of in producing an effect immediately depending on the will of the agent?

Hyl. I own I cannot.

Phil. How therefore can you suppose that an all-perfect Spirit, on whose will all things have an absolute and immediate dependence, should need an instrument in his operations, or, not needing it, make use of it? Thus, it seems to me that you are obliged to own the use of a lifeless inactive instrument to be incompatible with the infinite perfection of God; that is, by your own confession, to give up the point.

Hyl. It doth not readily occur what I can answer you.

Phil. But, methinks you should be ready to own the truth, when it hath been fairly proved to you. We indeed, who are beings of finite powers, are forced to make use of instruments. . And the use of an instrument sheweth the agent to be limited by rules of another's prescription, and that he cannot obtain his end but in such a way, and by such conditions. Whence it seems a clear consequence, that the supreme unlimited Agent useth no tool or instrument at all. The will of an Omnipotent Spirit is no sooner exerted than executed, without the application of means—which, if they are employed by inferior agents, it is not upon account of any real efficacy that is in them, or necessary aptitude to produce any effect, but merely in compliance with the laws of nature, or those conditions prescribed to them by the First Cause, who is Himself above all limitation or prescription whatsoever.

Hyl. I will no longer maintain that Matter is an instrument. However, I would not be understood to give up its existence neither; since, notwithstanding what hath been said, it may still be an *occasion*.

Phil. How many shapes is your Matter to take? Or, how often must it be proved not to exist, before you are content to part with it? But, to say no more of this (though by all the laws of disputation I may justly blame you for so frequently changing the signification of the principal term) I would fain know what you mean by affirming that matter is an occasion, having already denied it to be a cause. And, when you have shewn in what sense you understand *occasion*, pray, in the next place, be pleased to shew me what reason induceth you to believe there is such an occasion of our ideas?

Hyl. As to the first point: by *occasion* I mean an inactive unthinking being, at the presence whereof God excites ideas in our minds.

Phil. And what may be the nature of that inactive unthinking being?

Hyl. I know nothing of its nature.

Phil. Proceed then to the second point, and assign some reason why we should allow an existence to this inactive, unthinking, unknown thing.

Hyl. When we see ideas produced in our minds after an orderly and constant manner, it is natural to think they have some fixed and regular occasions, at the presence of which they are excited.

Phil. You acknowledge then God alone to be the cause of our ideas, and that He causes them at the presence of those occasions.

Hyl. That is my opinion.

Phil. Those things which you say are present to God, without doubt He perceives.

Hyl. Certainly ; otherwise they could not be to Him an occasion of acting.

Phil. Not to insist now on your making sense of this hypothesis, or answering all the puzzling questions and dif-ficulties it is liable to : I only ask whether the order and regularity observable in the series of our ideas, or the course of nature, be not sufficiently accounted for by the wisdom and power of God ; and whether it doth not de-rogate from those attributes, to suppose He is influenced, directed, or put in mind, when and what He is to act, by an unthinking substance ? And, lastly, whether, in case I granted all you contend for, it would make anything to your purpose, it not being easy to conceive how the external or absolute existence of an unthinking substance, distinct from its being perceived, can be inferred from my allowing that there are certain things perceived by the mind of God, which are to Him the occasion of producing ideas in us ?

Hyl. I am perfectly at a loss what to think, this notion of *occasion* seeming now altogether as groundless as the rest.

Phil. Do you not at length perceive that in all these different acceptations of *Matter*, you have been only sup-posing you know not what, for no manner of reason, and to no kind of use ?

Hyl. I freely own myself less fond of my notions since they have been so accurately examined. But still, methinks, I have some confused perception that there is such a thing as *Matter.*

Phil. Either you perceive the being of Matter immediately, or mediately. If immediately, pray inform me by which of the senses you perceive it. If mediately, let me know by what reasoning it is inferred from those things which you perceive immediately. So much for the perception. Then for the Matter itself, I ask whether it is object, *substratum*, cause, instrument, or occasion ? You have already pleaded for each of these, shifting your notions, and making Matter to appear sometimes in one shape, then in another. And what you have offered hath been disapproved and rejected by yourself. If you have anything new to advance I would gladly hear it.

Hyl. I think I have already offered all I had to say on those heads. I am at a loss what more to urge.

Phil. And yet you are loath to part with your old prejudice. But, to make you quit it more easily, I desire that, beside what has been hitherto suggested, you will farther consider whether, upon supposition that Matter exists, you can possibly conceive how you should be affected by it? Or, supposing it did not exist, whether it be not evident you might for all that be affected with the same ideas you now are, and consequently have the very same reasons to believe its existence that you now can have?

Hyl. I acknowledge it is possible we might perceive all things just as we do now, though there was no Matter in the world; neither can I conceive, if there be Matter, how it should produce any idea in our minds. And, I do farther grant you have entirely satisfied me that it is impossible there should be such a thing as Matter in any of the foregoing acceptations. But still I cannot help supposing that there is *Matter* in some sense or other. What that is I do not indeed pretend to determine.

Phil. I do not expect you should define exactly the nature of that unknown being. Only be pleased to tell me whether it is a Substance—and if so, whether you can suppose a substance without accidents; or, in case you suppose it to have accidents or qualities, I desire you will let me know what those qualities are, at least what is meant by Matter's supporting them?

Hyl. We have already argued on those points. I have no more to say to them. But, to prevent any farther questions, let me tell you I at present understand by *Matter* neither substance nor accident, thinking nor extended being, neither cause, instrument, nor occasion, but something entirely unknown, distinct from all these.

Phil. It seems then you include in your present notion of Matter nothing but the general abstract idea of *entity*.

Hyl. Nothing else, save only that I superadd to this general idea the negation of all those particular things, qualities, or ideas, that I perceive, imagine, or in anywise apprehend.

Phil. Pray where do you suppose this unknown Matter to exist?

Hyl. Oh *Philonous!* now you think you have entangled me; for, if I say it exists in place then you will infer that it exists in the mind, since it is agreed that place or extension exists only in the mind: but I am not ashamed to own my ignorance. I know not where it exists; only I am sure it exists not in place. There is a negative answer for you. And you must expect no other to all the questions you put for the future about Matter.

Phil. Since you will not tell me where it exists, be pleased to inform me after what manner you suppose it to exist, or what you mean by its *existence?*

Hyl. It neither thinks nor acts, neither perceives nor is perceived.

Phil. But what is there positive in your abstracted notion of its existence?

Hyl. Upon a nice observation, I do not find I have any positive notion or meaning at all. I tell you again, I am not ashamed to own my ignorance. I know not what is meant by its *existence,* or how it exists.

Phil. Continue, good *Hylas,* to act the same ingenuous part, and tell me sincerely whether you can frame a distinct idea of Entity in general, prescinded from and exclusive of all thinking and corporeal beings, all particular things whatsoever.

Hyl. Hold, let me think a little——I profess, *Philonous,* I do not find that I can. At first glance, methought I had some dilute and airy notion of pure Entity in abstract; but, upon closer attention, it hath quite vanished out of sight. The more I think on it, the more am I confirmed in my prudent resolution of giving none but negative answers, and not pretending to the least degree of any positive knowledge or conception of Matter, its *where,* its *how,* its *entity,* or anything belonging to it.

Phil. When, therefore, you speak of the existence of Matter, you have not any notion in your mind?

Hyl. None at all.

Phil. Pray tell me if the case stands not thus:—at first, from a belief of material substance, you would have it that the immediate objects existed without the mind; then that they are archetypes; then causes; next instruments; then occasions: lastly, *something in general*, which being interpreted proves *nothing*. So Matter comes to nothing. What think you, *Hylas*, is not this a fair summary of your whole proceeding?

Hyl. Be that as it will, yet I still insist upon it, that our not being able to conceive a thing is no argument against its existence.

Phil. That from a cause, effect, operation, sign, or other circumstance there may reasonably be inferred the existence of a thing not immediately perceived; and that it were absurd for any man to argue against the existence of that thing, from his having no direct and positive notion of it, I freely own. But, where there is nothing of all this; where neither reason nor revelation induces us to believe the existence of a thing; where we have not even a relative notion of it; where an abstraction is made from perceiving and being perceived, from Spirit and idea: lastly, where there is not so much as the most inadequate or faint idea pretended to: I will not indeed thence conclude against the reality of any notion, or existence of anything; but my inference shall be, that you mean nothing at all; that you employ words to no manner of purpose, without any design or signification whatsoever. And I leave it to you to consider how mere jargon should be treated.

Hyl. To deal frankly with you, *Philonous*, your arguments seem in themselves unanswerable; but they have not so great an effect on me as to produce that entire conviction, that hearty acquiescence, which attends demonstration. I find myself still relapsing into an obscure surmise of I know not what, *matter*.

Phil. But, are you not sensible, *Hylas*, that two things must concur to take away all scruple, and work a plenary assent in the mind? Let a visible object be set in never so clear a light, yet, if there is any imperfection in the sight, or if the eye is not directed towards it, it will not be distinctly seen. And, though a demonstration be never so well grounded and fairly proposed, yet, if there is withal a stain of prejudice, or a wrong bias on the understanding, can it be expected on a sudden to perceive clearly and adhere firmly to the truth? No, there is need of time and pains: the attention must be awakened and detained by a frequent repetition of the same thing placed oft in the same, oft in different lights. I have said it already, and find I must still repeat and inculcate, that it is an unaccountable licence you take, in pretending to maintain you know not what, for you know not what reason, to you know not what purpose. Can this be paralleled in any art or science, any sect or profession of men ? Or is there anything so barefacedly groundless and unreasonable to be met with even in the lowest of common conversation ? But, perhaps you will still say, Matter may exist; though at the same time you neither know what is meant by *Matter*, or by its *existence*. This indeed is surprising, and the more so because it is altogether voluntary, you not being led to it by any one reason; for I challenge you to shew me that thing in nature which needs matter to explain or account for it.

Hyl. The reality of things cannot be maintained without supposing the existence of Matter. And is not this, think you, a good reason why I should be earnest in its defence ?

Phil. The reality of things ! What things, sensible or intelligible ?

Hyl. Sensible things.

Phil. My glove, for example ?

Hyl. That or any other thing perceived by the senses.

Phil. But to fix on some particular thing; is it not a sufficient evidence to me of the existence of this *glove*, that I see it, and feel it, and wear it ? Or, if this will not do, how is it possible I should be assured of the reality of this thing, which I actually see in this place, by supposing that some unknown thing, which I never did or can see, exists after an unknown manner, in an unknown place, or in no place at all ? How can the supposed reality of that which is intangible be a proof that anything tangible really exists ? Or, of that which is invisible, that any visible thing, or, in general of anything which is imperceptible, that a perceptible exists ? Do but explain this and I shall think nothing too hard for you.

Hyl. Upon the whole, I am content to own the existence of Matter is highly improbable ; but the direct and absolute impossibility of it does not appear to me.

Phil. But, granting Matter to be possible, yet, upon that account merely, it can have no more claim to existence than a golden mountain or a centaur.

Hyl. I acknowledge it ; but still you do not deny it is possible ; and that which is possible, for aught you know, may actually exist.

Phil. I deny it to be possible ; and have, if I mistake not, evidently proved, from your own concessions, that it is not. In the common sense of the word *Matter*, is there any more implied than an extended, solid, figured, movable substance existing without the mind ? And have not you acknowledged, over and over, that you have seen evident reason for denying the possibility of such a substance ?

Hyl. True, but that is only one sense of the term *Matter*.

Phil. But, is it not the only proper genuine received sense ? and, if Matter in such a sense be proved impossible, may it not be thought with good grounds absolutely impossible ? Else how could anything be proved impossible ? Or, indeed, how could there be any proof at all one way or other, to a man who takes the liberty to unsettle and change the common signification of words ?

Hyl. I thought philosophers might be allowed to speak more accurately than the vulgar, and were not always confined to the common acceptation of a term.

Phil. But this now mentioned is the common received sense among philosophers themselves. But, not to insist on that, have you not been allowed to take Matter in what sense you pleased ? And have not you used this privilege in the utmost extent, sometimes entirely changing, at others leaving out or putting into the definition of it whatever, for the present, best served your design, contrary to all the known rules of reason and logic ? And hath not this shifting, unfair method of yours spun out our dispute to an unnecessary length ; Matter having been particularly examined, and by your own confession refuted in each of those senses ? And can any more be required to prove the absolute impossibility of a thing, than the proving it impossible in every particular sense that either you or any one else understands it in ?

Hyl. But I am not so thoroughly satisfied that you have proved the impossibility of matter, in the last most obscure abstracted and indefinite sense.

Phil. When is a thing shewn to be impossible ?

Hyl. When a repugnancy is demonstrated between the eas comprehended in its definition.

Phil. But where there are no ideas, there no repugnancy can be demonstrated between ideas?

Hyl. I agree with you.

Phil. Now, in that which you call the obscure indefinite sense of the word *Matter*, it is plain, by your own confession, there was included no idea at all, no sense except an unknown sense, which is the same thing as none. You are not, therefore, to expect I should prove a repugnancy between ideas, where there are no ideas: or the impossibility of Matter taken in an *unknown* sense, that is, no sense at all. My business was only to shew you meant *nothing;* and this you were brought to own. So that, in all your various senses, you have been shewed either to mean nothing at all, or, if anything, an absurdity. And if this be not sufficient to prove the impossibility of a thing, I desire you will let me know what it is.

Hyl. I acknowledge you have proved that Matter is impossible; nor do I see what more can be said in defence of it. But, at the same time that I give up this, I suspect all my other notions. For surely none could be more seemingly evident than this once was: and yet it now seems as false and absurd as ever it did true before. But I think we have discussed the point sufficiently for the present. The remaining part of the day I would willingly spend in running over in my thoughts the several heads of this morning's conversation, and to-morrow shall be glad to meet you here again about the same time.

Phil. I will not fail to attend you.

THE THIRD DIALOGUE.

Philonous.

TELL me, *Hylas*, what are the fruits of yesterday's meditation? Hath it confirmed you in the same mind you were in at parting? or have you since seen cause to change your opinion?

Hylas. Truly my opinion is that all our opinions are alike vain and uncertain. What we approve to-day, we condemn to-morrow. We keep a stir about knowledge, and spend our lives in the pursuit of it, when, alas! we know nothing all the while: nor do I think it possible for us ever to know anything in this life. Our faculties are too narrow and too few. Nature certainly never intended us for speculation.

Phil. What! say you we can know nothing, *Hylas?*

Hyl. There is not that single thing in the world whereof we can know the real nature, or what it is in itself.

Phil. Will you tell me I do not really know what fire or water is?

Hyl. You may indeed know that fire appears hot, and water fluid; but this is no more than knowing what sensations are produced in your own mind, upon the application of fire and water to your organs of sense. Their internal constitution, their true and real nature, you are utterly in the dark as to *that.*

Phil. Do I not know this to be a real stone that I stand on, and that which I see before my eyes to be a real tree?

Hyl. Know? No, it is impossible you or any man alive should know it. All you know is, that you have such a certain idea or appearance in your own mind. But what is this to the real tree or stone? I tell you that colour, figure, and hardness, which you perceive, are not the real natures of those things, or in the least like them. The same may be said of all other real things or corporeal substances which compose the world. They have none of them anything of themselves, like those sensible qualities by us perceived. We should not therefore pretend to affirm or know anything of them, as they are in their own nature.

Phil. But surely, *Hylas*, I can distinguish gold, for example, from iron : and how could this be, if I knew not what either truly was ?

Hyl. Believe me, *Philonous*, you can only distinguish between your own ideas. That yellowness, that weight, and other sensible qualities, think you they are really in the gold ? They are only relative to the senses and have no absolute existence in nature. And in pretending to distinguish the species of real things, by the appearances in your mind, you may perhaps act as wisely as he that should conclude two men were of a different species, because their clothes were not of the same colour.

Phil. It seems, then, we are altogether put off with the appearances of things, and those false ones too. The very meat I eat, and the cloth I wear, have nothing in them like what I see and feel.

Hyl. Even so.

Phil. But is it not strange the whole world should be thus imposed on, and so foolish as to believe their senses ? And yet I know not how it is, but men eat, and drink, and sleep, and perform all the offices of life, as comfortably and conveniently as if they really knew the things they are conversant about.

Hyl. They do so : but you know ordinary practice does not require a nicety of speculative knowledge. Hence the vulgar retain their mistakes, and for all that make a shift to bustle through the affairs of life. But philosophers know better things.

Phil. You mean, they know that they *know nothing*.

Hyl. That is the very top and perfection of human knowledge.

Phil. But are you all this while in earnest, *Hylas;* and are you seriously persuaded that you know nothing real in the world ? Suppose you are going to write, would you not call for pen, ink, and paper, like another man ; and do you not know what it is you call for ?

Hyl. How often must I tell you, that I know not the real nature of any one thing in the universe? I may indeed upon occasion make use of pen, ink, and paper. But, what any one of them is in its own true nature, I declare positively I know not. And the same is true with regard to every other corporeal thing. And, what is more, we are not only ignorant of the true and real nature of things, but even of their existence. It cannot be denied that we perceive such certain appearances or ideas; but it cannot be concluded from thence that bodies really exist. Nay, now I think on it, I must, agreeably to my former concessions, farther declare that it is impossible any real corporeal thing should exist in nature.

Phil. You amaze me. Was ever anything more wild and extravagant than the notions you now maintain: and is it not evident you are led into all these extravagances by the belief of *material substance?* This makes you dream of those unknown natures in everything. It is this occasions your distinguishing between the reality and sensible appearances of things. It is to this you are indebted for being ignorant of what everybody else knows perfectly well. Nor is this all: you are not only ignorant of the true nature of everything, but you know not whether any thing really exists, or whether there are any true natures at all; forasmuch as you attribute to your material beings an absolute or external existence, wherein you suppose their reality consists. And, as you are forced in the end to acknowledge such an existence means either a direct repugnancy, or nothing at all, it follows that you are obliged to pull down your own hypothesis of material Substance, and positively to deny the real existence of any part of the universe. And so you are plunged into the deepest and most deplorable *Scepticism* that ever man was. Tell me, *Hylas*, is it not as I say?

Hyl. I agree with you. *Material substance* was no more than an hypothesis, and a false and groundless one too. I will no longer spend my breath in defence of it. But, whatever hypothesis you advance, or whatsoever scheme of things you introduce in its stead, I doubt not it will appear every whit as false: let me but be allowed to question you upon it. That is, suffer me to serve you in your own kind, and I warrant it shall conduct you through as many perplexities and contradictions, to the very same state of Scepticism that I myself am in at present.

Phil. I assure you, *Hylas*, I do not pretend to frame any hypothesis at all. I am of a vulgar cast, simple enough to believe my senses, and leave things as I find them. To be plain, it is my opinion that the real things are those very things I see and feel, and perceive by my senses. These I know, and, finding they answer all the necessities and purposes of life, have no reason to be solicitous about any other unknown beings. A piece of sensible bread, for instance, would stay my stomach better than ten thousand times as much of that insensible, unintelligible, real bread you speak of. It is likewise my opinion that colours and other sensible qualities are on the objects. I cannot for my life help thinking that snow is white, and fire hot. You indeed, who by *snow* and *fire* mean certain external, unperceived, unperceiving substances, are in the right to deny whiteness or heat to be affections inherent in them. But I, who understand by those words the things I see and feel, am obliged to think like other folks. And, as I am no sceptic with regard to the nature of things, so neither am I as to their existence. That a thing should be really perceived by my senses, and at the same time not really exist, is to me a plain contradiction ; since I cannot prescind or abstract, even in thought, the existence of a sensible thing from its being perceived. Wood, stones, fire, water, flesh, iron, and the like things, which I name and discourse of, are things that I know. And I should not have known them but that I perceived them by my senses ; and things perceived by the senses are immediately perceived ; and things immediately perceived are ideas ; and ideas cannot exist without the mind ; their existence therefore consists in being perceived ; when, therefore, they are actually perceived there can be no doubt of their existence. Away then with all that Scepticism, all those ridiculous philosophical doubts. What a jest is it for a philosopher to question the existence of sensible things, till he hath it proved to him from the veracity of God ; or to pretend our knowledge in this point falls short of intuition or demonstration ! I might as well doubt of my own being, as of the being of those things I actually see and feel.

Hyl. Not so fast, *Philonous :* you say you cannot conceive how sensible things should exist without the mind. Do you not?

Phil. I do.

Hyl. Supposing you were annihilated, cannot you conceive it possible that things perceivable by sense may still exist?

Phil. I can; but then it must be in another mind. When I deny sensible things an existence out of the mind, I do not mean my mind in particular, but all minds. Now, it is plain they have an existence exterior to my mind; since I find them by experience to be independent of it. There is therefore some other mind wherein they exist, during the intervals between the times of my perceiving them: as likewise they did before my birth, and would do after my supposed annihilation. And, as the same is true with regard to all other finite created spirits, it necessarily follows there is an *omnipresent eternal Mind*, which knows and comprehends all things, and exhibits them to our view in such a manner, and according to such rules, as He Himself hath ordained, and are by us termed the *laws of nature*.

Hyl. Answer me, *Philonous*. Are all our ideas perfectly inert beings? Or have they any agency included in them?

Phil. They are altogether passive and inert.

Hyl. And is not God an agent, a being purely active?

Phil. I acknowledge it.

Hyl. No idea therefore can like be unto, or represent the nature of God?

Phil. It cannot.

Hyl. Since therefore you have no idea of the mind of God, how can you conceive it possible that things should exist in His mind? Or, if you can conceive the mind of God, without having an idea of it, why may not I be allowed to conceive the existence of Matter, notwithstanding I have no idea of it?

Phil. As to your first question: I own I have properly no *idea*, either of God or any other spirit; for these being active, cannot be represented by things perfectly inert, as our ideas are. I do nevertheless know that I, whom am a spirit or thinking substance, exist as certainly as I know my ideas exist. Farther, I know what I mean by the terms *I* and *myself;* and I know this immediately or intuitively, though I do not perceive it as I perceive a triangle, a colour, or a sound. The Mind, Spirit, or Soul is that indivisible unextended thing which thinks, acts, and perceives. I say *indivisible*, because unextended; and *unextended*, because extended, figured, movable things are ideas; and that which perceives ideas, which thinks and wills, is plainly itself no idea, nor like an idea. Ideas are things inactive, and perceived. And Spirits a sort of beings altogether different from them. I do not therefore say my soul is an idea, or like an idea. However, taking the word *idea* in a large sense, my soul may be said to furnish me with an idea, that is, an image or likeness of God, though indeed extremely inadequate. For all the notion I have of God is obtained by reflexion on my own soul, heightening its powers, and removing its imperfections. I have, therefore, though not an inactive idea, yet in *myself* some sort of an active thinking image of the Deity. And, though I perceive Him not by sense, yet I have a notion of Him, or know Him by reflexion and reasoning. My own mind and my own ideas I have an immediate knowledge of; and, by the help of these, do mediately apprehend the possibility of the existence of other spirits and ideas. Farther, from my own being, and from the dependency I find in myself and my ideas, I do, by an act of reason, necessarily infer the existence of a God, and of all created things in the mind of God. So much for your first question. For the second : I suppose by this time you can answer it yourself. For you neither perceive Matter objectively, as you do an inactive being or idea; nor know it, as you do yourself, by a reflex act; neither do you mediately apprehend it by similitude of the one or the other ; nor yet collect it by reasoning from that which you know immediately. All which makes the case of *Matter* widely different from that of the *Deity*.

Hyl. You say your own soul supplies you with some sort of an idea or image of God. But, at the same time, you acknowledge you have, properly speaking, no *idea* of your own soul. You even affirm that spirits are a sort of beings altogether different from ideas. Consequently that no idea

---

[1] The two speeches each of "Hylas and Philonous" which follow, were added to the last edition.

can be like a spirit. We have therefore no idea of any spirit. You admit nevertheless that there is spiritual Substance, although you have no idea of it ; while you deny there can be such a thing as material Substance, because you have no notion or idea of it. Is this fair dealing? To act consistently, you must either admit Matter or reject Spirit. What say you to this?

Phil. I say, in the first place, that I do not deny the existence of material substance, merely because I have no notion of it, but because the notion of it is inconsistent ; or, in other words, because it is repugnant that there should be a notion of it. Many things, for aught I know, may exist, whereof neither I nor any other man hath or can have any idea or notion whatsoever. But then those things must be possible, that is, nothing inconsistent must be included in their definition. I say, secondly, that, although we believe things to exist which we do not perceive, yet we may not believe that any particular thing exists, without some reason for such belief: but I have no reason for believing the existence of Matter. I have no immediate intuition thereof: neither can I immediately from my sensations, ideas, notions, actions, or passions, infer an unthinking, unperceiving, inactive Substance, either by probable deduction, or necessary consequence. Whereas the being of my Self, that is, my own soul, mind, or thinking principle, I evidently know by reflexion. You will forgive me if I repeat the same things in answer to the same objections. In the very notion or definition of *material Substance*, there is included a manifest repugnance and inconsistency. But this cannot be said of the notion of Spirit. That ideas should exist in what doth not perceive, or be produced by what doth not act, is repugnant. But, it is no repugnancy to say that a perceiving thing should be the subject of ideas, or an active thing the cause of them. It is granted we have neither an immediate evidence nor a demonstrative knowledge of the existence of other finite spirits ; but it will not thence follow that such spirits are on a foot with material substances: if to suppose the one be inconsistent, and it be not inconsistent to suppose the other ; if the one can be inferred by no argument, and there is a probability for the other ; if we see signs and effects indicating distinct finite agents like ourselves, and see no sign or symptom whatever that leads to a rational belief of Matter. I say, lastly, that I have a notion of Spirit, though I have not, strictly speaking, an idea of it. I do not perceive it as an idea, or by means of an idea, but know it by reflexion.

Hyl. Notwithstanding all you said, to me it seems that, according to your own way of thinking, and in consequence of your own principles, it should follow that *you* are only a system of floating ideas, without any substance to support them. Words are not to be used without a meaning. And, as there is no more meaning in *spiritual Substance* than in *material Substance*, the one is to be exploded as well as the other.

Phil. How often must I repeat, that I know or am conscious of my own being; and that *I myself* am not my ideas, but somewhat else, a thinking, active principle that perceives, knows, wills, and operates about ideas. I know that I, one and the same self, perceive both colours and sounds: that a colour cannot perceive a sound, nor a sound a colour: that I am therefore one individual principle, distinct from colour and sound; and, for the same reason, from all other sensible things and inert ideas. But, I am not in like manner conscious either of the existence or essence of Matter. On the contrary, I know that nothing inconsistent can exist, and that the existence of Matter implies an inconsistency. Farther, I know what I mean when I affirm that there is a spiritual substance or support of ideas, that is, that a spirit knows and perceives ideas. But, I do not know what is meant when it is said that an unperceiving substance hath inherent in it and supports either ideas or the archetypes of ideas. There is therefore upon the whole no parity of case between Spirit and Matter.

Hyl. I own myself satisfied in this point. But, do you in earnest think the real existence of sensible things consists in their being actually perceived? If so; how comes it that all mankind distinguish between them? Ask the first man you meet, and he shall tell you, *to be perceived* is one thing, and *to exist* is another.

Phil. I am content, *Hylas*, to appeal to the common sense of the world for the truth of my notion. Ask the gardener why he thinks yonder cherry-tree exists in the garden, and he shall tell you, because he sees and feels it; in a word, because he perceives it by his senses. Ask him why he thinks an orange-tree not to be there, and he shall tell you, because he does not perceive it. What he perceives by sense, that he terms a real being, and saith it *is* or *exists*; but, that which is not perceivable, the same, he saith, hath no being.

Hyl. Yes, *Philonous*, I grant the existence of a sensible thing consists in being perceivable, but not in being actually perceived.

Phil. And what is perceivable but an idea? And can an idea exist without being actually perceived? These are points long since agreed between us.

Hyl. But, be your opinion never so true, yet surely you will not deny it is shocking, and contrary to the common sense of men. Ask the fellow whether yonder tree hath an existence out of his mind: what answer think you he would make?

Phil. The same that I should myself, to wit, that it doth exist out of his mind. But then to a Christian it cannot surely be shocking to say, the real tree, existing without his mind, is truly known and comprehended by (that is, *exists in*) the infinite mind of God. Probably he may not at first glance be aware of the direct and immediate proof there is of this; inasmuch as the very being of a tree, or any other sensible thing, implies a mind wherein it is. But the point itself he cannot deny. The question between the Materialists and me is not, whether things have a *real* existence out of the mind of this or that person, but, whether they have an *absolute* existence, distinct from being perceived by God, and exterior to all minds. This indeed some heathens and philosophers have affirmed, but whoever entertains notions of the Deity suitable to the Holy Scriptures will be of another opinion.

Hyl. But, according to your notions, what difference is there between real things, and chimeras formed by the imagination, or the visions of a dream, since they are all equally in the mind?

Phil. The ideas formed by the imagination are faint and indistinct; they have, besides, an entire dependence on the will. But the ideas perceived by sense, that is, real things, are more vivid and clear; and, being imprinted on the mind by a spirit distinct from us, have not the like dependence on our will. There is therefore no danger of confounding these with the foregoing: and there is as little of confounding them with the visions of a dream, which are dim, irregular, and confused. And, though they should happen to be never so lively and natural, yet, by their not being connected, and of a piece with the preceding and subsequent transactions of our lives, they might easily be distinguished from realities. In short, by whatever method you distinguish *things* from *chimeras* on your scheme, the same, it is evident, will hold also upon mine. For, it must be, I presume, by some perceived difference; and I am not for depriving you of any one thing that you perceive.

Hyl. But still, *Philonous*, you hold, there is nothing in the world but spirits and ideas. And this, you must needs acknowledge, sounds very oddly.

Phil. I own the word *idea*, not being commonly used for *thing*, sounds something out of the way. My reason for using it was, because a necessary relation to the mind is understood to be implied by that term ; and it is now commonly used by philosophers to denote the immediate objects of the understanding. But, however oddly the proposition may sound in words, yet it includes nothing so very strange or shocking in its sense ; which in effect amounts to no more than this, to wit, that there are only things perceiving, and things perceived; or that every unthinking being is necessarily, and from the very nature of its existence, perceived by some mind ; if not by a finite created mind, yet certainly by the infinite mind of God, in whom " we live, and move, and have our being." Is this as strange as to say, the sensible qualities are not on the objects : or that we cannot be sure of the existence of things, or know anything of their real natures, though we both see and feel them, and perceive them by all our senses ?

Hyl. And, in consequence of this, must we not think there are no such things as physical or corporeal causes ; but that a Spirit is the immediate cause of all the phenomena in nature? Can there be anything more extravagant than this?

Phil. Yes, it is infinitely more extravagant to say a thing which is inert operates on the mind, and which is unperceiving, is the cause of our perceptions.[1] Besides, that

---

[1] In the first two editions the last sentence continued : " without any regard either to consistency, or the old known axiom, *Nothing can give to another that which it hath not itself.* Besides," &c.

which to you, I know not for what reason, seems so extravagant is no more than the Holy Scriptures assert in a hundred places. In them God is represented as the sole and immediate Author of all those effects which some heathens and philosophers are wont to ascribe to Nature, Matter, Fate, or the like unthinking principle. This is so much the constant language of Scripture that it were needless to confirm it by citations.

Hyl. You are not aware, *Philonous*, that, in making God the immediate Author of all the motions in nature, you make Him the Author of murder, sacrilege, adultery, and the like heinous sins.

Phil. In answer to that, I observe, first, that the imputation of guilt is the same, whether a person commits an action with or without an instrument. In case therefore you suppose God to act by the mediation of an instrument, or occasion, called *Matter*, you as truly make Him the author of sin as I, who think Him the immediate agent in all those operations vulgarly ascribed to Nature. I farther observe that sin or moral turpitude doth not consist in the outward physical action or motion, but in the internal deviation of the will from the laws of reason and religion. This is plain, in that the killing an enemy in a battle, or putting a criminal legally to death, is not thought sinful; though the outward act be the very same with that in the case of murder. Since, therefore, sin doth not consist in the physical action, the making God an immediate cause of all such actions is not making Him the Author of sin. Lastly, I have nowhere said that God is the only agent who produces all the motions in bodies. It is true I have denied there are any other agents besides spirits; but this is very consistent with allowing to thinking rational beings, in the production of motions, the use of limited powers, ultimately indeed derived from God, but immediately under the direction of their own wills, which is sufficient to entitle them to all the guilt of their actions.

Hyl. But the denying Matter, *Philonous*, or corporeal Substance; there is the point. You can never persuade me that this is not repugnant to the universal sense of mankind. Were our dispute to be determined by most voices, I am confident you would give up the point, without gathering the votes.

Phil. I wish both our opinions were fairly stated and submitted to the judgment of men who had plain common sense, without the prejudices of a learned education. Let me be represented as one who trusts his senses, who thinks he knows the things he sees and feels, and entertains no doubts of their existence; and you fairly set forth with all your doubts, your paradoxes, and your scepticism about you, and I shall willingly acquiesce in the determination of any indifferent person. That there is no substance wherein ideas can exist beside spirit is to me evident. And that the objects immediately perceived are ideas, is on all hands agreed. And that sensible qualities are objects immediately perceived no one can deny. It is therefore evident there can be no *substratum* of those qualities but spirit; in which they exist, not by way of mode or property, but as a thing perceived in that which perceives it. I deny therefore that there is any unthinking *substratum* of the objects of sense, and in that acceptation that there is any material substance. But if by *material substance* is meant only sensible body, that which is seen and felt (and the unphilosophical part of the world, I dare say, mean no more), then I am more certain of matter's existence than you or any other philosopher pretend to be. If there be anything which makes the generality of mankind averse from the notions I espouse, it is a misapprehension that I deny the reality of sensible things: but, as it is you who are guilty of that and not I, it follows that in truth their aversion is against your notions and not mine. I do therefore assert that I am as certain as of my own being, that there are bodies or corporeal substances (meaning the things I perceive by my senses); and that, granting this, the bulk of mankind will take no thought about, nor think themselves at all concerned in the fate of those unknown natures and philosophical quiddities which some men are so fond of.

Hyl. What say you to this? Since, according to you, men judge of the reality of things by their senses, how can a man be mistaken in thinking the moon a plain lucid surface, about a foot in diameter; or a square tower, seen at a distance, round; or an oar, with one end in the water, crooked?

Phil. He is not mistaken with regard to the ideas he

actually perceives, but in the inferences he makes from his present perceptions. Thus, in the case of the oar, what he immediately perceives by sight is certainly crooked; and so far he is in the right. But, if he thence conclude that upon taking the oar out of the water he shall perceive the same crookedness; or that it would affect his touch as crooked things are wont to do: in that he is mistaken. In like manner, if he shall conclude from what he perceives in one station, that, in case he advances towards the moon or tower, he should still be affected with the like ideas, he is mistaken. But his mistake lies not in what he perceives immediately and at present (it being a manifest contradiction to suppose he should err in respect of that), but in the wrong judgment he makes concerning the ideas he apprehends to be connected with those immediately perceived: or, concerning the ideas that, from what he perceives at present, he imagines would be perceived in other circumstances. The case is the same with regard to the Copernican system. We do not here perceive any motion of the earth: but it were erroneous thence to conclude, that, in case we were placed at as great a distance from that as we are now from the other planets, we should not then perceive its motion.

Hyl. I understand you; and must needs own you say things plausible enough: but, give me leave to put you in mind of one thing. Pray, *Philonous*, were you not formerly as positive that Matter existed, as you are now that it does not?

Phil. I was. But here lies the difference. Before, my positiveness was founded, without examination, upon prejudice; but now, after inquiry, upon evidence.

Hyl. After all, it seems our dispute is rather about words than things. We agree in the thing, but differ in the name. That we are affected with ideas from without is evident; and it is no less evident that there must be (I will not say archetypes, but) powers without the mind, corresponding to those ideas. And, as these powers cannot subsist by themselves, there is some subject of them necessarily to be admitted, which I call *Matter*, and you call *Spirit*. This is all the difference.

Phil. Pray, *Hylas*, is that powerful being, or subject of powers, extended?

Hyl. It hath not extension ; but it hath the power to raise in you the idea of extension.

Phil. It is therefore itself unextended ?

Hyl. I grant it.

Phil. Is it not also active ?

Hyl. Without doubt : otherwise, how could we attribute powers to it ?

Phil. Now let me ask you two questions : *First*, whether it be agreeable to the usage either of philosophers or others to give the name *Matter* to an unextended active being ? And, *Secondly*, whether it be not ridiculously absurd to mis-apply names contrary to the common use of language ?

Hyl. Well then, let it not be called Matter, since you will have it so, but some *third nature* distinct from Matter and Spirit. For what reason is there why you should call it Spirit ? Does not the notion of spirit imply that it is think-ing, as well as active and unextended ?

Phil. My reason is this : because I have a mind to have some notion of meaning in what I say : but I have no notion of any action distinct from volition, neither can I conceive volition to be anywhere but in a spirit ; therefore, when I speak of an active being, I am obliged to mean a spirit. Beside, what can be plainer than that a thing which hath no ideas in itself cannot impart them to me ; and, if it hath ideas, surely it must be a spirit. To make you comprehend the point still more clearly if it be possible : I assert as well as you that, since we are affected from without, we must allow powers to be without, in a being distinct from ourselves. So far we are agreed. But then we differ as to the kind of this powerful being. I will have it to be spirit, you Matter, or I know not what (I may add too, you know not what) third nature. Thus, I prove it to be spirit. From the effects I see produced I conclude there are actions ; and, because actions, volitions ; and, because there are volitions, there must be a will. Again, the things I perceive must have an existence, they or their archetypes, out of my mind : but, being ideas, neither they nor their archetypes can exist otherwise than in an understanding ; there is therefore an understanding. But will and understanding constitute in the strictest sense a mind or spirit. The powerful cause, therefore, of my ideas is in strict propriety of speech a *spirit.*

Hyl. And now I warrant you think you have made the point very clear, little suspecting that what you advance leads directly to a contradiction. Is it not an absurdity to imagine any imperfection in God?

Phil. Without a doubt.

Hyl. To suffer pain is an imperfection?

Phil. It is.

Hyl. Are we not sometimes affected with pain and uneasiness by some other being?

Phil. We are.

Hyl. And have you not said that being is a spirit, and is not that spirit God?

Phil. I grant it.

Hyl. But you have asserted that whatever ideas we perceive from without are in the mind which affects us. The ideas, therefore, of pain and uneasiness are in God; or, in other words, God suffers pain: that is to say, there is an imperfection in the Divine nature, which, you acknowledge, was absurd. So you are caught in a plain contradiction.

Phil. That God knows or understands all things, and that He knows, among other things, what pain is, even every sort of painful sensation, and what it is for His creatures to suffer pain, I make no question. But, that God, though He knows and sometimes causes painful sensations in us, can Himself suffer pain, I positively deny. We, who are limited and dependent spirits, are liable to impressions of sense, the effects of an external agent, which, being produced against our wills, are sometimes painful and uneasy. But God, whom no external being can affect, who perceives nothing by sense as we do, whose will is absolute and independent, causing all things, and liable to be thwarted or resisted by nothing; it is evident, such a Being as this can suffer nothing, nor be affected with any painful sensation, or indeed any sensation at all. We are chained to a body, that is to say, our perceptions are connected with corporeal motions. By the law of our nature, we are affected upon every alteration in the nervous parts of our sensible body; which sensible body, rightly considered, is nothing but a complexion of such qualities or ideas as have no existence distinct from being perceived by a mind: so that this connexion of sensations with corporeal motions means no more than a correspondence in the order of nature between two sets of ideas, or things immediately perceivable. But God is a pure spirit, disengaged from all such sympathy or natural ties. No corporeal motions are attended with the sensations of pain or pleasure in His mind. To know everything knowable is certainly a perfection ; but to endure, or suffer, or feel anything by sense, is an imperfection. The former, I say, agrees to God, but not the latter. God knows or hath ideas ; but His ideas are not conveyed to Him by sense, as ours are. Your not distinguishing, where there is so manifest a difference, makes you fancy you see an absurdity where there is none.

Hyl. But, all this while you have not considered that the quantity of Matter hath been demonstrated to be proportioned to the gravity of bodies. And what can withstand demonstration ?

Phil. Let me see how you demonstrate that point.

Hyl. I lay it down for a principle that the moments or quantities of motion in bodies are in a direct compounded reason of the velocities and quantities of Matter contained in them. Hence, where the velocities are equal, it follows the moments are directly as the quantity of Matter in each. But it is found by experience that all bodies (bating the small inequalities, arising from the resistance of the air) descend with an equal velocity ; the motion therefore of descending bodies, and consequently their gravity, which is the cause or principle of that motion, is proportional to the quantity of Matter ; which was to be demonstrated.

Phil. You lay it down as a self-evident principle that the quantity of motion in any body is proportional to the velocity and *Matter* taken together ; and this is made use of to prove a proposition from whence the existence of *Matter* is inferred. Pray is not this arguing in a circle ?

Hyl. In the premise I only mean that the motion is proportional to the velocity, jointly with the extension and solidity.

Phil. But, allowing this to be true, yet it will not thence follow that gravity is proportional to *Matter*, in your philosophic sense of the word ; except you take it for granted that unknown *substratum*, or whatever else you call it, is proportional to those sensible qualities ; which to suppose is plainly begging the question. That there is magnitude and solidity, or resistance, perceived by sense, I readily grant; as likewise, that gravity may be proportional to those qualities I will not dispute. But that either these qualities as perceived by us, or the powers producing them, do exist in a *material substratum* ;—this is what I deny, and you indeed affirm, but, notwithstanding your demonstration, have not yet proved.

Hyl. I shall insist no longer on that point. Do you think, however, you shall persuade me the natural philosophers have been dreaming all this while? Pray what becomes of all their hypotheses and explications of the phenomena, which suppose the existence of Matter?

Phil. What mean you, *Hylas*, by the *phenomena*?

Hyl. I mean the appearances which I perceive by my senses.

Phil. And the appearances perceived by sense, are they not ideas?

Hyl. I have told you so a hundred times.

Phil. Therefore, to explain the phenomena is to shew how we come to be affected with ideas, in that manner and order wherein they are imprinted on our senses. Is it not?

Hyl. It is.

Phil. Now, if you can prove that any philosopher hath explained the production of any one idea in our minds by the help of *Matter*, I shall for ever acquiesce, and look on all that hath been said against it as nothing; but, if you cannot, it is vain to urge the explication of phenomena. That a Being endowed with knowledge and will should produce or exhibit ideas is easily understood. But, that a Being which is utterly destitute of these faculties should be able to produce ideas, or in any sort to affect an intelligence, this I can never understand. This I say, though we had some positive conception of Matter, though we knew its qualities, and could comprehend its existence, would yet be so far from explaining things, that it is itself the most inexplicable thing in the world. And yet, for all this, it will not follow that philosophers have been doing nothing; for, by observing and reasoning upon the connexion of ideas, they discover the laws and methods of nature, which is a part of knowledge both useful and entertaining.

Hyl. After all, can it be supposed God would deceive

all mankind? Do you imagine He would have induced the whole world to believe the being of Matter, if there was no such thing?

Phil. That every epidemical opinion arising from prejudice, or passion, or thoughtlessness may be imputed to God, as the Author of it, I believe you will not affirm. Whatsoever opinion we father on Him, it must be either because He has discovered to us by supernatural revelation ; or because it is so evident to our natural faculties, which were framed and given us by God, that it is impossible we should withhold our assent from it. But where is the revelation? or where is the evidence that extorts the belief of Matter? Nay, how does it appear, that Matter, taken for something distinct from what we perceive by our senses, is thought to exist by all mankind ; or, indeed, by any except a few philosophers, who do not know what they would be at? Your question supposes these points are clear ; and, when you have cleared them, I shall think myself obliged to give you another answer. In the meantime let it suffice that I tell you, I do not suppose God has deceived mankind at all.

Hyl. But the novelty, *Philonous*, the novelty ! There lies the danger. New notions should always be discountenanced ; they unsettle men's minds, and nobody knows where they will end.

Phil. Why the rejecting a notion that hath no foundation, either in sense, or in reason, or in Divine authority, should be thought to unsettle the belief of such opinions as are grounded on all or any of these, I cannot imagine. That innovations in government and religion are dangerous, and ought to be discountenanced, I freely own. But, is there the like reason why they should be discouraged in philosophy? The making anything known which was unknown before is an innovation in knowledge : and, if all such innovations had been forbidden, men would have made a notable progress in the arts and sciences. But it is none of my business to plead for novelties and paradoxes. That the qualities we perceive are not on the objects : that we must not believe our senses : that we know nothing of the real nature of things, and can never be assured even of their existence : that real colours and sounds are nothing but certain unknown figures and motions : that motions are in themselves neither swift nor slow : that there are in bodies absolute extensions, without any particular magnitude or figure : that a thing stupid, thoughtless, and inactive, operates on a spirit : that the least particle of a body contains innumerable extended parts :— these are the novelties, these are the strange notions which shock the genuine uncorrupted judgment of all mankind ; and being once admitted, embarrass the mind with endless doubts and difficulties.   And it is against these and the like innovations I endeavour to vindicate Common Sense.   It is true, in doing this, I may perhaps be obliged to use some *ambages*, and ways of speech not common.   But, if my notions are once thoroughly understood, that which is most singular in them will, in effect, be found to amount to no more than this :—that it is absolutely impossible, and a plain contradiction, to suppose any unthinking being should exist without being perceived by a mind.   And, if this notion be singular, it is a shame it should be so at this time of day, and in a Christian country.

Hyl. As for the difficulties other opinions may be liable to, those are out of the question.   It is your business to defend your own opinion.   Can anything be plainer than that you are for changing all things into ideas ?   You, I say, who are not ashamed to charge me with *scepticism*.   This is so plain, there is no denying it.

Phil. You mistake me.   I am not for changing things into ideas, but rather ideas into things ; since those immediate objects of perception, which, according to you, are only appearances of things, I take to be the real things themselves.

Hyl. Things ! you may pretend what you please ; but it is certain you leave us nothing but the empty forms of things, the outside only which strikes the senses.

Phil. What you call the empty forms and outside of things seem to me the very things themselves.   Nor are they empty or incomplete, otherwise than upon your supposition that Matter is an essential part of all corporeal things.   We both, therefore, agree in this, that we perceive only sensible forms : but herein we differ, you will have them to be empty appearances, I real beings.   In short, you do not trust your senses, I do.

Hyl. You say you believe your senses ; and seem to applaud yourself that in this you agree with the vulgar.   According to you, therefore, the true nature of a thing is discovered by the senses. If so, whence comes that disagreement? Why, is not the same figure, and other sensible qualities, perceived all manner of ways? And why should we use a microscope the better to discover the true nature of a body, if it were discoverable to the naked eye?

Phil. Strictly speaking, *Hylas*, we do not see the same object that we feel; neither is the same object perceived by the microscope which was by the naked eye. But, in case every variation was thought sufficient to constitute a new kind or individual, the endless number or confusion of names would render language impracticable. Therefore, to avoid this as well as other inconveniences which are obvious upon a little thought, men combine together several ideas, apprehended by divers senses, or by the same sense at different times, or in different circumstances, but observed, however, to have some connexion in nature, either with respect to co-existence or succession; all which they refer to one name, and consider as one thing. Hence, it follows that when I examine by my other senses a thing I have seen, it is not in order to understand better the same object which I had perceived by sight, the object of one sense not being perceived by the other senses. And, when I look through a microscope, it is not that I may perceive more clearly what I perceived already with my bare eyes; the object perceived by the glass being quite different from the former. But, in both cases, my aim is only to know what ideas are connected together; and the more a man knows of the connexion of ideas, the more he is said to know of the nature of things. What, therefore, if our ideas are variable; what if our senses are not in all circumstances affected with the same appearances? It will not thence follow they are not to be trusted, or that they are inconsistent either with themselves or anything else; except it be with your preconceived notion of (I know not what) one single, unchanged, unperceivable, real nature, marked by each name: which prejudice seems to have taken its rise from not rightly understanding the common language of men, speaking of several distinct ideas as united into one thing by the mind. And, indeed, there is cause to suspect several erroneous conceits of the philosophers are owing to the same original: while they began to build their schemes not so much on notions as words, which were framed by the vulgar, merely for conveniency and dispatch in the common actions of life, without any regard to speculation.

Hyl. Methinks I apprehend your meaning.

Phil. It is your opinion the ideas we perceive by our senses are not real things, but images or copies of them. Our knowledge, therefore, is no farther real than as our ideas are the true representations of those originals. But, as these supposed originals are in themselves unknown, it is impossible to know how far our ideas resemble them ; or whether they resemble them at all. We cannot, therefore, be sure we have any real knowledge. Farther, as our ideas are perpetually varied, without any change in the supposed real things, it necessarily follows they cannot all be true copies of them : or, if some are and others are not, it is impossible to distinguish the former from the latter. And this plunges us yet deeper in uncertainty. Again, when we consider the point, we cannot conceive how any idea, or anything like an idea, should have an absolute existence out of a mind : nor consequently, according to you, how there should be any real thing in nature. The result of all which is that we are thrown into the most hopeless and abandoned Scepticism. Now, give me leave to ask you, First, Whether your referring ideas to certain absolutely existing unperceived substances, as their originals, be not the source of all this Scepticism ? Secondly, whether you are informed, either by sense or reason, of the existence of those unknown originals ? And, in case you are not, whether it be not absurd to suppose them ? Thirdly, Whether, upon inquiry, you find there is anything distinctly conceived or meant by the *absolute or external existence of unperceiving substances.* Lastly, Whether, the premises considered, it be not the wisest way to follow nature, trust your senses, and, laying aside all anxious thought about unknown natures or substances, admit with the vulgar those for real things which are perceived by the senses ?

Hyl. For the present I have no inclination to the answering part. I would much rather see how you can get over what follows. Pray are not the objects perceived by the senses of one, likewise perceivable to others present ? If there were a hundred more here, they would all see the garden, the trees, and flowers, as I see them. But they are not in the same manner affected with the ideas I frame in my imagination. Does not this make a difference between the former sort of objects and the latter?

Phil. I grant it does. Nor have I ever denied a difference between the objects of sense and those of imagination. But what would you infer from thence? You cannot say that sensible objects exist unperceived, because they are perceived by many.

Hyl. I own I can make nothing of that objection: but it hath led me into another. Is it not your opinion that by our senses we perceive only the ideas existing in our minds?

Phil. It is.

Hyl. But the same idea which is in my mind cannot be in yours, or in any other mind. Doth it not therefore follow, from your principles, that no two can see the same thing? And is not this highly absurd?

Phil. If the term *same* be taken in the vulgar acceptation, it is certain (and not at all repugnant to the principles I maintain) that different persons may perceive the same thing; or the same thing or idea exist in different minds. Words are of arbitrary imposition; and, since men are used to apply the word *same* where no distinction or variety is perceived, and I do not pretend to alter their perceptions, it follows that, as men have said before, *several saw the same thing*, so they may, upon like occasions, still continue to use the same phrase, without any deviation either from propriety of language, or the truth of things. But, if the term *same* be used in the acceptation of philosophers, who pretend to an abstracted notion of identity, then, according to their sundry definitions of this notion (for it is not yet agreed wherein that philosophic identity consists), it may or may not be possible for divers persons to perceive the same thing. But whether philosophers shall think fit to call a thing the *same* or no, is, I conceive, of small importance. Let us suppose several men together, all endued with the same faculties, and consequently affected in like sort by their senses, and who had yet never known the use of language; they would without question, agree in their perceptions. Though perhaps, when they came to the use of speech, some regarding the uniformness of what was perceived, might call it the *same* thing: others especially regarding the diversity of per-

sons who perceived, might choose the denomination of
different things. But who sees not that all the dispute is
about a word? to wit, whether what is perceived by different
persons may yet have the term *same* applied to it? Or,
suppose a house, whose walls or outward shell remaining
unaltered, the chambers are all pulled down, and new ones
built in their place; and that you should call this the *same*,
and I should say it was not the *same* house :—would we not,
for all this, perfectly agree in our thoughts of the house, considered in itself? And would not all the difference consist
in a sound? If you should say, we differed in our notions;
for that you superadded to your idea of the house the simple
abstracted idea of identity, whereas I did not; I would tell
you, I know not what you mean by the *abstracted idea of
identity ;* and should desire you to look into your own
thoughts, and be sure you understood yourself.——Why so
silent, *Hylas ?* Are you not yet satisfied men may dispute
about identity and diversity, without any real difference in
their thoughts and opinions, abstracted from names? Take
this farther reflexion with you—that whether Matter be
allowed to exist or no, the case is exactly the same as to the
point in hand. For, the Materialists themselves acknowledge what we immediately perceive by our senses to be our
own ideas. Your difficulty, therefore, that no two see the
same thing, makes equally against the Materialists and me.

Hyl. But they suppose an external archetype, to which
referring their several ideas they may truly be said to perceive the same thing.

Phil. And (not to mention your having discarded those
archetypes) so may you suppose an external archetype on
my principles; *external,* I mean, to your own mind;
though indeed it must be supposed to exist in that mind
which comprehends all things ; but then, this serves all the
ends of *identity,* as well as if it existed out of a mind. And
I am sure you yourself will not say it is less intelligible.

Hyl. You have indeed clearly satisfied me, either that
there is no difficulty at bottom in this point ; or, if there be,
that it makes equally against both opinions.

Phil. But that which makes equally against two contradictory opinions can be a proof against neither.

Hyl. I acknowledge it. But, after all, *Philonous,* when I consider the substance of what you advance against *Scepticism*, it amounts to no more than this :—We are sure that we really see, hear, feel ; in a word, that we are affected with sensible impressions.

Phil. And how are we concerned any farther ? I see this *cherry*, I feel it, I taste it : and I am sure *nothing* cannot be seen, or felt, or tasted : it is therefore *real*. Take away the sensations of softness, moisture, redness, tartness, and you take away the *cherry*. Since it is not a being distinct from sensations ; a *cherry*, I say, is nothing but a congeries of sensible impressions, or ideas perceived by various senses : which ideas are united into one thing (or have one name given them) by the mind ; because they are observed to attend each other. Thus, when the palate is affected with such a particular taste, the sight is affected with a red colour, the touch with roundness, softness, &c. Hence, when I see, and feel, and taste, in sundry certain manners, I am sure the *cherry* exists, or is real ; its reality being in my opinion nothing abstracted from those sensations. But if, by the word *cherry*, you mean an unknown nature, distinct from all those sensible qualities, and by its *existence* something distinct from its being perceived ; then, indeed, I own, neither you nor I, nor any one else, can be sure it exists.

Hyl. But, what would you say, *Philonous*, if I should bring the very same reasons against the existence of sensible things in a mind, which you have offered against their existing in a material *substratum* ?

Phil. When I see your reasons, you shall hear what I have to say to them.

Hyl. Is the mind extended or unextended ?

Phil. Unextended, without doubt.

Hyl. Do you say the things you perceive are in your mind ?

Phil. They are.

Hyl. Again, have I not heard you speak of sensible impressions ?

Phil. I believe you may.

Hyl. Explain to me now, O *Philonous !* how it is possible there should be room for all those trees and houses to exist in your mind. Can extended things be contained in that which is unextended ? Or, are we to imagine impressions made on a thing void of all solidity? You cannot say objects are in your mind, as books in your study: or that things are imprinted on it, as the figure of a seal upon wax. In what sense, therefore, are we to understand those expressions? Explain me this if you can: and I shall then be able to answer all those queries you formerly put to me about my *substratum*.

Phil. Look you, *Hylas*, when I speak of objects as existing in the mind, or imprinted on the senses, I would not be understood in the gross literal sense—as when bodies are said to exist in a place, or a seal to make an impression upon wax. My meaning is only that the mind comprehends or perceives them; and that it is affected from without, or by some being distinct from itself. This is my explication of your difficulty; and how it can serve to make your tenet of an unperceiving material *substratum* intelligible, I would fain know.

Hyl. Nay, if that be all, I confess I do not see what use can be made of it. But are you not guilty of some abuse of language in this?

Phil. None at all. It is no more than common custom, which you know is the rule of language, hath authorized: nothing being more usual, than for philosophers to speak of the immediate objects of the understanding as things existing in the mind. Nor is there anything in this but what is conformable to the general analogy of language; most part of the mental operations being signified by words borrowed from sensible things; as is plain in the terms *comprehend*, *reflect*, *discourse*, &*c.*, which, being applied to the mind, must not be taken in their gross original sense.

Hyl. You have, I own, satisfied me in this point. But there still remains one great difficulty, which I know not how you will get over. And, indeed, it is of such importance that if you could solve all others, without being able to find a solution for this, you must never expect to make me a proselyte to your principles.

Phil. Let me know this mighty difficulty.

Hyl. The Scripture account of the creation is what appears to me utterly irreconcilable with your notions. Moses tells us of a creation: a creation of what? of ideas? No certainly, but of things, of real things, solid corporeal substances. Bring your principles to agree with this, and I shall perhaps agree with you.

Phil. Moses mentions the sun, moon, and stars, earth and sea, plants and animals. That all these do really exist, and were in the beginning created by God, I make no question. If by *ideas* you mean fictions and fancies of the mind, then these are no ideas. If by *ideas* you mean immediate objects of the understanding, or sensible things which cannot exist unperceived, or out of a mind, then these things are ideas. But whether you do or do not call them *ideas*, it matters little. The difference is only about a name. And, whether that name be retained or rejected, the sense, the truth, and reality of things continues the same. In common talk, the objects of our senses are not termed *ideas* but *things*. Call them so still—provided you do not attribute to them any absolute external existence—and I shall never quarrel with you for a word. The creation, therefore, I allow to have been a creation of things, of *real* things. Neither is this in the least inconsistent with my principles, as is evident from what I have now said; and would have been evident to you without this, if you had not forgotten what had been so often said before. But as for solid corporeal substances, I desire you to shew where Moses makes any mention of them; and, if they should be mentioned by him, or any other inspired writer, it would still be incumbent on you to shew those words were not taken in the vulgar acceptation, for things falling under our senses, but in the philosophic acceptation, for Matter, or an unknown quiddity, with an absolute existence. When you have proved these points, then (and not till then) may you bring the authority of Moses into our dispute.

Hyl. It is in vain to dispute about a point so clear. I am content to refer it to your own conscience. Are you not satisfied there is some peculiar repugnancy between the Mosaic account of the creation and your notions?

Phil. If all possible sense which can be put on the first chapter of Genesis may be conceived as consistently with my principles as any other, then it has no peculiar repugnancy with them. But there is no sense you may not as well conceive, believing as I do. Since, besides spirits, all you conceive are ideas; and the existence of these I do not deny.   Neither do you pretend they exist without the mind.

Hyl. Pray let me see any sense you can understand it in.

Phil. Why, I imagine that if I had been present at the creation, I should have seen things produced into being— that is become perceptible—in the order prescribed by the sacred historian.   I ever before believed the Mosaic account of the creation, and now find no alteration in my manner of believing it.   When things are said to begin or end their existence, we do not mean this with regard to God, but His creatures.   All objects are eternally known by God, or, which is the same thing, have an eternal existence in His mind : but when things, before imperceptible to creatures, are, by a decree of God, perceptible to them, then are they said to begin a relative existence, with respect to created minds.   Upon reading therefore the Mosaic account of the creation, I understand that the several parts of the world became gradually perceivable to finite spirits, endowed with proper faculties ; so that, whoever such were present, they were in truth perceived by them.   This is the literal obvious sense suggested to me by the words of the Holy Scripture : in which is included no mention or no thought, either of *substratum*, instrument, occasion, or absolute existence. And, upon inquiry, I doubt not it will be found that most plain honest men, who believe the creation, never think of those things any more than I.   What metaphysical sense you may understand it in, you only can tell.

Hyl. But, *Philonous*, you do not seem to be aware that you allow created things, in the beginning, only a relative, and consequently hypothetical being : that is to say, upon supposition there were men to perceive them, without which they have no actuality of absolute existence wherein creation might terminate.   Is it not, therefore, according to you, plainly impossible the creation of any inanimate creatures should precede that of man ?   And is not this directly contrary to the Mosaic account ?

Phil. In answer to that, I say, first, created beings might begin to exist in the mind of other created intelligences beside men.   You will not therefore be able to prove any contradiction between Moses and my notions, unless you first shew there was no other order of finite created spirits in being before man. I say farther, in case we conceive the creation, as we should at this time a parcel of plants or vegetables of all sorts produced, by an invisible power, in a desert where nobody was present—that this way of explaining or conceiving it is consistent with my principles, since they deprive you of nothing, either sensible or imaginable; that it exactly suits with the common, natural, and undebauched notions of mankind; that it manifests the dependence of all things on God; and consequently hath all the good effect or influence, which it is possible that important article of our faith should have in making men humble, thankful, and resigned to their Creator. I say, moreover, that, in this naked conception of things, divested of words, there will not be found any notion of what you call the *actuality of absolute existence.* You may indeed raise a dust with those terms, and so lengthen our dispute to no purpose. But I entreat you calmly to look into your own thoughts, and then tell me if they are not a useless and unintelligible jargon.

Hyl. I own I have no very clear notion annexed to them. But what say you to this? Do you not make the existence of sensible things consist in their being in a mind? And were not all things eternally in the mind of God? Did they not therefore exist from all eternity, according to you? And how could that which was eternal be created in time? Can anything be clearer or better connected than this?

Phil. And are not you too of opinion, that God knew all things from eternity?

Hyl. I am.

Phil. Consequently they always had a being in the Divine intellect.

Hyl. This I acknowledge.

Phil. By your own confession, therefore, nothing is new, or begins to be, in respect of the mind of God. So we are agreed in that point.

Hyl. What shall we make then of the creation?

Phil. May we not understand it to have been entirely in respect of finite spirits; so that things, with regard to us, may properly be said to begin their existence, or be created, when God decreed they should become perceptible to intelligent creatures, in that order and manner which He then established, and we now call the laws of nature? You may call this a *relative*, or *hypothetical existence* if you please. But so long as it supplies us with the most natural, obvious, and literal sense of the Mosaic history of the creation; so long as it answers all the religious ends of that great article; in a word, so long as you can assign no other sense or meaning in its stead; why should we reject this? Is it to comply with a ridiculous sceptical humour of making everything nonsense and unintelligible? I am sure you cannot say it is for the glory of God. For, allowing it to be a thing possible and conceivable that the corporeal world should have an absolute existence extrinsical to the mind of God, as well as to the minds of all created spirits; yet how could this set forth either the immensity or omniscience of the Deity, or the necessary and immediate dependence of all things on Him? Nay, would it not rather seem to derogate from those attributes?

Hyl. Well, but as to this decree of God's, for making things perceptible, what say you, *Philonous*, is it not plain, God did either execute that decree from all eternity, or at some certain time began to will what He had not actually willed before, but only designed to will? If the former, then there could be no creation or beginning of existence in finite things. If the latter, then we must acknowledge something new to befall the Deity; which implies a sort of change: and all change argues imperfection.

Phil. Pray consider what you are doing. Is it not evident this objection concludes equally against a creation in any sense; nay, against every other act of the Deity, discoverable by the light of nature? None of which can we conceive, otherwise than as performed in time, and having a beginning. God is a Being of transcendent and unlimited perfections: His Nature, therefore, is incomprehensible to finite spirits. It is not, therefore, to be expected, that any man, whether *Materialist* or *Immaterialist*, should have exactly just notions of the Deity, His attributes, and ways of operation. If then you would infer anything against me, your difficulty must not be drawn from the inadequateness of our conceptions of the Divine nature, which is unavoidable on any scheme, but from the denial of Matter, of which there is not one word, directly or indirectly, in what you have now objected.

Hyl. I must acknowledge the difficulties you are concerned to clear are such only as arise from the non-existence of Matter, and are peculiar to that notion. So far you are in the right. But I cannot by any means bring myself to think there is no such peculiar repugnancy between the creation and your opinion : though indeed where to fix it, I do not distinctly know.

Phil. What would you have? Do I not acknowledge a twofold state of things, the one ectypal or natural, the other archetypal and eternal? The former was created in time ; the latter existed from everlasting in the mind of God. Is not this agreeable to the common notions of divines? Or is any more than this necessary in order to conceive the creation? But you suspect some peculiar repugnancy, though you know not where it lies. To take away all possibility of scruple in the case, do but consider this one point. Either you are not able to conceive the creation on any hypothesis whatsoever ; and, if so, there is no ground for dislike or complaint against any particular opinion on that score : or you are able to conceive it ; and, if so, why not on my principles, since thereby nothing conceivable is taken away? You have all along been allowed the full scope of sense, imagination, and reason. Whatever, therefore, you could before apprehend, either immediately or mediately by your senses, or by ratiocination from your senses ; whatever you could perceive, imagine, or understand, remains still with you. If, therefore, the notion you have of the creation by other principles be intelligible, you have it still upon mine ; if it be not intelligible, I conceive it to be no notion at all ; and so there is no loss of it. And indeed it seems to me very plain that the supposition of Matter, that is a thing perfectly unknown and inconceivable, cannot serve to make us conceive anything. And, I hope it need not to be proved to you that if the existence of Matter doth not make the creation conceivable, the creation's being without it inconceivable can be no objection against its non-existence.

Hyl. I confess, *Philonous*, you have almost satisfied me in this point of the creation.

Phil. I would fain know why you are not quite satisfied. You tell me indeed of a repugnancy between the Mosaic history and Immaterialism : but you know not where it lies.

Is this reasonable, *Hylas?* Can you expect I should solve a difficulty without knowing what it is? But, to pass by all that, would not a man think you were assured there is no repugnancy between the received notions of Materialists and the inspired writings?

Hyl. And so I am.

Phil. Ought the historical part of Scripture to be understood in a plain obvious sense, or in a sense which is metaphysical and out of the way?

Hyl. In the plain sense, doubtless.

Phil. When Moses speaks of herbs, earth, water, &c., as having been created by God; think you not the sensible things commonly signified by those words are suggested to every unphilosophical reader?

Hyl. I cannot help thinking so.

Phil. And are not all ideas, or things perceived by sense, to be denied a real existence by the doctrine of the Materialist?

Hyl. This I have already acknowledged.

Phil. The creation, therefore, according to them, was not the creation of things sensible, which have only a relative being, but of certain unknown natures, which have an absolute being, wherein creation might terminate?

Hyl. True.

Phil. Is it not therefore evident the assertors of Matter destroy the plain obvious sense of Moses, with which their notions are utterly inconsistent; and instead of it obtrude on us I know not what, something equally unintelligible to themselves and me?

Hyl. I cannot contradict you.

Phil. Moses tells us of a creation. A creation of what? of unknown quiddities, of occasions, or *substratum?* No, certainly; but of things obvious to the senses. You must first reconcile this with your notions, if you expect I should be reconciled to them.

Hyl. I see you can assault me with my own weapons.

Phil. Then as to *absolute existence;* was there ever known a more jejune notion than that? Something it is so abstracted and unintelligible that you have frankly owned you could not conceive it, much less explain anything by it. But, allowing Matter to exist, and the notion of absolute existence to be as clear as light, yet, was this ever known to make the creation more credible? Nay, hath it not furnished the atheists and infidels of all ages with the most plausible arguments against a creation? That a corporeal substance, which hath an absolute existence without the minds of spirits, should be produced out of nothing, by the mere will of a Spirit, hath been looked upon as a thing so contrary to all reason, so impossible and absurd, that not only the most celebrated among the ancients, but even divers modern and Christian philosophers have thought Matter co-eternal with the Deity. Lay these things together, and then judge you whether Materialism disposes men to believe the creation of things.

Hyl. I own, *Philonous*, I think it does not. This of the *creation* is the last objection I can think of; and I must needs own it hath been sufficiently answered as well as the rest. Nothing now remains to be overcome but a sort of unaccountable backwardness that I find in myself towards your notions.

Phil. When a man is swayed, he knows not why, to one side of the question, can this, think you, be anything else but the effect of prejudice, which never fails to attend old and rooted notions? And indeed in this respect I cannot deny the belief of Matter to have very much the advantage over the contrary opinion, with men of a learned education.

Hyl. I confess it seems to be as you say.

Phil. As a balance, therefore, to this weight of prejudice, let us throw into the scale the great advantages that arise from the belief of Immaterialism, both in regard to religion and human learning. The being of a God, and incorruptibility of the soul, those great articles of religion, are they not proved with the clearest and most immediate evidence? When I say the being of a *God*, I do not mean an obscure general cause of things, whereof we have no conception, but *God*, in the strict and proper sense of the word; a Being whose spirituality, omnipresence, providence, omniscience, infinite power and goodness, are as conspicuous as the existence of sensible things, of which (notwithstanding the fallacious pretences and affected scruples of Sceptics) there is no more reason to doubt than of our own being. Then, with relation to human sciences: in Natural Philosophy, what intricacies, what obscurities, what contradictions hath the belief of Matter led men into ! To say nothing of the numberless disputes about its extent, continuity, homogeneity, gravity, divisibility, &c.— do they not pretend to explain all things by bodies operating on bodies, according to the laws of motion ? and yet, are they able to comprehend how one body should move another? Nay, admitting there was no difficulty in reconciling the notion of an inert being with a cause, or in conceiving how an accident might pass from one body to another ; yet, by all their strained thoughts and extravagant suppositions, have they been able to reach the mechanical production of any one animal or vegetable body ? Can they account, by the laws of motion, for sounds, tastes, smells, or colours, or for the regular course of things ? Have they accounted, by physical principles, for the aptitude and contrivance even of the most inconsiderable parts of the universe? But laying aside Matter and corporeal causes, and admitting only the efficiency of an All-perfect Mind, are not all the effects of nature easy and intelligible ? If the *phenomena* are nothing else but *ideas ;* God is a *spirit*, but Matter an unintelligent, unperceiving being. If they demonstrate an unlimited power in their cause ; God is active and omnipotent, but Matter an inert mass. If the order, regularity, and usefulness of them can never be sufficiently admired ; God is infinitely wise and provident, but Matter destitute of all contrivance and design. These surely are great advantages in *physics*. Not to mention that the apprehension of a distant Deity naturally disposes men to a negligence of their moral actions, which they would be more cautious of, in case they thought him immediately present, and acting on their minds, without the interposition of Matter, or unthinking second causes. Then in *meta-physics :* what difficulties concerning entity in abstract, sub-stantial forms, hylarchic principles, plastic natures, substance and accident, principle of individuation, possibility of Matter's thinking, origin of ideas, the manner how two independent substances so widely different as *Spirit* and *Matter*, should mutually operate on each other ? what difficulties, I say, and endless disquisitions, concerning these and innumerable other the like points, do we escape, by supposing only Spirits and ideas ? Even the *mathematics* themselves, if we take away the absolute existence of extended things, become much more clear and easy; the most shocking paradoxes and intricate speculations in those sciences depending on the infinite divisibility of finite extension, which depends on that supposition. —But what need is there to insist on the particular sciences? Is not that opposition to all science whatsoever, that frenzy of the ancient and modern Sceptics, built on the same foundation? Or can you produce so much as one argument against the reality of corporeal things or in behalf of that avowed utter ignorance of their natures, which doth not suppose their reality to consist in an external absolute existence? Upon this supposition, indeed, the objections from the change of colours in a pigeon's neck, or the appearance of the broken oar in the water, must be allowed to have weight. But these and the like objections vanish, if we do not maintain the being of absolute external originals, but place the reality of things in ideas, fleeting indeed, and changeable; however, not changed at random, but according to the fixed order of nature. For, herein consists that constancy and truth of things which secures all the concerns of life, and distinguishes that which is real from the irregular visions of the fancy.

Hyl. I agree to all you have now said, and must own that nothing can incline me to embrace your opinion more than the advantages I see it is attended with. I am by nature lazy; and this would be a mighty abridgment in knowledge. What doubts, what hypotheses, what labyrinths of amusement, what fields of disputation, what an ocean of false learning may be avoided by that single notion of *Immaterialism!*

Phil. After all, is there anything farther remaining to be done? You may remember you promised to embrace that opinion which upon examination should appear most agreeable to Common Sense and remote from Scepticism. This, by your own confession, is that which denies Matter, or the absolute existence of corporeal things. Nor is this all; the same notion has been proved several ways, viewed in different lights, pursued in its consequences, and all objections against it cleared. Can there be a greater evidence of its truth? or is it possible it should have all the marks of a true opinion and yet be false?

Hyl. I own myself entirely satisfied for the present in all respects.   But, what security can I have that I shall still continue the same full assent to your opinion, and that no unthought-of objection or difficulty will occur hereafter?

Phil. Pray, *Hylas*, do you in other cases, when a point is once evidently proved, withhold your consent on account of objections or difficulties it may be liable to? Are the difficulties that attend the doctrine of incommensurable quantities, of the angle of contact, of the asymptotes to curves, or the like, sufficient to make you hold out against mathematical demonstration? Or will you disbelieve the Providence of God, because there may be some particular things which you know not how to reconcile with it? If there are difficulties attending *Immaterialism*, there are at the same time direct and evident proofs of it. But for the existence of Matter there is not one proof, and far more numerous and insurmountable objections lie against it. But where are those mighty difficulties you insist on? Alas! you know not where or what they are; something which may possibly occur hereafter. If this be a sufficient pretence for withholding your full assent, you should never yield it to any proposition, how free soever from exceptions, how clearly and solidly soever demonstrated.

Hyl. You have satisfied me, *Philonous*.

Phil. But, to arm you against all future objections, do but consider, that which bears equally hard on two contradictory opinions can be proof against neither. Whenever, therefore, any difficulty occurs, try if you can find a solution for it on the hypothesis of the *Materialists*. Be not deceived by words; but sound your own thoughts. And in case you cannot conceive it easier by the help of *Materialism*, it is plain it can be no objection against *Immaterialism*. Had you proceeded all along by this rule, you would probably have spared yourself abundance of trouble in objecting; since of all your difficulties I challenge you to shew one that is explained by Matter: nay, which is not more unintelligible with than without that supposition, and consequently makes rather *against* than *for* it. You should consider, in each particular, whether the difficulty arises from the *non-existence of Matter*. If it doth not, you might as well argue from the infinite divisibility of extension against the Divine prescience, as from such a difficulty against *Immaterialism*. And yet, upon recollection, I believe you will find this to have been often if not always the case. You should likewise take heed not to argue on a *petitio principii*. One is apt to say, the unknown substances ought to be esteemed real things, rather than the ideas in our minds : and who can tell but the unthinking external substance may concur as a cause or instrument in the productions of our ideas? But, is not this proceeding on a supposition that there are such external substances? And to suppose this, is it not begging the question? But, above all things, you should beware of imposing on yourself by that vulgar sophism which is called *ignoratio elenchi*. You talked often as if you thought I maintained the non-existence of Sensible Things : whereas in truth no one can be more thoroughly assured of their existence than I am : and it is you who doubt; I should have said, positively deny it. Everything that is seen, felt, heard, or any way perceived by the senses, is, on the principles I embrace, a real being, but not on yours. Remember, the Matter you contend for is an unknown somewhat (if indeed it may be termed *some-what*), which is quite stripped of all sensible qualities, and can neither be perceived by sense, nor apprehended by the mind. Remember, I say, that it is not any object which is hard or soft, hot or cold, blue or white, round or square, &c. ; —for all these things I affirm do exist. Though indeed I deny they have an existence distinct from being perceived ; or that they exist out of all minds whatsoever. Think on these points ; let them be attentively considered and still kept in view. Otherwise you will not comprehend the state of the question; without which your objections will always be wide of the mark, and instead of mine, may possibly be directed (as more than once they have been) against your own notions.

Hyl. I must needs own, *Philonous*, nothing seems to have kept me from agreeing with you more than this same *mistaking the question*. In denying Matter, at first glimpse I am tempted to imagine you deny the things we see and feel : but, upon reflexion, find there is no ground for it. What think you, therefore, of retaining the name *Matter*, and applying it to *sensible things?* This may be done without any change in your sentiments : and, believe me, it would be a means of reconciling them to some persons who may be more shocked at an innovation in words than in opinion.

Phil. With all my heart : retain the word *Matter*, and apply it to the objects of sense, if you please ; provided you do not attribute to them any subsistence distinct from their being perceived. I shall never quarrel with you for an expression. *Matter*, or *material substance*, are terms introduced by philosophers ; and, as used by them, imply a sort of independency, or a subsistence distinct from being perceived by a mind : but are never used by common people ; or, if ever, it is to signify the immediate objects of sense. One would think, therefore, so long as the names of all particular things, with the terms *sensible*, *substance*, *body*, *stuff*, and the like, are retained, the word *Matter* should be never missed in common talk. And in philosophical discourses it seems the best way to leave it quite out : since there is not, perhaps, any one thing that hath more favoured and strengthened the depraved bent of the mind towards Atheism than the use of that general confused term.

Hyl. Well but, *Philonous*, since I am content to give up the notion of an unthinking substance exterior to the mind, I think you ought not to deny me the privilege of using the word *Matter* as I please, and annexing it to a collection of sensible qualities subsisting only in the mind. I freely own there is no other substance, in a strict sense, than *Spirit*. But I have been so long accustomed to the term *Matter* that I know not how to part with it. To say, there is no *Matter* in the World, is still shocking to me. Whereas to say There is no *Matter*, if by that term be meant an unthinking substance existing without the mind ; but if by *Matter* is meant some sensible thing, whose existence consists in being perceived, then there is *Matter* :—this distinction gives it quite another turn ; and men will come into your notions with small difficulty, when they are proposed in that manner. For, after all, the controversy about *Matter* in the strict acceptation of it, lies altogether between you and the philosophers : whose principles, I acknowledge, are not near so natural, or so agreeable to the common sense of mankind, and Holy Scripture, as yours. There is nothing we either desire or shun but as it makes, or is apprehended to make, some part of our happiness or misery. But what hath happiness or misery, joy or grief, pleasure or pain, to do with Absolute Existence ; or with unknown entities, abstracted